Who Gets a Childhood?

WHO GETS A CHILDHOOD?

*Race and Juvenile Justice
in Twentieth-Century Texas*

WILLIAM S. BUSH

The University of Georgia Press   *Athens and London*

© 2010 by the University of Georgia Press

Athens, Georgia 30602

www.ugapress.org

All rights reserved

Set in Minion Pro and Myriad Pro by

Graphic Composition, Inc., Bogart, Georgia

Printed digitally in the United States of America

Library of Congress Cataloging-in-Publication Data

Bush, William S., 1967–

Who gets a childhood? : race and juvenile justice in twentieth-century Texas /

William S. Bush.

p. cm. — (Politics and culture in the twentieth-century South)

Includes bibliographical references and index.

ISBN-13: 978-0-8203-3719-7 (pbk. : alk. paper)

ISBN-10: 0-8203-3719-6 (pbk. : alk. paper)

1. Juvenile justice, Administration of—Texas—History—20th century.

2. Discrimination in juvenile justice administration—Texas—History—20th century.

3. Juvenile delinquents—Texas—History—20th century.

I. Title

HV9105.T4B87 2010

364.3609764—dc22   2010005961

British Library Cataloging-in-Publication Data available

FOR ALEX AND OLLIE,

WHO HAVE TAUGHT ME THE MOST ABOUT CHILDHOOD

CONTENTS

ACKNOWLEDGMENTS

This book has been nearly a decade in the making, and I have accumulated several debts along the way.

My deepest gratitude goes to David Tanenhaus, my colleague at the University of Nevada–Las Vegas for three years. David read countless chapter drafts, provided thoughtful feedback, and more than anyone encouraged me when I felt overwhelmed by or uncertain about this project. I also wish to thank all my former colleagues in the UNLV history department, many of whom read and commented on portions of this book or otherwise supported me: Elizabeth White Nelson, Eugene Moehring, Colin Loader, Andy Kirk, David Wrobel, Gregory Brown, Andy Fry, Jay Coughtry, Michelle Tusan, David Sproul, and the late Hal Rothman.

I have also benefited from scholarly exchanges with several distinguished historians of juvenile justice, childhood, and youth. It has been my privilege to participate in conference panels with Steve Schlossman, Paula Fass, Tamara Myers, Mona Gleason, Jennifer Trost, David Wolcott, Anthony Platt, Miroslava Chávez-Garcia, Adam Golub, Laura Mihailoff, and Mary Odem, each of whom shared valuable insights that have informed my thinking. I also wish to thank my dissertation committee at the University of Texas at Austin, particularly Mark Smith, Janet Davis, Julia Mickenberg, and King Davis, each of whom continued to support me during the lengthy revision process.

My research depended crucially on the assistance of archivists and library professionals. In particular I wish to thank Laura Saegert at the Texas State Library and Archives, whose encyclopedic knowledge of the history of crime and punishment in Texas was indispensable. A grant from the Spencer Foundation supported a critical portion of the research for this book, allowing me to access juvenile inmate correspondence from the early twentieth century. I also learned a great deal from juvenile justice professionals and children's advocates: Isela Gutiérrez and her colleagues at the Texas Criminal Justice Coalition; Scott Henson, whose blog Grits for Breakfast published some of my commentary on the ongoing reform efforts at the Texas Youth Commission (TYC); current and former TYC employees, especially Will Harrell; and Judge Jeanne Meurer and Jim Gobin of the Travis County Juvenile Justice Center in Austin, who allowed me to observe the juvenile court and detention center. I cannot emphasize enough the importance of my firsthand encounters, however limited, with the juvenile justice system. They forced me to rethink many of my original assumptions about the various characters in this book, and I believe this has resulted in a more nuanced and ultimately convincing account.

An earlier version of Chapter 4 appeared as "James Dean and Jim Crow: Boys in the Texas Juvenile Justice System in the 1950s," in *Lost Kids: Vulnerable Children and Youth in Twentieth-Century Canada and the United States*, edited by Mona Gleason, Tamara Myers, Leslie Paris, and Veronica Strong-Boag (University of British Columbia Press, 2009). I wish to thank the editors at UBC Press for a rigorous referee process that has resulted in a more focused chapter. I would also be remiss if I did not extend my deepest gratitude to Derek Krissoff, my editor at the University of Georgia Press, whose patience often seemed without limit, and to the blind reviewers for the Press, whose thorough critiques have produced a far more coherent manuscript than the original.

I am often asked if my scholarly interest in the history of juvenile justice is somehow autobiographical. My answer to that question is always no, thanks to the loving guidance of my mother, Maria Russo Bush, who raised my brother and me largely on her own, and to that of my father, Mitchell Kenneth Bush, who passed away tragically during my teenage years. Finally, my wife, Mary, has supported me throughout the duration of this project with unfailing love and generosity. I can never thank her and my parents enough.

Who Gets a Childhood?

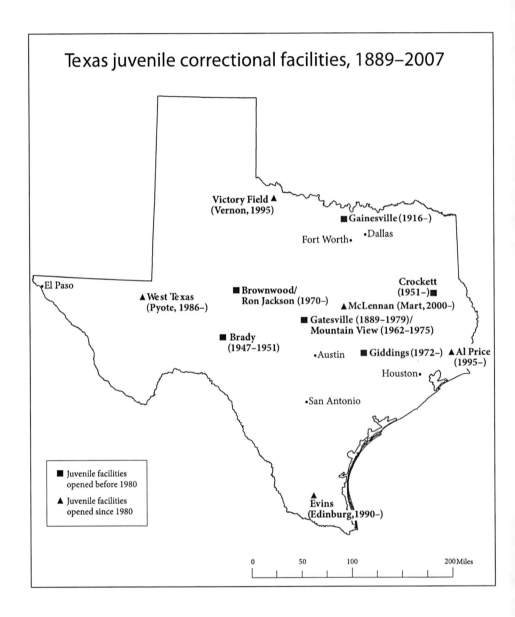

Texas juvenile correctional facilities, 1889–2007

Victory Field ▲
(Vernon, 1995)

■ Gainesville (1916–)

Fort Worth•   •Dallas

•El Paso

▲ West Texas
(Pyote, 1986–)

■ Brownwood/
Ron Jackson (1970–)

Crockett
(1951–)■

▲ McLennan (Mart, 2000–)

■ Gatesville (1889–1979)/
Mountain View (1962–1975)

■ Brady
(1947–1951)

•Austin   ■ Giddings (1972–) ▲ Al Price
(1995–)

Houston•

•San Antonio

■ Juvenile facilities
   opened before 1980
▲ Juvenile facilities
   opened since 1980

▲
Evins
(Edinburg, 1990–)

0   50   100   200 Miles

Introduction

Race, Childhood, and Juvenile Justice History

On February 16, 2007, an article on the *Texas Observer* Web site exposed a gruesome sex abuse scandal at the West Texas State School, a juvenile corrections facility in the remote town of Pyote, near Odessa. Over the next several weeks, news reports revealed that the school's assistant superintendent, Ray Brookins, and its principal, John Paul Hernandez, had coerced sexual favors from several juvenile inmates over a period of at least two years. Compounding the alleged crime was an inexplicably slow response from authorities. Between December 2003 and February 2005, staff complaints about Brookins's and Hernandez's suspicious behavior had fallen on deaf ears in the upper echelons of the Texas Youth Commission (TYC), the agency charged with administering the state's juvenile facilities.[1] Finally, in February 2005, Marc Slattery, a volunteer math tutor from nearby Midland, was approached by two students who wanted to confess "something 'icky.'" As Slattery later told a reporter, "I knew it must have been something bad if they had no word for it."[2] Slattery soon discovered that boys were being led into the administration building each night for forced encounters with Brookins, who had used his power to unilaterally lengthen or shorten youths' sentences to exact sex from inmates.

Appalled, Slattery contacted a Texas Ranger named Brian Burzynski, who launched an investigation. Within weeks, Burzynski had gathered sufficient evidence to charge both Brookins and Hernandez with multiple criminal charges. Instead, however, two years passed, during which the TYC forced both men to resign, a criminal case stalled in the offices of the local county prosecutor, and the United States Attorney's Office in San Antonio resisted numerous requests to take action. When news outlets finally broke the story, they portrayed a cover-up orchestrated by top administrators and enabled by, according to the *Dallas Morning News*, "a culture in which prison officials were free to abuse their power" and "punish children who tried to complain about them."[3] The story was subsequently picked up by the national media and mushroomed into a major scandal.[4]

The west Texas incident turned out to be only the tip of the iceberg. Subsequent investigations revealed over 2,000 confirmed allegations of staff-on-inmate violence between 2003 and 2006 and more than 60 instances of "suspicious" broken bones treated by medical personnel. An abuse hotline launched by the TYC immediately after the scandal broke amassed more than 1,100 complaints in less than a month. The TYC released nearly 500 youth inmates, mostly misdemeanants, and arrested, fired, or suspended numerous employees.[5] In March 2007, the U.S. Department of Justice declared that the violent conditions at the Evins Regional Juvenile Center in Edinburg, Texas, south of San Antonio in the Rio Grande Valley, violated the constitutional right of incarcerated youth to be adequately protected from harm while in state custody.[6] Along with complaints about lack of programming and sufficient staff, the report described Evins as having an assault rate five times the national average. Meanwhile, several inmates and their families launched personal injury lawsuits against the state.[7]

One of the most-watched cases was that of Shaquanda Cotton, a fifteen-year-old African American girl from the east Texas town of Paris, who received an indeterminate sentence (up to age twenty-one) for shoving a hall monitor in school. Portrayed in the national press as a victim of racially motivated sentencing, Cotton briefly became a symbol for civil rights advocates, who won her release at the end of March 2007. Cotton subsequently described the conditions at the Ron Jackson State Juvenile Correctional Complex in Brownwood for a feature in *Seventeen* magazine: "Seeing the barbwire fences and guards terrified me. I was given an orange jumpsuit and socks and taken to my quarters—a tiny room that had only a bed, a bookshelf, and a desk. Some of [the other inmates] had committed serious crimes, like murder."[8]

Public anger ran deep. While some critics denounced what they saw as a clear-cut case of racial profiling, others alleged a deliberate conspiracy against all juvenile offenders regardless of race or ethnicity. "Staff are being paid your tax money to rape your children," declared Randal Chance, a former TYC inspector, who described the agency as "a dynasty of corruption that condones the mistreatment of youth in its care."[9] For its part, the Texas legislature promulgated an overhaul of the TYC's governing board and administration and launched an investigation into the scandal's causes. As is often the case in such probes, the focus turned to individual failures: poor decisions, corrupt practices, budgetary choices. Much of the discussion focused on the TYC's "culture," which was often portrayed as uniquely insular, defensive, tolerant of abuses, yet impatient with outside criticism. Precious little attention was given to the agency's sixty-year history or the broader history of juvenile justice and corrections in Texas, which dates to the late nineteenth century.

This book seeks to tell that story and in the process explain how Texas's juvenile justice system reached its current place as one of the more controversial systems in the nation (although certainly not the only one plagued by abuse scandals). Throughout its long and troubled history, the Texas juvenile justice system has struggled with the tensions that historians argue have been built into juvenile justice since the founding of the nation's first juvenile court in Chicago a little over a century ago.[10] As we shall see, some reformers have advocated for the protection of youthful offenders from adult sanctions, punishments, and correctional environments. Others have viewed juveniles as little more than adult criminals in miniature and emphasized protecting the public from youth portrayed, at different historical moments, as gangsters, teenage terrorists, and most recently, super-predators. The youth inspiring such labels have tended to come from the most marginal populations—poor whites, African Americans, and Mexican Americans—who have also filled the dockets of juvenile courts, the cells of county detention centers, and the dormitories of large juvenile facilities.

The word "super-predator" was coined in 1995 by criminologist John J. DiIulio to describe remorseless "kids who kill." Citing statistical and anecdotal evidence of rising violent juvenile crime, he explained that the 1990s generation of youth suffered from a "moral poverty" that caused them to kill randomly, remorselessly, unpredictably. Moreover, he predicted an impending demographic bulge in the adolescent-age criminal cohort, warning that, unless this problem was addressed through tougher legal sanctions, the violent crime rate would continue to soar.[11] Critics denounced the term as racially charged and feared it would encourage racial profiling of inner-city youth by police departments. They also decried it for fanning the flames of an already extant panic that had caused many state legislatures to pass tougher juvenile sentencing laws and appropriate funds for the construction of "youth prisons"—precisely the kinds of facilities at the center of the recent sexual abuse scandal in Texas.[12]

Highly charged words such as "super-predator" do not appear in a cultural and historical vacuum. They resonate with the public for reasons involving collective historical memory, real and imagined, even if they fail to accurately describe the individuals and groups they single out for attention. The history of juvenile justice constitutes an important part of that shared experience, having helped shape popular and expert understandings about delinquent and at-risk youth, about the nature of childhood and adolescence, and about the place of various racial and ethnic groups within those categories. This book argues that uncovering the origins of the "super-predator"—both the rhetoric and the reality—requires an exploration of the historic relationship between race, juvenile justice, and importantly, childhood. The central failure of juvenile justice typically has stemmed from its chronic inability to shelter children and youth from the dangers, responsibilities, and experiences of the world of adult criminal justice.

According to historians of childhood, the notion of "protected childhood" animated the concerns of American social reformers as early as the 1820s.[13] During that era, the free school and Sunday school movements took root in several northern cities, while "houses of refuge" and reformatories were opened for the destitute, homeless, and delinquent youth who were beginning to appear on urban street corners. An emerging middle-class began to bear fewer children and to lavish greater attention on their individual children as new modes of child rearing gained a foothold in American social thought. Increasingly it was believed that a child's life should be characterized by education, play, and exploration rather than adult responsibilities such as wage labor or early marriage. By the end of the nineteenth century, middle-class "child savers" such as Jane Addams, Miriam Van Waters, Julian Mack, and Lewis Hine were advocating a laundry list of child-centered reforms: curfews, age of consent laws, child labor bans, compulsory education, playgrounds, and most notably, the juvenile court. Many of these reforms were aimed at extending the protections of childhood to working-class and poor children. Moreover, they sought to broaden the years of protection and semidependence on adults upward into the adolescent years, a reflection of the slowly spreading idea of adolescence itself at the turn of the twentieth century. One of its leading proponents, the Clark University psychiatrist and child-study movement leader Granville Stanley Hall, described the life stage of adolescence famously as a time of "storm and stress," a time of risk taking, rebellion, awkwardness, and self-discovery. Adolescents, he and other psychiatrists such as William Healy proposed, needed to be treated individually, especially when they ran afoul of rules, as seemed almost inevitable.

Early juvenile court judges, such as Denver's Ben Lindsey, helped to popularize the idea of the tough but fatherly juvenile justice official for whom understanding his wayward charges was a specialty. Meanwhile, courts for delinquent girls, headed by matronly figures such as Mary M. Barthelme of Chicago, preoccupied themselves with curbing the precocious sexuality of working-class girls, whose families were often recent arrivals to American industrial cities. However problematic and often contradictory these efforts could be, they drew on and helped legitimize the premise that children and adolescents should be protected from adult responsibility, as well as from adult sanctions, for their misdeeds. Recalling the case of an Italian immigrant youth arrested for stealing coal, Lindsey lamented "this business of punishing infants as if they were adults and of maiming young lives by trying to make the gristle of their unformed characters carry the weight of our iron laws and heavy penalties."[14] At its best, juvenile justice promised a way out of Lindsey's dilemma by offering individualized treatment instead of punishment.

Unfortunately, the descent from the lofty rhetoric to the gritty reality of juvenile justice was a precipitous one, as David J. Rothman and other historians have shown. Texas resembled many other states in its abject failure to live up to the promises of individualized treatment administered by caring, well-trained professionals. However, as this study demonstrates, it also confronted all manner of resistance from the juveniles placed in state custody. As early as the 1920s, youth were running away, refusing to obey orders, petitioning authorities for their release, or like Shaquanda Cotton, telling their stories to the news media. Although accessing the unmediated voices of children and youth is practically impossible, this book attempts to convey some sense of what juvenile inmates felt, thought, said, and did while confined in a variety of settings. Increasingly, youth, their parents, and other advocates began to employ the language of protected childhood to argue their case against mistreatment, poor physical conditions, or the lack of a homelike environment in juvenile facilities. Indeed, key moments of juvenile justice reform, particularly between 1910 and 1920 and in the 1940s and 1970s, specifically evoked the protections of childhood and adolescence to some degree. By contrast, calls for "law and order" reforms, such as tougher sanctions and prisons, have tended to rely on descriptions of juvenile offenders that make them out to be fully responsible adults—and just as dangerous as adult felons, if not more so.

Cycles of reform, resistance, and backlash form a constant feature in the landscape of Texas's juvenile justice history. In 1889, thanks to women reformers, Texas became the first state in the South to open a statewide reformatory for boys. However, it functioned as essentially a convict farm until reformers managed to lobby for a law to remake the institution into a training school with an educational program. But in what would become a recurring story, reforms could not be fully implemented. The chief obstacles to reform throughout the century were recalcitrant townspeople who staffed, ran, and protected the institutions and spendthrift legislators who were generally hostile to expenditures for the welfare of morally questionable groups like juvenile delinquents. However, again and again, such legislators opened the state purse to pay for the construction of secure institutions. Another problem was the transience of child advocates; until the 1970s, the state lacked any permanent children's rights or child welfare organizations that could maintain a consistent legal or media campaign for youth. Thus such work was often left to individuals or local groups that became temporarily interested in juvenile justice reform for a variety of reasons.

One of the most important features of this story is the repeated failure of juvenile justice to deliver on its promises of treatment, rehabilitation, and most significantly, protection. Throughout the period covered in this book, juveniles were subjected to all manner of abuses, prisonlike conditions, and exploitative labor requirements. In recent years, abuse scandals have become routine in youth prisons nationwide;

as of this writing, the Department of Justice is prosecuting lawsuits against nine states for unconstitutional conditions of confinement for juveniles.[15] As a result, the recent centennial anniversary of the juvenile court became an occasion for recrimination rather than celebration. Scholars, policy makers, and youth advocates have begun to rethink the recent trajectory toward punishment in juvenile justice.[16] At a time when new research on adolescent brain development strongly suggests that the progressives were correct in their belief that juveniles were too immature to be held fully responsible for their misdeeds, the cycle of juvenile justice reform appears to have produced an arbitrary, punitive, and ineffective system. It seems an opportune moment to explore that system's history.

ONE

The Other Lost Generation

Reform and Resistance in the Juvenile Training Schools, 1907–1929

In February 1927, Jimmy Jones, a sixteen-year-old inmate at the Texas State Juvenile Training School in Gatesville, convinced two parolees to smuggle letters to his father out of the institution.[1] Jimmy's odyssey into Texas juvenile justice had begun the previous October, when he was charged with "highway robbery with firearms."[2] That day, after working on the family farm, Jimmy had gone on a drinking excursion into the nearest town, San Marcos, just south of Austin. Armed with his father's revolver, an intoxicated Jimmy "went up the road a few miles, held up five Mexican men, got one dollar out of the crowd, and drove back to town," where he was arrested within minutes. Mr. Jones later speculated that Jimmy "must have thought himself a moving picture Hero of the West, under the influence of liquor." Jimmy's father was so angry that he "did not even hire an attorney" and gladly signed a court document declaring the boy "a Delinquent Child." A few months in Gatesville, he thought, would teach Jimmy "a lesson" about such reckless behavior.

Within days of his arrival at Gatesville, however, Jimmy attempted to escape.[3] In hot pursuit were bloodhounds led by Mr. Burleson, the Gatesville dog trainer. The dogs soon "treed" Jimmy, meaning they trapped him up a tree. When Jimmy tried to surrender, he was bitten in seven places. Upon Jimmy's return to Gatesville, he received "a run away busting," or "forty licks" with a black bat while three guards held him down. Jimmy then became a model citizen, building such a good conduct record that Gatesville staff made him a "trusty," the juvenile equivalent of the co-opted inmates in the adult prison system who helped guards maintain order in exchange for special privileges. However, Jimmy remained deeply unhappy. In addition to feeling "homesick," Jimmy loathed the meals of "beans and bread" and the constant threats of punishment for the pettiest mistakes in the classroom or the fields. He chafed at the institution's dishonest control of information. In his letters home, Jimmy explained, "[I've] got hold of some of the literature that Mr. Luck [the chaplain] sends you and half of it isn't true. He won't let us write anything against this place and won't let us ask to come home." He also remarked, "This place isn't what you think it is. . . . We are treated like dogs." Thus, Jimmy not only passed his request secretly; he also advised his father to respond in coded language. If he was willing to seek Jimmy's release, he was to write that he "got the new barn built," and if not, that he "got the new chicken house built." Jimmy expressed deep regret for his past misbehavior, insisting that he would "go straight" and renounce alcohol.

Moved by his son's plight, Jimmy's father took action. He visited Jimmy and was outraged by the scars and dog-bite marks that covered the boy's body. Mr. Jones confronted Gatesville officials about the matter and received contradictory explanations for the scars. The Gatesville parole officer, Lorene Moon, told him that Jimmy "fell out of a tree and scratched himself," while the superintendent, Charles E. King, explained that Jimmy "went through a barb wire fence."[4] After observing Mr. Jones in a heated argument with Moon and King, a sympathetic staff member quietly advised the angry father that reporting the incident would only place Jimmy in greater danger. But Mr. Jones already feared for his son's safety; immediately after his departure, staff "cursed [Jimmy] out" and threatened him so much that Jimmy was afraid to sleep at night. Angry and desperate, Mr. Jones brought his case before Texas Governor Daniel J. Moody Jr., the Texas Board of Control (TBC), the Texas Department of Public Safety, and Hays County Judge W. H. Thompson (who had committed Jimmy to Gatesville). Governor Moody's office took immediate action, ordering all documents related to Jimmy's case and sending a detail of Texas Rangers to Gatesville for a surprise inspection and an interview with Jimmy and other inmates.[5] Ranger J. E. McCoy examined Jimmy and found "scars and cuts" that "had the appearance of Dogbites."[6] However, he concluded that Jimmy's case was an aberration; McCoy took part in another dog chase and recapture during an escape attempt, during which he felt that dog trainer Burleson was "careful and watchful." Similarly, McCoy described Superintendent King as "very attentive in his duties and taking a great interest in the institution and its boys." McCoy reserved his only criticism for "Mr. Preston, who [did] the whipping"; McCoy reported that Preston illegally used a "large strap" and engaged in "bad policy" by enlisting other inmates to assist in whippings. McCoy's final report recommended that Preston "ought not to be connected with the Institution." The TBC quickly issued a policy directive reiterating an existing statutory requirement that whippings be closely supervised and circumscribed. However, with most of the Jones family's complaints explained away, no action was taken regarding Jimmy's case.[7]

News of the Rangers' investigation spread quickly, prompting letters to the TBC from former Gatesville employees. According to A. D. Chestnut, who had worked as a guard for two years, King had abolished a "Discipline Committee" put in place in the early 1920s to deal with inmate rule breaking. The replacement was "no trial no nothing except the bat."[8] Another former staff member, J. A. Farqhuar, reported that his brother-in-law's farm abutted the Gatesville property, from which he "could hear the lashes . . . and the boys screaming" from almost "a mile away."[9] The pressure for Jimmy's release mounted further when Hays County judge W. H. Thompson, who had sentenced him in the first place, issued his support for parole. This decision resulted from a personal visit to the judge from Mr. Jones, who made "a most pathetic appeal" on his son's behalf.[10]

Gatesville officials refused to yield to demands for leniency, regardless of their source. Superintendent King refused to parole Jimmy, insisting that he had not earned enough merit points to achieve rehabilitation. "We do not consider him to be the best boy we have by any means," declared King; he had yet to show "by good conduct that he can be a law abiding citizen."[11] This statement indicated that King would resist paroling him even when the committing judge, the TBC, and even the governor all wanted it done. An example had to be made to discourage other inmates from breaking the institution's stranglehold on information about itself to the outside world, as Jimmy had done. The counterattack continued with an attempted smear of Jimmy's family. In a letter to Judge Thompson, parole officer Moon accused Mr. Jones of lacking remorse for his son's crime.[12] Moon then erred revealingly, by complaining that Jimmy was receiving disproportionate attention compared to the many other boys committed from Hays County. This comment "irritated" Judge Thompson because, as he told Mr. Jones, most of those other commitments "were Negro Boys," and therefore, by virtue of his whiteness, Jimmy "would be entitled to some extra attention."[13] TBC board member H. H. Harrington denounced Moon's "indiscreet" letter and lamented that Gatesville "should be suspected of biased or prejudiced" treatment against a single inmate—a statement that clearly expressed an assumed "bias and prejudice" toward black juveniles.[14] Thus Moon's avenue of argument backfired badly. Within weeks, both Governor Moody and the TBC demanded "some definite action" from King.[15] Another meeting took place at Gatesville between King, Moon, Mr. Jones, and Jimmy, with no results. Finally, in August 1927, the TBC unequivocally ordered King to release Jimmy.[16]

Jimmy's case was exceptional only because he and his father managed to draw sympathetic attention to his plight. The vast majority of his fellow inmates, by contrast, practically disappeared from their families and communities. They comprised a "lost generation" of poor and working-class youth that rarely surfaced in public discourse during the second and third decades of the twentieth century. The dialectic of "reform and resistance" often invoked by historians of juvenile justice thus held two meanings in early twentieth-century Texas. Juvenile institutions such as Gatesville sought to reform inmates using a range of harsh methods, and yet, as this chapter illustrates, youth resisted their imprisonment in a variety of ways. At the same time, progressive child welfare advocates attempted to reform the way juvenile offenders were treated, both before and after they were charged with a crime. They successfully pushed for the creation of juvenile courts, detention centers, and juvenile probation departments. Most controversially, they attempted to reform the institutional treatment of juvenile offenders, only to confront bitter resistance from guards, townspeople, and elected officials.

Reforming the Reformatory

In 1886, after visiting youthful offenders incarcerated in the Rusk State Penitentiary, the Texas chapter of the Women's Christian Temperance Union launched a petition drive calling for the separation of juvenile and adult offenders. The following year, the Texas legislature passed an "Act providing for a House of Correction," and in August 1887, state commissioners purchased nearly seven hundred acres of land outside the town of Gatesville, located about two hours north of Austin in north-central Texas. "The lay of the land is most beautiful," wrote one commissioner, "and commands the most beautiful and picturesque scenery we have ever had the pleasure of witnessing."[17] Gatesville opened its doors in January 1889, followed by others in Virginia (1889), Kentucky (1891), and Alabama (1900).[18] The initial campus was comprised of two buildings "fitted with all modern appliances, an engine and engine house, electric light machine," and a "first-class" laundry. With an "imposing appearance and pleasing to the eye," the campus buildings, according to state officials, had "scarcely a resemblance to a prison."[19] The superintendent, "Captain Ben E. McCulloch," presided over a farm labor program that began with eighty-six inmates. An apocryphal story that appears several times in Gatesville's history held that the first two inmates had a footrace to see which of them would be the first official resident. Eager for the anticipated jobs the institution would provide, local residents helped pay for the land, whose cost exceeded the state's own appropriation.

Founded in 1854, the town of Gatesville was located on a former military base that had demarcated the white-Indian frontier until about 1880. Economic development in Gatesville and surrounding Coryell County revolved around cattle ranching, lumber, and cotton cultivation. After 1882, the Texas and St. Louis Railway Company's "Cotton Belt" express passed through Gatesville regularly, transporting cattle and cotton products between the Texas hinterlands and the Mississippi River. The population was sparse, numbering just short of seventeen thousand in 1890, the year after the House of Correction opened its doors. It was also overwhelmingly white, according to the county's official history, with few African Americans

THE WHITE ROAD.

Figure 1. Entrance to the Texas State Juvenile Training School, Gatesville, Texas, 1921. (*Biennial Report of the State Juvenile Training School*, 1913–14 [Austin, 1914]. Courtesy of the Texas State Library and Archives Commission.)

before or after the Civil War. At that time, there were few plantations and fewer than three hundred slaves, although this had not diminished the county's support for the Confederacy. In the 1860 presidential election, the county had voted for the pro-slavery Democrat John C. Breckenridge and had voted to secede from the Union the following month.[20] By the 1880s, the major issues facing the region were poverty and temperance. With 42 percent of all farms worked by tenants, Baptist and Methodist reformers focused on saloons—Gatesville alone had ten of them— which were blamed for regular outbreaks of lawlessness, including lynchings.[21]

Despite nearly nonexistent records, one can infer that the Gatesville House of Correction bore some marks of these immediate surroundings. Boys spent most of their days laboring in fields surrounded by barbed wire, or "Texas fence," the cheaper alternative to rock fencing chosen by most area farmers (figure 1). In a 1917 interview, one longtime guard recalled the scene when he first began working at Gatesville, in 1903:

> Then we had something like 150 boys, ranging in age from about fifteen to about twenty one years old. . . . At that time this institution was regarded more as a prison. We required more work and less schooling. In fact during the spring and fall months we had no school. All the time of the boys was devoted during these two seasons to manual labor, and for this reason we farmed more intensively, raised large crops and

from a financial standpoint made the institution more profitable. At that time the inmates were guarded with guns.[22]

Demographically, juvenile delinquents in Texas presented a stark contrast to the urban immigrants from eastern and southern Europe who preoccupied progressive child savers in northern cities such as Chicago, Milwaukee, or Boston. A large plurality of inmates were white, black, or of Mexican origin, the children of rural poor families who had recently migrated to growing cities such as Houston, Dallas, Galveston, and San Antonio. "The Gatesville boy," declared a 1914 report, "is essentially a town boy."[23] That same report included a survey of boys' family backgrounds, in which 119 of 195 respondents listed their mother's occupation as "housekeeper." The leading occupations for fathers were, in descending order, "unknown," "railroad men," "laborers," and "farmers." A parent had died in nearly two-thirds (113) of the boys' families, and just under half (74) of the parents had criminal records. Most of the boys had moved at least once and lived on rented property.[24]

A second distinguishing feature of juvenile justice in Texas was the Jim Crow system of racial and ethnic discrimination that resulted in unequal treatment of African American juvenile inmates (and later those of Mexican origin). This pattern manifested itself in disparate ways according to gender. Black males were vastly overrepresented in the Gatesville inmate population. When Gatesville had opened in 1889, African Americans comprised 46 of the first 68 inmates, all of whom were transferred from the adult prison system. Although Gatesville admitted inmates regardless of race or ethnicity, it strictly segregated every aspect of their daily lives: housing, schooling, dining, and religious services. As a result, by 1917, about 250 black inmates crowded into Harris Hall, the Jim Crow congregate dormitory built to house about half that number.[25] By contrast, when the state opened its first and only training school for girls before World War II, it excluded black females altogether. Black girls charged with committing a crime in this period may have had their cases heard in local juvenile courts, but the available remedies were limited to the county jail or release back into the community, which posed their own distinct dilemmas (examined in chapter 3).

These demographic and policy features interacted in startling ways as the overall numbers of incarcerated juvenile delinquents rose steadily throughout the second and third decades of the twentieth century. Like the nation as a whole, Texas experienced "youth problems" stemming from broader social and cultural changes. Young people in this period enjoyed unprecedented opportunities to engage in unsanctioned activities away from the prying eyes of adults, in the "rumble seats" of automobiles, on the polished wood floors of urban dance halls, or in the darkened spaces of movie houses.[26] Adolescents and their parents clashed over these activities more than anything else in the 1920s, according to sociologists Robert and Helen Lynd in their classic study *Middletown*.[27] But many working-class and impoverished youth also desired access to fast cars, stylish clothes, and the new sites of leisure and consumption that nourished the growth of an American youth culture.

The new mobility also drove more-enduring social upheavals, propelling internal migrations within the South that brought large numbers of young people into Texas's cities. By the 1920s, many young families from Texas, Arkansas, Louisiana, and northern Mexico were migrating from small towns to cities such as Dallas, Houston, Galveston, and San Antonio. Poor whites, as well as African Americans and migrants of Mexican origin, moved to the cities in search of work in the emerging oil, shipping, cotton, construction, and manufacturing sectors. While many southern blacks migrated north, thousands in east Texas and Louisiana chose to move to Houston or Dallas. Not only was Texas the only southern state to realize a net gain in black population in the first half of the twentieth century, but a large portion of those new migrants were teenagers and young adults. Increasingly by the 1920s, urban youth cultures emerged that crossed borders of race, ethnicity, and class, prompting harsh responses from the all-white police forces that defended the rigid social order of Jim Crow segregation. In Houston, police raids on juke joints and "sweeps" of underage boys in black neighborhoods helped propel disproportionate numbers of African American youth into Gatesville, a pattern that would continue into the postwar era.[28]

Women's reform organizations played a central role in pressuring the legislature to improve the treatment of juvenile offenders. The Texas Federation of Women's Clubs, the Young Women's Christian Association, and the Texas Congress of Mothers mounted a series of child-saving campaigns in the first decades of the century. In the 1920s, these associations pooled their efforts to form the Joint Legislative Council, or the "Petticoat Lobby." They achieved many legislative victories, including laws providing for public kindergartens (1907 and 1917), local school taxes (1908), regulation of child labor (1911), compulsory schooling to age fourteen (1915), and mother's pensions (1917). Collectively, these activities embodied what one historian of Texas women's movements has called "social motherhood," an extension of women's traditional role in the home; at the local level, so-called municipal housekeepers such as the Houston Housewives League and the Dallas Federation of Women's Clubs pressured city governments to provide sanitation services, pure milk and water supplies, parks, and playgrounds to impoverished areas.[29]

In 1907, the Juvenile Delinquency Court Act established juvenile courts for offenders under sixteen years old and required parental notification of charges.

The law lacked concrete guidelines for court procedure, probation, or sentencing. Judges, for example, were not required to compile "social histories" or to provide any background information to Gatesville authorities should a boy be institutionalized. The lack of indeterminate sentencing reflected a distinctive feature of the Texas law, which designated juvenile courts as criminal rather than civil proceedings. Unlike the nation's first juvenile court in Chicago, the Texas version emphasized punishment over rehabilitation and criminal responsibility over child protection. Like their adult counterparts, youths incarcerated in the Gatesville reformatory could gain their release in one of three ways: completion of sentence, a "recall" issued by the sentencing court jurisdiction, or a governor's pardon.[30]

Even as they elaborated a juvenile court system, reformers focused their attention on Gatesville, decried by the Texas Federation of Women's Clubs as "an instrument of torture."[31] In 1909, the legislature removed the reformatory from the penitentiary system and renamed it the State Institution for the Training of Juvenile Delinquents, which later became simply the State Juvenile Training School.[32] The change, as it turned out, was in name only. In November 1912, the Gatesville superintendent, W. H. Adams, decided that the institution's new mission required the abolition of exotic forms of corporal punishment. Adams outlawed "pulling toes," in which boys were forced to stand holding their toes with their hands indefinitely; and "bustings," in which boys were made to stand with their arms held over their heads while a guard "flogged" them with a bat. This policy provoked a revolt from the institution's guards, who initially expressed their displeasure by allowing, and possibly encouraging, over two dozen escapes over a three-day period. Ultimately, they all walked off the job, forcing Superintendent Adams to recruit local citizens (many of whom publicly supported the guards) to serve in their place.[33] A *Dallas Morning News* reporter labeled Gatesville "a hybrid institution" that had not shed the "stigma of prison."

> In and around it there is much of the insignia of a State's prison. Attaches as well as
> the citizens of the neighborhood speak of the institution as "the reformatory" and
> of its inmates, not as "students" or "cadets," but as "prisoners" or "convicts," and
> one hears all such terms as "putting up time," "busting," etc., employed as familiarly
> as they are in a penitentiary. Also the boys have numbers. . . . In fact, the State is
> attempting to conduct at Gatesville a combined reformatory and juvenile training
> school, an effort doomed to failure.[34]

The crisis prompted a visit from Texas governor Oscar B. Colquitt, who toured the institution along with representatives of the Texas State Conference of Charities and Corrections (TSCCC). It was, by all accounts, a bleak place, consisting of two dormitories, a school building, a guardhouse, a kitchen and dining hall, a power plant, a chapel, a superintendent's residence, and assorted barns and livestock houses. The inventory included three "Kentucky dogs" for tracking escapees, and 644 feet of "Texas fence"—barbed wire—which surrounded the grounds.[35] An apocryphal-sounding story described their visit to the institution's tailor shop, where boy inmates made prison uniforms. Reportedly, Colquitt held up a pair of poorly stitched trousers and, "touched with pity and compassion for the creature who might have the shapeless garment to wear," asked the superintendent why he could not "have them made a little neater."[36] The governor's question echoed those being asked by the national movement toward training schools, which embarked on a new, more "scientific" approach to juvenile rehabilitation that emphasized education over punishment. In January 1913, Colquitt appointed two TSCCC women to a reconstituted Gatesville Board of Trustees, which issued a report that led to the passage of a sweeping new juvenile act in 1913. The bill declared that Gatesville was now an educational rather than a penal institution, which should "include common school, as well as industrial, or agricultural branches."[37] Gatesville became the destination for boys convicted of both criminal and status offenses, including "delinquency, dependency, incorrigibility or truancy."[38] The juvenile court now had original jurisdiction over all offenders under the age of seventeen, regardless of the severity of their offense. Although the court would remain classified as a criminal proceeding until 1943, it now was required to issue indeterminate sentences "between one and five years" for individuals up to the age of twenty-one. Like the training school, the Texas juvenile court would function as a hybrid institution that combined features of adult and juvenile justice.

The law's contradictions gave rise to a series of habeas corpus appeals filed on behalf of juvenile delinquents. For example, in April 1919, the Texas Court of Criminal Appeals considered the case of a thirteen-year-old boy named Raymond Brooks who had been committed to Gatesville for the crime of "stealing twenty empty grain sacks worth ten cents each."[39] The appeals court noted that the indeterminate sentence potentially could last "three years more" than if "he was sixteen and charged with murder," because the juvenile court rules now applied even in capital cases. The court also noted that Brooks's father had not been notified of the charge and had been prevented from retaining a lawyer. In siding with Brooks, the court stated that juvenile offenders were entitled to legal representation. A similar case extended juveniles' right to post bail while a case was pending.[40] Although such appeals were rare, they provoked complaints from the Gatesville superintendent about being "hauled into court" because of a perceived legal loophole in the sentencing requirements, which implied that juvenile delinquents were wards of the state but also retained constitutional rights reserved for adult defendants. Gatesville officials viewed these cases as incursions into their proper sphere of authority and complained about them throughout the second and third decades of the century.

Adding to the uncertain legal status of juvenile proceedings was the haphazard establishment and operation of local juvenile courts. In general, urban juvenile courts more faithfully adopted the features recommended by national reformers. For instance, by the 1930s, Houston, Galveston, and Dallas each had established a separate juvenile court with an elected judge, a juvenile probation department, and a separate juvenile detention center. The juvenile courts in Houston and Dallas also retained the services of a child guidance clinic. By contrast, smaller towns typically offered few if any services. In rural areas, juvenile cases might be heard once or twice a month in the nearest district court. Accused juveniles awaiting trial in such locations typically languished in the county jail along with adult offenders. Such practices were hardly unique to Texas; a 1918 survey conducted by the U.S. Children's Bureau revealed that only 4 percent of all juvenile courts served rural areas, with another 16 percent in smaller cities.[41]

Regardless of the venue through which a youth was adjudged, the final destination increasingly remained the same: the training school. For boys, that meant Gatesville, which, according to the first survey produced by the board of trustees, did not operate according to any written program and merely served as "a convict farm for boys under 16 years of age."[42] After studying training schools in other states, the board members adopted the philosophy that "the institution [was] for the benefit of the boys, and not the boys for the benefit of the institution."[43] Hiring decisions were to be based on educational background rather than political or personal "influence," starting with the new superintendent, A. W. Eddins. A native of Alabama, Eddins had graduated from the Sam Houston Normal Institute in 1894 and spent the previous decade as the school superintendent for nearby Falls County.[44] Eddins typified the training school superintendents of the era, who wielded near-total institutional authority and exercised substantial public influence much like juvenile court judges such as Denver's Ben Lindsey. The typical superintendent was "practically supreme"; according to an appraisal of the nation's training schools published by the U.S. Children's Bureau, he made "decisions on all subjects, issue[d] all orders, supervise[d] all departments, [and] passe[d] on all questions of standards and scientific work," including all parole and release decisions.[45] Versed in educational psychology, Eddins delivered public speeches invoking G. Stanley Hall's view of adolescence as a "savage stage" in human evolution. In a November 1913 address at the Fort Worth meeting of the TSCCC, he sympathetically described Gatesville boys as "the most misunderstood, misrepresented and mistreated" group in Texas and outlined plans for a new dormitory building, a "trades" building for vocational education, and the hiring of professionally trained teachers and a school principal.[46]

The institution's first academic curriculum offered classes at the elementary, intermediate, and advanced levels.[47] In 1915, the state board of education certified the training school as an independent school district, which made public education funds available for teachers' salaries and school supplies. These funds, along with private donations, enabled the school to open a lending library, which quickly amassed a collection of over two thousand books, magazines, and newspapers. Eddins introduced extracurricular programs that simulated those emerging in public high schools across the nation. Historians have explored how such activities became sites of social and cultural conflict in urban high schools and Indian boarding schools during this period. Devised to foster conformity and citizenship, school sports, academic clubs, and governance bodies were sometimes imbued with unsanctioned and oppositional meanings by students.[48] In the case of Gatesville, the evidence is somewhat inconclusive. Juvenile inmates regularly participated in sports and music clubs that functioned in isolation from their counterparts in public schools; for instance, baseball and football teams competed against adult amateur and semiprofessional clubs rather than high school varsity squads. Photographs of the Gatesville football and baseball teams resemble scenes one might find in "normal" high school yearbooks, although the backdrop is a gray building rather than an athletic field (figure 2). Similarly, a school newspaper, *State Boys*, begun in 1914, appears to have been less an organ for adolescent journalism or any authentic expressions of the boys than a propaganda organ touting the institution's progress (figure 3). Few articles survive from this four-page weekly newspaper assembled and published by the boy inmates "for families and the public," other than the most blatantly pro-administration editorials with titles like "Some Advantages of the Boys Committed to This Institution."[49]

The modernization of the curriculum also affected religious services, which became more elaborate than in the past. In the first year of Eddins's administration, Gatesville conducted eight separate Sunday school classes divided by grade levels. The Gatesville chaplain, a Methodist, invited a local Catholic priest and a Jewish rabbi to visit on a monthly basis. Choir classes, as well as special holiday services, joined religious training with the curricular and extracurricular offerings in a larger program of social uplift. The institution's lack of a chapel, which caused the more extensive Sunday services to be held in regular classrooms, reinforced this integration of religious and secular activities.[50]

Another key facet of the program was military discipline, maintained under the leadership of a commandant who organized the boys into drill companies. Formations, marches, flag ceremonies, khaki uniforms, and salutes became part of everyday life. Once a week, the "State Boys' Batallion" (*sic*) put on public drill performances, accompanied by a thirty-piece marching band also comprised of inmates, in what surely must have seemed like spectacular evidence of the institution's improvements. A widely reprinted editorial, "Better Boys," praised the military program for instilling discipline, respect for authority, responsibility, and pa-

BASEBALL TEAM

Figure 2. Gatesville baseball team, 1917. (*Biennial Report of the State Juvenile Training School*, 1917–18 [Austin, 1918]. Courtesy of the Texas State Library and Archives Commission.)

triotism.[51] "Goodbye Gatesville, Hello France," exclaimed a 1917 audit report, on the eve of American entry into World War I, suggesting that one purpose of the program may have been to prepare delinquent boys for military service.[52] Entwined with the military program was a merit and demerit system that measured inmates' progress toward rehabilitation. Well-behaved boys could be promoted to the rank of "cadet captain," which put them in charge of their own company. Boys who had progressed the furthest toward their release slept in a newly christened "honor cottage"; soon they would meet with the new Gatesville parole officer, whose job was to review case files once a boy had served an informal mandatory minimum sentence of one year. Gatesville officials touted this system as a major improvement on the "black bats" and "dark cells" of the reformatory.[53] In the more humane training school, corporal punishment was banned "except as a last resort to maintain discipline"; even then, it was restricted to no more than twenty blows with an implement that would not cause "bodily injury" and was to be administered only in the presence of the superintendent and a nurse.[54]

Of special importance to reformers was the hiring of women teachers educated in normal schools and universities to replace men who had functioned as little more than prison guards. According to Mrs. E. W. Bounds, a member of both the TSCCC and Gatesville boards, women teachers exercised a "civilizing" and

STATE BOYS

VOLUME 1   GATESVILLE TEXAS MAY 13th, 1916   NUMBER 24

SOME ADVANTAGES OF THE BOYS COMMITED TO THIS INSTITUTION

(By ~~████~~

Most people have the wrong impression of this institution. They think it is about the same thing as the penitentiary, but they are mistaken—it ts a training school for boys. Boys are not sent here to be punished for their crimes, but to teach them to be better boys in the future.

When a boy is sent to this institution he doesn't think of the advantages he will have when he gets here; because the majority of the boys sent here do not have the proper care at home, and their parents or guardians let them do as they please at home. We have several good trades let the boy to learn, and if he will act right while he is here, he will soon have a good job that will be a benefit to him when he gets on the "outside."

THE BLACKSMITH SHOP.

This is but one of the many good trades a boy can learn while here.

The boys do all of the repair work on the farm implements, and shoe horses. There has been several boys left since the first of the year who have good jobs in blacksmith shops, two of the boys at present are making $15. per week.

TAILOR SHOP.

The institution has it's own tailor shop. They work about fifteen boys in this department. They make all the pants, shirts and all other wearing apparel for the boys, and make suits for the boys to wear home when they leave. They are under supervision of an experienced tailor.

THE LIBRARY.

The boys have a nice library here in charge of the Chaplain of the institution. Two boys are detailed to this department whose duty it is to see that each boy receives the book that he prefers to read. These books are given to the boys on Thursday's of each week to be read and returned to the library on the following Wednesday. The boys are allowed to receive magizines and papers of all kinds. The library has about 2,000 volumes of books.

CHAPEL.

We also have church services every Sunday morning at 10, o'clock. Our chaplain speaks to us about our Sunday School lesson, and then we go to our Sunday School rooms. We have song services in the afternoon. We enjoy this very much.

After the song service we have the military drill. This is a good thing for the boys which perhaps they would not g'et if they were on the "out side,"—because most of them would not be in school, as military is taught in most all public schools, especially in the larger cities where most of the boys are sent from.

THE SCHOOL.

While the boys are here they go to school half a day and work the other half.

This institution employs eight teachers and we use the same books as are used in the public schools. The books are prescribed by the State Board of Education, with the exceptions of a few studies above the eighth grade.

PRINTING OFFICE.

The boys print a four-page paper that is gotten up by the boys of the institution. And also print

---

Boy O' Mine.

I'm writing these lines, dear boy o' mine,
    To try and engrave on your tender heart,
A token of strength as a living start,
    For I love you well, O boy o' mine.

In the years to come small boy o' mine,
    You'll pass near shadows of shame and crime,
You'll be tempted and lured full many a time,—
    Its the test of worth, dear boy o' mine.

I'm praying to God, O boy o' mine,
    To guide you safely thru treacherous ways,
To steady your hand, to lighten your days,—
    And to make you a MAN, good boy o' mine.

But in weal or woe, small boy o' mine,
    I'm always your dad and I'm always glad,
To share your burdens or sorrows sad—
    Its part of my love, dear boy o' mine.

If you rise to the heights of power and fame,
    I'll laugh in the thought that you're a part of me,
And my soul will ring with a melody,
    Of a fathers love, brave boy o' mine

—Unidentified.

Figure 3. *State Boys* masthead, May 1916. (Box 2007/203–17, Records, Texas Youth Commission. Courtesy of the Texas State Library and Archives Commission.)

"maternal influence" over the boys in the absence of their mothers. For evidence, she pointed to improved cleanliness and hygiene and a more nurturing environment. Bounds contrasted cafeteria meals of the past, in which boys dined in enforced silence "like herded cattle" seated on two by fours, under the watch of men "lounging around . . . aimlessly smoking, chewing, and spitting tobacco," against the new atmosphere of "polite and ordinary conversation" over freshly pressed tablecloths, under the watchful eyes of "lady teachers."[55]

Such tender sentiments rarely extended to the growing numbers of African American inmates, a feature that the Texas juvenile justice system shared with other southern states.[56] According to a 1923 federal census of children in institutions, half of all black delinquents were placed in prisonlike settings (prisons, jails, workhouses, or reformatories), compared to only about a fifth of their white counterparts.[57] The roots of such disparities ran back to slavery and shaped the thinking of child savers who created juvenile justice and corrections. Put simply, white reformers did not include black children in the emerging idea of modern childhood, and unequal treatment largely persisted despite the strenuous efforts of African American reformers. Rather than malleable "blank slates" capable of being rehabilitated, black children and adolescents were viewed by many whites as "hard clay" fit only for manual labor and social control, as Geoffrey K. Ward has noted.[58] Thus juvenile courts and institutions discriminated against African Americans by allocating fewer resources for their treatment, which had the effect of narrowing the range of options to punitive ones such as incarceration. For example, the only published book-length study to date of southern juvenile justice illustrates how the Memphis juvenile court increasingly resolved African American delinquency cases by commitment to the city's detention center, which quickly became "a predominantly black institution" and "a holding station and short-term jail."[59] Similarly, when Gatesville first opened in 1889, African Americans comprised forty-six of the first sixty-eight inmates, all of whom were transferred from the state prison system.[60]

The 1913 Juvenile Act mandated "that the white boys shall be kept, worked and educated entirely separate from the boys of other races, and shall be kept apart in all respects." That same year, Gatesville opened its "Negroes' Institute," which included a dormitory and school building. "The negro boys' campus is some distance from the main campus," read later reports, "and segregation from the white boys is as complete as though there were two separate institutions."[61] Out of a dozen teachers on staff, the only one assigned to black students was Tom Gerald, the former night watchman, who lacked any formal training in education. Within a few years, overcrowding exacerbated this inadequate arrangement. By 1917, the black dormitory built to house 125 boys held nearly twice that number. The rise in

INTERIOR DAIRY BARN

Figure 4. "Interior Dairy Barn." (*State Juvenile Training School Pictorial Review*, Gatesville, Tex., 1933.)

Equipped with cement mangers, floors and gutters, steel stanchions and other modern and sanitary devices. The dairy barn is sufficiently large to care for 108 cows at one time.

black commitments reflected a national increase in the numbers of black youth in juvenile courts; for instance, in 1928, African Americans comprised only 5 percent of the nation's juvenile population but 16 percent of all reported juvenile court cases.[62] Ill-prepared to handle this influx of black inmates, Texas officials refused to expand the availability of either dormitory or classroom space. As a result, only about half of all black inmates were permitted to attend school, and those who did were forced to divide their days evenly between the classroom and the cotton field. Meanwhile, black inmates over the age of sixteen received no schooling at all, instead toiling in fields or farmhouses much as their predecessors had during the reformatory era (figure 4). This pattern of inadequate or nonexistent schooling for black inmates persisted throughout the first half of the century.

The problem of black overcrowding gave rise to calls for transforming Gatesville into an all-white institution and placing the growing number of black delinquents in a Jim Crow training school. In response to numerous pleas from Gatesville officials, the 1917 legislature passed a statute that established a "State Training School for Negro Boys" and even provided for the legal transfer of black inmates, but failed to appropriate any funds for it.[63] This symbolic gesture made Gatesville staff apoplectic with frustration. During testimony before the legislature in 1924, the Gatesville school principal, Della McDonald, complained bitterly that black inmates "were never supposed to have been placed" in Gatesville, which had "no provision" for black schooling.[64] The measure confused one county judge, who in a July 1923 case sentenced a black teenager named George Brown to spend a year in the nonexistent Jim Crow training school. With an irony that was probably unintended, the Texas Court of Criminal Appeals reversed the decision while declaring that the legislature "surely" had not intended "to lay down one procedure for boys of one race and another procedure for those of another race."[65]

These racial disparities reflected differences of degree rather than kind. Generally, Gatesville's program never really broke away from the assumptions of the reformatory era, when all the institution's boys were viewed as "inmates" rather than "students." Hard labor, congregate housing, rigid discipline, and the use of untrained staff as "guards" rather than "mentors" persisted during what proved to be a short-lived period of reform. Such shortcomings stood in sharp relief against the more progressive institution for delinquent girls that also opened in this period in Gainesville, located north of Dallas near the Oklahoma border. Delinquent girls presented Texas reformers with a distinct set of challenges related less to preserving public safety and more to safeguarding traditional family and gender roles.

Preparing for Future Womanhood

When it opened in 1916, the Gainesville institution's stated mission was "to provide a home for delinquent and dependent girls where they [might] be trained in those useful arts and sciences to which women are adapted," to inculcate a sense of "the sacredness of the responsibility of parenthood and wifehood," and "to prepare them for future womanhood and independence."[66] These tasks seemed within reach because, in contrast to its male counterpart, Gainesville served a much smaller inmate population and enjoyed more consistent and superior leadership. Situated on 160 acres, Gainesville received a total of 232 girls in its first four years.[67] By 1920, its average daily population was seventy-one girls, with a median age of fifteen. The vast majority came from cities, including nearly half from the nearby Dallas–Fort Worth area alone. New arrivals underwent medical, dental, and intelligence screenings, which revealed that nearly all of them needed attention for preventable illnesses. One third suffered from venereal disease, a reflection of the leading offense categories of sexual delinquency and "incorrigibility," which typified national patterns of female delinquency as well as the ways in which child savers attempted to control adolescent female sexuality.[68] In response, Gainesville's planners devised a program to encourage appropriate feminine behaviors, starting with private housing accommodations. In contrast to the congregate dormitories that persisted at the boys' training school, Gainesville adopted cottages, each of which included ten private bedrooms and a space for the cottage matron.

Gainesville's progressive mission was largely the brainchild of its first director, Carrie Weaver Smith, a native of the South who had earned a medical degree in the Northeast. Born in Fayetteville, Georgia, in 1884, Smith graduated from the Pennsylvania Women's Medical College in Philadelphia in 1910.[69] During her twelve-year tenure at Gainesville, she distinguished herself on the national stage as an expert on female delinquency. In 1922, *The Survey*, the leading national publication of social work, featured Gainesville prominently in an article titled "Where Girls Go Right." Miriam Van Waters, the nationally known referee of the Los Angeles Juvenile Court, praised Gainesville as one of the "most progressive" of the thirty state training schools she visited on a national survey.[70] "Dr. Carrie Weaver Smith has probably gone further than anyone else in stressing the school side of the program," exclaimed Van Waters, alongside a photograph of Gainesville girls preparing doughnuts in a "domestic science" class.[71] So focused was Gainesville on providing "individualized" instruction that institution-maintaining labor was performed by hired male workers, rather than by the girls themselves, in stark contrast to the practice at Gatesville. As the following Van Waters anecdote suggests, Smith's program encouraged the cultivation of both "feminine" sensitivity and individual identity, hallmarks of normative female adolescence:

> In the Texas State School a tiny, inexpensive outhouse has been built as a museum. Here the girls take specimens that they have collected on walks. One girl is detailed as curator. Jennie, a tall, angular girl, with a rebellious jaw and horny elbows, stooped as we were walking through the tall dried grass. She was working on something with infinite pains.
>
> "There," she said, "I have teased it out." She held up the shining, cast-off skin of a snake. "That is for the museum. It is as fine work as combing out babies' hair, but I didn't break it."
>
> The discovery of one's personal and unique relation to the commonplace is surely an element in the process of "finding oneself" which is so necessary in the restoration of the delinquent girl.[72]

The article also noted the absence of corporal punishment and the inclusion of sex education, both topics about which Smith wrote and spoke widely. In 1920, she delivered a major address to the National Conference of Social Work, titled "The Unadjusted Girl," which blamed adults for female delinquency.[73] Many of the girls charged with sexual delinquency were victims of adult males, often relatives, who had escaped legal or moral sanction. These "children of squatters" living in "covered wagons" and "shotgun houses," she asserted, were surrounded by "moral and physical filth." So impoverished were the girls that their first letters home often began thus: "I have a room and a dresser all to myself." Smith frequently invoked eugenicist thought, asserting that most delinquent girls were the products of "unspeakable" homes headed by "unfit" or "mentally defective" parents. In her view, state laws restricting marriage might prevent such poor parentage. To illustrate the point, Smith often told vignettes such as the one about the fifteen-year-old girl who had sauntered into Smith's office and insisted that at home she was accustomed to "having half a pint of whiskey and two packages of 'Camels' a day."[74]

Smith's impassioned advocacy on behalf of delinquent girls fed into her blunt criticism of the lack of resources that hampered Gainesville's rehabilitation program. While the institution was still under construction, Smith spent several weeks inspecting conditions at the Dallas County Industrial Girls' Home. Blood tests uncovered a tainted food supply that had infected several girls with hookworm; interviews with inmates revealed the use of chains and whips in medieval-style punishments.[75] In her later reports to the legislature, Smith wryly complained that she was forced to search outside Texas for qualified teachers and social workers because of a shortage of academic programs, inadequate salary scales, and the low social status accorded to such careers in the state. Nevertheless, Gainesville established a widely admired curriculum that included academic, vocational, and moral programming. In addition to home economics, the vocational department offered more career-related training for such "women's jobs" as stenography, typewriting, and bookkeeping. The girls also took required classes in baby and child care and attended a twelve-part lecture series on "sex hygiene." A devout Christian, Smith sought to "arouse the unawakened religious sense" of the girls, two-thirds of whom had attended church regularly prior to their adjudication.[76] Bible instruction and religious assemblies took place twice a week, supplementing lengthy Sunday services.

The emphasis on moral uplift shaped extracurricular activities as well. By 1920, the institution had established local charters from both the Young Women's Christian Association and the Girl Scouts of America (GSA). The first correctional school ever to apply for a GSA charter, Gainesville reported having three troops with fifty-four girls, and in its early years awarded over three hundred merit badges for "homemaking, canning, cooking, home nursing, athletics, farming, first-aid, and home economics."[77] For its participants, the GSA provided an experience, described as "a simplified form of army drill," that was roughly equivalent to the military-style program of their male counterparts in Gatesville.[78] They wore uniforms, went on nature hikes, and engaged in patriotic activities such as making flags. At the same time, the GSA gave girls a semblance of "normal" childhood life; members took several field trips to local stores, movie theaters, and outdoor picnic sites. They also played sports such as tennis, basketball, volleyball, and croquet. These girls were most likely to move expeditiously into the "Texas Cottage," which housed girls who had earned the opportunity for parole consideration. Decorated with furniture and a Victrola phonograph player donated by a local women's Bible-study group, the cottage prepared girls who, in their own words, were "Going from Texas to Texas," in part by allowing them to attend Sunday services in the town church.[79]

In contrast to the institution for delinquent boys, which attempted to superimpose a training-school model on a correctional structure, Gainesville's program began with the assumption that its charges were children and adolescents who could be rehabilitated. The emphasis on privacy, adult mentoring, education, and adolescent development distinguished Gainesville's program as one devoted to juvenile rehabilitation. Gainesville also enjoyed a substantially lower inmate population and well-educated leadership, all of which contributed to its strong public reputation into the mid-1920s. However, Gainesville's successes began to erode under social and political pressures that affected the institutions for both delinquent boys and girls. In 1925, Superintendent Smith left to run the Maryland State School for Girls. In the 1930s, she directed the National Training School for Girls in Washington, D.C., mounting a public campaign for improved conditions that won the support of Eleanor Roosevelt, who was "so appalled" that she invited the girl inmates to tea on the White House lawn and helped convince Congress to appropriate one hundred thousand dollars for improvements.[80] However, in 1937, a "free-for-all fight" between "white and colored inmates" led the D.C. Board of Commissioners to fire Smith for being "too lenient." Smith finally retired from the field of juvenile corrections to run a bookstore until her death in 1942.[81]

The Retreat of Progress

Public and especially political support for the rehabilitative treatment of juvenile offenders proved to be short-lived. The training schools became enmeshed in the increasingly polarized world of Texas state politics, particularly the Democratic machines associated with James ("Pa") and Miriam ("Ma") Ferguson.[82] During his controversial governorship (1915–17), the charismatic James Ferguson, no supporter of correctional reform for adults or juveniles, appointed political loyalists to the Gatesville Board of Trustees. In March 1915, a divided board produced a tie vote over whether to retain "reform" superintendent Eddins, who in turn resigned "due to political conditions."[83] His replacement was Charles E. King, a "practical businessman and farmer" whose main qualification appears to have been his loyalty to Ferguson.[84] Under King's stewardship, progressive reform at Gatesville essentially came to a halt amid new building construction to house more juvenile inmates. Notably, in 1917, Gatesville christened a "Ferguson School Building" equipped with "ten large rooms, an auditorium with stage and motion picture booth and equipment." A proposed Jim Crow institution for black delinquent boys was to be named the Ferguson State Farm.[85] King's tenure of office followed that of his patrons. In 1917, the Texas legislature impeached and removed Ferguson on corruption charges; four years later, King resigned due to an abuse scandal (described later in this chapter). However, in 1925, King was reappointed during the administration of Governor Miriam "Ma" Ferguson, who had won election with her husband's backing. King promptly went to work for the Fergusons, pressuring Gatesville staff to vote for the incumbent in the 1926 election. When twenty employees refused, King fired them, tarring them as "Ku Kluxers," a reference to Ferguson's opponent in the previous election, Judge Felix Robertson, who had been endorsed by the newly resurgent Ku Klux Klan.[86] The accusation made little sense, however, because Ferguson's opponent in 1926 was the young state attorney general, Daniel J. Moody Jr., who was no Klansman and had the support of good-government reformers. Staff members vehemently denied any affiliation with the Klan and levied countercharges that King encouraged staff to disregard restrictions on drinking, gambling, and whipping boys.[87] After Moody won election, prominent Gatesville residents petitioned him to fire King, or as they put it more colorfully, to "get rid of this Fergusonism." King, they insisted, had turned the training school into "a partisan political machine," hiring, firing, and even contracting with local businesses who expressed loyalty to the Fergusons.[88]

Such complaints typically ended up in the hands of a new government body, the Texas Board of Control, established by the legislature in 1920 to oversee all the state's "eleemosynary" institutions for dependent populations.[89] Adopted by many other states, this governance model attempted to remedy abuses thought to stem from overly autonomous superintendents of institutions for the deaf, blind, mentally ill, dependent, and delinquent populations.[90] For instance, the TBC was given equal share in the superintendent's unilateral authority to make parole decisions. However, in practice, the TBC depended completely on the superintendent for information about individual inmates. Moreover, the superintendent retained the final say; no inmate could be paroled without his or her consent. Physically remote from Gatesville and Gainesville, the TBC divided its attention between several institutions, resulting in fairly lax regulation. While the Gatesville trustees had been comprised of eight members who met monthly, the TBC's three members held quarterly meetings. This general decline in oversight resulted in less frequent and less thorough reports submitted by superintendents throughout the 1920s and 1930s. Lengthy narrative descriptions of activities vanished; by 1932, the average annual report shrank to only about a page long, belying the untrammeled growth of the inmate population (table 1).

King's political alliances could not protect him from public anger following the brutal murder of an inmate by a staff member, early on the morning of Sunday, September 25, 1921. The victim, fifteen-year-old Dell Thames, of Beaumont, had arrived in Gatesville the previous Wednesday and had been in trouble ever since with the "drill master," H. G. Twyman.[91] Twyman had beaten Thames repeatedly for "falling down and refusing to drill"; an investigation later showed that the boy's

Table 1. New admissions to Gatesville, 1910–1935

Year	1910	1915	1920	1925	1930	1935
	277	493	822	1,042	1,085	1,371

Sources: *Biennial Report of the State Juvenile Training School* (1910–18); *Report of the State Board of Control* (1920–36).

body was so covered in bruises that he was probably physically unable to stand and march. Prior to Sunday services, the boys convened for morning drill under the supervision of two inmates, Eddie Stokes and Joe Thomas, who were acting as "sub-officers." When Thames again refused to cooperate, Stokes and Thomas escorted him to Twyman, who ordered them to bring the boy to "the picket, a small covered stand about eight by ten feet with open sides, used as a seat for guards," which doubled as a punishment area. While Stokes and Thomas looked on in shock, Twyman "deliberately choked" their fellow inmate while muttering phrases like "Do you feel yourself slipping?" and "I liked to have got you that time." After Thames passed out on the ground, Twyman "picked up his body and choked out of him any remaining spark of life."

News of the incident provoked a furor. Several mothers of Gatesville inmates petitioned the governor to release their sons for their own safety. The Texas Congress of Mothers demanded King's firing, echoed by prominent critics within the system such as Judge Ed S. Lauderdale of the Dallas County Juvenile Court and Superintendent Carrie Weaver Smith of Gainesville.[92] The subsequent murder investigation included both a courtroom trial and a public hearing run by the TBC. Both were covered in dramatic fashion by the state's newspapers, with the parents of the deceased boy and his accused killer each in attendance at the Coryell County District Court. Twyman claimed that Stokes and Thomas had framed him and even boasted to other inmates that they "had put one over on the Captain." However, several staff members and inmates lined up to testify against Twyman, including the school nurse who had examined Thames immediately after his death. Twyman was convicted of murder and received a ten-year prison sentence, although the Texas Court of Criminal Appeals subsequently reduced this charge to accidental manslaughter and ordered that his sentence be lowered accordingly. Meanwhile, in November 1921, King resigned as superintendent, complaining that he did so under pressure of "unjust and sensational publicity" and an allegedly partisan investigation by Governor Pat Neff.[93] Not once in his lengthy and self-pitying resignation letter (lamenting the absence of "the appreciation" that he felt "the public ought to give" him) did King express any regret for the death of inmate Thames. This horrific episode exposed the routine and unchecked use of physical force and discipline against boy inmates and indicated the limits of the much-touted reforms of recent years.

The Thames case also illustrated the frequency of inmate deaths at Gatesville. At least sixteen boys, ranging in age from thirteen to twenty years old, died and were buried in the institution's cemetery between 1900 and 1920. Official causes of death included being "struck by lightning" and drowning in the nearby Leon River, but the vast majority of fatalities resulted from disease.[94] Eight boys died during the Spanish flu epidemic of 1918–19, which spread rapidly through crowded dormitories until three hundred boys came down with full-blown cases of influenza. That same year's tally of illnesses included fifty cases of smallpox and forty cases of malaria.[95] In contrast, Gainesville reported sixty influenza patients without fatalities, which Superintendent Smith chalked up to the institution's cottage-style housing and emphasis on hygiene, measures that probably contained the spread of the illness.[96] Another factor contributing to Gatesville's generally high rate of serious illness was probably the menu, which was heavy on starches and low on meats, fruits, and vegetables. As late as 1936, the weekly dinner menu consisted chiefly of bread, beans, and milk, eliciting complaints from boys about skimpy meals that reminded them of "the pen."[97]

The official death toll omitted boys who contracted lethal diseases in the institution but died at home. Such was the case of Leland Wilson, who lived on a farm in rural Electra, just west of Wichita Falls in north-central Texas. When Leland was a toddler, his father died, leaving his widowed mother behind to run the family farm and raise Leland and his older sister. In February 1925, at the age of fourteen, Leland was committed to Gatesville on a charge described as "theft" in official correspondence and "mischievousness and misdirected boyish energy" in the *Dallas Morning News*.[98] Leland quickly established a reputation in Gatesville as a troublemaker. Responding to a parole request from Leland's sister in April 1927, Gatesville parole officer Moon called him "one of the worst boys" there. During the first month of his incarceration, Leland had attempted escape twice, wrecking two state vehicles in the process. Since then, according to Moon, he had "been guilty of burglary, petty thefts, selling stolen articles and numerous other offenses." Leland also refused to work, having "absolutely proven so sorry" on each work assignment that staff had found it "necessary to continually change him from one to the other."[99] In light of these circumstances, what followed proved highly suspicious.

On July 6, 1927, Leland was admitted to the institution's hospital for "heart trouble" after complaining for weeks of chest pains and labored breathing. Two months later, Leland's mother received a note from the Gatesville nurse alerting her to her son's condition. The note assured Mrs. Wilson that the boy was "in no immediate danger" and "would be up if [they] let him"; however, the note continued, "We just thought you should know . . . as you never know what heart trouble does."[100] According to the nurse, the only reason for the delay in informing Leland's family was Leland himself, who "insisted" that the news would unnecessarily "excite" his mother. But the boy's condition worsened; within weeks, Leland was granted a medical furlough—a temporary leave of absence that required his return to Gatesville upon recovery from illness. An outside doctor found that Leland's left lung was "covered with pus" and concluded that he had "had tuberculosis for six months." Mrs. Wilson wrote a scathing letter to Governor Moody demanding Leland's unconditional release:

> I didn't know in institutions like that, that boys were allowed after contracting a
> disease like T.B. to remain in ignorance of their condition and almost dead before
> thare [sic] parents were notified. I am just a poor woman—I get my living from the
> Government and my husband's been dead five years and I feel like I should have
> [been] told of Leland's condition. Miss Moon . . . said Leland was a bad boy the
> worst boy there and perhaps he was—but he is a human and she probably withheld
> his sickness from me because of her grudge.[101]

In response, officials at both the TBC and Gatesville moderated their stance ever so slightly. Although they admitted fault for Leland's illness and allowed him to remain out on furlough, they refused to grant either parole or release. "His record shows clearly that he ought to remain there until he learns how to behave himself," asserted TBC official H. H. Harrington. "I am sorry that this young man seemingly does not merit and appreciate [your] love and confidence."[102] Gatesville superintendent King produced a physician's statement blaming Leland for not notifying doctors of his condition. "At no time did he appear dangerously sick," recounted the Gatesville doctor, Ralph Bailey; indeed, "he was well nourished, strong and had been begging to leave the Hospital for over a week."[103] Unable to afford the cost of sending Leland to a sanitarium, the optimal treatment center for tuberculosis in the 1920s, Mrs. Wilson instead allowed him to take a job working in a local bakery through the month of November. However, Leland suffered a relapse shortly before Christmas and was dead within days. In her final letter to state officials, Mrs. Wilson requested information for a life insurance policy to cover her son's funeral expenses and delivered a bitter lament: "When Leland went to the school he was a clean healthy boy and I shall never get over his death knowing what caused it."[104]

In part, the blame for Leland's fate could be laid at the doorstep of Gatesville's structural deficiencies: overcrowded, unsanitary conditions; inadequate medical services; and obtusely rigid policies regarding parental notification and release. However, to focus only on these elements is to ignore the more fundamental ways in which commitment to state custody revoked the protections and privileges of childhood. Leland was at bottom a prisoner rather than a ward, a laborer rather than a student, and an adult rather than a juvenile. When push came to shove, preserving the institution was more important than saving the life of a single adolescent whose transgressions, by many accounts, stemmed from immaturity rather than deliberate criminality. Leland's case presents in a microcosm the dissipation of reform energies calling for individualized rehabilitation that had peaked over a decade earlier. By the late 1920s, parents and other advocates for youth began to mount demands for better treatment of juvenile inmates, employing the language of protected childhood.

"A Crime against Childhood"

Between the departure of reform superintendent Eddins in 1915 and the death of inmate Leland Wilson in 1927, Gatesville dramatically increased its use of regimentation and surveillance. By the mid-1920s, the average inmate performed military drills for 28 hours a month and 330 hours annually. In school, English classes required each boy to write at least one letter per week to his family. The teachers, supervised by the Gatesville chaplain, H. E. Luck, screened all these letters. They also opened and read all incoming mail; in 1924, Luck estimated that they read about five thousand letters each month. Superintendent King touted this practice as both educational and helpful; teachers, he insisted, could not truly help the boys without access to their deepest "sorrows" and "joys" as expressed in their private correspondence. Luck went further, advancing the questionable claim that boys secretly wanted their private mail read by teachers.[105] The meticulous attention to monitoring the boys' daily actions and even their thoughts reflected a preoccupation with maintaining order that increasingly resembled the policies of prison. Indeed, when Texas prison officials offered to devise a fingerprinting system for Gatesville, officials jumped at the opportunity. The rationale, according to a spokesman for the Texas Prison Bureau of Identification, was that the prisons receive "a large amount of young inmates . . . that have served time in the Reformatory," and "since the young man, or better, boy, does start his carrer [sic] in the Reformatory, I think it to be of great importance, that his record should also start there."[106] The idea was endorsed by everyone except the Texas legislature, which refused to fund it.[107]

Just below inmate control on the list of institutional priorities was labor, which eclipsed schooling and brought the development of Gatesville's education program to an abrupt halt. A 1936 study revealed that 97 percent of whites and 94 percent of blacks were working below grade level, with three-fourths of inmates having fallen more than two years behind.[108] Out of 381 boys over the age of fourteen, 103 had not progressed beyond the third grade. As a result, the academic high school served a meager 28 students, all of whom were white. Much of the curriculum consisted of subjects such as spelling, table etiquette, "story hour," and current events. Even Sunday services had slipped, offering lifeless sermons for "disinterested" boys. Although Gatesville provided "plenty of Bibles" for "practically every boy," the books went unread and the boys proved "indifferent" during Sunday school classes. Extracurricular activities seem to have provided one bright spot; Gatesville's fifty-piece marching band practiced twice a day and traveled several times a year to give performances. The baseball and football teams remained active, although they competed against local amateur teams rather than high schools. The inmate newspaper, *State Boys*, also continued to publish. However, the optimism witnessed twenty years earlier had declined. In a 1936 opinion survey, teachers described most inmates as "incapable" of working at grade level because of innate deficiencies in intelligence. This view was widely held nationally; the 1930 White House Conference on Children and Youth reported that "90 per cent of the children admitted to correctional institutions" were "retarded from one to seven years."[109]

Nevertheless, state education officials occasionally registered their displeasure with Gatesville in ways that suggested the blame lay less with the inmates than with their teachers. In 1929, a teacher named Donald Gregg was fired for cursing in class and leaving campus without permission to attend a college basketball game. Gregg appealed his termination, unsuccessfully, to the Texas State Board of Education. The May 1929 decision issued by state superintendent S. M. N. Marrs reserved its harshest criticisms for Gatesville rather than Gregg, who in Marrs's view exemplified the kind of unqualified teacher routinely placed in an already difficult educational environment. Observing that "the atmosphere surrounding the institution" contributed "to coarseness, vulgarity, and obscenity," Marrs declared that "the students are not receiving the kind of training they deserve." If Gatesville was going to call itself a "training school," he urged, then "this district should be treated as a school district, not as a penal institution."[110]

This criticism demonstrates the blurring that often took place between education and labor, principally under the guise of vocational education. The offering of formal courses in auto repair, carpentry, and printing seemed to emulate the vocational curriculum developing in many urban high schools during the interwar era.[111] On the surface, Gatesville seemed to be training youth from the same poor and working-class backgrounds that concerned urban education reformers. Observers expected that the development of job skills would improve morale, reduce recidivism, and generally bolster the institution's ability to foster genuine rehabilitation. National juvenile justice experts concurred, citing the vocational programs set up in urban high schools loosely based on progressive educators' emphasis, led by John Dewey, on "experiential" learning models, or "learning by doing." But

Figure 5. "Gatesville Laundry—Boy Operating Pressing Machine." (*Third Annual State Eleemosynary Schools Exhibit and Fatstock Show Catalog*, April 10–11, 1946, Camp Mabry, Austin, Texas. Courtesy of the Texas State Library and Archives Commission.)

these experts also warned that vocational education alone was no panacea and had to go hand in hand with smaller class sizes; more precise inmate classification procedures based on age, offense, and psychological interviews; and a diagnostic intake that would uncover the "special aptitudes" of individual inmates and allow for solid placement decisions. Without these additional measures, priorities could easily be reversed, with vocational education driven by the needs of the institution rather than of the child, reducing the program to the "drudgery" of child labor.[112]

Even during the height of reformism around 1910, institution-maintaining labor had persisted at Gatesville, and it only expanded during the King administration. The vocational program masked a veritable factory powered by the forced labor of juvenile inmates (figure 5). In the year 1926 alone, the Gatesville tailor shop produced 38,316 garments; the shoe shop repaired 4,295 pairs of shoes; the laundry washed and ironed the uniforms of 733,000 inmates and 55,207 employees; the plumbing shop performed over 2,300 jobs; the printing office produced over 86,000 official documents (along with 48 issues of *State Boys*); the barber shop gave over 10,000 shaves and 11,000 haircuts to boys and men; the bakery made over 265,000 loaves of bread; and the dairy provided 47,203 gallons of milk and 14,500 pounds of butter. That same year, boy laborers were leased out to work on about

Table 2: Proceeds from inmate labor, Gatesville State Juvenile Training School, 1909–1926

Year	Cotton	Other	Labor fees	Total
1909–10	$6,041.60	$1,085.26	$477.15	$7,604.01
1911–13	$13,139.90	$742.60	$3,120.14	$17,002.64
1913–14	$3,614.00	$1,676.75	$5,282.62	$10,573.45
1917–18	$8,317.00	$244.36	$7,092.21	$15,654.41
1918–20	$13,562.15	$6,382.47	$5,155.78	$25,100.40
1921–24	unreported	unreported	unreported	$37,903.14
1925–26	unreported	unreported	unreported	$12,407.74

Source: *Biennial Report of the State Juvenile Training School* (1910–18); *Report of the State Board of Control* (1920–36).

2,300 acres of farm land owned by at least 5 local farmers. The overall proceeds from "labor, farm products, [and] industrial departments" totaled nearly $12,500, a number made all the more striking when set against Gatesville's listed expenditures for that year, which were $14,736.[113] In other words, the boys' labor quite literally paid the salaries of their jailers. Moreover, the annual income generated by cotton cultivation on state land and leasing fees collected from private farmers went into a "farm product fund" that was used for expenditures not covered by legislative appropriations. Although the amount fluctuated somewhat (table 2), it is clear that agricultural labor formed the backbone of Gatesville's daily regime as well as its financial health.

The official discourse surrounding boy labor blurred the distinction between retribution and rehabilitation. A March 1928 editorial in *State Boys* lauded the "Manual Training Program" as "better than the courts" at inculcating discipline and a love of work.[114] Farm labor particularly was praised as "one of the greatest curative agents" for inmates, especially the growing number coming to Gatesville from metropolitan areas by the late 1920s.[115] "More than ninety percent are City boys," wrote Superintendent King in 1927, who believed boys benefited from "work out in the open air and sunshine . . . as near nature as possible."[116] These representations tapped into widely shared notions about farm labor's ability to morally uplift wayward boys. Much like the Children's Aid Society of the previous century and the Civilian Conservation Corps of the 1930s, the Gatesville farm program purported to inculcate habits of discipline, honesty, and the Protestant work ethic. As usual, however, the reality departed starkly from such lofty rhetoric; employees and inmates alike viewed the "Farm Squad" as the least desirable labor placement. According to the 1936 study, new inmates received mandatory farm assignments for the first two months, after which they could work their way up to a vocational placement. Well aware that most boys were "not good prospects for future farmers," the staff used field assignments as a form of punishment for bad behavior.[117]

Farm labor fell most heavily on African American inmates, whom superintendent King described as "grown in size and . . . nearly grown in age." In an especially revealing 1927 letter, King explained to TBC chairman R. B. Walthall why it was "good . . . to send these boys out in squads of fifteen or twenty, with an attendant, to work for nearby farmers": "I personally know some of the best negro farmers in this country, who learned what they know about their business at this place. If these boys are not taken care of in this way, they must be kept at the institution and taught to play games, but I must confess that a buck negro looks better to me with a goose-necked hoe in his hand than he does with a baseball bat or golf club."[118]

This designation of black inmates for the harshest, lowest-status labor may have reflected social arrangements outside the institution, but it did not sit well with everyone. One such critic was Lyman J. Bailey, a white probation officer from Travis County (Austin). In April 1928, Bailey visited the office of TBC chairman R. B. Walthall. Accompanying Bailey was Kevin James, a fifteen-year-old black juvenile who had spent the previous two years in Gatesville for an unspecified offense. By all accounts, James was a model inmate; Gatesville parole officer Moon described him as "well behaved" and noted that he had been paroled "to assist his mother in making a living."[119] James, with Bailey's support, complained that he personally had spent two years working in the fields while receiving no schooling whatsoever. Claiming that James's experience was typical for black inmates, Bailey requested an official investigation. Already well aware of this situation, Walthall nevertheless went through the motions of filing an official inquiry with Gatesville parole officer Moon. She disputed James's story, stating that he had attended school regularly and "had reached the third grade" by January 1928.[120] However, Moon also admitted that "only the smaller ones" received schooling, due to long-standing shortages of classroom space: "We are doing the best we can."[121] Walthall relayed this information to Bailey without further comment, ending the complaint.[122]

Inmate protests aided by parents, or worse, lawyers (deemed "meddlers" in one report), elicited biting contempt from Gatesville officials, who blamed the 1913 Juvenile Act for a small upsurge in habeas corpus petitions. Official reports portrayed lawyers who dared interfere with the quasi-parental work of juvenile courts and training schools as confidence men exploiting the misguided fears of their clients, who were often impoverished families. "The class of people from whom most of the delinquent children come is credulous, quick to believe and listen to stories of imaginary evils existent in institution life," declared one report, "and often conceive themselves to have been encroached upon and mistreated in their private life."[123] In the end, according to this narrative, the victim of such appeals was the wayward child: "No one ever did anything but harm to a boy who got his release before he merited his parole."[124]

Undoubtedly this characterization of fee-for-service attorneys held some kernel of truth, although the available evidence is insufficient to be certain. However, the revival of progressive political clout after the January 1927 inauguration of reform governor Dan Moody sparked a new round of reforms in the state's prison system and emboldened critics of Gatesville. Moody began to stack government agencies with reformers, including the TBC, which voted in August to cease hiring out boy inmates to local farmers as convict laborers. Gatesville officials balked at the idea, fearing an uprising from local farmers and an inability to maintain order without the bludgeon of field labor. Initially, the TBC conceded to these objections, leaving the question "entirely to [Gatesville's] judgment and discretion."[125] But reformers based in Galveston caught wind of the compromise and launched a public attack on the practice of juvenile convict leasing, which began with an editorial in the *Galveston Tribune* that asked, "[Why] we must make peons of the unfortunate boys, most of whom have been denied childhood's greatest boon, in order to pay the salaries of their keepers."[126] The editorial accused Gatesville of sanctioning a form of "slavery" that constituted a "crime against childhood."[127] A second salvo appeared two days later, authored by Rabbi Henry Cohen, a well-known humanitarian activist who had worked alongside the "Petticoat Lobby" on numerous reform initiatives throughout the 1920s. Governor Moody had just appointed Cohen to the newly created Texas Prison Board, which went on to institute rehabilitative measures such as inmate classification, a grievance system, mental health testing, and correctional education. In the *Tribune*, Cohen pointed out that the legislature had outlawed convict leasing in the adult prisons over a dozen years earlier yet tolerated the practice for juveniles. He lambasted Gatesville's claims to the title of "training school" and asked, "What sort of 'training' would one imagine this could be?"[128]

In response, TBC chairman H. H. Harrington published a lengthy letter in the *Tribune*. He defended local farmers who had come to depend on the boys' labor to harvest the cotton crop. The sudden loss of this labor, he warned hyperbolically, would cause a "calamity" comparable to the 1901 hurricane that had destroyed Galveston. Warning that the Gatesville superintendent "had no way of keeping these boys busy," Harrington then issued this startling justification:

> I would like to call your attention to the fact that there are about two hundred and fifty negro boys; most of them husky fellows that have been used to work all their lives. Many of the white boys are practically grown in stature, if not in years. I submit the thought that work is not inimicable [sic] to reformation. . . . Traveling over the

highway this week from Austin to Gainesville I was impressed with the rush to the cotton fields. In many fields I saw children picking cotton. In many instances, apparently whole families were engaged in this work. Is it any more, or as much, a reproach to our civilization in hiring out, under the State's name, big husky boys, black or white, to work for the State than it is to find free men and farmers reduced to the necessity of employing their children to pick cotton in order that debts may be paid and the meager supplies of life be furnished?[129]

In a private letter to Harrington, Cohen reiterated his "unequivocal" opposition to juvenile convict leasing. He also expressed faith that the boys were "in good hands" with Harrington, which seemed to be vindicated when the TBC issued a second directive to Gatesville superintendent King to halt the practice at the end of the harvest season.[130]

Around this time, Cohen received a telephone request from Judge Charles G. Dibrell of the Galveston Juvenile Court regarding a "little fellow" named Joey O'Connor who had just returned home from a two-year stay at Gatesville.[131] Joey's mother, a young waitress in Galveston and a widow, had become alarmed at the bruises on her eleven-year-old son's body and his apparent fear of speaking about how he had gotten them. The Gatesville guard who put Joey on the train home had "cautioned him not to tell anything 'about the State' to the Juvenile Judge in Galveston, or to any other person." Dibrell then took a sworn affidavit, which revealed that Joey had been whipped five times in two years, twice while he was working in cotton fields. Joey had received "a severe whipping" for standing up and stretching to relieve a sore back and another time "because he did not pick enough cotton to satisfy the guard." As a "white boy" and particularly young, Joey was treated "far better" than most, which for Dibrell and Cohen suggested that the norm was much worse. They forwarded Joey's deposition to the TBC, asking for an investigation. Superintendent King's response was to remind his superiors that Joey lived in a home headed by a single mother who had remarried and separated once already, asking that the TBC "take into consideration the breeding of the boy and the environment under which he was brought up." These insinuations apparently fell on deaf ears; not only did the TBC maintain the ban on juvenile convict labor, but it also fired King for the second time that decade.

The appointment of King's successor, Earl H. Nesbitt, did little to stem the tide of criticism. One of the fiercest was J. P. Mestrezat, a former probation officer and an executive officer of the El Paso branch of the Boy Scouts of America. In March 1929, Mestrezat helped start a club for boys who had returned from Gatesville and were at risk of re-offending. Mestrezat discovered that sixty-nine local boys had been paroled in the previous fourteen months, all of Mexican origin, and all but three with American citizenship. Most of them had been committed on dependency rather than delinquency charges. Founded with nine charter members (a number that quickly swelled to twenty-six), the club's aims were "recreation, friendship, and jobs"—and keeping the boys off the "thin ice" that separated "solid citizenship" from "a life of crime."[132] The club provided members with an identification card and a sponsor, intended to protect them from being "picked up by the police" for frivolous reasons and to help them find employment. To local whites who viewed the boys as an alien menace to public order, Mestrezat emphasized that they were "El Paso boys, though 'Mexican,' just as surely as though they were Anglo-Saxon boys."[133]

Mestrezat noticed that Gatesville had brutalized the boys without preparing them for even the most rudimentary employment. He complained publicly to the El Paso Juvenile Board and to Governor Moody that Gatesville "masqueraded under the name of a training school" while forcibly extracting institution-maintaining labor.[134] "Repression," not limited to whippings, fostered "bad habits" in the boys. In response, the TBC cited the 1913 law, which allowed for supervised whippings, and simply ignored the criticism of vocational training. Mestrezat was unable to make headway with authorities in either El Paso or Austin, but he did fire off a final letter to the TBC in which he declared that "the Texas system of juvenile correction [was] vicious" and constituted "a violation of the rights of the child." Admonishing lawmakers and officials who were "too quick to defend the system," Mestrezat implored the TBC to "bring the juvenile procedure of the state out of its medieval situation."[135]

These types of protests became more common between 1927 and 1928, as the TBC under the Moody administration collected complaints against Superintendent King, a Ferguson appointee. Individual cases sometimes attracted support from local elites for a variety of reasons. For example, the Robert Oil Corporation became involved in the case of an employee's child, fifteen-year-old Sam Davis of Breckenridge, just west of Dallas. Charged with delinquency, Sam had "borrowed" parked cars on at least two occasions in order to give rides home to girl-friends. Each time, Sam had parked the car, undamaged, near its original location; however, the Stephens County judge had sentenced him to "at least two years" in Gatesville. According to his family and an oil company attorney, Sam suffered from a variety of medical ailments, including epilepsy and "chronic stomach and kidney troubles."[136] The latter caused bedwetting, for which Sam was beaten regularly by guards. In a letter to Governor Moody, the attorney requested Sam's release "as a matter of justice and humanity." It was wrong, he asserted, to hold a "mental defective" like Sam "strictly accountable for his actions."[137] Moreover, one of the borrowed cars in question was a company vehicle belonging to Robert Oil, which supported Sam's parole. Superintendent King denied the allegations of abuse and resisted Sam's release, which forced attorneys to appeal to the county judge to recall Sam, which he did in short order.[138] The case illustrates how protests against the juvenile justice system that invoked the language of protected childhood could produce different results. Mestrezat's appeals on behalf of adolescents of Mexican origin in El Paso fell on deaf and even hostile ears, while the white child of an oil company employee managed, albeit with some difficulty, to win release on the basis of the need for individualized treatment and the unfairness of applying full standards of criminal responsibility.

Other cases stemmed from sympathy for widowed mothers rather than concerns about protecting childhood innocence. A doctor in Sterling City, halfway between San Angelo and Midland, sent a notarized statement that he had been treating a Mrs. Johnson for over a year. Her "mental and nervous condition" had been "caused by her separation from her baby boy." According to the doctor, it was "doubtful whether medical treatment [could] save her life unless her mind [was] relieved from the worry and dread."[139] In another case, Mrs. M. H. Witt mounted a petition for her son's release. Destitute and facing a foreclosure of the family farm, Mrs. Witt managed to convince about three dozen local citizens to sign her petition. "The time has come for we as citizens of this community to do something," it read, "to hold the home together."[140] Many of the signers listed their occupations: farmer, rancher, mail carrier, blacksmith, merchant, ranch hand. Both mothers met with blanket refusals from the TBC and Superintendent King, accompanied by a bluntly dismissive tone. Mrs. Witt, for instance, was told that her son was "lazy and would not be of any assistance to his mother if released." The state's insensitivity to family situations was far reaching. Hank Richards, of rural Normangee, about 125 miles east of Gatesville, was committed without parental notification for "stealing a calf." The staff threatened Hank with "severe punishment" because his mother sent him one dollar a month. At the end of Hank's second year in confinement, his father became seriously ill, prompting his mother to request parole. Gatesville officials granted this request, but only on the condition that she "furnish transportation" and keep Hank in school, even though he had reached the age of eighteen.[141] Another boy, Charles Baker of Wichita Falls, was denied furlough to visit his mother on her deathbed. Charles's case prompted the TBC to criticize Gatesville for "keeping boys in the institution too long" but resulted in no further action.[142]

These were more typical cases than those of boys from relatively privileged backgrounds, such as Sam Davis or Jimmy Jones, who were able to win release. Their collective plight, however, received attention from an unexpected place: Hollywood.

Routine Destruction

In 1929, the Hollywood filmmaker Cecil B. DeMille released his last silent picture, titled *The Godless Girl*. The film told the story of a group of "modern" teenagers who form an atheist club in their high school, which leads them into delinquent behavior and ultimately into their local juvenile court, where they are sentenced to extended terms in a juvenile training school. After evoking the culture wars of the 1920s, the film spends about half of its running time in the harsh, prison-like setting of the training school. Viewers saw extreme regimentation, unsanitary conditions, and exotic forms of physical abuse—the punishment, ostensibly, for young would-be rebels who emulated the bohemian attitudes popularized in films such as *It* (1927) and novels such as *The Great Gatsby* (1924). The social realism of the training school scenes drew on several months of research conducted at actual training schools across the nation. On DeMille's orders, employees of his production company had spent months interviewing guards and former inmates, shooting film footage of facilities, and in some instances, taking jobs temporarily to observe up close the daily routines of juvenile inmates.[143] In fall 1927, George Ellis, a DeMille agent, visited Gatesville, worked as a guard for a few days, and hired a Dallas-based cinematographer to film "the method of receiving new recruits, the changing of citizen clothing to prison uniforms, the clipping of the hair, the counting and checking up at meals, the marching off to bed and the saying of prison prayers."[144] Of particular interest to Ellis and DeMille was the electrified "iron prison fence" surrounding Gatesville, which they specifically included in the film.

After completing his research and filming for *The Godless Girl*, Ellis gave an interview to the press in Austin, during which he criticized several aspects of Gatesville. Incensed, Superintendent King fired off an angry letter to DeMille's studio, only to be rebuked by TBC chairman Harrington.[145] However, King need not have worried. Despite its relatively graphic portrayals of abused juvenile inmates, the film was widely panned as sensationalistic, earned little money, and failed to galvanize any substantial public concern about conditions in training schools.[146] Indeed, the *Dallas Morning News*, one of the state's largest metropolitan newspapers, initially refused to publish the fact that DeMille had based some of *The Godless Girl* on Gatesville. Shortly after printing that information, the *News* published a feature article lauding Gatesville as a "place of beauty and usefulness" that provided a "healthful environment."[147] The piece profiled boys who tearfully resisted being released to their families and former inmates who had gone on to successful careers. Photographs showed neatly dressed, attentive-looking boys cooking and baking in an orderly kitchen and milking cows in a dairy that might have been mistaken for a typical family farm.

Contrasting such uplifting scenes was a gruesome accident a few months later, involving a black inmate, which was handled in such a detached fashion by Gatesville officials as to seem almost routine. Early on the morning of December 8, 1929, a squad of black boys was "grubbing" (clearing) land near the Leon River for planting.[148] They were chopping trees with axes under the supervision of a white guard, who reported hearing "a noise like two axes striking together." The guard "turned just in time to see both boys drop to the ground"; they had struck each other accidentally. One boy suffered a deep wound to his head that was bleeding profusely. The guard left him in the field and rode his horse nearly a mile away to "the negro building" to call for a car. A local doctor examined the boy in the institution's hospital and urged the recently appointed Gatesville superintendent, Earl H. Nesbitt, to take him to a surgeon.[149] Nesbitt had him brought to the Baptist Sanitarium, located about forty miles away in Waco. Although the Gatesville guard's report claimed that the boy was conscious and walking easily, the Waco surgeon described the boy upon arrival at the hospital as being "in a profound coma" and "suffering severe shock, so much so that [they] were not able to offer surgical services for several hours."[150] The axe had caused a four-inch-long wound that cut all the way into his brain, requiring the removal of "a portion of detached brain tissue." Within a day, the boy was dead, having suffered brain damage "too great for one to survive."[151]

Of all the terrible cases in the Gatesville records, this one stood out for several reasons. While many of his white peers began their respective days in an academic classroom or a vocational workshop, this boy was made to perform hazardous field labor on a muddy riverbank. It took over an hour for a doctor to examine his ultimately fatal wound and several more hours before the boy reached a proper hospital. Starkly reminiscent of the era when the institution was known as a "house of correction" rather than a "training school," the scene might have horrified the progressive women reformers of the two decades earlier, except for one thing: the victim was black. Even the most enlightened proponents of juvenile rehabilitation had failed to include African American juveniles in their plans. Embedded in the universal rhetoric of emerging developmental categories of childhood and adolescence were distinctions of race, ethnicity, and class that surfaced in expert and popular responses to the problem of juvenile delinquency in the early twentieth century. The routine destruction of individual lives in Gatesville, whether through death, physical abuse, or psychological damage, was even more pronounced for the lowest-status offenders. The newspapers and archives did not record the names of black inmates or their families because they simply failed to register in the minds of officials, experts, or opinion makers as belonging to the mission of rehabilitating wayward youth into good citizens. These juveniles were not juveniles but problems to be warehoused into overcrowded dormitories or assets to be exploited in the cotton fields until they could take their expected place in the adult prison system.

Even in the face of this overwhelming failure, however, one important legacy paid dividends later. The official embrace of rehabilitation as the main goal for juvenile justice and corrections survived the 1920s and, in succeeding years, intermittently raised the public's expectations. As we have seen, in the late 1920s, when Gatesville failed to live up to that vague standard, critics invoked visions of childhood stolen through the abuse or neglect of the state. Increasingly this criticism drew on the insights of a new field of inquiry, children's mental health, and the development of noninstitutional, community-based responses to juvenile delinquency, to which we now turn.

TWO

Socializing Delinquency
Child Welfare, Mental Health, and the Critique of Institutions, 1929–1949

On September 1, 1941, the Texas Board of Control simultaneously fired the superintendents of both the boys' and the girls' training schools. The move came in the aftermath of yet another round of abuse scandals, which had resulted in legislative investigations and bad publicity in the late 1930s. However, the immediate cause for the firings was the publication of two audit reports commissioned by the TBC, which portrayed both schools as little more than prisons. Observers with long memories surely would have found the reports' descriptions depressingly familiar. The auditor summed up Gatesville's "entire atmosphere" as "one of prison and penal confinement," in which boys of all ages and offense categories crowded into "deplorable" dormitories with "open shower and toilet facilities placed in one corner of the room with no screen or partition separating them from the sleeping quarters."[1] The academic school lacked basic educational materials and trained teachers, while the "non-existent" vocational program served mainly to provide institution-maintaining labor. Whether toiling in fields or workshops or shuffling silently into broken-down cafeterias and dormitories, the boys experienced nothing but "regimentation and repression," for which the report blamed the staff, described as "well educated mule skinners." Earl H. Nesbitt, the Gatesville superintendent, spent most of his time "trading, buying, and selling mules and other livestock" instead of giving "his full time and effort to the rehabilitation of the boys." In short, the institution had changed little, and perhaps even regressed, since the cycle of reform and rollback examined in the previous chapter.[2]

Similar complaints filled the auditor's report on Gainesville, which clearly had declined since the progressive administration of Carrie Weaver Smith. However, the Gainesville report included something new: an emphasis on the staff's lack of "knowledge of child psychology."[3] While both reports cited the need for "individualized treatment," the Gainesville audit specifically called for substituting "patient redirection" for physical discipline and incorporating the lessons of "child guidance" into the training schools' rehabilitation program. Although applied more to girls than to boys in these particular reports, the lens of child psychology began to cast training school conditions in an entirely different light. These reports reflected the growing influence of two distinct but related trends that emerged unevenly in the first half of the twentieth century in Texas: the growth of an expansive concept of child welfare, which favored community-based prevention and diversion programs over large institutions; and an emerging concern for children's mental health, which reframed juvenile delinquency and rehabilitation in psychological rather than moral terms. By the 1940s, a new generation of child savers regarded the training schools as irredeemably backward not only for their abusive physical conditions but also for the emotional damage they wreaked on child and adolescent development. No longer would reformers settle for warehousing delinquent youth in institutions; instead, they invoked a broadly conceived notion of community responsibility in calling for the "socializing" of delinquency, to borrow the legal scholar Michael Willrich's term. During the 1930s and 1940s, cities such as Dallas and Houston became laboratories for the idea that delinquency grew from environmental rather than individual roots and called for solutions based on treatment rather than punishment. The commitment to shared social responsibility for ills such as poverty and delinquency only grew during the Great Depression and World War II, lending further impetus to new reforms in the administration of juvenile justice and corrections in Texas.[4] In 1949, the Texas legislature enacted the Texas Youth Development Act—a dramatic about-face that threatened to put Texas in the forefront of juvenile justice and corrections nationwide.

Sweeping juvenile justice reform at the statewide level in the 1940s would not have been possible without the changes wrought at the local level in preceding decades. Collectively, local and state reforms reflected the impact of an emerging discourse of childhood protected by a caring community and preserved through the new science of children's mental health. Although not embraced by all, hotly contested, and even contradictory at times, this discourse drove the campaigns for youth recreation and against whipping juvenile inmates that are described in this chapter. Some advocates extended their concern to youth of Mexican origin and African American youth, while others continued to draw distinct lines separating white from nonwhite, middle class from working class, rural from urban, and the salvageable from the permanently damaged. The path to the tipping point of major reform, explored in this chapter, was fraught with disagreement as Texans began to grapple with the question of when and which juvenile delinquents deserved the benefits and protections of modern childhood and adolescence.

"Delinquency Begins with the Community"

Services for delinquent and dependent children emerged in northern cities during the early nineteenth century, sponsored by a mixture of public and private funds. During the Progressive Era, municipal governments in Chicago, Boston, and New York created professionally staffed agencies to provide services such as mother's pensions, playgrounds, adoption, foster care, and juvenile justice. After 1899, when the nation's first juvenile court opened in Chicago, urban child welfare services increasingly revolved around juvenile justice. Like the municipal courts created at roughly the same time, the juvenile court sought to uncover and address "the root social causes" of crime and delinquency. Child welfare agencies formed a key part of this endeavor. They referred children to juvenile court, provided information for the "life histories" compiled for individual children, and offered noninstitutional placement options for juveniles such as supervised parole or foster care. In both the quest to unearth delinquency's causes and the making of rehabilitation plans, the therapeutic methods of psychiatry, psychology, and social work played a key role in formulating ideal if not always practiced procedures. Under what became the favored model, trained social workers researched a child's family, school, and neighborhood in compiling a life history; psychologists measured a child's intelligence and personality using a battery of standardized tests; and psychiatrists met with the child in therapy sessions designed to uncover hidden mental or emotional disorders. Adopted in uneven fashion in juvenile courts across the nation, these procedures reflected the consensus among juvenile justice experts that, as a U.S. Children's Bureau report on national standards stated in 1923, courts "should have a scientific understanding of the child," devise treatment plans "adapted to individual needs," and try as best as possible to "keep . . . the child in his own home and his own community."[5]

In the South, where urbanization came somewhat later, child welfare developed differently. In cities such as Memphis and Houston, private agencies provided the bulk, although not all, of the child welfare services to local juvenile courts. The Jim Crow social order shaped child welfare such that separate white and black organizations emerged, although the "black child savers" often worked on much smaller budgets and thus were unable to provide anything approaching equal assistance to black children. In Memphis, the inauguration of the juvenile court in 1910 exacerbated a public-private divide that mirrored racial inequality. Over the next few decades, private agencies provided child welfare and institutional care for white children, while the government, in the form of the juvenile court and the juvenile training school, served mostly black youth. The overt exclusion of "at-risk" and delinquent African Americans from most resources distinguished the South regionally and represented a way of limiting the social boundaries of protected childhood to whites only.[6]

Urbanization began to develop in Texas around the turn of the century, as agriculture and cattle ranching gave way to large-scale industry, centered in the Dallas–Fort Worth and Houston-Galveston metropolitan areas. Overall, the state's urban population increased eightfold, from 349,511 in 1890 to 2,911,389 by 1940, the year when urban residents first comprised a majority in the state (by 1960, the number had more than doubled again to 6,963,114). Between 1890 and 1940, Dallas's population grew from 38,067 to 297,734, while in Houston the figures were, respectively, 27,557 and 384,514. Houston's population soared in the twentieth century, reaching over 1.5 million by 1980 and making it the largest city in Texas and one of the five largest cities in the United States.[7] The city's preeminence resulted from an aggressive business class and some good fortune. In 1900, a deadly hurricane devastated the port city of Galveston and eliminated a potential economic rival; one year later, the massive Spindletop oil strike spurred lucrative refinery- and petroleum-related industries. The opening of the Houston Ship Channel in 1914 transformed Houston into the Gulf Coast's most active port city. By World War II, the city's landscape was dominated by oil tankers, refineries, and petrochemical factories manufacturing key materials such as synthetic rubber for the war effort. Significant federal wartime investments would set the stage for continued economic growth in aerospace, communication technology, and related sectors, as Houston became one of the nation's largest urban centers and a symbol of the Sun Belt region.[8]

Although government contracts underwrote much of the city's growth, Houston's entrepreneurial elite aggressively promoted a brand of "frontier capitalism" that eschewed government regulation and taxpayer-funded services. Instead, the city's power elite, dubbed the "big rich" in a profile by longtime Houston journalist George Fuermann, sponsored charitable agencies to meet the city's rapidly expanding needs. According to Fuermann, the "wild and wonderful philanthropic race" was nothing more than "a hobby of the city's Big Rich." Most historians have echoed this characterization of Houston as a city dominated by a wealthy class bitterly opposed to government activity in the public sphere, causing the city to suffer from Gilded Age–era disparities of wealth and poverty well into the twentieth century.[9] A few influential families, however, opposed this dynamic, embracing what one historian has called the "city as a whole" philosophy, which maintained that the residents of different neighborhoods and by extension distinct social classes shared a responsibility for the community's larger well-being. A coterie of progressive elites pushed for the development of progressive schooling, public libraries, a city symphony, public housing projects, and social welfare programs to aid the needy.[10] From these impulses sprang much of Houston's child welfare infrastructure around the turn of the century, which grew with the city's exploding population in subsequent years. Coordinating much of this work was the United Charities, founded in 1904 by a group of wealthy women led by Estelle B. Sharp, a recent arrival from Dallas, where she had participated in that city's movement for public kindergartens. In March 1915, the city government replaced this agency with the Houston Foundation, which used both public and private funds to coordinate the work of private charities, allocate funds for specific needs, and collect statistics on social conditions in order to analyze their causes. The foundation's work reflected the political unpopularity of tax-supported social welfare. In its first year of operation, the foundation received $26,000 from the city, an amount dwarfed by a single donation of $200,000. In 1917, the foundation's Social Service Bureau oversaw and staffed five private agencies at a cost of $36,000, less than half of which came from the city government. "Sorely underfunded" and "pitifully understaffed," the foundation struggled to ameliorate conditions of poverty without addressing its root causes. Funding improved after 1922, when the foundation was replaced by the Houston Community Chest, which had expanded its annual budget to $600,000 by 1931, enabling it to widen its scope of activity.[11]

One of the key agencies supervised by both the Houston Foundation and the Community Chest was the Houston Settlement Association (HSA), which brought the approach of the national settlement house movement to local conditions.[12] According to an oft-repeated story, the HSA sprang from a single incident that occurred one afternoon in 1903, when a schoolteacher named Sybil Campbell discovered a small child sleeping alone on the front steps of the Rusk Day School. Located in the Second Ward on Houston's East End, the school's once-fashionable neighborhood had fallen into disrepair as old-stock whites had moved away, to be replaced largely by Jewish immigrants, many of whom worked at nearby cotton mills. The child told Campbell her mother was at work and her older sibling was inside the school taking classes. Appalled, Campbell contacted Alice Graham Baker, wife of banker and attorney James A. Baker and president of the local branch of the Texas Federation of Women's Clubs. Campbell and Baker spearheaded the formation of the HSA, which sponsored a kindergarten and day nursery at Rusk for the children of working mothers. Influenced by Jane Addams's Hull House in Chicago, the HSA expanded its efforts to relieve the "health hazards, moral laxness, and drab lives" of the area's children. The HSA embarked on a project to transform Rusk into a "socialized school" offering a range of services beyond education. In its early years, Rusk housed a walk-in clinic, a day nursery, supervised recreation, and a night school for adult students.[13] Echoing Addams's belief that "recreation alone can stifle the lust for vice," Rusk opened an outdoor playground as a healthy outlet for youthful energies and an arts and crafts program to inculcate "culture."[14]

Figure 6. Rusk Settlement House, 1947. (Corrine Tsanoff, *Neighborhood Doorways* [Houston, 1958]. Courtesy of Neighborhood Centers, Inc., and the Center for American History at the University of Texas at Austin.)

The settlement movement arrived in other parts of Texas as well; "neighborhood houses" opened under similar auspices in Dallas (1903) and Fort Worth (1908), while evangelical women opened "mission houses" in several Texas cities, aimed at providing social assistance and converting Mexican and Mexican American families from Catholicism to Protestantism.[15] Interclass cooperation, a key feature of the settlement movement nationally, in Texas drew together white philanthropists, middle-class social workers, and working-class populations of diverse racial and ethnic backgrounds. Under the sponsorship of the Houston Foundation, the HSA opened the Bethlehem "Colored" Settlement in 1917 and began serving a largely Mexican and Mexican American clientele at Rusk. In the 1920s, as Mexican immigrants transformed the community into the Segundo Barrio, Rusk adapted its services, emphasizing "Americanization" programs such as English-language classes for immigrant mothers.[16]

Long an impoverished area, the neighborhood around Rusk declined significantly due largely to official neglect. During the 1920s, the city razed several residential blocks to make way for industrial development, making Rusk into an island hemmed in between Buffalo Bayou (an industrial canal at the city's center) and the Southern Pacific railroad yards (figure 6). Exacerbating these conditions were budget shortfalls, reflecting cuts in the HSA's major source of financial support, the Community Chest, whose donor base dried up during the Great Depression. City officials and opinion makers began to associate Rusk's area and the population of Mexican origin generally with the growing problem of juvenile delinquency.[17] Mexican American organizations, often with the support of Rusk or other private agencies, responded by forming social clubs for youth and advocating for fair treatment of alleged juvenile offenders. For example, Club Femenino Chapultepec, sponsored by the local YWCA, offered job placement services to girls who spoke English and had earned their high school diplomas. The most influential of these groups, and most indicative of the "Mexican American generation" that came of age in the 1930s, was the League of United Latin American Citizens (LULAC) Chapter 60, founded in 1934 in the Magnolia Park area, adjacent to Rusk's neighborhood. Led by Mexican American businessmen and professionals, the LULAC advocated for civil rights, formed "junior" auxiliary chapters for teenagers, and defended youth of Mexican origin publicly from growing accusations of gang involvement and criminality.[18]

The construction of delinquency as a "Mexican" problem was part of a general increase in public awareness of the problem of juvenile delinquency. In the late 1930s, the city mounted its first substantial investments in delinquency prevention and juvenile justice. Leading the charge was Roy Hofheinz, who at the tender age of twenty-two won election to the state legislature from Harris County. In 1935, he spearheaded legislation creating a county juvenile board, consisting of county judges and a juvenile probation department. Two years later, Hofheinz himself took over the juvenile judgeship he had helped to create and became a champion of alternatives to institutionalization. "Anything which approaches a home environment," he stated in a 1938 speech, "is better than institutional care." With Hofheinz's support, the juvenile board instituted a juvenile detention center for boys, and in July 1941 the police department launched a crime prevention division to deal separately with juvenile offenders. Part of Hofheinz's support for these reforms stemmed from his conviction that juvenile justice and delinquency prevention were "social" rather than individual problems. Like Ben Lindsey, the Denver juvenile judge who gained a national reputation in the second and third decades of the century, Hofheinz spun folksy anecdotes about individual delinquents in his courtroom, such as the many boys he sentenced to attend Sunday school and to take jobs working for local businesses. Portraying himself as a surrogate father to "his boys," Hofheinz urged the public to view them as misguided adolescents rather than budding criminals. "No youngster is born mean," he characteristically insisted. "When they go bad, it is because you and I thought our responsibility to the community ended with our own children." Hofheinz curried his own "cult of judicial personality," extending beyond Harris County to the national stage, as the first southern juvenile judge to address the National Probation Association and the National Association of Juvenile Judges. During a 1939 visit to New York for the National Juvenile Agencies Association meeting (at which he gave a keynote address), Hofheinz appeared on a national radio broadcast to discuss alternatives to institutions with former New York governor and presidential candidate Al Smith.[19]

However, Hofheinz seems to have moderated his views somewhat during World War II, a time when the city was in the grip of a panic over "gang warfare" between three rival "Latin-American" gangs in the Second Ward, called the Black Shirts, the Long Hairs, and the Snakes. Violence reached a crescendo in early 1943, when the local newspapers reported several beatings, stabbings, and murders. Evoking the Los Angeles media coverage of the Zoot Suit Riots, the Houston press portrayed the gangs as "alien hoodlums" who should be deported. At other times, editorials likened them to adult mobsters, as when the *Houston Post* complained about "imitation Chicago wop gangsters, shooting, cutting, and beating people." In response, the police inaugurated a series of raids on dance halls and honky-tonks, which resulted in mass arrests of youth explicitly "profiled" by their race, ethnicity, and attire.[20] The police's crime prevention division also created a "Latin-American squad" of Spanish-speaking and Mexican American officers. These two initiatives reflected divergent missions of establishing relationships with youth gangs similar to those forged by "curbside counselors" in Chicago and New York City while simultaneously identifying and removing those same youth from the streets. Either the Houston police department's traditional function of upholding the Jim Crow order clashed with delinquency prevention imperatives, or mass arrests of Mexican American youth comprised a part of those imperatives; the record is unclear. As the historian Edward J. Escobar has shown in his study of Los Angeles, police departments in the Southwest played key roles in defining Mexican Americans as "criminal" in the early twentieth century.[21] Directed overwhelmingly at nonwhite youth, the mass arrests fueled a spike in the number of Mexican origin youth who were arrested and sent to the state training school at Gatesville. According to a 1944 study, youth of Mexican origin "were known to the police in much larger number than their proportion in the total population would indicate." This conclusion was based on an estimate that Mexicans and Mexican Americans comprised about 5 percent of the city's overall population and 13 percent of all "known" juvenile delinquents (for the years 1939–44, the number of juvenile offenders averaged five thousand annually). In raw figures, white and African American juveniles outnumbered youth of Mexican origin, but their respective percentages were generally proportional

Table 3. Persons known to Houston Crime Prevention Division by race and ethnicity, 1941–1943

Year	Anglo-American		Mexican American		African American	
	Number	Percent	Number	Percent	Number	Percent
1941	2,016	61.3	427	13.0	844	25.7
1942	2,503	59.0	661	15.6	1,080	25.4
1943	5,281	63.3	1,143	16.4	1,401	20.3

Source: Houston Council of Social Agencies, "Juvenile Delinquency in Houston: A Preliminary View," *Social Statistics* 1, no. 2 (December 1944), Houston Metropolitan Research Center.

Table 4. Harris County Juvenile Court cases and institutional commitments, 1939–1943

Year	Male		Female	
	Cases	Commitments	Cases	Commitments
1939	166	100	73	33
1940	155	96	95	60
1941	188	84	128	67
1942	210	127	128	54
1943	134	86	120	66
Total	853	493	544	280

Source: Houston Council of Social Agencies, "Juvenile Delinquency in Houston: A Preliminary View," *Social Statistics* 1, no. 2 (December 1944), Houston Metropolitan Research Center.

with their share of the overall population (see table 3). Even more striking were the implications of statistics on juvenile court cases and their outcomes, which suggested that youth of Mexican origin were institutionalized disproportionately as well. Although few cases actually received a formal disposition in juvenile court, between half and two-thirds of cases resulted in institutionalization (see table 4). Added to these statistics was the juvenile court's "policy adopted of commitment of Latin-American boys to institutions" to stem the tide of gangs.[22]

These growing concerns about gangs clearly challenged reformers who advocated community-based solutions for juvenile delinquency and in some cases pushed them toward the use of juvenile institutions. However, residents of the areas targeted by police countered portrayals of Mexican American youth as inherently criminal. Representatives of the LULAC served on the citywide Delinquency and Crime Commission formed in 1944 to address the gang problem and urged the provision of better schools and recreational services in their neighborhoods. At the same time, the LULAC and like-minded groups organized youth activities on their own, such as the "Junior LULAC 60," which began sponsoring dances and live music shows, sometimes at the Rusk Settlement House, in the late 1940s and into the 1950s.[23] A measure of the feeling among Mexican Americans came from Abigail Gonzalez Cavasos, a resident of the Second Ward, who answered a *Houston Post* editorial demonizing Mexican American gangs with this letter:

> We realize how big a problem these gangs are and we are willing to cooperate to abolish them. We also realize, and wish others would too, why these boys have become a problem. It is a pent-up disgust against discrimination that has been with us for years. Have you ever been made to wait while a salesgirl waits on others when you were there first? Have you ever been at a restaurant and have the same thing happen? Do you know that there is at least one company that will employ those of Mexican extraction only as laborers and with no opportunity for promotion? I could fill page after page with such incidents that happen too often to be accidents. What would you do on such occasions? Walking out is pretty good but it does not satisfy one's pride.[24]

Child welfare agencies mounted their own counteroffensive, led by the Houston Community Chest, whose director, Elwood Street, was outspoken in his support of community programs for at-risk youth. Street's advocacy often reflected nationwide fears about unsupervised and out of control "teenagers"—a new word in the American lexicon that conveyed a widening acceptance of adolescence as a life stage characterized by diminished responsibility, semidependence on adults, and education rather than labor. In 1943, the federal Office of Community War Services began funding the establishment of local "teen canteens," adult-supervised youth recreation clubs governed jointly by adults and teenagers.[25] Under the auspices of the Community Chest, Houston's Club 506 opened in March 1944, with the *Houston Post* proclaiming, "Houston's teenagers will come into their own when the new Teen-Age canteen opens." Over four hundred "dancing" and "screaming" teenagers packed the club on its opening night, following a ribbon-cutting ceremony by Houston mayor Otis Massey.[26] The growing usage of the word "teenager" provided an important context for the ongoing debate about juvenile delinquency. If the answer for the misbehavior of the children of (largely white) soldiers and defense-plant workers was to provide supervised recreation in the form of the teen canteen, then perhaps a similar solution applied to nonwhite youth. Were they not also "teenagers"?

For his part, Community Chest director Elwood Street responded to this question in the affirmative, as epitomized in an editorial titled "Delinquency Begins with the Community," which appeared only two months after the opening of Club 506. Instead of blaming delinquency on individual juveniles and their families, he argued, "we should consider delinquent, that *community*, which allows to exist conditions which produce delinquency." Street asserted that "no one is completely responsible for what he does because he is a product of the strange and incalculable interplay of heredity and environment."[27] Such statements echoed the findings of interwar social scientists, particularly those at the University of Chicago, whose influential studies had concluded that delinquency was a product of individual, social, and environmental causes. Houston's child welfare advocates borrowed two particular arguments from the Chicago school. In urging improved city services to dilapidated "delinquency areas," they explained that the neglected physical environment contributed to higher levels of juvenile crime. They also transplanted Chicago studies of the "cultural conflict" between immigrant parents and "Americanized" children, substituting Mexico for southern and eastern Europe.[28] The Community Chest and its social welfare agencies presented narratives and images of a pluralistic society in which the general ideal of a healthy childhood applied to children of all racial and ethnic backgrounds. The Community Chest's monthly newsletter, *Our Community*, described the work of these agencies. On one page, a YMCA poster featured black and white children smiling together, while photos showed a "Latin-American" Girl Scout troop at Rusk Settlement, a youth painting class at the Jewish Community Center, and a "Teen-Age Club" of African American girls at Hester House in the predominantly black Fifth Ward.[29]

Street explored these subjects in his weekly radio program titled *Little Journeys to the Homes of the Great War-Time Services*.[30] In an April 1944 broadcast, he featured the Rusk Settlement House, set amid "an island of small unpainted, ramshackle wooden houses, unpaved streets and alleys," cleaved by "rutted channels" of "bluish-green, noisesome sewage." Street interviewed a Spanish-language teacher and a white social worker who extolled the "great value in living [there] and making common cause with the people of the neighborhood." Urging listeners to view Rusk's clientele, the residents of the Second Ward, as "good Americans all," Street described the area's "inescapable connection with [Houston's] great community." Rusk not only offered education, child care, and medical care; it also assisted residents in petitioning for city services such as paved streets, working sewers, adequate streetlights, and police protection. The residents stressed the importance of improving the quality of life for their children, or "the worthy citizenship of the future," as Street put it. By linking wartime child welfare with broader democratic citizenship, the broadcast implicitly evoked the "Double-V" campaign of black and Latino civil rights groups nationwide, which equated victory over Nazism abroad with victory over racism at home. In the words of a Community Chest directory of youth services, "leadership of youth in wartime" represented "a fighting line in this total war."[31]

Street's broadcast concluded with a brief interview with the leader of Rusk's parent organization, newly hired HSA director Franklin Israel Harbach. A graduate of the University of Pennsylvania, Harbach had spent over a decade working as an assistant director and "Boy's Worker" at the Henry Street Settlement on the Lower East Side of New York City. Reflecting the empathetic tradition of the settlement house, Harbach described a summer during college when he worked at Bethlehem Steel: "I always was very happy I had this experience when I was young because I had an opportunity to work with people who were living a different life than I was accustomed to. You can read about them, you can be sorry for them, you can be concerned about them, but until you really know what's going through their mind as they work at a tiresome job you do not know them."[32]

Epitomizing the settlement movement's emphasis on interclass cooperation, Harbach cultivated working relationships with Houston's philanthropists as well as Mexican American community leaders. His effective advocacy won residents many of their demands; in his first years, the city built new playgrounds, installed streetlights, and provided more policing in the Second Ward. In Harbach's hands, Rusk became a go-between for the police department and local youth gangs, with the occasional boy serving his probation under the supervision of a Rusk social worker. After 1948, Rusk hired local young men to work with "at-risk" youth in exchange for a modest college scholarship, as Harbach explained to the LULAC Council 60's president, Felix Tijerina, "to help our boys from Rusk help their own people."[33]

This burst of reform activity in Houston reflected the growing conviction in many localities by the end of World War II that delinquency was best handled in a community rather than an institutional setting, with emphasis on saving at-risk youth from institutionalization rather than on closing down institutions. To do so, however, required not only a genuine effort to improve core infrastructure in housing, education, employment, but also the provision of child welfare services, which were becoming increasingly specialized. Indeed, the HSA had hired Franklin Harbach partly out of a desire for an experienced, well-connected, and professionally trained social worker who could be entrusted with administration of a multimillion-dollar endowment, a sudden windfall that HSA's trustees wished to spend effectively. Until 1950, when the University of Texas opened its School of Social Work, most of the state's child welfare professionals and paraprofessionals had attended school outside Texas or had received training in a related discipline. Lagging somewhat behind other parts of the country, Texas by the 1940s began a steady professionalization of child welfare and juvenile justice. Much of the impetus for this movement stemmed not only from a search for alternatives to institutions but also from enthusiasm about the new field of children's mental health, or "mental hygiene" as it was still known, which promised to put medical authority behind such abstract endeavors as delinquency prevention and juvenile rehabilitation.

Children's Mental Health

> Juvenile delinquency, more than any one problem, has awakened communities to the need for coordinated effort in solving their problems. When they become aroused about any one condition, communities soon discover that all of the human relationship problems are interrelated. Housing projects cannot operate successfully unless day care programs for children and recreational facilities for youth have been developed. Crime prevention cannot be successfully established in a police department unless the case and group work agencies are cooperating in a preventive program.[34]

A growing number of Texans agreed with the sentiments expressed here, which appeared first in a *Dallas Morning News* series on wartime delinquency in April 1943 and subsequently in a pamphlet distributed to a mailing list of thousands of subscribers. The publisher was the Hogg Foundation for Mental Hygiene, which had begun work in February 1941 "to improve the mental hygiene of the people of Texas." In the process, the foundation tirelessly promoted mental hygiene all over the state. In its first three years, the foundation sponsored public lectures in 152 communities, reaching an estimated audience of 400,000 people; it also gave training seminars in 40 college classrooms, as well as 70 elementary and high schools. The foundation's director, Robert Lee Sutherland, described by a contemporary as "a circuit-riding preacher for mental health," personally had driven to 56 counties to spread the gospel in some 460 lectures. During the war, the foundation assisted at least a dozen local governments in setting up comprehensive delinquency prevention plans that included vocational, recreational, and clinical services for youth and in-service training for adult providers. It was instrumental in popularizing the idea that any effective delinquency prevention program should both nurture a child's emotional "adjustment" to existing social norms and construct a "healthy" social and physical environment for that adjustment. In this way, the foundation signaled the merger of social responsibility, government action, and a distinctly psychiatric perspective regarding the needs of children, which would have major ramifications for juvenile justice policy.[35]

The Hogg Foundation took its inspiration largely from the National Committee for Mental Hygiene (NCMH), a reform organization founded in 1909 in New York City. Initially the NCMH advocated sweeping changes in the care and treatment of the mentally ill in asylums and mental hospitals. Its first leader, former mental patient Clifford Beers, had gained national recognition for his 1907 memoir, *A Mind That Found Itself*, which described his own experiences in a Connecticut mental hospital. However, within a few years, the NCMH began to shift its focus from institutional to community settings. The amorphous phrase "mental hygiene" came to connote the prevention of mental illness through the therapeutic treatment of emotional disorders. A generation of American psychiatrists, led by Adolph Meyer, director of the Phipps Clinic at Johns Hopkins University, embraced mental hygiene in part because it expanded their authority beyond the narrow confines of mental institutions. To its proponents, mental hygiene seemed applicable to practically all aspects of everyday life, from family relationships to the quality of one's education, employment, and housing. By the 1920s, the NCMH was conducting statewide mental hygiene surveys—including one of Texas in 1925—that focused mainly on an array of infrastructural features such as schools, clinics, social welfare services, housing, employment, roads, and sanitation services.[36]

Mental hygiene experts devoted a great deal of attention to childhood, the life stage during which they believed most mental and emotional disorders began.[37] Although they were, like most American psychiatrists and psychologists, influenced by Sigmund Freud's teachings, mental hygienists widened their focus beyond the internal drives or intensive mother-child relationships that preoccupied most Freudians. Instead they followed the lead of Meyer and William Healy, a child psychiatrist who worked with the Chicago Juvenile Court and the Judge Baker Clinic in Boston. Meyer developed the technique of "psychobiology," which analyzed mental disorders by gathering information about an individual's medical, family, and community histories. Similarly, Healy's 1915 book about his work in Chicago, *The Individual Delinquent*, argued that each case was unique and required a comprehensive investigation. During Healy's tenure there, the Chicago Juvenile Court had pioneered the use of an interdisciplinary team comprised of a psychiatrist, a psychologist, and a social worker.

The NCMH adopted this method in its child guidance demonstration clinics, which promoted the idea that a large number of children had hidden emotional problems that could lead to serious disorders or even delinquency. Between 1921 and 1927, with funding from the Commonwealth Fund of the Rockefeller Foundation, the NCMH's Division on the Prevention of Delinquency opened demonstration clinics in eight cities. In most cases, these clinics proved so popular that city governments or local charities gladly funded them after the NCMH's trial period ended; by 1942, the number of clinics had risen from eight to sixty. Ironically, despite the NCMH's touting of child guidance clinics as "delinquency prevention," many of them did not work in a close or sustained way with juvenile courts. Clinicians quickly concluded that juvenile court referrals, even those who had not been officially adjudged delinquent, were already beyond help. Instead, clinics actively solicited referrals of what were called "predelinquent" children from child welfare agencies, schools, or parents; these children, it was believed, were younger and more amenable to treatment. This focus greatly broadened the potential client base for child guidance and expanded the types of behaviors that could be treated. According to one historian, a partial list of "predelinquent" disorders included "disobedience at home, negativism, stubbornness, rebelliousness, temper displays, stealing from parents, truancy, failure to get along with other children, school failure, sleep disturbances, fears, excessive fantasy."[38] Thus, child guidance blurred the line between obviously "at-risk" youth from the urban working classes (the original clientele), "the everyday child" of all social classes "showing ordinary signs of misbehavior any parent might anticipate," and "children brought voluntarily by middle-class mothers."[39] Meanwhile, child guidance practitioners popularized their work in a host of books, magazines, newspapers, and radio broadcasts during the 1920s and 1930s. The federal Children's Bureau, established in 1912, also published numerous pamphlets on child guidance. At the local level, clinics put on public demonstrations, lectures, and training for a variety of audiences. Child guidance thus added much to the discourse but little to the practice of delinquency prevention; the same could be said for juvenile rehabilitation.[40]

This national pattern held true generally in Texas, where two child guidance clinics opened, in Dallas (1923) and Houston (1929). The NCMH sponsored the Dallas clinic but complained that the city's "undeveloped services" limited its ability to work with "predelinquent" children.[41] Nearly all its initial referrals came from "an ethnically homogenous group" of white parents and educators, as indicated by a brochure urging "anyone" to refer a "problem child" for clinical attention.[42] By contrast, the Houston Child Guidance Center, which was not affiliated with the NCMH, served a wider array of children. Of the 514 new cases accepted in its first two years, over half came from social agencies (263), roughly a quarter from families (127), and very few from public schools (56) and juvenile courts (23). The complaints, however, typified the broad range of behaviors labeled as disorders by the child guidance movement, with the most common ones being "disobedience," "temper tantrums," "nervousness," "lying," "distractibility and inattention," and "poor group adjustment."[43] During World War II, the clinic expanded its purview further as the Bureau of Mental Hygiene, offering treatment to adults and children suffering from the dislocations and stresses of wartime. The clinic responded to Houston's rising juvenile delinquency problem by providing consultant services to the juvenile court, mainly psychological testing, while accepting few referrals of "difficult" cases.

Although the Houston clinic's overall contribution to delinquency prevention remained small, its significance lay in its role as a springboard for the formation of the Hogg Foundation, which in turn would have a major impact on the statewide conversation about juvenile justice reform in the 1940s. The chief financier behind both the clinic and the foundation, Ima Hogg, was one of Texas' most revered and energetic philanthropists and became a leading spokesperson for children's mental health. "Miss Ima," as she was known to her many admirers, hailed from one of Texas's oldest political families.[44] Her father, James Hogg, had served as Texas governor from 1890 to 1895, crusading against "the interests" and pushing successfully for the regulation of railroads, banks, and insurance companies. As a child, Ima traveled with her father on numerous official trips, including visits to "schools for the blind and deaf" and "prisons for mentally ill people." According to one biographer, the governor "had great compassion for these individuals, and he read research on mental problems in hopes that one day they could be cured."[45] These visits made a deep impression on Ima, as she recalled later in a 1970 interview:

> I was also very much interested in mentally ill people in hospitals. . . . My father was very interested, also. . . . And often I went through with him and I'd hear him say to the superintendent or the doctor, "What can be done for these people? What are you doing?" And then I used to sit with them, many of them, and entertain them. I enjoyed talking with a lot of them, and they were all so homesick. They'd say they didn't belong there—their families sent them because they wanted to get rid of them . . . that was always in the wards where they weren't so mentally ill . . . they were disturbed people, melancholy people. I used to visit a great deal at the asylum. And I had little girl friends out there, you know, at the asylum where they had children. . . . I was at the hospital all the time. . . . I was free to go into the wards any time I wanted to.[46]

These visits were cut short by tragedy. In 1895, Ima's mother, Sallie Stinson Hogg, fell ill with tuberculosis. At age thirteen, Ima served as her mother's caregiver until she passed away later that year, in what proved to be the first of several extended periods of caring for dying loved ones, including her father James Hogg (1905–6), her brother Will (1930), and her brother Mike (1941). After her father's death, Ima suffered a deep depression that was allayed by long visits to New York City (1906) and Europe (1907). Her continued study of music with some renowned teachers gave Ima her first experience with philanthropy. In 1913, Ima organized the first Houston Symphony and began prolonged fund-raising and publicity campaigns. According to her biographers, Ima cultivated an attitude about the symphony that was at once populist and avant-garde; she "composed dissonant music," purchased several pieces of then-controversial European modern art, and built a substantial collection of American Indian art. Later in life, she sponsored music programs for underprivileged children and often insisted that the symphony should belong to the masses as well as the classes. Like many modern women of her generation, Ima intuitively included the arts, or "anything that contributes to a wholesome life," in her understanding of mental health.[47] Ima Hogg first encountered the mental hygiene movement shortly after World War I, when she became one of the victims of the Spanish flu pandemic of 1918. Her doctors interpreted some aftereffects, including a bad case of insomnia, as "nervous exhaustion" and sent Ima to see a neurologist in Philadelphia.[48] In 1925, she visited the psychiatrist and child guidance proponent Austin Riggs in Massachusetts, who connected her to the NCMH. She returned to her home in Houston to mount fund-raising drives for the Houston Child Guidance Center, which opened with Community Chest support in 1929. Wanting to promote mental health on a wider scale, Ima spent the 1930s negotiating with the University of Texas at Austin to devote a multimillion dollar bequest from her brother Will toward a mental hygiene foundation.

After a lengthy search, the new foundation hired as its first director Robert Lee Sutherland, who was then teaching at Bucknell University. Prior to that, Sutherland had earned a doctorate in Christian theology and ethics at the University of Chicago. His dissertation, supervised by sociologist Ernest K. Burgess, was a study of Chicago's black churches that employed both the social survey and participation-observation methods.[49] In the late 1930s, Sutherland took over the "Negro project" of the American Youth Commission (AYC), a division of the Commonwealth Fund devoted to studying the plight of children and youth during the Depression. At the AYC, Sutherland oversaw the publication of a series of books on "caste and class" authored by John Dollard, Allison Davis, E. Franklin Frazier, and Charles S. Johnson. Using interviews, social surveys, and participation-observation techniques, these studies examined how legalized inequality and individual bigotry impeded the healthy "personality development" of African American children and youth.[50] This work placed Sutherland at the center of spiraling national concerns about youth as well as race. Many Americans feared that the economic crisis had produced a "youth crisis." Countless thousands of young people, displaced from their homes, were riding the rails, even after the New Deal administration of President Franklin Roosevelt inaugurated two major initiatives, the Civilian Conservation Corps (1933) and the National Youth Administration (NYA) (1935). In a 1935 article in the *Journal of Social Hygiene*, Eleanor Roosevelt confessed her "real terror": "We may be losing this generation." Some observers went so far as to suggest that idle American youth could provide a constituency for homegrown versions of the Hitler Youth. In his book about the "world problem" of youth, W. Thatcher Winslow, the NYA's assistant director, wrote, "In Italy and Germany youth marches in uniform to martial music." Similarly, Homer Price Rainey, president of the University of Texas, warned that it was "often the depressed, embittered, or unstable youth who most quickly follows the demagogue." Rainey, who had supervised Sutherland at both the AYC and Bucknell, suggested his appointment at the Hogg Foundation in 1941.[51]

Sutherland brought a distinctly progressive perspective to the foundation, linking mental hygiene to broad notions of social responsibility. In his public speeches and writings, he argued that policymakers and industrialists, as well as schools and social agencies, helped shape "environmental factors which determine the social rewards and punishments which surround the development of the child and determine the goals toward which he will strive." In interviews with AYC researchers, however, African American children and youth had expressed their belief that their horizons for adult accomplishment were much lower than those of their white peers. Sutherland warned that the children of African American and Mexican American families suffered from "institutionalized patterns" of inequality.[52] Though he usually stopped short of the explicit language of the AYC studies, Sutherland was essentially claiming a child's right to mental health similar to the controversial position staked out by Charlotte Helen Towle, a psychiatric social work professor at his alma mater, the University of Chicago. In her 1945 training manual for staff at federal assistance agencies, titled *Common Human Needs*, Towle argued that all people should enjoy a right to food, shelter, and health care, which in turn would lead to widespread psychological well-being.[53] Denounced as promoting socialism, the book was removed from distribution by the federal government, only to be reprinted widely by the American Association of Social Workers. However, the episode underscored the ease with which child advocacy could be tarred as "socialistic," as it often would be during the Cold War. Sutherland wisely tempered any criticisms he might have felt (none appear in his private correspondence) with a vague, optimistic message of improved quality of life that tapped into his audience's shared experiences of the recent past.

During the Depression, affirmative government action guided by experts had helped ameliorate poor living conditions; the notion emerged that large administrative bureaucracies could offer solutions to intractable social problems. As the intellectual historian Elizabeth Borgwardt has shown, the war amplified that viewpoint by broadening the horizons of millions who left their homes to work in defense plants or serve in the military.[54] The connection between physical and mental health and the role governments could play in ensuring both seemed more obvious than they ever had before. "Everywhere," wrote Sutherland in the foundation's 1945 blueprint for community mental health, "there are basic problems of human relationship. They appear in the growing-up difficulties of children, in the quest for harmony within families, in the conflict between social and economic groups, and in the personal failure and maladjustment of some adults."[55] Distributed to dozens of city and county governments in Texas, this plan proposed sweeping actions, from installing guidance counselors in the public schools to providing adequate sanitation and water services to all neighborhoods. The infrastructure of "preventive" mental health had broadened far beyond the clinic, reshaping public consciousness about the possibilities for government action, even in a state that historically had opposed it.

Despite its potentially controversial claims, the expansive advocacy of children's mental health and of a shared social responsibility for the well-being of even the most outcast youth combined to create a new kind of consensus in the 1940s. The timing could not have been more propitious for the state's juvenile training schools, which became sites of struggle between scientific reformers, old-line officials, and an increasingly watchful public.

"Children Not Fully Responsible for What They Do"

On August 29, 1942, Judge Roy Hofheinz of Houston delivered the opening address at the annual meeting of Texas's district and county judges. The meeting's major theme was the improvement of working relations between local juvenile courts, probation departments, and the Gatesville State School for Boys. Indeed, the meeting was held at Gatesville, at the invitation of its new superintendent, Robert N. Winship Jr., whom Hofheinz praised lavishly for inaugurating "tremendous strides" toward "the rehabilitation of youngsters."[56] Most of the judges in attendance concurred, having spent the day walking "unescorted," singly and in groups, around the Gatesville complex. Hofheinz marveled at the absence of "lock-step formations and other efforts to destroy the initiative of youngsters," hallmarks of past years. In their place, Winship had begun building a more individualized program staffed with professionals trained in child psychology, education, social work, and sociology. He had created the new staff position of "youth counselor" to offer boys individual therapeutic attention and inaugurated a "sociological department" to compile case files as well as more precise statistical data on the inmate population. Largely haphazard in the past, individual record keeping now included a thirty-six-part schedule for logging more detailed information about an inmate's offense, education, and family histories. Plans were afoot to hire a psychologist, who would conduct behavior and intelligence testing.[57] Much of the day's discussion focused on tying these efforts more closely to those of local agencies in the hopes of facilitating more sophisticated intake and release plans.

Winship seemed an ideal fit for this daunting task. A former schoolteacher, he had run a well-known Boy Scout camp at his family ranch in Junction, about 140 miles west of Austin, where the Texas Hill Country begins to give way to the more arid, rocky landscape of western Texas. In hiring Winship, the TBC touted him as an expert in "modern ideas of dealing with delinquent boys."[58] His public speeches outlined a broad vision of delinquency prevention and rehabilitation that echoed the rhetoric of children's mental health advocates. "The local community," he told a meeting of the Texas Division of Child Welfare, must devise "reasonable health, recreational, social and other advantages for all children whether they were from this side or the other of the railroad track."[59] Too often, this lack of services made commitment of a boy to Gatesville a first choice instead of a "last resort, as it should be." Boys often arrived as blank slates, unless they came from one of the five counties in the state that sent along case histories. This lack of information undermined the possibility of individual rehabilitation, virtually ensuring that benchmarks for progress would be based on conformity to institutional routines and rules, which in turn exacerbated the use of corporal punishment to maintain order. Further slowing a boy's release was the lack of supervision in the community; by 1941, only 16 of the state's 254 counties offered any semblance of juvenile probation services, and even many of those, lamented Winship, remained "wholly unequipped" according to national standards set forth by the U.S. Children's Bureau.[60] In an interview with the *Fort Worth Star-Telegram*, Winship explained his general philosophy:

> We do not regard the boys here as having committed crimes. They are, rather, delinquent boys who are in need of guardianship above and beyond what they are getting at home. This means that instead of their being punished like adults, they are regarded as being children and not fully responsible for what they do. They are somewhat like a boy who is sick. Such a boy has something wrong with him physically, but these boys have something wrong with them because they are sick socially, and need help where the proper guidance in the community has failed.[61]

Winship's reforms pleased most juvenile justice professionals as well as the legislative committee charged with supervising Gatesville's reforms. In February 1943, the Committee to Investigate State Eleemosynary and Reformatory Destitution reported "a great improvement in . . . the morale of the boys," citing the replacement of "inhumane punishment" with "the merit system plan."[62] However, not everyone shared this enthusiasm. Longtime employees, some of whom had worked at Gatesville since the 1920s, resigned in protest of Winship's wholesale prohibition of corporal punishment—a reaction reminiscent of the 1912 staff revolt against a short-lived ban on "whippings" (see chapter 1). In early 1942, these disgruntled former employees launched a whisper campaign against Winship, alleging that he was allowing the inmates to escape "nearly every day," harass women in town, molest one another, and curse staff with impunity. A petition with ninety-one signatures from "prominent Gatesville citizens," including an alderman, claimed that the county lived in "a constant state of fear," with boys "invading" homes and stealing cars daily.[63] Citing these charges, the area's legislators, state senator Karl L. Lovelady and state representative Earl Huddleston, filed official requests for Winship's removal.[64] Although some local citizens, including Gatesville mayor C. E. Gandy, rallied to Winship's defense, the damage was done.[65] On February 3, 1942, the TBC held a hearing in which Winship faced his accusers—a group of four former employees and their attorney.[66] Winship's critics made allegations that ranged from the improbable to the bizarre, including assertions that 148 boys had escaped in the previous 153 days and that a group of boys had "sodomized a mule." What these examples showed, they claimed, was the failure of the merit system to maintain discipline. Staff testimonials turned bitter when recounting instances of disobedient or disrespectful behavior, especially when it came from African American or "Mexican" inmates. When one black inmate mockingly told Edwin Elms, a sixty-three-year-old Gatesville native who had worked for the school since 1921, that he "had no authority" anymore, Elms quit in disgust, informing Winship that he "would not work under a man that thought more of a negro than he did of [him]." According to another longtime staff member, Otis Beard, "The negroes got to where when you told them to do anything they would laugh at you and there was nothing you could do about it." Worst of all, for Beard, was R. B. Johnston, the school sociologist in charge of black inmates, who "would take the negroes word instead of [his]" in disputes and "would call negroes up and ask how he was being treated." D. F. Farqhuar, whose father had worked at Gatesville in the 1920s, complained about "a Mexican boy whistling at ladies." Each of them agreed that a return to "whipping the boys would correct the situation." The meeting ended in shouting, after which the TBC advised Winship to reinstate corporal punishment; he refused to do so.[67]

The situation deteriorated further over the next year, as relations between Winship and the local townspeople degenerated into open hostility. Excursions to downtown Gatesville became occasions for chilly stares and awkward conversations. Described as "unfriendly" and "very cold" publicly, Winship also ordered his staff not to speak with legislators, especially his chief critic, Representative Huddleston.[68] In June 1943, Texas governor Coke Stevenson received an emotional petition for Winship's removal endorsed by Gatesville's legislative delegation, the editor of the local Gatesville Messenger, the Chamber of Commerce, Coryell County judge Floyd Zeigler, and a women's group in the First Methodist Church.[69] In a face-to-face meeting, the TBC explained to Huddleston that Winship had the "universal approval" of "probate authorities in Texas" as well as unspecified "national authorities on juvenile problems."[70] However, it was agreed that Winship would be transferred to a different institution. The decision abruptly became moot in early September, when Winship died following a car accident.[71]

Winship's successor, R. E. "Ed" Blair, came from a very different background. A native of rural Ellis County, near Dallas, Blair had spent most of his career at Daniel Baker College, a Presbyterian school in central Texas, where he coached football and taught history. Just before accepting a position at Gatesville, he had worked on the staff of the Corsicana State Home, an institution for orphaned boys. After becoming Gatesville superintendent, Blair quickly set about restoring old modes of discipline. In March 1944, two boys caught trying to escape on horses were beaten so badly that one of them was hospitalized. News of the incident reached Tarrant County (Fort Worth) judge Clarence O. Kraft, who had committed one of the would-be escapees. At Kraft's insistence, the TBC launched a formal investigation but quickly shifted its focus to uncovering the judge's informant. Kraft had learned of the beatings from R. B. Johnston, the school sociologist and a holdover from Winship's administration, who resigned in protest over the affair. Within weeks, Johnston found himself the subject of a sexual abuse investigation; Superintendent Blair produced testimonies from several boys accusing him of coercing sexual favors in exchange for favorable work placements and accelerated release recommendations. One former inmate described, in graphic detail, how he and other boys had rendezvoused with Johnston in downtown Austin after their release. Johnston protested his innocence and claimed that Blair was retaliating to "keep him quiet"; however, the TBC believed the charges and helped bring about a grand jury investigation in Coryell County. The pressure caused Johnston, a married man with a son fighting in the European theater, to suffer a nervous breakdown. Writing from a mental institution, he threatened to commit suicide if the allegations were made public. The case was eventually dropped, but the door clearly had been shut on the effort to modernize Gatesville, at least for the time being.[72]

Personal scandals also undermined reform efforts at the girls' training school in Gainesville during the early 1940s. Hired, like Winship, in September 1941, Superintendent Mary A. Stone had been a public school teacher and a staff worker at the Austin State School, an institution for mentally retarded women and children. Stone seems to have made little effort to address the problems that had brought about her hiring. In August 1942, the Texas Division of Child Welfare reported that Gainesville still lacked a "trained social worker" and had not provided any meaningful intake or parole procedures. The report singled out the girls' housing for special criticism, noting that the "cottages" denoted the floors of "large two and three story buildings"; each floor, in other words, constituted a "cottage" (see figure 7). Individual bedrooms, much touted over the years, resembled jail cells. Sparsely furnished with dilapidated beds and desks, the rooms included barred windows and windowless doors that were locked from the outside each night. In lieu of overnight access to bathrooms, girls were given chamber pots; for more

Figure 7. "Gainesville State School for Girls, building with swingset." (Box 1999/016-098, Records, Texas Youth Commission. Courtesy of the Texas State Library and Archives Commission.)

serious emergencies, however, they were left on their own because staff often slept out of earshot of any possible cries for help. Girls who attempted to flee these conditions received harsh punishments. The worst offenders had their heads shaved before being confined to the "reflection room," a steel cell, and fed a Spartan diet of bread and water.[73] Stone's dismissal barely a year into her administration came not as a result of these practices but because of a criminal indictment for depositing paychecks for fictitious employees into her personal bank account. In 1943, the Cooke County (Gainesville) Court sentenced Stone to two years in the state penitentiary.[74]

The interim superintendent, Margie Mizell, lasted less than a year and did nothing to further state recommendations for improved rehabilitation services. Indeed, the school failed even to provide adequate clothing for girls upon their release. So appalling was the girls' "very poor clothing" that the girls' counselor of the Austin Police Department purchased new outfits at her own expense.[75] Even more damning was the account of a staff whistle-blower named Bell Turner Johnson, who wrote the following account one month after being hired as a housemother:

The place is desperately in need of a superintendent with some understanding of the adolescent girl and who would not use discipline methods that have in most instances been responsible for the girl leaving home. When a girl attempts to "run," she is entitled to some sort of trial, an attempted understanding instead of being flattened out on a table whipped in Gestapo fashion, then locked in her room and fed a cup of skimmed milk and two slices of bread for fourteen to thirty days. I thought such brutal methods of discipline belong to the dark ages, for they are in direct opposition to all that has been written on the subject of delinquency for the last forty years. . . . Nothing in the way of constructive work can be done until a new superintendent with specialized training in the "teen-aged girl" is brought here.[76]

Johnson's claims, which echoed the conclusions of prior investigations, reflected the aforementioned paucity of trained professionals in relevant disciplines such as social work in Texas. Her note became an embarrassment when its accusations were publicized in the local Gainesville newspaper. An irate superintendent Mizell wrote to the TBC asking for guidance on how to respond. In a revealing bit of advice, TBC chairman Baker suggested, "The best answer . . . is no answer at all. Do not let this matter disturb you at all. Just run your school like it ought to be, and everything will come out all right in the end."[77] As it had in the case of Gatesville reform superintendent Winship, the TBC was acting as an agent of the status quo. Indeed, Winship was the exception to the typical superintendent hired by the TBC, in that he was a genuine reformer. The sum total of the TBC's actions strongly suggest that its overarching imperative all along had been bureaucratic self-preservation, which extended to defenses of the troubled institutions under its supervision. Although this strategy of ignoring and outlasting critics had worked in previous decades, it was now wearing thin with a public whose expectations had been raised by the spread of ideas about children's mental health, child welfare, delinquency prevention, and juvenile rehabilitation. This brand of public impatience was expressed clearly during the brief and controversial tenure of Mizell's successor, Pearl Chadwell, hired in September 1943.

For nearly a dozen years prior to becoming Gainesville superintendent, Chadwell had supervised the women's dormitories at the University of Texas. There she had demonstrated "great strength and . . . unusually fine judgment in handling girls," according to education professor Charles F. Arrowood, who wrote one of two faculty references that positively gushed over Chadwell's unique understanding of "Texas girls" and "Texas people."[78] However, this experience failed to prepare her for running a training school for delinquent girls. Consider, for example, the case of fifteen-year-old Anne Ricks of Crockett, in east Texas, who was committed to

Gainesville on June 4, 1943, for "incorrigibility."[79] Anne's case had been heard in a jury trial, in direct contravention to the core tenet of juvenile justice that emphasized "root causes" over proof of a specific crime beyond a reasonable doubt. The jury had adjudged her "a delinquent child" and sentenced her to "one year—not to exceed the time she shall reach the age of twenty-one." During an April 1944 visit, Anne's mother informed Chadwell that she expected her daughter's release at the end of one year—that June. Chadwell's reaction was to immediately write Houston County judge Will McLean, who had sent Anne to Gainesville, for a supporting opinion. Meanwhile, as Anne's expected release date approached, her parents threatened to sue for false imprisonment, securing legal representation from a high-powered personal friend of the family: Jonathan B. Sallas, Crockett's representative in the Texas legislature. Sallas wrote Chadwell several times requesting Anne's release, only to be told in the most patronizing tone that Anne had not "made a proper adjustment" by earning sufficient merit points. After more than a month of these fruitless exchanges, Anne's father confronted Chadwell in person. The superintendent refused to budge, insisting that Anne must "make her records"; in a perhaps misguided attempt to reassure him, Chadwell explained that Anne had been "rather defiant at first" but was "making considerable progress of late." Even a request from Judge McLean, written in the presence of Anne's increasingly frustrated parents, failed to change Chadwell's mind. Finally, Sallas wrote directly to TBC chairman Baker, who instructed Chadwell to release Anne immediately or face criminal charges herself. When Chadwell protested that "the reason why [Anne] needs more training" was that she "has made the boast that she has always had what she wanted," Baker tersely reiterated his order, advising her to "always interpret court orders most favorably to the delinquent child."

Staff who openly criticized Chadwell's policies were either fired or pressured to resign. "Junior sociologist" Selma Jones, whom Chadwell had blamed for instigating the dispute with the Ricks family, quit after being accused by other staff of "always complaining" and sowing discontent among the girls. On the same day, "Commercial Teacher" Lucy T. Furlow resigned in protest of "unfair conditions."[80] As we have seen, long-festering divisions among institutional staff tended to bubble to the surface after the hiring of a new superintendent. In this instance, however, the fault line clearly fell between those who embraced the philosophy of juvenile rehabilitation and those who adhered to a more traditional custodial philosophy. That Chadwell fell into the latter category was revealed during a December 1945 inspection. Several teachers told TBC staff member Erwin K. Stork that Gainesville "was a reformatory and not a school."[81] One teacher referred to the girl inmates as "poor trash"; when a mortified Stork asked her to explain further, she simply remarked, "That is all they are." Stork patiently reprimanded the teacher but found to his horror that the local townspeople shared her opinion. Convinced that Gainesville's wards were "bad influences" on local children, schools and businesses had banned them from their premises—a complete reversal from the more cooperative relations established during the tenure of Carrie Weaver Smith. Largely cut off from the outside world, viewed with contempt and hatred by their teachers and housemothers, the girl inmates were immersed in an atmosphere that was more desolate and "institutional" than at any time in the school's history. At the outset of his inspection, Stork was struck by "the absolute idleness of the girls"; he described a large number of girls "with nothing to do but sit on their bed and stare out of a window." So complete was Chadwell's policy of mandatory silence that laughter was prohibited even at the weekly motion-picture show. Stork watched girls sit quietly through a "hilarious Mickey Mouse comedy." Many girls had engaged in self-mutilation, "inscribing or cutting with any sharp object the initials or name of her purported lover into her flesh." In some cases, the names belonged to other girls, indicating to Stork an epidemic of "homo-sexual relationships," particularly between "Mexican and white girls." Stork presented no evidence to corroborate this claim, which reflected long-standing concerns about "deviant" femininity in the institution. His suggestion that Gainesville segregate "the Mexican girls as a class" tempered the report's call for more humane treatment. "These girls are human beings," Stork exclaimed, "and are not as delinquent as they are dependent on someone for proper teaching." The report recommended the hiring of a psychiatrist as well as the replacement of staff or their reeducation to view the girls as "students" instead of "inmates."

Around this time, the walls began to close in on the defenders of the training schools, particularly the boys' school at Gatesville. Demands for action came from practically every corner of Texas and from groups of various political persuasions. In a 1946 speech to the Corpus Christi Jaycees, district judge Paul A. Martineau denounced Gatesville as "a terrible place where criminals are made" and swore that he would never commit another delinquent boy to state custody.[82] The Waco Humane Society called for an end to the "many instances of useless whipping, amounting to cruelty."[83] During prior uproars, the state's customary response was to invite reporters on tours of the institutions, which usually had resulted in positive press used to counter critics. In October 1946, the *Dallas Morning News* ran just such an article, which praised Gatesville's "father-to-son attitude" and derided critics who "harassed" staff with "unfounded rumors of brutality."[84] This time, however, positive reviews failed to stem the tide; requests poured in to state offices from individuals and church groups for an end to "punishments . . . not worthy of a democratic and Christian state."[85] In early 1947, members of the Democratic Women's Club of Dallas "cornered" Representative Pat Wiseman in his capitol office, demanding action from the House Legislative Investigating Committee on Eleemosynary and Reformatory Institutions, which Wiseman chaired. On March 4, Wiseman led a four-member delegation on a surprise visit to Gatesville. Like earlier investigators, they found unsanitary conditions: water-damaged dormitory walls, open-air toilets that caused entire sleeping areas to reek of feces, and food "served by boys who dipped it out with bare hands."[86] However, they discovered something even more troubling:

> The day of our visit two boys had made attempts to escape; upon recapture, the boys were struck several times in the face by the bare fist of employees. Then their clothes were stripped off and they were given several lashes with a leather strap, which left them bruised and blue from the treatment. *In order to prevent our seeing these boys, they had been transferred from the hospital to the County jail. When we tried to see them at the jail, we found that we could not get in, due to the face that the Deputy Sheriff was unable to come to town, and the Sheriff, who had left orders that the jail was not to be opened by anyone except himself, could not be located anywhere. We began trying to see the boys at 11 o'clock A.M., and finally succeeded in getting in the jail to see them at 6 o'clock P.M.*[87]

Immediately, Gatesville's defenders sprang into action. Three days after the House inspection, TBC chairman Carlos C. Ashley visited Gatesville to question the same inmates who had alleged abuse. They were covered in bruises, which one sixteen-year-old boy with "the remnant of a black eye" attributed to Superintendent Blair personally.[88] After ordering the inmates to pull their pants down so he could examine them further, Ashley concluded that the leather strap was "not a severe instrument of punishment at all" compared to the past. The boys, he felt, had exaggerated for credulous politicians. According to Ashley's report, they admitted plans to assault the guards and escape the institution and agreed that "they had done wrong, and deserved punishment." Ashley also pointedly disputed Blair's alleged role, which if true would have stained his reputation as a tough but compassionate administrator. Before returning to Austin, Ashley interviewed various "well known citizens" of Gatesville, including the sheriff and county judge Floyd Ziegler, all of whom described Blair as "the best Superintendent the institution ha[d] ever had." The institution, they claimed, was "in the best condition that they ha[d] ever known it." Blair bolstered this benign narrative with his own version of events, which directly contradicted each key point in the House report. Rather than a beating, the would-be escapees had received a "light paddling," under careful supervision, for which they "thanked" Blair.[89] Cataracts, instead of blows to the face, were responsible for one boy's black eye. Blair also invoked an argument that would become well worn in subsequent years: visits from outside authorities harmed the very juveniles they purported to help. The "disruptive" inspection had incited "general unrest among the boys," leading to more punishments.[90]

The inspection's findings were made public in late April, provoking a flurry of action in the legislature. Senator Fred Harris of Dallas sponsored a bill "to abolish corporal punishment in all forms." A second bill proposed the creation of a "State Penal and Eleemosynary Commissioner" to ensure the "humane and equitable treatment" of inmates. Initially, the bills seemed likely to succeed. Newspapers highlighted the House report's descriptions of the Gatesville beatings, the attempted cover-up at the county jail, and the concluding statement that conditions at both training schools fell "far below the standards required of a subdivision of a civilized nation." However, the TBC mounted an effective counteroffensive. Publicly, the TBC distributed its own favorable report, while the freshman representative from Coryell County, Sid Gregory, warned that the proposed bills would result in the inmates "taking over" the institutions. Indeed, as a former Gatesville employee, Gregory was surely in a position to know. In the gallery were over one hundred spectators from Gatesville bent on preserving the established order. Behind the scenes, newly installed TBC chairman Hall H. Logan lobbied individual legislators, with assistance from Gatesville judge Ziegler. Senators watered down the antiwhipping bill with amendments and ultimately defeated it. Instead, a seemingly innocuous bill passed authorizing a seven-member commission appointed by the governor to examine the laws governing the training schools and recommend changes. Gatesville's defenders breathed a sigh of relief; in August 1947, TBC chairman Logan thanked Ziegler for his help with their "mutual fight." He also ordered Blair and Gainesville superintendent Chadwell to reduce the use of corporal punishment and produce monthly reports on the number of whippings. In his letter to Ziegler, Logan touted the planned creation of two "honor companies" at Gatesville and the expansion of the "industrial training" program.[91] So preoccupied were Gatesville's defenders with preserving the status quo that they failed to realize that they had won the battle but lost the proverbial war.

The Best Interests of the Institution

Even as the TBC pushed for these well-worn piecemeal reforms, Chairman Logan knew such balms would fail to soothe the consciences of reformers for whom the institutions had become embarrassingly backward. He consulted with the superintendents of boys' training schools in Nebraska, Illinois, and California. Although each school prohibited corporal punishment, the consensus opinion was that encoding such a ban in law would encourage the inmates to misbehave. More important, explained Nebraska superintendent Hugo Carroll, was an institutional culture of treatment that discouraged violence, which no statute could remedy. Carroll described how he had hired a former Gatesville employee; however, he explained, "[I] had to fire him, because you couldn't make him believe that you can handle a kid without beating him up."[92] What was needed was wholesale reform on a scale unprecedented in Texas' history, but this was unlikely to happen from within the TBC. The dilemma was captured best in a thank-you letter to the TBC from the Gatesville citizens who had defended the institution before the legislature. It stated that "local citizens" were glad to help "any time the best interest of this institution [was] at stake"—a stunning variation on the founding principle of juvenile justice.[93]

More was at stake than any of Gatesville's supporters realized. In November 1947, Texas governor Beauford H. Jester announced the formation of the Texas Training School Code Commission. All the appointees came from outside the training school system and were experienced hands in the fields of child welfare and mental health. Their task—to find "a realistic approach" to not only "the training and rehabilitation of youthful offenders" but also "the problem of juvenile delinquency" itself—was sufficiently open ended to potentially overturn the established regimes at Gatesville and Gainesville.[94] The convergence of abuse scandals with a new understanding of words like "prevention" and "rehabilitation," spread by urban child welfare agencies, juvenile justice experts, and children's mental health advocates, created a historic moment of possibility for the most sweeping juvenile justice reforms yet.

THREE

Juvenile Rehabilitation and the Color Line
The Training School for Black Delinquent Girls, 1943–1950

At the very moment when the training schools were coming under attack in Texas, a decades-long push to open an institution for black delinquent girls finally achieved success with the opening of the Brady State School for Negro Girls in 1947. Located at a reconverted German prisoner-of-war camp in west central Texas, the Brady school appeared to respond in part to calls for equal treatment for delinquent black girls. Despite the publicized abuses of juvenile inmates over the years, civil rights groups had feared that for some female offenders, the alternative to institutionalization was much worse. Girls who committed violent offenses were often thrown in county jails or adult prisons, while those found guilty of sexual or status crimes were simply released back into the community. Neither resolution had pleased African American leaders, who viewed the inattention to rehabilitating black girls as one facet of the state's general slighting of public safety in predominantly black neighborhoods. Until World War II, the state legislature remained largely indifferent to the problem. This state of affairs changed during and immediately after the war due to escalating pressure from black civil rights advocates, white social reformers, juvenile justice professionals, and (strangely enough) military officials—each of whom offered conflicting visions of the problem of black female delinquency and of what this particular training school should do about it. Also, while most black and some white reformers expressed the traditional progressive concern for protecting children and youth from the dangers of the adult world, other advocates for the training school were clearly motivated primarily by concerns for public safety. These conflicts spilled over into the school's inaugural years, which were fraught with tension between black and white employees and between adult staff and girl inmates. The local population, which was predominantly white, also played a role in shaping public discourse surrounding the rehabilitation of black delinquent girls that was strikingly similar to the role played by townspeople in Gatesville and Gainesville. As we shall see, the results were mixed. On the whole, the school for black delinquent girls at Brady (later at Crockett) fared much better than its counterparts for white and Mexican American youth in providing a program of education and treatment. However, it accomplished this by excluding the most difficult cases and by embracing a fairly conservative model of racial uplift.

The seeds for Brady were planted much earlier, in 1916, when the legislature first created the school for white girls at Gainesville. The school's director, Carrie Weaver Smith, urged the legislature to create an institution for black girls.[1] At the same time, the Texas Association of Colored Women's Clubs (TACWC), founded in 1905 in Gainesville, also began a campaign for a black girls' school.[2] In the 1920s, the effort gained the support of the all-white Texas Federation of Women's Clubs, which had been instrumental in pushing prior juvenile court and training school legislation, and the Joint Legislative Council, an umbrella organization of reform groups. While the TACWC began raising funds for a privately run school, the Texas branch of the Atlanta-based Commission on Interracial Cooperation (CIC) lobbied the legislature and raised public awareness. The school's cause was taken up briefly by the CIC's director, Jessie Daniel Ames, a former suffragist and antilynching activist who took on the state's powerful Ku Klux Klan throughout the decade. In 1927, this interracial coalition of women's reform groups managed to convince the legislature to authorize the construction of a training school for black girls. Authorization, however, did not amount to much. Like the proposed school for black boys a decade earlier, the legislature withheld all funding for the school, reducing it to a mere idea, an unfunded mandate. This decision reflected more than just a particularly blatant example of the racial segregation and discrimination of the Jim Crow era; it was, more fundamentally, a refusal to include African American youth in the emerging categories of childhood and adolescence. At Gatesville this belief expressed itself through separate and unequal treatment within the institution, while in this instance it surfaced as the refusal to provide services altogether. Indeed, the lack of even the miserly funding levels afforded for white juvenile rehabilitation left black youth in the hands of adult justice at a time when lynching still posed a major threat. In Texas, lynchings claimed the lives of nearly 500 people, including 349 African Americans, between 1882 and 1930.[3] Along with public accommodations, schooling at every level was strictly segregated during the period. Thus the landscape of opportunities for expressions of protected childhood and adolescence was less promising for African American than for white children and youth. However, after 1927, black and white activists continued to agitate for the school's construction, and they found unexpected allies in the state government and the United States Army by the time of World War II.

"A Menace to All Our Men and Boys"

In May 1938, an eighteen-year-old African American woman named Christel Gibson got into an argument with a white police officer on a Houston city bus and was arrested on a charge of disturbing the peace. The local branch of the National Association for the Advancement of Colored People (NAACP) sprang into action. Only months earlier, the organization had launched a youth council initiative specifically to recruit younger members and to address issues facing African American children and youth. Within days, an NAACP Youth Council attorney had Gibson's charges dropped; the officer, it turned out, had "literally run berserk" in arresting her in what the *Houston Defender* termed "a frame-up."[4] Although the incident galvanized long-standing complaints about police brutality against Houston's black community, it also underscored the paucity of options for black youth charged with delinquency.[5] At an event commemorating the first anniversary of the NAACP's Houston Youth Council, speakers linked the two problems. Gibson's attorney pointed out that she had been facing "a long sentence in a county jail"; R. O. Lanier, dean of the Houston College for Negroes, warned that "juvenile delinquency . . . [was] on the increase among Negroes, with no corrective or protective institution provided for their commitment and reformation."[6]

This issue preoccupied Youth Council branches in other Texas cities as well, including Austin, Dallas, Seguin, El Paso, and San Antonio.[7] Often a branch's interest stemmed from a single incident, as it had in Houston. For example, in May 1939, the Bexar County (San Antonio) Court convicted a sixteen-year-old girl named Odessa Haywood for the murder of another girl in a knife fight. A jury sentenced Haywood to a term in the girls' training school at Gainesville, only to learn that it was a white-only institution, which led the county judge to complain publicly that the state should "make some provision" for black delinquent girls—a concern echoed in that year's report of the Texas Board of Control, which suggested adding a "Negro unit" at Gainesville.[8] During a lengthy appeals process sponsored by the NAACP San Antonio Youth Council, the girl languished in the county jail because the local juvenile detention center also excluded blacks. The council appealed to the national office for assistance, only to be told that overt NAACP involvement would doom any campaign to fund a training school for black girls.[9] Nevertheless, these local Youth Councils joined existing pressure groups such as the TACWC in making the problem visible to public officials.

This activism seemed to pay off in 1941, when the legislature appropriated sixty thousand dollars for the construction of a training school for black girls. However, the funds were never put to use, and their availability expired in September

1943. According to TBC chairman Weaver Baker, the war was to blame. The War Production Board had "flatly turned down" TBC requests for building materials, and skyrocketing labor costs rendered the amount appropriated inadequate.[10] This latest failure elicited angry complaints from local officials, who argued that black delinquent girls were growing in number and becoming an increasingly dangerous threat to public safety. "In every county there are young negro girls who are delinquent," declared Maude H. Gerhardt, a Corpus Christi probation officer, "and should be given the benefits of the 'Training School' plan."[11] Under such conditions, complained the Nueces County attorney, it was "useless to attempt prosecution" of black female offenders.[12] Judge Charles Dibrell of the Galveston juvenile court wrote the TBC twice in two years requesting advice about the same girl, who was arrested for "ten burglaries of private residences" and who had served about "a year's time in jail in the past three years."[13]

Sensing an opportunity, reform advocates pressed the TBC for quick action. Leading public officials and civic organizations in Dallas, Houston, Austin, Nagodoches, and San Antonio signed petitions urging the TBC to include a new training school in their budget request to the legislature.[14] Like prior complaints, these petitions portrayed black delinquent girls as a threat to public safety and focused secondarily on the girls' rehabilitation and moral uplift. Contradictions sometimes surfaced between the existing Jim Crow racial order, with its concomitant presumptions about African American "deviance," and more progressive ideals of child welfare put forth by interracial groups as well as some African American organizations. Nowhere did these notions clash more noticeably than in lengthy written requests sent by members of the Houston power elite, many of whom sat on the boards of the city's privately run welfare agencies. For instance, William Ryan, a prominent attorney, assistant chairman of the Houston Council of Social Agencies, and board president of the all-black Hester House, wrote on behalf of "the responsible white people" who wished "to keep the negro problem in hand" lest it "develop into a serious menace."[15] Ryan focused particularly on the most widespread concern about female sexual delinquency during the war, the problem of the "V-girls," underage girls whose relations with soldiers were blamed for the spread of venereal disease on military bases. Across the nation, hysterical press accounts of the so-called khaki-whackies portrayed the girls as prostitutes. Historians have noted that this problem, while real, was largely overblown in the press and underlined the well-established "gendering" of delinquency categories, which equated any precocious sexual activity with either prostitution or exploitation.[16] One reason for this phenomenon in Houston seems to have been a conflation of adolescent and adult females. In 1943, the Eighth Service Command of the United States Army complained publicly that its bases in Houston ranked fifth out of twenty-six cities in the

Gulf South for rates of venereal disease. At the army's urging, the city began to offer clinical services, but only for white and "Mexican" girls.[17] The absence of clinical services, along with the exclusion of black delinquent girls from the county detention home and the state training school, lent Houston's V-girl panic a distinctly racial cast. Thus reform advocates such as Ryan lobbied the state by evoking fears of adolescent black females having sex with soldiers and generally running wild:

> There is in Houston a group of from 40 to 60 to 75 negro girls from 12 to 16 years of age who are responsible for a great deal of the venereal infection prevalent among soldiers who visit this community—both negro soldiers and white soldiers. The only thing we can do about them is to confine them for a temporary period in the venereal disease clinic until they are no longer infectious but immediately thereafter they go back to their old ways and we have records of negro girls 13, 14, and 15 years of age who have been picked up by the police officers and treated as many as seven times in six months, each time for a new infection.[18]

A similar statement was issued by the Texas Social Welfare Association (TSWA), which asserted that the girls "[are] engaged in prostitution" and "for the most part . . . [have] no parents and no homes as we understand the term so there is no natural restraint."[19] The TSWA claimed to have received "many complaints" from across the state, especially Houston, about what it termed this "menace to all our men and boys."[20] Such depictions drew on time-worn stereotypes about uncontrollable black sexuality and social scientific literature on the "disorganized" communities and families from which black children came.[21] They also expressed a belief among whites that precocious sexuality among black girls posed a threat to public safety and called for a law and order solution. Rarely, if ever, was the girls' rehabilitation placed at the center of the discussion, as it traditionally had been for white girls and even girls of Mexican origin charged with sexual delinquency. White reformers such as Marjorie Wilson of the TSWA frequently claimed that the proposed school was "very long overdue," contrasted the options for black and white girls to show the need, and invoked "the welfare of our children," but rarely expressed concern for the girls as individuals.[22] Similarly, the Houston Retail Merchants Association complained that "a group of young negro women, all known to the police," were responsible for a wave of shoplifting and purse snatching in downtown department stores. "Several of them have been prosecuted and convicted but had to be released and allowed to run free," the association lamented, "because there is no house of correction" for them—a phrase that captured the business community's growing frustration with the situation.[23]

The public safety issue gave the school the impetus it needed to finally win funding from the legislature, eighteen years after the school's initial authorization. In spring 1945, the legislature approved a TBC budget appropriating $150,000 for the new school, more than twice the amount approved in 1941. The budget included provisions for a "Negro advisory board" comprised of prominent black women, which passed over the objections of legislators from rural areas thanks in part to lobbying from TBC chairman Baker and leading social welfare advocates.[24] Another key reason for the bill's passage was its endorsement by the United States Army, which presented documentation purporting to demonstrate the problem of venereal disease among soldiers stationed in Houston. To expedite the school's opening, the army offered Camp Brady, a recently decommissioned prisoner of war camp located about 115 miles northwest of Austin, as a site for the school. The Brady site solved several lingering problems for the TBC, especially those involving labor and building materials, which were projected to be nearly insurmountable even with the newly authorized funds. Symbolically, however, Brady represented a bizarre progression in which African American girls would inhabit a facility that recently had held Nazis, including hundreds of soldiers from Rommel's Afrika Korps, who had fought for the subjugation of the "inferior races" of Africa.[25] To locate a Jim Crow school for black girls at such a site was to turn on its head one of the lesser-known recommendations of Gunnar Myrdal's influential book *An American Dilemma*, published just as the Texas legislature was considering funds for the school.[26] This exhaustive study, based on years of research by a veritable army of social scientists, detailed the yawning gulf between an "American creed" of equality and the realities of segregation and discrimination. The book argued, among other things, that "one of the most flagrant violations of the spirit . . . of equal treatment" in the South was the lack of training schools for delinquent black girls.[27] As if to amplify the point, some local residents soon raised objections to the placement of delinquent black girls near the largely white town of Brady. One Brady attorney, writing to Texas Governor Coke Stevenson, complained that the institution should be located in east Texas, where "the vast majority of our Negroes live."[28] Foreseeing the possibility of a local backlash, the TBC solicited the support of Congressman O. C. Fisher, whose district included Brady, and the town's business leaders.[29] By summer 1946, the army had turned over the property to the TBC, and plans were under way to open the school the following spring.

For many juvenile justice professionals, though, the new school could not open soon enough. Between summer 1945, when the bill passed the legislature, and February 1947, when the school opened its doors, the TBC was flooded with letters from juvenile courts, probation departments, and child welfare agencies. "We very often have negro girls under the age of 18 years, who are unruly and cause a great deal of trouble," stated the Taylor County (Abilene) judge, "and there is no place to send them."[30] Some letters addressed specific cases, such as that of a thirteen-year-old girl in Galveston who was being held in the county jail "pending acceptance of her in an institution."[31] In small towns such as Palestine, officials viewed the school as a placement option for their "unusual cases" of delinquent black girls.[32] Conversely, black child welfare workers espoused very different concerns. For example, Marzelle Hill, a Dallas County probation officer who would subsequently sit on the "Negro advisory board" for the Brady school, emphasized "the welfare of Negro girls."[33] Hill called the absence of a training school "distressing and deplorable" and urged the TBC to speed things up, a sentiment echoed by Janie Jones, "a Negro case worker" in Fort Worth.[34]

Similarly, the response of African American organizations and individuals went beyond merely expressing support for the Brady school and offered specific suggestions about the school program. Black input had contributed indispensably to the school's authorization, had been included in the appropriation bill in the form of the advisory board, and continued in the planning period of 1945–46. A case in point was the Dallas-based Texas Negro Chamber of Commerce, whose chairman, Antonio Maceo Smith, recently had helped lead the state NAACP in its successful challenge to the white primary in the Supreme Court case *Smith v. Allwright* (1944).[35] While congratulating the TBC for its successful negotiations with the state legislature and the army, Smith argued that the school's staff should "be selected from members of the Negro race. We are not prompted by selfishness or false pride in making this suggestion. It is offered in a spirit of helpfulness and cooperation, and if justified on the same basis that members of the white race are selected to staff institutions that serve white people. There are many well trained and qualified Negroes for such positions and we offer our services, if called upon, to point out some of them to you."[36]

Echoing these views was Houston's Fifth Ward Civic Club, which urged the TBC to expedite the school's opening because "the need [was] urgent."[37] In July 1946, the TACWC, now renamed the Texas Federation of Colored Women's Clubs (TFCWC), celebrated the school's imminent opening at its fortieth annual meeting in Austin. The TFCWC's outgoing president, Mrs. V. C. Tedford, recalled how the organization had lobbied the legislature and mounted letter-writing campaigns every year since 1927.[38] The TBC had just announced the appointees for the Brady Advisory Board of Negro Women, of which there were no TFCWC members. The organization demanded representation and got it when the TBC appointed two of its trustees to key positions. Mrs. U. V. Christian, who ran the Crescent School of Beauty Culture in East Austin (and "has direct contact with girls") and sat on the Interracial Commission of the University Methodist Church, was made chairwoman of the advisory board, and Mrs. Iola Winn Rowan, the incoming TFCWC president (1947–51) and a graduate of the all-black Prairie View Normal and Industrial College just outside Houston, was appointed as Brady's first superintendent.[39] Rowan seemed an ideal fit for the position: a matronly black educator focused more on "uplifting the race" than challenging white authority. However, as subsequent events would show, black and white professionals held very different ideas about juvenile rehabilitation for delinquent black girls. Their clashes would ignite controversy in Brady's early years. Moreover, black and white authorities alike quickly found the girls they wanted to reform to be quite resistant to the diagnoses and remedies prescribed for them.

"We Build the Ladder by Which We Rise"

Brady accepted its first referrals on February 14, 1947, and housed about thirty girls by summer in a physical space that was unique compared to the training schools at Gatesville and Gainesville. Designed to accommodate over three thousand prisoners, the Brady camp covered 360 acres and included two hundred buildings, many of which were torn down during the first school year. Remodeling and construction activities were constant features, as were the workers themselves: a crew of twenty to thirty black men from the Austin State Hospital supervised by a small group of whites from Brady. With 150 beds, the former hospital building was converted to the main dormitory and became the center of the school. Academic and vocational facilities, however, lacked adequate equipment for much of the school's first year and hampered fulfillment of the school's mission. The 1927 legislation had called for training in "the useful arts and sciences to which women are adapted . . . to prepare them for future usefulness and economic independence," specifying "nursing, sanitation and hygiene, and moral and religious training."[40] This gendered conception of female rehabilitation mirrored the Gainesville program for white and Mexican American girls. But Brady's program also promoted racial uplift, or a specific brand of self-help ideology embraced by much of the black middle-class and epitomized by the official school motto: "We Build the Ladder By Which We Rise," a play on the TFCWC slogan, "Lifting As We Climb." Self-help, as the historian Kevin Gaines has noted, represented a strategy that sometimes compromised with white presumptions of black inferiority and other times complemented civil rights activism.[41] Symbolizing those boundaries were the school buildings, named for Booker T. Washington, George Washington Carver, Sojourner Truth, and Urissa V. Christian (chairwoman of Brady's black advisory board).[42] Superintendent Rowan struck an accommodationist tone when, scarcely a month after opening its doors, Brady participated enthusiastically in National Negro Health Week, an event founded by Washington in 1915 "to stress the health needs of his race and to encourage the Negro to take advantage of existing health facilities in his community."[43] In a March 30, 1947, radio broadcast, Rowan promoted the event and detailed the harrowing health statistics for African Americans compared to whites. She blamed higher rates of tuberculosis, syphilis, and infant mortality not on racism or segregation but rather on blacks themselves, emphasizing "poor personal hygiene, bad housing, insanitary environment," and "the lack of health education among Negroes."[44] Thus Brady's school program that week consisted of a series of lectures on hygiene, venereal disease, nutrition, and the life of Washington; a cleaning campaign on the school grounds; and, plays, essays, and songs devoted to health and safety.[45]

To its proponents, the self-help vision of racial progress seemed to complement the goal of juvenile rehabilitation. By steering wayward girls on the path to good citizenship, Brady would serve the dual purposes of redeeming youth and uplifting the race. But even these relatively uncontroversial goals foundered on the contradictions underlying the school's creation. On the one hand, many white officials and opinion makers viewed it as a correctional facility to house the so-called prostitutes plaguing city streets, who were in reality older, streetwise girls uninterested in cooperating with the Brady project; on the other hand, many reformers, black and white, had high hopes for a genuine rehabilitation program on the order of Gainesville. Caught between these two imperatives, Rowan and her staff also had to overcome the blatantly second-class status of the institution. Nothing reflected that status more than Rowan's bitter struggles to obtain needed funds and materials for her program, which themselves turned on ugly interracial conflicts among employees.

The TBC decided quite early in the planning stages to hire an all-black female staff to work with the girls and an all-white male staff to handle the school's finances and physical plant. This plan proved utterly disastrous. From the outset of her regime, Brady superintendent Rowan found herself under attack from the institution's white employees. Leading the charge against her was Carl M. Tibbitts, a Brady grocer whom the TBC hired as the school's business manager. On the eve of the school's opening, Tibbitts made the first of what would become several allegations of mismanagement against Rowan, in this instance accusing her of using a state vehicle to haul her refrigerator to Dallas and back for repairs.[46] Tibbitts also seems to have presented himself to the press as the contact person for information about Brady. In a lengthy feature on the school, the *San Angelo Standard-Times* quoted him at length without bothering to interview Superintendent Rowan or any other employee.[47] Tibbitts's comments were so inappropriate that they earned him an official reprimand from the TBC, but they revealed much about the prevailing attitudes toward staff authority and the meaning of rehabilitation.[48] According to Tibbitts, Brady was the first training school of its kind in the South (of schools in the North, he noted, "They throw them all together and make no line between the color of the children") and would be able to house up to five hundred girls. The "30 or 40" families of black employees to be housed on the Brady grounds were to serve as "the layer between the girls and the eight or ten white families that [would] make up the top flight administrative personnel." Girls who earned sufficient merit points for good behavior would earn "limited furloughs . . . to work in homes around Brady." Indeed, stated Tibbitts, "several Brady families have already made requests for girls."[49] He envisioned Brady essentially as an employment agency providing black labor to local whites.

However, although this portrayal flatly contradicted the chain of command envisioned by Superintendent Rowan, it seemed to find support in the institution's official parole and release policies. Girls were to be released only to either a "suitable home" or "a position where she [would] be self-supporting."[50] Employees were required not only to follow specific rules but also "to render cheerful and loyal cooperation to the Superintendent." Such assertions of authority rankled Tibbitts, who squabbled with Rowan over her power to hire and fire white employees, a ban on alcohol on the grounds, and a rule against smoking cigarettes around the girls. At one point, Rowan felt compelled to provide Tibbitts with a written job description of his duties as the school's "Storekeeper-Accountant," which prompted him to deliver the following outburst to the TBC:

> We have all leaned over backwards trying to make this Institution go, and I might add we have waited on Negros [*sic*] more without griping than we would have done for whites, and when we are presented with such [rules] from a colored person with an impudent, important, air, it's just pretty hard to take. In fact, the white employees, I mean all of them . . . have all helped to bear out this burden, but most of them are fastly getting fed up with trying to cooperate under such.
>
> We have just had this past week a committee of three gentlemen from the State Legislator, and one of their questions was how can white people take orders from a Negro Superintendent. They also stated this was "Texas" and we were "Texans," and they thought it badly out of line.[51]

For her part, an equally frustrated Rowan urged the TBC to "discontinue" the "dual administration" at the school, which had "handicapped" and "frequently embarrassed" her.[52] She also invited the black advisory board to make a surprise inspection in April 1947. Appalled at the level of staff infighting, the board warned the TBC that it had caused "unrest" among the girls, a problem further compounded by the lack of appropriate space or equipment for schooling.[53] Act quickly, urged the board, or the "lack of cooperation or understanding" would result in a major incident of some sort. The TBC opted to ignore this advice; its initial response was to question the competence of Superintendent Rowan by instructing her in patronizing terms to order equipment and to submit educational plans for courses in "homemaking, cosmetology, tailoring, and secretarial training."[54] A month later, staff tensions were on full display at a June meeting of the advisory board, as Rowan and Tibbitts exchanged charges and countercharges while board members and TBC chairman Hall H. Logan attempted to mediate. It quickly became evident that the school program was being held up not by Rowan's lack of planning but instead by Tibbitts's unofficial policy of subjecting all of Rowan's purchase requests to a nine-day review process. In short, Rowan could not get any of the equipment she needed because Tibbitts constantly suspected her of incompetence or even corruption. Once again, the TBC mustered an utterly tone-deaf response by severely limiting Rowan's authority. Decreeing that "construction work should always be a responsibility relegated to a man," TBC chairman Logan informed Rowan that she was "segregated to the supervision of the students and the educational work."[55] The episode also revealed the lack of power wielded by the advisory board, which openly expressed its disapproval of the TBC's decision to no avail. This inadequate resolution allowed Brady's obvious racial tensions to fester until the situation finally led to a violent incident in the hottest month of a typically hot Texas summer.

"I Guess I'm Crazy Now"

The daily disrespect shown by whites toward black employees and professional staff had a corrosive effect on the institution, particularly for the delinquent girls who were there, ostensibly, to learn proper respect for adult authority. Instead they learned to manipulate the simmering animosities between the staff and to issue verbal and sometimes physical challenges to their housemothers and teachers. This trend in turn threatened to push Brady toward a more custodial rather than educational regime, even with an extraordinarily low student-to-staff ratio (roughly five to two that summer). Brady's initial philosophy had discouraged the use of solitary confinement and corporal punishment, even though both were permitted in the official staff guidelines. Indeed, Brady touted the absence of locked doors, bars on windows, and high-security fences, claiming that its merit system of rewards for good behavior and "minor punishments" such as scrubbing floors or loss of privileges prevented disorder. Officially, Brady claimed that "only" 19 girls attempted to escape in the school's first year, an average of 1.6 each month.[56] Monthly discipline reports submitted by Rowan to the TBC between August 1947 and June 1948 claimed that no girls had been whipped or beaten.[57] However, discipline quickly became a problem; in late April 1947, Rowan requested permission to convert an abandoned guardhouse building into "a place for solitary confinement and punishment."[58] The TBC not only supported the move but encouraged it as an alternative to whipping because of the abuse scandals then surfacing at Gatesville and Gainesville (see chapter 2).[59]

The cause of Rowan's and the TBC's conversion to solitary confinement was a small group of older girls, ages seventeen and eighteen, who proved unwilling to follow the rules. According to employees and the girls themselves, they frequently argued with housemothers and teachers, spoke out of turn in classes, complained about the food, sneaked off to smoke cigarettes with black and white construction workers, and ran away from the institution.[60] At the center of this group was a seventeen-year-old girl from Fort Worth named Rose Thompson, who had been adjudged a delinquent for forging checks and stealing clothes.[61] Shortly after Brady received approval for a solitary cell, Rose tried to escape. In short order, she was caught and imprisoned in the county jail, where a doctor found her so "unruly and uncooperative" that he recommended leaving her in jail indefinitely, or at least until she could be placed in a maximum security cell.[62] However, this resolution was unsatisfactory for two reasons: it undercut the rationale for Brady's existence, and it cost too much—the county jail threatened to charge the state a daily fee. By July 1947, Rose was back at Brady, where she clashed bitterly with the African American school principal, Pete Harrell. According to later testimony from staff and students (including Rose herself), she also threatened a housemother with a knife and a steel pipe on separate occasions. Finally, on July 19, Rose and three other girls ran away from Brady. A housemother who saw them leaving, rather than attempt to stop them, warned the girls to flee Texas because, as she chillingly put it, "You belong to the state."[63]

It was late at night when the girls slipped across the barbed-wire fence surrounding the school. One girl claimed that they used the school's ladder, while the others described sustaining cuts and scratches from climbing over without it; the girls also had carved each other's names as well as boyfriends' names into their arms. Their plan was to hitch a ride to a relative's house in the "colored part" of Brady, located several miles away from the school. After riding a short way with three "Mexican" men, who allegedly tried to extort money from them, the girls convinced a black cab driver to take them the rest of the way. The girls reached their destination at sunrise, then spent the day shuttling between a couple of different families in town. Late that night, the girls were taken to Rose's uncle's home in Brownwood, about forty-five miles north of Brady. Unaware that his niece had just escaped from state custody, Rose's uncle fed the girls and paid for a hotel room. By the next morning, however, he became suspicious and decided to make a few phone calls. Suspecting trouble, Rose called a taxi, and the girls left town; over the next several days they hitchhiked and walked until they reached Rose's home in Fort Worth. On July 26, a full week after escaping from Brady, the girls were arrested by local police. The wife of a married man who ran a barbeque restaurant and with whom Rose had been carrying on an affair had reported the girls to authorities. Three weeks later the girls were returned to the McCullough County Jail, in downtown Brady, while the school's construction crew finished converting a guardhouse into a secure isolation cell.

The story thus far illustrates why at least some of the girls clashed with Rowan and her staff. The two groups were separated by yawning differences of class, region, and generation. Most of Brady's wards came from working-class neighborhoods in Texas's largest cities. Of the sixty-three total admissions in 1947, thirty-one of them came from Houston, with several others coming from the Dallas–Fort Worth area—the places whose civic leaders had complained the loudest about the need for a school such as Brady.[64] The adult staff, meanwhile, not only tended to be hired from rural areas but also was comprised of members of the black middle class. Many of them were college educated and, given the spread of children's mental health into the academic curriculum in the early 1940s, probably viewed their mission as one of mentoring "damaged" children and instructing them in the rules of bourgeois respectability. However, many of the "problem" girls already had assumed some adult roles and responsibilities and had little use for a program geared in part toward "civilizing" wayward juveniles. All the girls had worked for wages before being committed to Brady. Moreover, three of the four escapees in Rose's party were parents themselves, and two of them later told investigators that they were married. Rose herself was the only childless member of the escape party, while at least two of her companions had joined her only in the hopes of reaching their own homes in other parts of the state. Thus, despite Brady's aspirations to provide individualized treatment, its program matched up poorly with the actual lives led by the girls, some of whom had been committed on status crimes. One of the escapees, a wife and mother, had been sent to Brady from a Corpus Christi juvenile court for a mere curfew violation. In such a situation, resistance or escape may have seemed like logical responses, while disciplinary punishment for such transgressions might call for even more drastic action. A cycle of defiance and retribution that had escalated for months finally exploded at the end of August, when the girls were returned to Brady.

At about two o'clock on the afternoon of August 28, Brady police brought Rose back to the school. Officials placed her in the newly renovated "detention cottage," which was in reality a barren isolation cell with a barred window looking out onto a yard across from the administration building. It was especially hot that afternoon, but according to Rose, her repeated requests for food and water went ignored. Although this claim is hard to verify, punishing runaways with sparse rations was an established policy at Gainesville and could very likely have been employed in this case. After several hours, a young white maintenance worker took pity on Rose and slipped her some water. He may also have given her a cigarette and some matches, which she used to set a fire inside the cottage. That evening, Rowan returned from the county jail with one of Rose's accomplices to find students rushing toward her yelling that the detention cottage was on fire. Large plumes of smoke rose out of the cottage, but before Rowan could act, she was confronted by a white assistant to her antagonist Tibbitts. He demanded to know where the keys to the cottage were, shoved her aside, then retrieved the keys from Rowan's office, all the while screaming profanities, threats, and racial epithets. Tibbitts and firefighters arrived in time to see Rose and her rescuer emerging from the smoking cottage. While police took Rose back into custody, Tibbitts nearly had a physical altercation with Pete Harrell, the school principal, whose role in the incident was hotly disputed. Rose claimed that as the fire spread, Harrell stood outside her window with a shotgun, taunting her and ignoring pleas from white workers about the location of the cell key. The exchanges between black and white staff became so heated that Rowan ordered all her employees to retreat to her quarters.

Still fuming, Tibbitts placed a phone call to the TBC offices, then got in his truck and drove directly to Austin. Soon afterward, Rowan followed him, setting up yet another dramatic confrontation in the TBC offices the next morning. Tibbitts spun a predictable tale of black indolence and incompetence. Rowan countered by pointing out that firefighters had found cigarette butts and matches in the cell. That evidence, coupled with the school's prior history of unsanctioned smoking among white workers and black girl inmates, suggested quite clearly to Rowan what had happened. She went much further, arguing that Tibbitts's crew regularly manipulated the most disgruntled girl inmates against her staff. The entire incident, she concluded, stemmed from their "difficult relations," and she warned that her staff felt "quite unsafe" at Brady. However, this explanation failed to satisfy one questioner, TBC member Tom DeBerry, who felt that Rowan, as superintendent, should have taken a more active role in responding to the fire instead of retreating to her cottage:

DEBERRY: The information I was trying to get was whether, regardless of the bi-racial situation down there and as to whether the conditions at that time justify you in not taking any more active part.

ROWAN: Maybe I am a coward.

DEBERRY: It was fear then. You were afraid you would become involved in something that would result in some hurt or abuse to you, is that it?

ROWAN: That is correct. . . . As I said some time back, our working conditions there are not pleasant at all and if something can be explained to me that will help me to either stay out of the way or do the right thing, I would appreciate it.[65]

The girls' testimony, meanwhile, unwittingly lent support to Rowan's allegations. Girl inmates not only admitted to smoking and fraternizing with the white workers; they also described them as the only sympathetic adults at the institution. In Rose's view, the black teachers and housemothers harbored a vendetta against her in particular and the other girls in general. During the fire, she felt "more angry than . . . scared," vowing that she preferred the penitentiary to Brady. "I'm not going to let my own color mistreat me," she warned. "I try to be nice but if they mistreat me you all are going to hear about it even if you don't hear no more than I broke up some property." Rose was about to get her wish; already Brady officials had taken steps to have her transferred to the state mental hospital in Austin. The day before Rose's deposition, she had undergone a medical examination by the institution's doctor, who pronounced her "mentally unbalanced." "She will never improve," he continued, and "given an opportunity she would do bodily harm to anyone that is connected with the school."[66] Rose mocked this diagnosis during her TBC interview:

> They sent the doctor . . . out here at the school. . . . He said, "You sick?" I said, "No, sir. I guess I'm crazy now." Most of the girls that run off, they say they're crazy and they got more sense than [the staff] got. I said, "I guess I'm crazy now." He say, "Yes, that's what they say. You want to go to Austin to the crazy house?" . . . I said anything they want to do is all right, just so I'll not be mistreated. I can't keep them from sending me but if I go I'll prove I wasn't crazy just because people mistreated me.[67]

Despite Rose's removal from Brady, she seems to have succeeded in hastening the end of Rowan's administration. In subsequent months, the TBC, the black advisory board, and some black staff members complained that discipline was slipping.[68] The record is unclear about whether Rowan withered under the likely strain of negotiating the color line that undermined her professional authority with her own staff as well as the girls. However, she delegated to the Brady head nurse, Emma G. Harrell (wife of the school principal), the task of running the National Negro Health Week campaign in spring 1948. Unlike in the previous year, the radio broadcast included more strident civil rights language, quoting from President Harry Truman's Committee on Civil Rights, which had just issued a controversial report calling for sweeping federal action to end lynching, integrate the military, ensure voting rights, and strengthen the Civil Rights Division of the Department of Justice. The report, titled *To Secure These Rights*, also denounced inequality in education, housing, and employment, as damaging to the nation's "conscience, self-interest, and survival in a threatening world."[69] Thus Harrell's radio broadcast blamed poor health statistics for African Americans on "the manner of living imposed upon [them] by society" and called for "State and Federal legislation" to remedy the inequities.[70]

Harrell's ascendance came as the TBC grew increasingly disenchanted with Rowan, who in their eyes had lost control of the institution. On May 4, 1948, TBC chairman Hall Logan visited the school and spoke with a few "incorrigible" girls who had "beat up on some of the housemothers" and "flatly refused to do any work."[71] Two girls told him without hesitation "that they would run away at the first opportunity." Concluding that Rowan had "too much feeling for the girls," Logan called for "a definite program of two or three hours of good hard work" each day. This episode was the last straw for Rowan, who resigned two days later, claiming "physical and mental strain."[72] Her frustration went far beyond unpleasant personal encounters with whites; a full year after Brady had opened its doors, it still lacked the necessary equipment to begin any of its planned vocational programs. The reasons were the same as they had been a year earlier. Funds were relatively plentiful, with thousands of budgeted dollars going unspent. Persistent obstruction by Brady's white staff, enabled by the TBC, had sabotaged Rowan's administration. In solidarity with Rowan, a few teachers and housemothers walked off the job. The news of Rowan's abrupt resignation and its causes enraged African American observers. Marzelle Hill of the Brady advisory board, who had been one of the leading advocates for opening the school, insisted that the TBC at least avoid a repeat performance by endowing the next superintendent with greater authority.[73] Finding a replacement proved difficult, however; few black professionals wanted to suffer through the same indignities that Rowan had endured. The acting superintendent, Emma Harrell, reported to the TBC that "rumors" of "serious trouble" at Brady had rendered it "very hard to employ anyone."[74] Harrell had managed to hire two teachers, but they quit without explanation within days. Brady's soured reputation among African Americans stemmed largely from a biting critique that appeared in the editorial column of Carter Wesley, who published both the *Dallas Express* and the *Houston Informer*, two of the most widely read black newspapers in Texas. After visiting Brady and interviewing both Rowan and Tibbitts, Wesley concluded, "The women of Texas, who have worked for this home for girls, have been rooked by the politicians."[75] That the system of "dual control" had placed Rowan in "an impossible situation" was more obvious to Wesley than it had been to the TBC. African Americans, he argued, "should have been protesting vociferously against such a situation in a Negro school since it was established." Barring a major policy shift, he predicted that "the current situation at Brady [would] fail in all of its purposes."[76]

"Check upon Yourself"

But the school not only survived; it grew rapidly, admitting more delinquent girls each year and developing what was by most measures solid programs in academic and vocational education. The person most responsible for this turnaround was Emma Harrell, who had the superintendent's position thrust on her in June 1948. Harrell was far more successful than her predecessor in procuring funds and supplies for vocational programs in homemaking, cosmetology, and secretarial skills. She also installed a more defined point system measuring progress toward rehabilitation and more rigorous forms of discipline, including a secure cell block and corporal punishment. Harrell pushed successfully for the separation and sometimes the removal of older offenders such as Rose Thompson from the institution. Indeed, when authorities at the Austin State Hospital attempted to have Rose returned to Brady in January 1949, Harrell enlisted the TBC in preventing it.[77] Harrell's other major achievement in this early period was helping to persuade the legislature to relocate the school near the town of Crockett, in east Texas, closer to the majority of the state's black population. The move took place almost seamlessly in December 1950, after which the school consistently remained out of the headlines at a time when the state's other juvenile training schools were the subjects of recurring abuse scandals. The patterns that ultimately proved successful at Crockett began with Harrell's administration at Brady, to which we now turn.[78]

Much like Gainesville under Carrie Weaver Smith in the second and third decades of the century, Brady sought to foster "a family-like atmosphere."[79] The girl inmates were housed in three dormitories separated by age (12–14, 15–16, and 17–18 years), each with two housemothers. Girls wore blue uniforms modeled on nurses' attire and staffed a sewing department responsible for making and mending all official clothing. In general, vocational courses focused on the women's pursuits most associated with conventional marriage: beauty, cleaning, cooking, and child rearing. At the same time, the courses also attempted to prepare girls for wage labor in similarly "gendered" fields such as hairstyling, typing, and domestic service—the latter of which, in the South, was reserved largely for African Americans. In February 1949, Brady's cosmetology school was licensed by the Texas State Board of Cosmetologists; later that year, it launched a "Homemaking Department to develop character and skill in the making of a well-managed home."[80] In 1949, the school held its first commencement ceremony in which four girls were awarded vocational degrees in cosmetology.[81] The state accredited Brady's academic program as a Rural Elementary School, even though nearly all the girl inmates were of high school age. Out of seventy-three girls tested for "mental ability and educational achievement" in 1948, only nine scored at grade level, with the remainder ranked at "defective," "borderline," or "dullness" levels on the scale.[82] Nevertheless, Brady included several trappings of a "normal" high school, including basketball, speech, and spelling teams that competed in interscholastic tournaments with other all-black public schools in 1948 and 1949. The school's chorus performed at nearby churches and occasionally on the local Brady radio station, most notably singing carols during a Christmas musical broadcast. With Harrell's encouragement, the girls elected a student council, which began meeting in October 1948. That same month, the Brady Parent-Teacher Association held its first meeting, with "several of the girls' mothers and friends" in attendance.[83] This suggestion of openness to parent involvement contrasted starkly with the practiced secrecy of the state's other training schools.

Reports of these extracurricular activities appeared in the *Brady News*, a mimeographed student newspaper inaugurated in November 1948. Much like the Gatesville newspaper before the First World War, this one predictably parroted official slogans about hard work, honesty, and setting long-term goals. It published the school honor roll, as well as a gossip column titled "Violets and Brickbats" that alternately praised girls' achievements and pilloried their misdeeds. Sometimes the paper challenged conventional paths to adulthood for African American women in what was still a Jim Crow society at the dawn of the civil rights era. One editorial encouraged girls to aspire to be "successful in any field"; another one urged girls to ignore the messages fed them by "society," and instead explore their "inner and outer self" to discover what it called "the real you."[84] Superintendent Harrell herself declared the school's mission to produce "future women . . . who will earn the right to be regarded as women . . . who shall have the qualities of triumphant leadership."[85] While it is difficult to read too much into such lofty rhetoric, one can infer some optimism. The world seemed to be changing, and the Jim Crow order was on the defensive. By 1950, President Harry Truman had ordered the desegregation of the United States Army, Jackie Robinson had broken the color line in major league baseball, and the Supreme Court had ordered the University of Texas Law School to open its doors to African American students. A growing body of scientific literature argued that school inequality had bred low self-esteem and lowered expectations for African American children (see chapter 2). The *Brady News* expressed this sense of hopefulness but at the same time displayed a critical perspective on the girls' own predicament:

One of the main causes of "Juvenile Delinquents" is too strict "Discipline." Parents often believe that if a child is not allowed to mingle with others, and is severely punished for everything he does is a good method for rearing children [sic]. Why? Because it worked in the days of their youth. . . . Remember that in childhood the foundation of your child's "personality" is being laid and their life's habits are formed. Do not let your mothers be found guilty of being responsible for more "Juvenile Delinquents." . . . Remember this is 1949 not 1899, when you were coming up, we live in a modern and dangerous world. Make your child the best of what ever they are.[86]

Clearly, at least some of the girl inmates had bought into the program and were helping to shape it for their own purposes. For example, one article invoked the school's "Human Relations" course in criticizing teachers' responses to misbehavior. "Regimentation has an unhealthy effect upon emotional growth," advised the piece. "We must, if we are to make a success of our educational work devote more serious attention . . . to helping our young girls strive for emotionally [sic] maturity."[87] Even editorials seemingly devoted to timeworn maxims, such as "Check upon Yourself," may have taken on more nuanced meanings for the girls and the staff. The short essay instructed girls to focus on self-improvement rather than criticizing others and preached the virtues of self-control.[88] The relative embrace of such messages by the girls suggests that, under Harrell's more disciplined and focused program, shared resistance to Jim Crow overshadowed the girls' resistance to the training school itself, and that juvenile rehabilitation fused with an expectation of more-genuine black citizenship. As Harrell observed in 1950, "We have a responsibility made new and doubly solemn by the march of events."[89]

Fulfilling that responsibility, however, meant removing the most troublesome girls, a policy Harrell began advocating just before becoming superintendent. In May 1948, she prepared a report on eleven girls described as "constant trouble makers."[90] Ranging in age from fourteen to eighteen years old, these girls' case summaries provide a window into the mixture of moral and medical diagnoses employed at Brady. The report blamed several of these girls for the spread of "homosexual practices," taking as evidence fights over "girlfriends" and incidents in which girls were caught in bed together. However, the most violent girls were diagnosed as "sexual inverts," a term coined by nineteenth-century sexologists that meant, roughly, "unwomanly."[91] Girls who were especially defiant, argumentative, or physically aggressive seem to have fallen into this category. For example, one girl was depicted as "a definite sexual invert . . . which has resulted in fights and quarrels." Another so-called sexual invert had "participated in gang fights" and was "an agitator, a habitual runaway . . . stubborn, given to tantrums or to outbursts of rage."[92]

In many instances, the report's language slipped uneasily between portrayals of child and adult behaviors, reflecting an uncertainty about whether these adolescent girls should be treated as cunning, adult criminals. One girl, who tested with an IQ of 47 ("frankly 47 may be a little more than it should be"), was "definitely a pathological liar." Another "insecure" girl with an "inadequate personality" suffered from low self-esteem yet also had "no respect for authority" and would "never be able to adjust to any organized environment." These girls tended to be serial offenders who had received so many demerits that they had no hope of earning an early parole. For instance, one girl's list of offenses between September 1947 and May 1948

Table 5. Whippings by age, Brady State School, July 1948–September 1949

Age	12	13	14	15	16	17	18	Total
Whippings	6	12	27	7	6	10	1	69

Source: Chairman Hall H. Logan files, Board member's files, Records, Texas State Board of Control, Archives and Information Services Division, Texas State Library and Archives Commission, Austin.

Table 6. Whippings by infraction, Brady State School, July 1948–September 1949

Infraction	Escape	Insubordination	Homosexuality	Total whippings
	5	62	2	69

Source: Chairman Hall H. Logan files, Board Member's files, Records, Texas State Board of Control, Archives and Information Services Division, Texas State Library and Archives Commission, Austin.

included smoking cigarettes, attempting escape (twice), fighting, arguing with the housemother in her dormitory, refusing to wear her uniform, and being caught in bed with another girl. Her final offense of the period came during an argument with another girl over a dress; when a housemother tried to mediate the dispute, she "told the matron to kiss her ass" and received "30 days in Detention Cottage and 3 days on bread and milk."[93] Ultimately, Harrell argued successfully that "this type of girl should not be with the girls who [were] trying to adjust themselves."[94]

A few months later Harrell amplified her views with a second report detailing the offenses committed by twenty older girl inmates, fifteen of whom came from Houston (9), Dallas/Fort Worth (3), or San Antonio (3).[95] A full eleven of them had been charged as sex offenders. Some of the more serious offenses included armed robbery, aggravated assault, and theft. Almost all of them had attempted escape from Brady at least once. "These girls are not interested in school," declared Harrell, and "it would be better if they did not go."[96] In response, the TBC advised Harrell that girl inmates between the ages of eighteen and twenty-one could be transferred to prison if they ran away and committed another crime outside school grounds.[97] Although no transfers appear in the record, it seems likely that Harrell took advantage of this policy to rid Brady of girls who, in her view, exerted "a very bad influence on the younger girls."[98]

However, discipline problems were hardly limited to the older offenders, as the school's whipping reports demonstrate (see tables 5 and 6).[99] Unlike her predecessor, Harrell had few reservations about corporal punishment, which consisted of twelve "strokes" or "licks" for each infraction. At an institution that admitted 118 inmates in 1948 and 150 in 1949, there was a total of 69 whippings during that period. With an average monthly population of about 80 and records that leave unclear the number of repeat infractions, one can conclude that most girls did not encounter corporal punishment at Brady.[100] Its increasing usage, though, especially for the vague infraction of "insubordination," suggests that maintaining order was a constant problem even at this relatively quiescent institution. Reports often listed girls in groups for "insubordination" along with related charges of "cursing," "agitation," or "disobedience."

Harrell had brought order to an unstable, precarious enterprise by spring 1950, when the legislature approved a proposal to relocate the school on 125 acres of farmland in Houston County, near the town of Crockett.[101] The new site was located just north of the state prison in Huntsville, a short drive from Prairie View College. Anticipating the creation of new jobs, the Crockett Chamber of Commerce had backed the move; however, as news spread, protest letters arrived at the TBC offices from some of the town's white residents. Attorneys at two different law firms complained that Crockett would "become known as a 'Negro Town.'"[102] According to one critic, "at least 90% of the adult citizens" opposed the school, with opinions ranging from "very hostile" to "bitter."[103] The *Houston Post* later reported that a group of Crockett citizens attempted to incorporate the site, which was located just outside city lines, to prevent the school's opening.[104] But such maneuvers amounted to little; the school's credibility and importance were well established with the legislature. No serious policy maker wished to return to a period when the only available options for black delinquent girls were adult jail or release back into the community. Even the local Crockett newspaper gave favorable coverage of the school's opening in early 1951 and heaped praise on Harrell for running a "model institution" years later.[105] For vastly different reasons, black and white Texans had finally come to an agreement of sorts on the desirability of a training school for black delinquent girls.

A Mixed Accomplishment

Despite Harrell's accomplishments at Brady, the goal of juvenile rehabilitation remained elusive, even in conventional terms. The transition of paroled girls back to noninstitutional life posed one of the most enduring problems. In December 1948, Harrell informed the TBC that over half of the girls in the school's "Honor Cottage" were ready for parole but had no place to go due to "unsuitable" or nonexistent homes.[106] This problem existed for all the state's training schools but proved especially acute for Brady, and later Crockett, due to the lack of public and private resources for African American child welfare. It underlined the fact that the school's entire history, from the exclusion of black girls from Gainesville in the second decade of the century, to the separate school's conception in the

1920s, its long-delayed funding in the 1940s, and its sometimes difficult operation in the postwar era, functioned under the constraints of Jim Crow segregation and inequality. Indeed, the State of Texas did not integrate its girls' training schools until September 6, 1966, when two buses shuttled girls and employees between Gainesville and Crockett.[107] Until that time, the "badge of inferiority" identified by the Supreme Court remained in place for a marginal juvenile population already labeled as delinquent.

Despite these obstacles, the school would be widely praised as the best run of the state's institutions for juvenile delinquents. Ironically, this good reputation rested partly on a pattern of benign neglect; allotted lower budgets and fewer physical resources, Crockett maintained a much lower inmate population than its counterparts, as well as more favorable staff-to-inmate ratios. Harrell's early success in excluding the more troublesome and difficult girl inmates would continue throughout the period, helping to ensure relative institutional tranquility. Thus Crockett remained generally free from controversy, even as the public's attention focused largely on the predicament of the training school for boys at Gatesville, due to a perceived explosion in the rate of juvenile delinquency among boys. The consequences, explored in the next chapter, were far more sweeping and immediate for African American youth in the 1950s.

FOUR

James Dean and Jim Crow

The Failure of Reform and the Racialization of Delinquency in the 1950s

On February 6, 1949, Texas Governor Beauford H. Jester and the seven members of the Texas Training School Code Commission held a much-anticipated press conference in Austin (see figure 8). After eighteen months of study, the commission had written a bill that proposed to go far beyond its original mandate to repair the state's broken juvenile training schools. With great fanfare, it announced plans for "the most extensive youth program ever developed" in Texas, the South, the Southwest, and even the nation.[1] The legislation would create a new state agency, the Texas State Youth Development Council (TSYDC), tasked with overseeing a sweeping reduction in the training school population while aiding local governments in inaugurating a plethora of community-based prevention and rehabilitation programs. Armed with statewide authority, staffed with trained experts and professionals, the TSYDC promised to eradicate the intractable abuses of the past and begin anew with "modern" approaches to delinquency. Beginning in September 1949, the TSYDC's first year of work reflected its unprecedented optimism and energy. Trained field workers fanned out across the state, advising hastily formed "community youth councils" about the creation of blueprints for intertwined juvenile justice, child welfare, and recreation services. So rapid was the TSYDC's ascent to a position of authority that, mere months after its formation, the agency's leadership was chosen to represent Texas at the 1950 White House Conference on Children and Youth, where it was hailed as a model worthy of emulation by other states. A historic breakthrough seemed to have taken place. At long last, proclaimed TSYDC chairman Walter K. Kerr, "many children and youth will have a fairer opportunity for development of a healthy personality."[2]

The breathtaking speed with which the TSYDC took shape reflected a host of converging national trends, not the least of which was growing opposition to institutions for dependent populations. One of the more critically acclaimed films of the late 1940s, *The Snake Pit*, portrayed the nation's mental hospitals as places

Figure 8. Governor Beauford H. Jester (seated) signing HB 705, July 5, 1949, creating the State Youth Development Council, with members of the Training School Code Commission, sponsors of the bill in the House and the Senate, the lieutenant governor, and the speaker of the House. Standing from left: S. L. Bellamy, Walter K. Kerr, R. L. Proffer, Leslie Jackson, Davis Clifton, Pearce Johnson, Durwood Manford, Rebecca Townsend, Sid Gregory, A. M. Aikin, and Allan Shivers. (Box 1999/087-3, Records, Texas Youth Commission. Courtesy of the Texas State Library and Archives Commission.)

that caused rather than alleviated insanity.[3] The newly formed National Institute of Mental Health, along with the American Psychiatric Association, campaigned for federally subsidized community mental health clinics as substitutes for the asylum. Leading the anti-institutional charge was journalist Albert Deutsch, whose 1948 book, *The Shame of the States*, indicted the quality of care in mental hospitals. In 1950, Deutsch published *Our Rejected Children*, which applied the same muckraking technique to the nation's juvenile training schools. With painstaking detail, Deutsch described sterilizations, beatings, and exotic punishments such as "hydrotherapy," a scientific-sounding term for spraying a high-pressure hose at a boy inmate's back from close range. Readers of this litany of seemingly limitless horrors would have been hard-pressed indeed to disagree with Deutsch's contention that the training school had become "a disgraceful blot on a democratic and rich society."[4]

Lending urgency to the training school crisis were predictions of a looming explosion in juvenile delinquency. One of the leading proponents of this notion was Richard Clenenden, who served as consultant on training schools for the United States Children's Bureau, and later as executive director of the Senate Subcommittee to Investigate Juvenile Delinquency. In "The Shame of America," a five-part series published in the *Saturday Evening Post* in 1955, Clenenden recounted lurid crimes committed by teenagers across the nation. Citing the baby boom, he warned that annual juvenile arrests would reach the astronomical number of two million by 1960. This improbable figure, which would have comprised a nineteen-fold increase over juvenile arrests in 1955, reflected a gulf between perception and reality.[5] As the historian James Gilbert has shown, Americans consistently ranked delinquency just behind Communist subversion on their list of pressing public concerns during the 1950s, despite relatively low figures for juvenile crime.[6] One explanation for this phenomenon was delinquency's newfound ubiquity; unlike in prior eras, it seemed to surface in the emerging middle-class suburbs as often as it did in urban slums. "Juvenile delinquency today is everybody's problem," admonished Clenenden. Like Communist spies lurking next door, "the delinquent may be any child you know, including your own."[7]

This sort of thinking dramatically altered the image of juvenile delinquency. More than at any time in the past, the public face of the juvenile delinquent in the 1950s was white and middle class. In the suburbs, national commentators discovered a separate teenage culture of consumption that seemed to threaten adult authority and traditional values.[8] Sympathetic observers suggested that more-affluent teenagers were largely misunderstood by parents who were themselves ill-equipped for modern child rearing. The most influential of these portrayals, the 1955 film *Rebel without a Cause*, explored the fuzzy border between "normal" adolescent rebellion and "serious" delinquency in a comfortable Los Angeles suburb. Told from the point of view of its teenage characters, led by James Dean's Jim Stark, the film depicts delinquency almost entirely as the product of bad parenting. Indeed, the film begins with Jim's parents bickering pointlessly at the juvenile hall, where Jim has been charged with underage drinking. Absent, needlessly authoritarian, self-absorbed, materialistic, or overly permissive, the parents in this film are replacing the "root causes" once found in poverty, inequality, racial or ethnic conflict, and a ghetto environment. Revealingly, the only capable adult authority to appear in the film is a police psychiatrist, Officer Roy, who dispenses the kind of patient, tough, one-on-one mentoring advocated by postwar juvenile justice reformers.[9] Relentlessly psychological, the postwar approach to delinquency separated "salvageable" youth such as Jim Stark from the more hardened offenders who rarely surfaced in public discourse. An invisible line divided juvenile *delinquents*, who were entitled to the privileges and protections increasingly attached to the life stage of adolescence, from juvenile *offenders*, who were more likely to be incarcerated in facilities that remained, despite the best efforts of reformers, prisons in every sense of the word.

In Texas, the redeemable youth appeared when it was time to tout progress toward rehabilitation; by contrast, the dangerous offender served as a reminder that secure institutions remained necessary. Who was this dangerous offender? Throughout the 1950s, the incarcerated juvenile population skyrocketed, driven by dramatic increases in the numbers of African American and Mexican American youth. Always overrepresented in the juvenile inmate population, nonwhites actually came to outnumber whites in the state's training schools by 1965. Under budgetary and social pressures to focus on institutions, the TSYDC's early optimism quickly collapsed; within a decade of its creation, the agency reverted to little more than an updated version of the regime it had sought to replace, supervising an ever-expanding archipelago of large institutions. Inside their walls, new forms of racial discrimination and segregation joined the old. While the symbol of James Dean defined the juvenile delinquent on the outside, Jim Crow remained a persistent presence within juvenile justice.

Attacking "an Insoluble Problem"

On June 19, 1948, the Texas Training School Code Commission gathered in Austin for a meeting with Richard Clenenden, who had just spent the previous week touring the training schools at Gainesville and Gatesville.[10] He politely but firmly suggested that a major overhaul was in order. The institutions were too large and, as a result, too dependent on outmoded mechanisms such as farm labor and the merit system for the maintenance of order.[11] In the past, he recounted, juvenile institutions had experimented with a range of programs, with little success. Now, however, they were "no longer working in the dark." Traditional training schools had long stood in the way of the goal of offering individualized treatment; therefore, they should be phased out. In their place, Clenenden recommended "small-sized" facilities housing anywhere from 50 to 150 juveniles and including outdoor camps, group homes, and vocational centers, as well as "penal-type" institutions for the most serious offenders. The ideal location for these new facilities, he suggested, was not an isolated rural backwater like Gatesville but the metropolitan areas from which most delinquents came—a policy that was a major break with the past. Traditionally, for a juvenile, a commitment to training school custody meant the severing of nearly all contact with family and community, for reasons only partly stemming from the institutions' remote locations. The official presumption held that the family and the neighborhood were to blame for delinquent behavior. As we have seen, strict limits on visitation, censorship of correspondence, and stingy parole practices combined to remove families from the rehabilitation process. By the late 1940s, however, a leading national expert such as Clenenden could urge the commission to include families at every stage of the rehabilitation process, from intake to progress meetings to parole. In a state as vast and demographically diverse as Texas, he warned, a more dispersed program was especially crucial:

> It is almost inconceivable for me to be able to believe that there are not on the streets of El Paso and even more so on the streets of smaller towns in that vicinity, as well as in the Brownsville vicinity, a group of children in need of treatment. But if I were the Judge down there and had the thing of arranging transportation seven or eight hundred miles, why, I believe I would be inclined to let them run around as long as possible rather than try to make any such trip; get up there, separated such a distance from the family they can't be visiting the school, no opportunity to become personally acquainted with the families. As a matter of fact, can't even become personally acquainted with the Judges in the courts that they are serving. Actually, it seems to be very definite that . . . you will want to scatter the training schools out over the state.[12]

Clenenden's suggestions were well received, in part because the commission's membership included virtually no representatives of the training schools themselves. Mrs. Raymond Fonville and Rebecca Townsend represented child welfare groups in Houston and Dallas, respectively. Chairman Leslie Jackson, dean of the Baylor University Law School, was widely considered to be sympathetic to the plight of impoverished youth. S. L. Bellamy, an Austin juvenile probation officer and president of the Texas Probation Association, had worked for five years as the assistant superintendent of Gatesville in the late 1930s. However, the person most receptive to Clenenden's comments, indeed the one who had brought him to Austin, was the commission's vice-chairman, Walter Kinsolving Kerr, its driving force and main public spokesperson. The son of a lumber and cotton businessman, Kerr had starred on his high school football team in Teague, Texas, and at the University of Texas had served as president of the University Light Opera Company for three years while studying for a law degree, which he obtained in 1937. Instead of practicing law, however, Kerr moved to New York City to pursue his ambitions for a career in theater or radio. Within a year, he returned with a new bride and opened a law practice in Lufkin. Soon he was working on the staff of Democratic governor Coke Stevenson, a job that brought Kerr to Austin, which was in the midst of reforming its county services for juveniles. In 1948, Kerr joined with the well-respected Travis County judge Harris Gardner in the design of a new juvenile detention center in south Austin, earning a master's degree at the University of Texas along the way. During this period, Kerr became the pastor of the Central Methodist Church in downtown Austin. From his post as chairman of the church's social-action committee, Kerr gained access to local and state power brokers that would prove invaluable when it was time to shepherd the commission's proposed TSYDC bill through the legislature.[13]

Even as he built his political connections in the legislature, Kerr traveled outside the state on a fact-finding mission to learn more about the latest approaches to juvenile delinquency. In February 1948, he attended the annual meeting of the American Prison Association (APA) in New York City. There he met with training school superintendents from various states and, with a group of APA officials, toured the Children's Village and Warwick Training School facilities in New York, which were among the nation's best-known juvenile institutions.[14] Kerr subsequently visited the nation's capital, where he inspected the Federal Training School for Delinquents. He also met with Clenenden and Katherine Lenroot at the Children's Bureau and with Attorney General Tom Clark, who had led an important national conference on juvenile corrections in 1946. Clark had declared that training schools "should be considered as specialized stations" in an "integrated system" where "a punitive philosophy [had] no place."[15] During this time, Kerr was introduced to Austin MacCormick of the Osborne Foundation, probably the leading correctional education expert and prison reformer in the country. His 1931 book *The Education of Adult Prisoners* had sparked a correctional education movement in penology that dovetailed with the introduction of mental health principles in inmate classification and segregation practices. An advocate for replacing mass custody with individualized treatment, he denounced the "prisonization" inculcated in offenders by traditional lockstep regimes. During the 1930s and 1940s, MacCormick worked as a much-sought-after consultant for states seeking to reform their juvenile and adult correctional institutions, publishing a multivolume survey of the nation's training schools. He visited Texas several times between 1948 and the 1970s and eventually became the state's principal outside evaluator for its training schools.[16]

MacCormick's main activity in reforming training schools occurred during his work with the American Law Institute (ALI). Founded in 1923 in Philadelphia, the ALI had promulgated what became known as the "youth authority" movement during the 1930s and 1940s. In 1941, California became the first state to adopt a version of the ALI's draft legislation, the Model Youth Correction Authority Act. Authored by a panel of renowned experts that included MacCormick, child psychologist William Healy, and sociologist Sheldon Glueck, the Model Act proposed the creation of a state agency to coordinate the disposition and treatment of youthful offenders aged sixteen to twenty-one. The Model Act also envisioned a "Delinquent

Minor Court," separate from both the juvenile and the criminal court, to adjudge this particular age group, from which ALI studies had shown the majority of violent and serious offenders came. Driven by a desire to extend the rehabilitative ideal upward chronologically, from the juvenile to the young adult offender population, the ALI was forced to make compromises in order to see its Model Act put into practice at the state level. In California, public attention had focused on the juvenile training schools, which had been rocked by gruesome inmate deaths and mass escapes in the late 1930s. Instead of young adult offenders, the California Youth Authority (CYA) focused on improving conditions for its juvenile wards. During World War II, the CYA helped reform the state's training schools and worked closely with local communities to devise delinquency prevention and juvenile justice programs. Because of its early success, the CYA replaced the Model Act as the standard-bearer for modern juvenile justice and corrections administration. By 1950, five states, including Texas, had inaugurated state agencies based on the CYA, with the advice of ALI consultants.[17]

In its final report to the legislature, the Texas Training School Code Commission praised the CYA model while lamenting the lack of progress in its own state. Much as they had in the Progressive Era, local communities relied overwhelmingly on private charities, which sponsored eighty-two private child-care institutions and thirty child welfare agencies. By contrast, out of the state's 254 counties, only 3 housed juvenile offenders in separate detention facilities, and only 24 offered any semblance of probation or parole services. Indeed, parolees themselves often filled out their own paperwork unaided; as the commission noted, "A letter from a parolee stating that he or she is doing very well may precede by only a few days the child's return to the institution."[18] Traditionally all-purpose county courts, rather than specially designated juvenile courts, handled the bulk of juvenile cases, and their decisions followed no clear standard. In many instances, the report asserted, commitments to training schools stemmed from arbitrary reasons that had nothing to do with a demonstrated need for institutional care.[19] Worst of all, according to the commission, was the possibility that placement in a training school steered juveniles ever more directly on the path to a criminal career. A 1948 survey sponsored by the commission found that over half of Gatesville's inmates were repeat offenders, while nearly two-thirds of the state's adult prisoners described themselves, tongue firmly in cheek, as "graduates" of Gatesville. Echoing previous surveys, the commission's final report described Gatesville as a house of horrors, with unsanitary cafeterias and hospitals, a dangerously neglected physical plant, and abusive punishments that included "severe whipping," excessive solitary confinement, and in extreme cases, the "water cure," in which guards fired a high-pressure hose at the groin from point-blank range, a brutal variant of the abuse chronicled by Albert Deutsch. So widespread was word-of-mouth knowledge about Gatesville that several county judges confessed to dismissing all but the worst male delinquency cases. The girls' school at Gainesville fared little better; the same commission study reported that a third of its inmates were recidivists. In June 1948, a delegation that included Austin MacCormick, the commission membership, state representative Pat Wiseman, and members of the Dallas Democratic Women's Club (proponents of the antiwhipping bill in the previous legislative session) made a surprise visit to find girls "chained around the ankles with large log chains."[20]

The commission's draft legislation proposed to remedy these formidable problems by placing all state and local juvenile justice agencies under the TSYDC's supervision. The TSYDC would be charged with devising diagnostic, classification, and treatment programs based on child psychology rather than penology. Each child adjudged delinquent in juvenile court was to be sent to a single diagnostic center for one month, where an intake team of trained professionals would formulate a rehabilitation plan based on a psychiatric interview and observation, a battery of psychological and intelligence tests, and a life history provided by local authorities. From there the child might be placed in any number of facilities that were to be constructed in the next few years. Ideally, the diagnostic center would have the option of sending juveniles to community-based programs run locally. Thus, the TSYDC's other key task was to assist local governments in organizing what would later be known as diversion programs. The stated goal was to reduce sharply the activity of existing training schools, while expanding the overall facilities for delinquent youth. Although completely phasing out Gatesville and Gainesville was never seriously considered, they were expected to jettison "the whole correctional system and philosophy" of mass custody and control:[21]

> The Commission wishes to emphasize that maintenance of discipline in a mass-custody institution, with untrained personnel, presents an insoluble problem. Because it is a mass-custody institution, combining the dangerous with the trustworthy, the first responsibility of the institution becomes custody. It must prevent the dangerous from running away. It thus forces the entire staff to be first of all guards, and it divides the population inevitably into the watchers and the watched. Life becomes an endless series of countings, of unlocking and relocking doors, of forming lines to go to classes, to work, to eat, to play. As always under repression, the human spirit rebels, plots endlessly to escape. In turn, the administration introduces more "discipline," and this degenerates sooner or later into brutality.[22]

In this statement, one can discern the impact of multiple tours of the state's training schools, the opinion of national experts, and a genuine desire to revolutionize the treatment of at-risk and delinquent youth. Thus it is hardly surprising that the commission's proposed legislation and its impending passage touched off a bitter power struggle in the most unreconstructed of the state's training schools: Gatesville. The drama pitted Superintendent Ed Blair and his local supporters against the Texas Board of Control, which retained authority over the training schools until the TSYDC formally took charge in September 1949. In response to mounting public criticism, punctuated by a series of exposés in the *Amarillo Times*, the TBC ordered Blair to halt corporal punishment and to cooperate with the hiring of a school psychologist, an educational director, and a certified accountant.[23] Each of these orders elicited bitter resistance. In November 1948, finalists for the educational director position visited Gatesville and were so appalled by what they saw—a school in utter disrepair and an openly hostile superintendent—that they immediately withdrew their applications.[24] Around this time, the TBC managed to hire a school psychologist, John Freeman, from Baylor University, who administered intelligence and behavior tests to 369 inmates between December 1948 and May 1949. Freeman also developed individual case files, which provided the basis for educational placements within the institution as well as parole recommendations upon release, earning him the gratitude of numerous local law enforcement agencies.[25] However, Freeman found his efforts frustrated by Blair and his staff. The longtime school principal, who lacked any teaching experience or credentials, openly ignored Freeman's placement recommendations, while the lack of any "follow-up program" inhibited his ability to track inmates' progress in or out of the institution. Freeman's frequent complaints subjected him to intimidation; shortly after his arrival at Gatesville, he discovered that a 250-pound guard named "Tiny" Hodges (whom Freeman suspected was mentally retarded) was spending several hours a day lurking outside his private residence on the Gatesville grounds, which frightened his wife and daughter. Put off by an atmosphere he later described as one of "abject fear" and frustrated with "people who [had] no sincere concern for the boys," Freeman left Gatesville in June 1949.[26]

Freeman's resignation came amid intensified tensions. New allegations of abuse led to a surprise visit from TBC chairman Hall Logan in late April. He inspected the punishment area, known as the "bull pen," and found a veritable arsenal of torture: a "newly cut" tree branch; "two iron straps approximately three feet long . . . with ends wrapped in cloth for handles;" several broom poles; and, "two long boards . . . trimmed down and fashioned for beating the boys."[27] In one of the "colored" buildings, Logan, "tipped off by one of the boys," discovered hidden behind a wall "three or four well-shaped paddles." An incensed Logan demanded that Blair fire several guards, the school principal, and "the grossly incapable white teachers in the colored school."[28] Blair refused and threatened to resign. Within days of the incident, on April 30, a conveniently timed mass escape of twenty inmates made news headlines. Whether or not Blair had engineered the breakout, as some suspected, it offered a reminder to critics that juvenile inmates were dangerous. But it failed to deter public and official criticism. On May 18, Logan recommended that the TBC remove Blair before the TSYDC assumed control in September. This report was followed immediately by an equally harsh review from the Austin Juvenile Probation Department. Both evaluations concluded that Blair's staff were "merely interested in custodial care" and were "not capable of rehabilitation of boys."[29] Underscoring the prevailing view, a sixteen-year-old serial burglar made headlines by asking a Dallas juvenile judge to send him to Gatesville because he "heard you could learn a lot about crime there."[30]

A second set of allegations emerged during two formal hearings in Austin on May 25 and June 6. The school's recently hired accountant, James Teague, revealed that Blair had his wife and the wives of several key staff members on the payroll. Moreover, the institution's single largest supplier of goods was the Gatesville Ice Company, whose owner, attorney Harry Flentge, had led local opposition to the antiwhipping bill in the previous legislative session, when, as Teague acidly put it, "Gatesville marched on Austin to save the great and noble work your Superintendent has been doing."[31] Teague recounted a litany of attempts to discredit or intimidate him over the previous months. Blair and assistant superintendent M. B. Kindrick had cornered him in an empty office; they had spread a rumor among the inmates that Teague was a "dope fiend"; and they had sent their mentally unbalanced enforcer Hodges to Teague's residence with a warning to "be careful."[32] The task of carrying out such threats fell not to Blair's "henchmen" among the staff, according to one office assistant, but to boy inmates who were promised "freedom" in exchange. Several informants testified that Blair routinely manipulated inmates' behavior for his own purposes, reflecting his overall disdain for them: "Let me tell you that Mr. Blair believes in cruelty. One night when Mr. Blair was talking to me about [name], he told me, don't feel sorry for these boys. I did when I first started working with them. You can't do anything for these boys. He said, this is nothing but a holding station for these boys until they are old enough to go to the pen."[33]

Local Gatesville citizens sprang to Blair's defense, issuing a public statement through the Coryell County grand jury blaming "the school's runaway problem" on restrictions against corporal punishment. Describing Blair as "a high-class gentleman with the best interest of this institution and his community at heart," the grand jury asserted that "bad boys must be disciplined." News reports quoted Blair stating that the TBC had "tied his hands" by banning all whippings, even for escapees, thereby opening the floodgates.[34] The politics of these gestures were unmistakable, for they took place while the TSYDC bill was making its way through the legislature, with strong support from Governor Jester. Although Blair's defiance infuriated the TBC, its members disagreed over whether to remove him, and after weeks of debate, including a heated meeting with Blair, ultimately allowed him to remain in his post. By then, the TBC's days in charge of Gatesville were numbered; the TSYDC bill was on its way to the governor's desk for his signature. Better to leave Blair in his post, the thinking went, rather than have the superintendent position replaced twice in a six-month span, although the TBC did pass along a stern warning to the new agency about Blair's shortcomings.[35] Indeed, in November 1949, the TSYDC removed Blair but promoted his assistant, M. B. Kindrick, in his place.[36] The TBC's choice to take the path of least resistance thus allowed holdovers from the old regime to remain at Gatesville and helped embolden continued resistance to policy reforms, which would contribute to an array of formidable obstacles confronting the TSYDC in the 1950s.

"A Freckle-Faced Boy"

Between 1949 and 1955, the TSYDC was divided into two directorates, focused respectively on "Institutions" and "Community Services." Viewed as "the point of conception" for delinquency, the local community represented the TSYDC's "primary concern."[37] In fact, the word "delinquency" appeared nowhere in the introductory text of the enabling legislation, which defined the TSYDC as an agency "for the protection, care, and training of children and youth."[38] The TSYDC was required by statute to gather data and "focus public attention" on community needs; to "strengthen the family in meeting its responsibilities"; to coordinate services throughout the state; and to assist local authorities in developing juvenile justice, probation, and prevention programs. To fulfill these daunting tasks, the TSYDC divided the state into four regions, each headed by a "field consultant." In its first year alone, TSYDC field consultants visited nearly 200 of the state's 254 counties, armed with a written blueprint for the development of "community youth councils."[39] The blueprint included a written constitution and an organizational plan for committees on schools, recreation, juvenile court, family, and religion. The TSYDC also provided an array of more-direct services. It demonstrated how to develop an individual case study in 32 county courts; compiled "comprehensive" surveys of 4 counties; and helped create 2 county probation departments. Part of this effort involved standardizing the "irregular" practices of juvenile courts across the state. Local juvenile courts hosted in-service training seminars on "best practices" and received new "face sheets" intended to accompany juveniles committed to TSYDC custody. However, the major focus for field consultants was supervised recreation; out of some seven hundred incorporated communities, only about twenty provided organized public recreation services. The TSYDC persuaded dozens of local governments to build playgrounds and swimming pools and to develop summer and after-school programs. "Thousands of children are prone to join the 'street corner society,'" admonished the TSYDC in its first annual report. "Our future depends largely upon how we use our leisure time."[40] The invocation of William Foote Whyte's pioneering participant-observation study of young men in an Italian slum in Boston suggests that the TSYDC was taking as its model for recreation those programs oriented toward urban, working-class youth, such as those in Houston described in chapter 2, and that it was aware such youth could join organized gangs in the absence of alternative choices.[41] "Most of the delinquency of the state comes in the larger cities," declared TSYDC chairman Kerr at a press conference in Fort Worth in February 1949, "and it will be those cities that will benefit most."[42]

One measure of the program's importance to reformers came when the TSYDC announced the appointment of S. L. Bellamy to the position of director of community services. Prior to serving on the Code Commission, Bellamy had worked as a juvenile probation officer in Austin and Houston. However, even earlier Bellamy had been the assistant superintendent at Gatesville during a five-year period (1937–41) notorious for abuse investigations. This past elicited a storm of protest from the Democratic Women's Club of Dallas, the group largely responsible for exposing the chain of abuse scandals that led to the formation of the TSYDC. A tense confrontation took place in November 1949; a group of women led by Mrs. William B. Crawford passed out photographs of bruised Gatesville inmates purportedly taken in 1941. Either Bellamy himself had "indulged in brutality," they claimed, or he "probably had sanctioned this unusual punishment." In his own defense, Bellamy assured them that he had been "vitally opposed" to corporal punishment, referring to his years at Gatesville as "the most trying experience of [his] career." This expression of remorse compensated for Bellamy's unacceptable association with the training schools, which in the eyes of the Dallas women disqualified him from heading the community services program. Over the reformers' protest, the TSYDC unanimously approved Bellamy for the position, thus inaugurating a pattern over the next few years by which some reform groups would be left to criticize the agency from the outside looking in.[43]

The heated nature of this dispute reflected the importance of public relations for the new agency. The TSYDC's mission faced an uphill battle on two scores. First, it called on citizens to invest tax dollars in areas where they had been reluctant to do so previously; second, the beneficiaries of those funds were juvenile delinquents, who had to be portrayed sympathetically in order to merit public support. The TSYDC's goal, as expressed by Chairman Kerr in 1951, was "to be in a position to develop and control public opinion in matters pertaining to youth work."[44] In 1950, "to focus attention on the problem of juvenile delinquency," the TSYDC began publishing a monthly newsletter, the *Key*, which was distributed across the state.[45] That same year, Kerr appeared on a statewide radio broadcast with Texas governor Allan Shivers to promote the availability of the TSYDC's field workers to local communities. Favorable news articles lauded community programs begun with TSYDC aid, including in some cases recreation centers initiated by teenagers themselves. The TSYDC earned enough respect to serve as the "go-to" source for news quotes on practically every youth-related issue imaginable, from child-support payments to the moviegoing habits of teenagers. In the process, Kerr and his compatriots helped "normalize" delinquency for their public audiences, which in turn seemed to lend further legitimacy to the TSYDC. In a joint radio address, Kerr and Shivers touted the "trained field workers" available to communities all over the state and described the TSYDC's mission as "boiling down to two words—character development"—a generic-sounding staple that audiences would recognize from Boy Scouts, public schools, and ROTC programming.[46] At the same time, this effort tended to elicit a fairly unprecedented level of sympathy for the plight of certain kinds of delinquent youth. In a 1950 editorial celebrating the TSYDC's mission of "salvaging what can be salvaged," the *Austin Statesman* stated:

> The most tragic aspect of the delinquency docket is that more often than not the conditions which bog a youngster's feet in this sordid path are not of his own making. Organized society has learned that the remedy is not the harsh processes of punitive justice in dealing with a boy or girl pushed by environment or home conditions into truancy and delinquency, but rather a correction of the conditions making his or her life what it is. Texas in just the past short time has gone beyond that to the concept that even when it first contacts a youngster well along the way to juvenile crime, hating society, in many cases it can help him readjust himself to a useful and self-respecting place in that society. . . . A freckle-faced boy, no matter how straight his mind would be, if given a chance, has no chance to grow up there to self-respect and a decent place in society. He is important, not only to himself but to society as a whole. . . . Human values call for some sort of organized effort by organized society to see that the child shall have at least the chance of normal life, or education, happiness and usefulness.[47]

These well-meaning narratives distinguished between "salvageable" children who were first-time or nonviolent offenders and older, hardened delinquents believed to be beyond help. They also implied, sometimes with little subtlety, the economic, racial, or ethnic background of the merely misguided child. Versions of the "freckle-faced boy" evoked in the *Austin Statesman* editorial quoted here appeared several times during this period. In 1949, he had graced the cover of the Code Commission's official report, which was circulated at press conferences across the state (figure 9). With neatly combed hair, white, freckle-faced, and clearly preadolescent, "Bill" wears a Western belt buckle over a tucked T-shirt emblazoned with a cowboy. His determined stare toward the horizon, taken from a lower, heroic camera angle, perhaps aroused a sense of collective purpose or evoked nostalgia

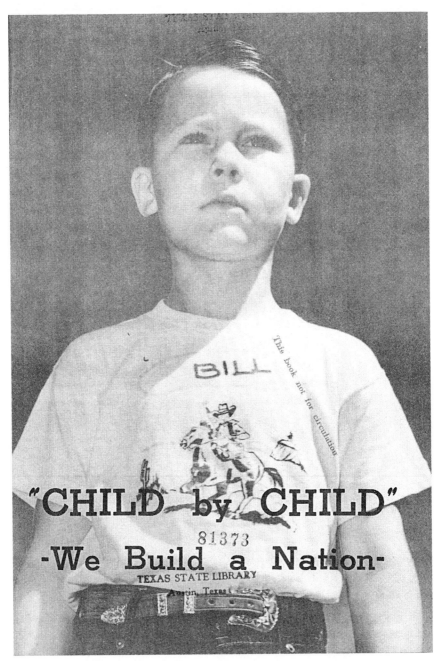

Figure 9. Cover, *Child by Child We Build a Nation: A Youth Development Plan for the State of Texas* (Austin: Texas Training School Code Commission, 1949). (Courtesy of the Texas State Library and Archives Commission.)

Where Credit Is Due

See Editorial, 'Juvenile Delinquents.'

Figure 10. "Where Credit Is Due." Tyler Morning Telegraph, May 5, 1951. (Sam Nash cartoon reprinted with permission of the *Tyler Courier-Times-Telegraph*, Tyler, Texas. Image courtesy of the Texas State Library and Archives Commission.)

for a rural childhood uncomplicated by the state's urbanization and industrialization. A similar image, titled "Man of Tomorrow," had appeared on the cover of the June 1944 issue of *Our Community*, the monthly newsletter of the Houston YMCA. For this special issue devoted to the problem of delinquency in the city's poorest neighborhoods, a freckle-faced boy gazed upward, wide-eyed and admiringly, at a father figure whose hand rested on the boy's shoulder. The image more closely resembled the unsupervised and largely white children whose parents were occupied in military and factory labor during World War II, and who had inspired the "teen canteen" movement, than the youth-gang members and "hoodlums," overwhelmingly nonwhite, who had filled the headlines of Houston's newspapers during that same period, as we have seen.[48] This was a measure of both the influence of community-based youth programs developed in previous decades and of the images and narratives that came to be associated with such programs, which carried over into the TSYDC era (see figure 10).

A striking feature in these reformist narratives and images was the complete absence of African American or Mexican American youth, itself a reflection of three key contexts in the TSYDC's early years. The TSYDC's initial orientation toward community-based prevention encouraged a focus on "predelinquent" youth rather than juvenile inmates in the state's training schools, where nonwhites were a substantial and fast-growing population. Thus it made sense for the TSYDC to present younger, more innocent-appearing children as exemplars. Second, the TSYDC was in part created by reformers whose experiences with local programs had inculcated in them an inclusive "color-blind" outlook that tended to be fairly superficial in practice. Although the TSYDC frequently insisted generically on fair treatment for every child regardless of "race, color, or creed," it tended to omit the roles of racial discrimination and economic inequality in discussions of delinquency. Thus not only African Americans and Mexican Americans but also to a lesser extent poor whites—always overrepresented within the white offender population—were rhetorically excluded from the "nation" and "community" envisioned in the lofty language employed by the TSYDC. Meanwhile, as we shall see, the language of crime and punishment, as well as more punitive policies and programs, increasingly were reserved mainly for nonwhite juveniles. These dual discourses had the combined effect of "racializing" delinquency, with therapeutic rehabilitation offered to one group and correctional retribution for the other.

The final critical context for understanding both the acceptance of the TSYDC's ideas generally and the racialized way in which they were implemented was the popularization of the idea of adolescence. As explained by the era's most influential child psychologist, Erik H. Erikson, adolescence was a life stage characterized by the identity crisis, a period of self-discovery, role experimentation, and internal struggle. In the early postwar era, the "teenager" became one of the most commented on cultural phenomena in American life; as adolescents attended high school at the unprecedented rate of 90 percent and became more dependent than ever on adults to a later age, Erikson's thesis seemed to explain a great deal of what was actually happening in everyday life. In a telling formulation, Erikson referred to adolescence as "normal semicriminality," suggesting that teenagers were likely to test legal as well as social boundaries in their quest for a coherent identity.[49] Occasional misbehavior could be tolerated, as long as it did not escalate into full-blown "maladjustment," which could then call for clinical or even judicial intervention. By highlighting such middle-class "predelinquents," the TSYDC thus echoed popular sentiments while domesticating a historically unsolvable dilemma and making it seem manageable. In place of Stanley the jack-roller, the working-class, urban, "ethnic" juvenile delinquent of early twentieth-century social science, the TSYDC constructed a younger, native-born, even less threatening version of

James Dean, who suffered from purely psychological problems of self-esteem or inadequate parenting.[50] This misguided boy-next-door appealed to reformers and audiences alike because of his familiarity. With a fatherly hand on his shoulder, he elided the messy, intractable problems associated with the actual population of juvenile delinquents. Like mental health and illness, normative adolescence and delinquency came to exist on a continuum that could be molded through a range of scientific interventions.[51]

The TSYDC demonstrated just such an intervention to the public with its "mobile diagnostic clinic," which toured the state for five months in 1951. The idea arose out of the failure to establish a permanent reception center for the diagnosis of adjudged delinquents committed to state custody, about which there had been some disagreement. Harold J. Matthews, the TSYDC's director of institutions, had argued for the creation of at least three diagnostic centers, located in Austin, Dallas, and Houston, rather than one.[52] He predicted that a single center would quickly become overcrowded, which in turn would hamper "individualized consideration" of cases and, echoing earlier warnings, would make transportation expensive and impractical. "It would be difficult," he suggested, to maintain "the four main classifications of white girls, colored girls, white boys, and colored boys," not to mention distinctions based on age or behavior. For as long as a month, children would undergo a rigorous screening process that included a physical examination, intelligence and psychological tests, and interviews with a case worker and a psychiatrist. Staff would keep a behavior record of each child and compile "a family and social history." Matthews's plan foundered, however, on the inability to secure facilities due in large part to the legislature's refusal to finance the venture—even though the TSYDC was required by statute to provide diagnostic services. Although each institution would provide some limited diagnostic services separately, the TSYDC's scope would be limited by its status as a division within several existing state agencies, rather than as an independent agency in its own right, until 1957, when Gatesville became the site for the main intake, classification, and diagnostic center for boys.[53]

Therefore, the mobile clinic represented a last-ditch attempt to demonstrate the utility of diagnostic screening of delinquents. Clearly modeled on the child guidance demonstrations of the 1920s, the mobile clinic treated 152 children in six locations between March and August 1951. The locations—San Antonio, Texarkana, Tyler, El Paso, Edinburg, and Nacogdoches—encompassed both urban and rural areas and were chosen for their general lack of psychological services for children and youth. Typically, the arrival of the mobile clinic took on the features of a public event; in a temporary space reserved in or near the local county courthouse, reporters and citizens from the surrounding area gathered to question a three-person team of clinical psychologist, psychometrist, and social worker. The team then spent several days "treating" children before and after their court hearings.[54] A summary report described "a few of the 'delinquent' children the Clinic examined" mainly as victims of parental neglect and abuse, which led to compensatory or "acting out" behavior that in turn landed them in juvenile court.[55] There was "Susan," the daughter of alcoholics, who was pawned off on relatives, causing her to perform poorly in school and seek "affection" through sexual liaisons. "Tom and Bill," two brothers from a "good, well-to-do home," compensated for their busy parents' frequent absence by going on crime sprees late at night. Even "Alec," who lived in a "slum," suffered less from poverty than from being raised by a single mother who worked and dated several men. Like the others, regardless of their social background, Alec's biggest problem was low self-esteem rooted in family disorders. Of the clinic's 152 child patients, 105 came from families marred by "divorce, separation, desertion, or death"; 113 of them "were rejected by their own parents"; and 141 "had weak or inadequate parents." Sexual abuse, usually by a relative, marred the lives of over half of the girls examined by the clinic. Once again, the relentless focus on emotional problems seemed to be a double-edged sword. On the one hand, it promised a more humane exploration of the interior life of youth who previously might have been simply committed to state custody; on the other, it encouraged a reductive flattening of the complex root causes of delinquency. However, although the mobile clinic received favorable press, it ran out of funding at the end of August 1951 and failed to win budgetary support from the legislature.

The impression that the TSYDC was modernizing its facilities received further confirmation from a series of attention-getting reforms at Gainesville, promulgated by a new superintendent with a progressive reputation. Having gone through four superintendents in the previous decade, the TBC in March 1949 appointed Maxine Burlingham, a University of Texas graduate and a longtime probation officer in nearby Fort Worth. Burlingham earned widespread praise for hiring professional caseworkers, revamping intake and discharge procedures, and launching a nursing school. This "new deal for girls' reform," as one newspaper put it, included therapeutic programs for "social adjustment."[56] For instance, in a class on "family relationships," girls wrote and performed autobiographical plays intended to show them "where they erred." Observers noted that laughter had replaced the "dreariness, resentment, and boredom" of previous administrations. An expanded beauty and cosmetology program encouraged "womanly" habits, an improvement on "a type of homosexuality which took the form of some girls dressing and acting like boys" in the past. Burlingham sought to deter these behaviors by reviving the policy of Gainesville's first superintendent, Carrie Weaver Smith, of encouraging off-campus activities. Trips to swimming pools, churches, and parks, as well as "special" destinations like the circus or the skating rink, became rewards for good behavior and among the privileges denied for disobedience. "The girls have something interesting to do at all times," observed TSYDC members who visited Gainesville, which they compared favorably to "a small college" or "a boarding school."[57] So well-received were Burlingham's reforms that the TSYDC began promoting Gainesville as an exemplar of a modern juvenile institution. On the last weekend of May 1950, Gainesville held an open house that was attended by girls' families, reporters, and TSYDC board members. The event further underlined Burlingham's insistence that "the state school girls" be viewed as generally normal girls rather than social deviants. "We have created a love for beautiful things," stated the event program, "have improved mental health, and have learned to think beautiful thoughts."[58] Violations of school rules were still punished, but progressively. In place of the shackles, "reflection rooms," and forced haircuts of her predecessors, Burlingham employed a four-tier discipline system: denial of privileges, restriction to bedrooms, "cocktail parties" ("a stiff dose of castor oil" supervised by a physician), and last, "10 to 12 strokes with a leather strap on the lower part of the buttocks."[59] To most observers at that time, these policies represented a vast improvement over an abusive past that was hopefully long gone. Unfortunately for would-be reformers, however, implementation of genuine education and rehabilitation programs in the training schools would prove to be far more difficult than they imagined.

"A Head-On Clash between the Old and the New Thinking"

Juvenile inmates and their families were the first to puncture the positive bubble of media attention surrounding the TSYDC. The most dramatic protest occurred in February 1952, when a Houston attorney named Kenyon Houchins filed a series of habeas corpus petitions on behalf of girls incarcerated in Gainesville.[60] One of Houchins's clients was a Houston waitress named Reba Willis, whose sixteen-year-old daughter had spent 186 of the previous 210 days locked in the very same steel-lined isolation cell that notoriously had been known as the "reflection room." After clashing repeatedly with Superintendent Burlingham, Willis told a Houston judge that she feared her daughter had "cracked from the strain" of solitary confinement.[61] When Houchins arrived at Gainesville with a court order for the girl's release, he discovered that Superintendent Burlingham had personally driven the girl to Wichita Falls and had her committed to a state mental hospital. For several days, the girl's whereabouts were unknown to her mother and her attorney, giving the appearance of foul play. During a subsequent court hearing, a rapt audience of reporters and child welfare activists listened as the "attractive, strawberry-blonde girl" described how two men had held her down while a third one beat her with a leather strap; how Burlingham had dosed her with Nembutal, a sedative from a class of barbiturates known colloquially as "goof balls"; and how she and other girls routinely inhaled the fumes from glue and lighter fluid and engaged in self-mutilation as an outlet for their unhappiness.[62] These lurid stories convinced the judge to release the girl to the care of a county psychiatrist, while the Houston Housewives League charged Burlingham with "cruel and inhuman treatment in violation of the child's constitutional rights."[63] Perhaps the most forceful condemnation came from another of Houchins's clients, a Gainesville escapee, during an emotional interview with a reporter:

> I'll kill myself before I'm returned. I've been punished enough. It's not a corrective institution. It's a place of punishment. I've seen girls as young as 12 and 13 suffer treatment that shouldn't be given a hardened criminal. . . . You're not there long before you learn a lot of things that can hardly be called corrective. . . . I needed help, not punishment. I was emotionally upset. The school doesn't have provisions to take care of girls who need counseling. Instead, when a girl gets upset and makes a scene they put her in her room and lock the door and leave her there until she becomes resigned to the place.[64]

Burlingham denied none of these charges, countering that Houchins's clients were mentally ill, physically aggressive, and unsuited for a juvenile rehabilitation program. After an investigation that included a surprise visit from Texas governor Allan Shivers, the TSYDC concurred, fully supporting Burlingham. "Some girls are so far gone," fretted TSYDC executive director John Winters, that "we hardly know what to do with them."[65] Burlingham never denied the charge of corporal punishment, having recorded sixteen beatings the previous year. In her view, it was a necessary bulwark against inmate-on-staff violence. For her, the worst aspect of the incident was that it led to a temporary moratorium on beatings, which in turn incited widespread disobedience within the institution. "Scared and intimidated," Burlingham's staff allegedly stood by helplessly while girls erupted in "near-rebellion" and "insurrection."[66]

For Gainesville, such incidents were rare and did not recur throughout the 1950s and 1960s. By contrast, from the TSYDC's first day of operation, the boys' school at Gatesville remained mired in various permutations of controversy. Locals simmered with resentment over the replacement of former superintendent Blair, whom the TSYDC fired in December 1949, with James Atlee, a former area supervisor for the state Welfare Department with no "actual institutional experience."[67] The *Gatesville Messenger* denounced the change as "outside meddling" by Austin bureaucrats "not familiar with the tremendous task . . . of attempting to instill the ideals of law-abiding citizenship in some of the boys of a more hardened criminal nature."[68] A hostile citizenry, at least initially, was the least of Atlee's problems. Practically everything about Gatesville was "outmoded" or "unsafe," from its buildings to its records. Atlee's first report to the TSYDC included a laundry list of defects: an academic school that had lost its accreditation; an unqualified staff; a recreation program "consisting entirely of movies"; no placement or counseling services; "no facilities for classification or segregation"; a vocational program that continued to emphasize agricultural labor; and a "retribution-oriented program of discipline."[69] However, Atlee's first attempts at reform—which included a ban on corporal punishment and the removal of the facility's old barbed-wire fencing—provoked the same problems that had befallen previous reform-minded superintendents. Within months, he became the target of bitter complaints that relaxed discipline had sparked a wave of escapes. In June 1950, the Coryell County grand jury demanded that the state compensate local property owners for burglaries and damages caused by escapees, whom they claimed had grown in number to forty-seven a month, nearly twice the official statistics, which showed that runaways had dropped from a monthly number of twenty-nine in 1949 to twenty-six in 1950—still a high figure.[70] Interpreting these criticisms as "no worse than they had ever been," the TSYDC issued a public statement of support for Atlee: "We hope that future legislative help would enable the school . . . to properly classify . . . those difficult youngsters who lead escapes, steal cars, carry guns and are so emotionally and mentally disabled as to require special care."[71]

This statement vastly underestimated the powder keg that was local anger, which found its spark on the morning of August 15, 1950, when a fourteen-year-old African American inmate named Walter Johnson escaped from Gatesville.[72] Johnson was a first-time offender who had been committed only three weeks earlier for robbing several grocery stores in Austin. Within hours, he turned up at the nearby home of a fifty-five-year-old white farmer named Walter Mack. After arriving home on his tractor, Mack opened his door to find Johnson standing in the front room holding "his Winchester rifle." According to news accounts, Mack "pleaded with the Negro not to shoot him" and attempted to flee, only to be shot in the back. Johnson helped Mack inside, laid him on his bed, and went in search of help. Soon Johnson wandered onto the grounds of Fort Hood, directly to the south of Gatesville, where he allegedly "pulled a cocked rifle" on a military policeman "and demanded to be driven to the Austin highway." Soldiers took Johnson into custody and attended to the stricken Mack, who survived the shooting but spent several weeks in the hospital. Reportage on the incident was so laced with anger that it clouded the actual chain of events, but one thing was certain: the spectacle of a black escapee shooting down a white farmer in his own home—a crime that might have resulted in a lynching in some parts of the South a mere four years before the infamous murder of Emmett Till in Mississippi—infuriated Gatesville's citizenry. Two days after the incident, "an angry crowd of 200 Coryell County farmers and businessmen" crowded into the county courthouse to vent their anger at Gatesville superintendent Atlee and TSYDC director Winters, who each addressed the group. The "ugly mood" was captured best by the response to a forty-five-minute speech by Atlee explaining the "trend toward rehabilitation" in juvenile corrections and the "grim picture" at the institution, which would require a major investment to rebuild. "The best thing to do," yelled one farmer, "is spend $25 on leather instead of a million on buildings." Others declared "open season" on runaways, threatening to shoot them on sight.[73] Shouting Atlee and Winters down, the crowd demanded the reinstatement of whipping, the dispatching of a detail of inmates to work Mack's land while he recuperated, and the construction of an electrified barbed-wire fence. Otherwise, they insisted that the school should be relocated, preferably near "those Dallas clubwomen" who had pushed for the hated reforms.[74]

In response, the TSYDC proposed to give the "Gatesvilleites" precisely what they wished for: the removal of the training school. Shortly after the Johnson-Mack affair, at the TSYDC's request, Richard Clenenden of the U.S. Children's Bureau and Bertram Beck of the American Law Institute visited Gatesville. Both experts reiterated the advice that Clenenden had given the commission in 1948, to replace the large, mass-custody institution with smaller, regionally located ones. Accordingly, at its September meeting, the TSYDC endorsed a plan to break up Gatesville into four separate facilities, each of which would replace mass-custody dormitories with single-room cottages. In November 1950, TSYDC chairman Kerr unveiled a pricey $2,250,000 budget request for the new facilities. The plan received favorable news coverage throughout the state. "At last," rejoiced the *Austin American*, "after precisely 61 years in which official neglect has made Gatesville a prep school for the state penitentiary," the state was willing to invest in "a brighter day."[75] Younger, more vulnerable youth would be protected from "the toughies," resulting in less restrictive, less prisonlike settings. On closer inspection, however, the plan relied on classification criteria that revolved around levels of custody rather than juveniles' stage in the rehabilitation process. The designations of three of the four facilities included a "maximum" security facility for "boys who [could not] accept an open setting or ordinary treatment methods," and "medium" and "minimum" facilities for "the most hopeful and trainable boys." The plan called for a fourth institution for "Negro boys" that would include a secure "detention cottage." Ironically, in the name of a brand of "segregation" associated with scientific rehabilitation, the TSYDC strove to realize the aspirations of its embittered predecessors for racial segregation in the form of a separate Jim Crow training school.[76]

Unlike its predecessors, however, the TSYDC relied on "scientific" rather than purely racial arguments. Although the TSYDC had lacked funding for agency-wide diagnostic services, it had been able to hire a clinical psychologist at Gatesville, who began to conduct intelligence and psychological tests on inmates in 1950. This had allowed Superintendent Atlee to blame not only the Johnson escape but also institutional failures generally on a high number of "feeble-minded Negroes." In September 1950, he estimated that 75 of the 132 black inmates at Gatesville fit this description. "Many of the runaways were feeble-minded," he argued, "or the other boys whose segregation is felt so necessary."[77] The Gatesville testing regime had formed the centerpiece of the diagnostic center envisioned by the TSYDC to screen juvenile commitments for placement decisions and rehabilitation plans. However, the tests were neither unbiased in content nor administered equally. Although the actual questionnaires used at Gatesville no longer exist, they likely resembled the Binet tests on which they were based, which historians have shown were so skewed in favor of the well educated that their use in World War I draft screenings had suggested that over half of all American soldiers were mentally retarded.[78] In this instance, African American inmates were particularly set up to fail these exams. Saddled with a broken academic school program generally, Gatesville had never seriously pretended to educate its black inmates, as we have seen. Moreover, in 1950, the first TSYDC exams were administered to all the African American inmates but, allegedly due to "time constraints," only to "sample groups" of white and Mexican American inmates (there is no indication of how these samples were taken). This choice raises questions because whites comprised 48 percent of Gatesville's admissions in 1950, followed by blacks (28 percent) and Mexican Americans (24 percent). The results confirmed the existing opinions of TSYDC administrators: The average intelligence quotient for black inmates, 65, placed them in the "feeble-minded" category; less than 10 percent tested at "normal" or above. The mean score, respectively, of Mexican Americans at 85 ("borderline") and whites at 91 ("low normal") made them better candidates for rehabilitation.[79] More-extensive tests given the following year produced similar results (see table 7). This time, in addition to measurements of intelligence and attitude scales, the tests included the Bennett Hand-Tool Dexterity Test, which evaluated boys' performance in timed tasks; an Educational Achievement Test administered to white and Mexican American boys only; and an Adjustment Test given to girls only.[80]

Even more revealing was the TSYDC psychologist's analysis of these results. Low scores for white boys on the intelligence test, he advised, should "not be taken at face value" because they suffered from "poor environment, lack of opportunity, [and] lack of parental love and guidance" rather than inherent "low mental capacity."[81] Language barriers, in the TSYDC's view, helped explain "Latin American"

Table 7. Average intelligence quotient scores of Texas State Youth Development Council inmates, 1950–1951

	White	Mexican American	African American
Boys	92.8	82.7	69.0
Girls	94.9	83.3	64.8

Aggregate scores from Gatesville, Gainesville, and Brady/Crockett training schools.
Source: *Second Annual Report of the State Youth Development Council* (1951), 52.

boys' scores. However, no such considerations appeared in the section on "feeble-minded Negroes," a phrase that quickly became a mantra in TSYDC complaints, which in substance diverged little from the 1920s. The TSYDC would spend much of the ensuing decade trying to have the entire population of black inmates transferred to mental hospitals or prisons. This troubling record leaves it unclear which black inmates were genuinely suffering from epilepsy, mental retardation, or mental illness, and which were simply victims of prejudicial treatment at the TSYDC's hands. The state's institutions for the mentally retarded were either white only or in the early stages of admitting African American patients. Howard E. Smith, the director of the Board for Texas State Hospitals and Special Schools, informed the TSYDC board in September 1950 that he was negotiating to gain access for some of Gatesville's black inmates; one year later, however, nothing had changed.[82] In 1952, the Abilene State Hospital and the Austin State School, both of which housed epileptic and mentally retarded individuals, began accepting black referrals, if only a small number.[83] That same year, the TSYDC issued a policy directive that cited state law to the effect that "feebleminded, epileptic, and insane children" could not be admitted to any juvenile training school.[84] Regardless of the extent to which this problem truly existed, the TSYDC's advocacy of the Gatesville "break-up" produced two overlapping racial arguments: African Americans were overrepresented among those inmates who were too violent and dangerous to participate in a therapeutic rehabilitation plan; and they were, in essence, too mentally retarded (or "psychopathic") to benefit from treatment. The TSYDC insisted, at least as strenuously as had its predecessors in the Progressive Era, on the complete segregation of black inmates from the rest of the population.

In spring 1951 the plan to divide Gatesville into four separate facilities went before the legislature, where it garnered a tepid response. Lacking the kind of grassroots support that had powered recent reform campaigns, the plan instead was promoted by the less compelling figures of state bureaucrats. Having more or less pushed away its putative allies in the reform community, the TSYDC now found itself alone. Pleas similar to those that had spurred the agency's creation now fell on deaf ears. Citing a survey showing that 53 percent of state prison inmates were "graduates" of Gatesville, O. B. Ellis, the general manager of the Texas Department of Corrections, urged the legislature to "eliminate the 'school for crime.'"[85] The TSYDC's Winters testified that smaller facilities located near cities would attract more trained professionals and reduce the "sensation" surrounding escapes. In impassioned testimony before the Texas Senate, Superintendent Atlee described inmate gangs as an outgrowth of conditions that he called "worse than Huntsville" (the state prison):

> The beds, rows on rows of them in bare dormitories, are behind steel wire, similar to that used to enclose the cages in a zoo. Outside this cage sits an attendant. His job is to see that the boys behave. But if a sex deviate, in the blazing light of the overhead bulbs, makes a move, the attendant may lose his life if he opens the cage door to stop it. Things are that tough in the "training school," where the boys are supposed to be steered from the path of crime. . . . In the past nobody seemed to care what happened to the school or the boys in it. Somebody permitted construction of a school building which has no rest room for students. Each morning and afternoon, school stops and the boys are marched two blocks away to outside toilets behind the row of dormitories. Because they must be treated like prisoners in many respects, [the boys] have adopted many prison ways. The large, flat area behind the dormitories, a sort of gathering place, is called the "yard." . . . A normal haircut is a "citizen's haircut," to distinguish it from a head shave. A knife, or any instrument for stabbing purposes, is a "jigger." A "fire buggy" is anything that will make fire.[86]

In May 1951, the expanded TSYDC budget bill went down to defeat, largely due to opposition from Texas governor Allan Shivers, who favored diverting funds to the construction of hospitals. Instead, the TSYDC received an appropriation of $669,000, a fraction of the requested amount.[87] Not only did Gatesville remain intact; it would continue to grow exponentially throughout the next two decades, forcing the TSYDC to abandon its commitment to community-based rehabilitation and prevention programs. Budgetary requests, submitted and negotiated at each biennial legislative session, reflected a renewed emphasis on large institutions. In May 1953, for instance, Gatesville received "one of the best appropriations in its history" while the noninstitutional TSYDC positions of director of community service, recreation consultant, clinical psychologist, as well as the four field representatives were slated for elimination.[88] By 1955, budget cuts forced the TSYDC to abandon completely its advising and grant programs for local juvenile courts, civic groups, and youth recreation clubs. Thus, less than a decade after its inception, the TSYDC's once diverse, albeit partially implemented, scope of activity narrowed to a single task: the management of the state's three juvenile training schools at Crockett,

Table 8. Gatesville admissions by race and ethnicity, 1935–1965, in five-year increments, with raw numbers and percentages of total

Year	White	Mexican American	African American	Total
1935	281 / 51.1	92 / 16.7	177 / 32.2	550
1940	185 / 40.0	104 / 22.4	174 / 37.6	463
1945	269 / 47.0	144 / 25.2	158 / 27.8	572
1950	300 / 48.3	149 / 24.0	172 / 27.7	621
1955	395 / 44.8	239 / 27.1	247 / 28.0	881
1960	678 / 37.1	473 / 25.9	672 / 36.8	1,825
1965*	736 / 32.3	640 / 28.1	895 / 39.3	2,274

*1965 figures include the Mountain View State School for Boys, which opened in 1962.

Sources: *Texas Juvenile Court Research Reports*, vol. 3 (Austin, 1948); *Annual Report of the Texas State Youth Development Council* (1949–57); *Annual Report of the Texas Youth Council* (1957–71).

Gainesville, and especially Gatesville, which experienced a startling increase in its inmate population over the next decade. Maintaining order at the training schools in the face of this rapid increase would come to occupy all of the TSYDC's attention for the remainder of the decade.[89]

In the 1950s, the total number of Gatesville admissions nearly tripled, from 621 to 1,825, with the bulk of that increase coming after 1955 (see table 8). That year, a survey revealed that the adolescent-age population had grown by 13 percent, while the number of delinquency cases had risen by 51 percent. The estimated delinquency rate in Texas jumped from fifteen per thousand in 1953 to nineteen in 1955 and twenty-three in 1964.[90] The state's rapid postwar urbanization also played a role; nearly half of all TSYDC referrals came from the nine largest counties, led by Harris County (Houston). Delinquency serious enough to warrant institutionalization remained largely the province of adolescent males, with the sex ratio widening from three boys for each girl committed to four by 1960. Moreover, police departments referred over 95 percent of all male commitments, but only about a quarter of female.[91] Thus, in contrast to the official imagery of delinquency, the typical juvenile delinquent remained male, urban, and working class, a social background that differed little from previous decades. The only major change in the demography of the juvenile delinquent population occurred at Gatesville, where the number of African American and Mexican American juveniles rose precipitously, helping to drive the overall population numbers. Nonwhite offenders, as we have seen, had comprised a disproportionate share of the inmate population from Gatesville's inception. However, the trend became much more pronounced after World War II, when white juveniles grew in raw numbers but shrank as a percentage into a distinct minority of the overall inmate population. In 1950, the percent-

Table 9. Resolution of male delinquency cases in Texas juvenile courts by race, 1958, with raw numbers and percentages of total*

	White**	African American	Total
Official	2,799 / 85.4	479 / 14.6	3,278
Unofficial	11,829 / 84.4	2,180 / 15.6	14,009
Total cases	14,628 / 84.6	2,659 / 15.4	17,287

*Based on 124 of 264 (61 percent) of counties reporting.
**The "white" category includes Mexican American cases.
Source: *Texas Juvenile Court Statistics for 1958* (Austin, 1959).

age of African American inmates (27 percent) ran more than twice their share of the state's general population of fifteen to nineteen year olds (13 percent).[92] By 1955, according to the TSYDC's own statistics, black male adolescents were three times as likely as their white counterparts to be incarcerated in Gatesville.[93]

By the early 1960s, black inmates comprised the largest group even in raw numbers, a stunning development that has more or less persisted to the present day. The reasons for this disproportionate confinement of nonwhite offenders were suggested in a 1958 survey of juvenile court decisions in roughly half of Texas's counties. According to these data, over three-fourths of all juvenile cases handled "officially" involved white offenders (table 9). Tried in formal proceedings at a rate commensurate with their share of the overall population, African American juvenile offenders nevertheless were far more likely to be committed to an institution.[94]

As the decade unfolded, demoralization set in at the TSYDC. Meetings became shorter, less frequent, and less well attended; in 1953, the TSYDC moved to cut its membership in half, from six to three.[95] Forced to abandon its lofty goals for delinquency prevention and rehabilitation, the agency found itself saddled with the same large, dysfunctional institutions that it had once hoped to marginalize. Worse yet, the institutions were growing at an uncontrollable pace, their walls bulging with "tougher" juveniles from precisely the same social groups that the TSYDC had expressly tried to exclude from its most progressive plans for institutional rehabilitation. Few responses were available to a fund-starved TSYDC. In 1953, it proposed a plan (never realized) to bill parents for the costs of incarceration; one version of this idea called for authorization for the TSYDC to withdraw funds directly from Social Security, Aid for Dependent Children, or other government checks.[96] The next year, the TSYDC won an appropriation for "security treatment centers" to isolate the most antisocial inmates—an expanded version of the "reflection rooms" at Gainesville. "Our program is breaking down," admitted Gatesville superintendent

Herman Sapier. "About all we can concentrate on is custodial care."[97] Adding to Sapier's troubles was Gatesville's slowly crumbling physical plant, featured in a 1955 series in the *Austin Statesman*. In one photograph, boy inmates crowd together in "stacked" bunk-beds; in another, a silhouetted boy broods in front of a vast empty field that was "the barren 'recreation area.'" "Goals Lofty, Cash Lagging" read one indicative headline.[98] "It is obvious," stated TSYDC chairman Kerr, "that we have many buildings which should be razed and replaced with safe and modern structures."[99]

The most significant construction to take place in the late 1950s, however, came not from public funds but as the result of a private fundraising drive spearheaded by the Dallas Grand Jury Association and sanctioned by the TSYDC, which hoped the good publicity would raise support for legislative funds. Between 1957 and 1959, the group received about two hundred thousand dollars in donations for the installation at all three training schools of interdenominational chapels, which, according to TSYDC member Lewis Nordyke, would provide "untold comfort and inspiration."[100] In the end, this well-meaning gesture was overshadowed by enduring problems caused by overcrowding and underfunding. At Gatesville, inmates could now kneel on an altar of shag carpet and polished wood in search of salvation (figure 11), a refuge from a harsh institution. Meanwhile, outside Gatesville's walls, a new initiative emerged to "get tough" on juvenile offenders, led by the TSYDC itself.

"A Twilight Zone between Adolescence and Adulthood"

The decline of the TSYDC's reformist bent coincided with the growing influence of James Aubrey Turman. A former army captain, engineer at the DuPont Corporation, and graduate of Abilene Christian College, Turman earned his master's degree in educational psychology at the University of Texas. His master's thesis, completed in January 1951, extolled the potential benefits of school desegregation while admiringly quoting a litany of prominent antiracist scholars, including Gunnar Myrdal and Gordon Allport.[101] At the same time, however, he was working as a clinical psychologist for the TSYDC's mobile clinic and the diagnostic testing programs and advocating the removal of "feeble-minded Negroes" from Gatesville. That year, Turman left the TSYDC for a similar position in the Child Welfare Division of the Texas Department of Welfare. In January 1955, the TSYDC hired Turman as its consultant for juvenile delinquency, a position that previously had entailed working with various community agencies and organizations. Those functions, as noted earlier, had been slated for elimination by the legislature. Turman advised the TSYDC that it should focus on its institutions rather than pursue the reinstate-

Figure 11. "Religious Service at Gatesville," undated, ca. early 1960s. (Photographs, ca. 1960–78, box 1999/087-11, Records, Texas Youth Commission. Courtesy of the Texas State Library and Archives Commission.)

ment of community programs. Overcrowding at Gatesville had already reached crisis levels, forcing the daily release of at least two boys, regardless of their progress toward rehabilitation, to compensate for new admissions, which averaged two each day. This "revolving-door" tactic failed to stem the tide; although the typical stay dropped from fourteen to nine months during this period, the facility's average daily population exceeded capacity by at least two hundred.[102] Therefore, Turman argued that the TSYDC "could not expect any appreciable decrease in commitments" and should plan accordingly.[103]

The legislature concurred, refusing once again to fund a TSYDC budgetary request for community work, this time for thirty juvenile parole officers. Commenting on the legislature's rejection, board member Weldon Hart, chairman of the Texas Employment Commission, noted that the TSYDC had lost its popular mandate for community-based work in the face of steadily rising juvenile crime rates: "Much of the original enthusiasm and public interest had been lost."[104] In Austin, some suggested "doing away" with the TSYDC and placing the training schools under the authority of either the Department of Welfare or the Department of Corrections. As high-level staff either saw their positions eliminated or resigned to take jobs elsewhere, Turman's role in the agency grew. By 1956, Turman had taken on the additional position of director of institutions, putting him atop both of the major divisions within the TSYDC. That same year, Turman completed his doctoral studies in clinical psychology, cementing his professional as well as bureaucratic authority.[105] At the end of 1956, the TSYDC named Turman "executive director" to represent the agency to an increasingly hostile legislature, which was due to consider the TSYDC's future in the upcoming spring session. A measure of Turman's political savvy came in the conditions he demanded in order to accept leadership of the TSYDC:

> He thanked the Council for their consideration and confidence but stated that since he was well aware of the responsibilities and intense pressures that the job entailed, he could only accept the position with the complete confidence and cooperation of the Council. He indicated that any action on his part in this capacity would be as the representative of each Council member individually as well as the Council collectively. He stated that he could not accept these responsibilities without unanimous cooperation, confidence and support of the Council, as well as the superintendents, and that if they did not place full confidence in his ability and integrity, that he would be unable to accept the position they had offered.[106]

In January 1957, the TSYDC sponsored a policy conference on juvenile delinquency in Austin. Out of that meeting came a proposal to reorganize the TSYDC as an independent agency in charge of the three juvenile training schools and three institutions for dependent children in Waco, Austin, and Corsicana. By April, the legislature and Governor Price Daniel had endorsed the idea. When the new Texas Youth Council (TYC) began work that fall, Turman was the consensus choice for executive director. With a board of directors that had been reduced from six to three and met less frequently, Turman wielded far more power than his predecessors in the 1950s. One of his first actions was to continue a "get tough" effort he had begun behind the scenes within the TSYDC. "Certain juveniles have taken advantage of the law," he had argued previously, "escaped punishment, and flaunted the juvenile law in the faces of law enforcement officers . . . with the knowledge that they could not be prosecuted as adults."[107] At Turman's urging, the TSYDC had recommended that the legislature make it easier to transfer older juvenile offenders to adult court.

This argument found a willing audience due to a rash of violent juvenile crimes. The most dramatic incident took place on Christmas night in 1957, when four Gatesville parolees joyriding in a stolen car shot and killed a fifteen-year-old teenager named Jay Evans in his own front yard, in the upscale West University Place neighborhood of Houston. The assailants in this drive-by shooting, ranging in age from sixteen to eighteen, had a combined record of seventy-four arrests. Their leader, Stuart "Sandy" Lumpkin, whose father worked as a superintendent at an oil drilling and refinery equipment company, had stopped the car when he thought he had heard Evans shout an insult at him. According to one eyewitness, Lumpkin walked up to Evans and shot him three times in the forehead at close range, then fled. The next night, Lumpkin phoned in to a radio broadcast to complain about a news announcer who had referred to the killers as "a pack of rats." Within hours, Lumpkin had confessed the crime to his father, and the four boys had surrendered to police. One Houston county judge called for lowering the age at which a juvenile could be tried as an adult from seventeen to fifteen. Meanwhile, the dead boy's parents organized the West University Place Committee to Assist in the Elimination of Juvenile Crime, warning that "any family's child, even yours" could be a victim of "teen-ager terrorism." Within weeks, the Houston parent's group issued a "blueprint" that recommended trying violent juvenile offenders in criminal courts and building more maximum-security training schools. The plan was circulated to twenty-five city mayors, all the state's district judges, members of the legislature, and the governor.[108] Parents' groups, who once had championed greater protections for delinquent youth, now led the charge for tougher punishments in order to safeguard their own children from what they perceived as a more violent and street-hardened generation.

For the TYC, a waiver provision allowing juvenile courts to transfer certain cases to criminal court promised to alleviate the overcrowding problem at Gatesville. But it also offered an opportunity to reverse years of budgetary neglect. Thus, in the midst of the latest cycle of outrage over juvenile delinquency, TYC director Turman urged the construction of "an interim reformatory" for older juvenile offenders. In a major speech to a convention of state judges and law enforcement officers, Turman described these offenders as inhabiting a "twilight zone between adolescence and complete adulthood."[109] Endorsing the Houston parent's group blueprint, Turman called for the expanded certification of adolescents to adult court. "In some instances," he suggested, juvenile offenders were "overprotected . . . at the expense of society."[110]

This view seemed to be confirmed in the eyes of many observers by the brutal murder of a Gatesville guard in August 1961. A staged fight lured the victim, forty-three-year-old Billy Malone, a retired air force mechanic, into the sleeping area of a dormitory around midnight. Nine boys attacked Malone, beating him to death with a baseball bat before fleeing the facility. An uproar ensued, led by local attorney and longtime Gatesville defender Harry Flentge, who blamed

Figure 12. Exterior photo of Mountain View during construction, 1962. (Photographs, ca. 1960–78, box 1999/087-11, Records, Texas Youth Commission. Archives and Information Services Division, Texas State Library and Archives Commission.)

"theory-happy psychologists" who ran the training schools by "remote-control" from Austin. To mollify critics, the legislature eagerly appropriated over $2.5 million for a youth prison that far exceeded the funds it had been willing to approve for smaller, community-based programs a few years earlier. This new facility, the Mountain View State School for Boys, would "be surrounded by a heavy double fence, barbed-wire topped" (figure 12).[111]

The Contours of Failed Reform

Rarely has a social reform effort started with as much promise and ended as dismally as the Texas State Youth Development Council and its successor, the Texas Youth Council, in the 1950s. An agency launched from a campaign to reduce sharply the use of large, prisonlike institutions became the leading advocate for the construction of ever-larger, more secure facilities that resembled prisons even more than had their predecessors. A public mobilized behind the extension of protected childhood and adolescence to some previously excluded groups gave way to a fearful clamor for tougher sanctions against juvenile offenders increasingly portrayed as quasi-adult "others" in public discourse. However, this episode represented much more than merely the latest swing of the pendulum in the political history of juvenile justice. It reflected fundamental social, cultural, and political changes that can be explained only partially by the story told in this chapter. We have seen that the reform movement had fatal flaws that planted the seeds of its own undoing. By seeking to exclude the "difficult" cases from its conception of the typical juvenile delinquent, the TSYDC made it impossible to rally public sympathy for the youth who increasingly came to dominate its inmate population. Stigmatizing its African American, and to a lesser extent Mexican American, juvenile inmates as uniformly incapable of rehabilitation prevented the agency from pursuing policies to assist those groups and thus left it ill equipped to deal with their exploding numbers by the end of the decade. By marginalizing key local constituencies from its decision making, the TSYDC fatally sabotaged its ability to pressure the legislature for budgetary support—a self-inflicted wound that rendered an already difficult task practically impossible. Ultimately, the TSYDC gained as an agency only when its director, James Turman, became a leading spokesperson for a "get-tough" campaign that violated many of the stated ideals on which the agency had been founded.

The other side of this story can only be told at the local level, where many of the broad changes charted in this chapter were lived by ordinary citizens, and where the policies argued about in the legislature and the media were put into practice. In the next chapter, we return to Houston, where dramatic shifts in demographic, residential, political, and economic patterns had major consequences for social thought and policy on juvenile delinquency. As we shall also see, the rollback of progress at the TSYDC resulted in innovation being left to local jurisdictions, which were not always uniformly in favor of tougher sanctions.

FIVE

"Hard to Reach"

The Politics of Delinquency Prevention in Postwar Houston

On the afternoon of December 6, 1956, representatives from Houston's juvenile court met with the TSYDC board in Austin. It was a moment of crisis for the TSYDC. Several of its key administrative personnel had resigned in recent months, while the Gatesville superintendent, Herman Sapier, had asked to be relieved of his duties. Much of the discussion that morning had revolved around a proposal in the legislature to shutter the agency permanently. The board had voted to make James Turman the new executive director of the TSYDC to better represent the agency before the legislature. Turman had accepted the board's unanimous vote only on the condition that he receive its "total support" at all times, a demand that was put to an immediate test by the Houston delegation. Led by juvenile court judge J. W. Mills and chief juvenile probation officer Paul Irick, the Houston group was there to share news of their recent creation of the state's first domestic relations court and their expansion of juvenile probation services. They also wanted to know what the TSYDC's future plans were, given the statewide rise in juvenile crime. Mills made clear that he was no admirer of the TSYDC's move toward large institutions; he had been "disturbed" at having to commit a child recently to TSYDC custody for an indeterminate period. He asserted that the TSYDC should "decentralize" the training schools and locate smaller facilities near large cities, such as Houston, in partnership with city governments. For good measure, he excoriated the idea of lowering the age at which a juvenile could be tried as an adult—an idea Turman had championed in recent TSYDC board meetings and would soon promote publicly—as "a big mistake." Turman blandly rebutted this assertion by citing "pressure in some areas to revise juvenile laws" and rejected Mills's suggestion about regional facilities as too expensive. The meeting ended cordially but with little having been accomplished.[1]

However, this episode was noteworthy for what it revealed about the lack of relationship between the TSYDC and local jurisdictions and the distinct perspectives fostered by that widening gulf. As we have seen, the rise of community-based child welfare, recreation and mental health services in the 1920s, 1930s, and 1940s had helped nurture demand for reform in the statewide administration of juvenile justice, which in turn contributed to the creation of the TSYDC. When budgetary restrictions and internal ideological shifts led the TSYDC to retreat from its short-lived work with local reformers, those groups were forced to seek support elsewhere for new policies, programs, and innovations. This chapter focuses on Houston, picking up where chapter 2 left off chronologically in the early 1950s, just as the TSYDC was fading from the local scene. It explores the impact of rapid growth, suburbanization, and racial and ethnic conflict on the politics of juvenile delinquency in the state's largest—and by 1960, the nation's fifth largest—metropolitan area.

The most notable local campaign against juvenile delinquency received sponsorship not from the TSYDC but from the federal government. Inaugurated in 1962, Houston Action for Youth (HAY) was funded initially by the President's Committee on Juvenile Delinquency and Youth Crime and later under the Community Action Program of the War on Poverty. As we shall see, it was bedeviled by some of the same types of representational issues that had surfaced during the TSYDC's early media campaigns. Although a disproportionate number of youth in Houston's juvenile justice system were African American and Mexican American, HAY chose to portray the problem of juvenile delinquency as largely white, middle-class, and psychological in orientation. Once HAY began working with actual at-risk youth in some of Houston's roughest areas, however, the agency moved to embrace the theory of the "culture of poverty," which had its own problems. Overall, Houston's reformers, while flawed in ways that echoed the TSYDC's shortcomings, could not escape a confrontation with social, economic, and political root causes for delinquency that had gone ignored at the state level through much of the postwar era. In some instances, even well-meaning reform efforts echoed the TSYDC's practice of implicitly or overtly constructing two categories of youth: irredeemable quasi adults, framed in "cultural" and behaviorist terms; and less dangerous teenagers deserving of protection and forgiveness.

"Just Where Do We Lose Hold on Our Boys?"

The broad context for Houston's response to postwar delinquency was the city's rapid growth, by every measure, and the political struggles this growth touched off over the allocation of social services. As a major port city and home to oil and petrochemical industries, Houston became a center for defense plants and military bases. Job-seeking migrants flooded Houston during the war, to the tune of over ten thousand a month, according to the Texas office of the U.S. Census.[2] The city's rapid growth continued unabated after the war; between 1940 and 1960, Houston moved from twentieth to fifth on the Census Bureau's list of largest Standard Metropolitan Statistical Areas. Twice the city doubled its size through the annexation of burgeoning suburbs, in 1949 and 1956. Houston's physical expansion was not matched by a sea change in the attitudes of its political leadership toward social services. Faced with housing shortages, city fathers blocked public housing projects; enamored with unrestricted growth, they abhorred zoning as "socialistic"; suspicious of tax-financed social services, they merely tolerated private agencies dependent on inadequate allowances from local charities; saddled with one of the nation's highest murder rates, they steadfastly maintained the smallest police force of any big city in the nation.[3] If, as local journalist George Fuermann once noted, Houston represented an updated version of frontier capitalism, its underbelly revealed stark disparities between rich and poor. The "big rich" resided in exclusive subdivisions such as the tony River Oaks, while a largely nonwhite underclass languished in ramshackle industrial neighborhoods deserted long ago by "white ethnics" for the greener pastures of planned subdivisions.[4]

Competing with laissez-faire ideology for sway over public policy was a broader notion of the common good, which urban historian Robert Fairbanks describes as the idea of "the city as a whole."[5] In his study of public housing in Dallas, Houston, and San Antonio, Fairbanks argues that during the 1930s, urban reformers convinced skeptical publics of the interconnectedness of neighborhoods. They portrayed social ills such as delinquency and crime as contagions easily spread across the city and insisted that public housing was one of many infrastructural improvements that could halt such "diseases" in their tracks. In this spirit, the Houston Housing Authority was created in 1938 with the support of both the city council and the mayor's office. It completed four housing projects before running into tough opposition after the war. Realtors and builders led a campaign that resulted in a 1951 ordinance effectively halting any further public housing. According to Fairbanks, this action marked the redefinition of the city's traditional mission, replacing a shared social good with an emphasis on individual and group rights in the 1950s.

These broad changes formed the major themes of a city-sponsored investigation into the causes of juvenile delinquency in 1954. The report was commissioned by Mayor Roy Hofheinz, the city's once-celebrated juvenile court judge, who had won election the previous year. The mayor's Juvenile Delinquency and Crime Commission was strongly influenced by the ongoing inquiry at the national level by the United States Senate.[6] Its report decried the influences of popular culture and illicit drugs, echoing the national outcry over the "seduction of the innocent" by unscrupulous media moguls and drug peddlers. However, it also placed substantial blame on rapid, unplanned suburbanization, a process that was especially pronounced in Harris County. Indeed, the report's three major sources of information—the Harris County Juvenile Probation Department, the Crime Prevention Division of the Houston Police Department, and the Houston Independent School District—each were grappling with dramatically expanded geographic coverage that made data gathering extremely difficult. With a growing overall population, the report predictably documented an increase in juvenile crime. However, it found that the bulk stemmed from nonviolent and status offenses of younger boys aged thirteen to fifteen who had recently moved to the suburbs.[7] Indeed, this age group accounted for 80 percent of all delinquent boys and 64 percent of all girls referred to the Juvenile Probation Department. Similarly, while the number of recidivists reported by the Crime Prevention Division had remained static in the prior five-year period, first offenders had increased by 87 percent, indicating a rise in less serious rather than "hard-core" cases. The report concluded by admonishing "a crisis psychology in the area of delinquency . . . that involves scaring ourselves with specters . . . of a generation of drug addicts and immoral youths."[8] Statistics were deceptive and unclear, it warned, and should instead bolster "community sanity." According to the report, Houston's delinquency problem had broadened along with its population growth but had not hardened into serious youth crime.

To commission member Franklin Harbach, the director of the Houston Settlement Association, the new suburbs were just as "disorganized" as inner-city areas and thus provided breeding grounds for a different brand of "hard-to-reach," if more affluent, teenagers.[9] "The movability [sic] of people," he wrote to Texas senator Lyndon B. Johnson, represented "one of the major problems of this generation."[10] Harbach's concerns echoed themes of suburban isolation and alienation often explored in the popular literature of the 1950s. According to David Riesman, author of the influential study *The Lonely Crowd* (1950), suburban youth were far more likely to grow up unmoored from the traditions once reinforced in tight-knit urban communities. More susceptible to the influence of peers or popular culture, middle-class teenagers suffered from an "other direction" that caused alienation but rarely resulted in a criminal career—a view shared by many of Riesman's contemporaries as well as much of Houston's political leadership, which in any case was not eager to spend money on the problem.[11]

In response to the commission's findings, the Houston Settlement Association mounted a major overhaul to its traditional mission, renaming itself the Neighborhood Centers Association of Houston and Harris County (NCA). From its central headquarters in Ripley House, a settlement opened in Houston's historically impoverished East End in 1938, the NCA operated youth recreation and vocational programs in seven different locations ranging from southeast Houston into the

Figure 13. "Teen-Age Dance at Pasadena, 1950s." The lack of community felt by the parents of suburban children and teenagers helped expand the traditional mission of the settlement house to include upwardly mobile families. (Corrine Tsanoff, *Neighborhood Doorways* [Houston, 1958]. Courtesy of Neighborhood Centers, Inc., and the Center for American History at the University of Texas at Austin.)

more prosperous suburban ring on the city's west side. The agency began to sponsor events for a more upscale clientele, hosting teenage dances (figure 13) reminiscent of the wartime teen canteens. While these sorts of supervised recreational programs had a long history, the new attention to suburban youth corresponded with the NCA's decision to jettison the word "settlement" from its name. Not only did this seemingly superficial change avoid any association with the stigma of charity; it also signaled the detachment of the NCA from its historic roots in neighborhood and community. By the 1950s, professional staff typically held advanced degrees and were less likely to inhabit the facility, which pioneers such as Jane Addams had once emphasized as crucial to developing interclass empathy and understanding. In its place, the NCA offered a more detached brand of professional service delivery that attracted national attention.[12] The NCA stood on the cutting edge of a national trend, as indicated by the election of its director, Franklin Harbach, to the presidency of the National Federation of Settlements in 1947. Founded in 1911, with Addams herself as its first president, the federation had served as the umbrella organization of the nation's settlement houses. Throughout the 1950s, the national organization looked to its Houston chapter as a model for fundraising, service delivery, and especially working with Latino populations, which were growing in northern cities. Ironically, given its growing interest in white suburban youth, the NCA expanded its reach beyond national as well as neighborhood borders due to its historic work with Latino communities. In cooperation with the U.S. Children's Bureau, the Pan-American Child Congress, and, later, the Agency for International Development, Harbach launched a training program that brought Latin American social work students to intern at settlement houses in Houston, San Antonio, and New Orleans.[13] "The southwestern city," enthused Harbach, echoing Chicago school sociologist Robert Park, offered "a natural laboratory for Anglo and Latin relationship."[14] It also provided lessons for coping with laissez-faire government. Lacking in publicly funded social services, these cities approximated "countries not so highly developed" far more than "the highly organized centers of the East and Middle West," forcing social workers to devise creative means of providing services.[15]

As the decade progressed, however, popular culture and suburban alienation proved to be inadequate explanations for the problem of juvenile crime. According to the FBI's authoritative *Uniform Crime Reports*, between 1955 and 1960 the nation's juvenile arrest rate rose by nearly 50 percent, double the increase of the juvenile-age population. Although nonviolent offenses comprised most of this growth, the numbers for violent crimes against persons such as murder, aggravated assault, and manslaughter had risen one and a half times more than the growth in eligible population.[16] In 1960 alone, offenders under the age of twenty-one comprised more than a third (37 percent) of all the nation's criminal homicide arrests. Similarly alarming figures obtained for the under twenty-one population in the categories of robbery (47 percent); assault (39 percent); and rape (42 percent). In Harris County, juvenile delinquency rose faster than the national average cited by the FBI. Between 1952 and 1962, the county's overall juvenile population doubled from 156,930 to 308,159. However, delinquency referrals to the juvenile probation department tripled from 2,030 to 6,010.[17]

An examination of the figures for 1962, the year that Houston launched its federally funded antidelinquency campaign, reveals that the rise in juvenile crime statistics was being driven by property crimes rather than status offenses, by male rather than female offenders, and by a disproportionate number of African American and Latino offenders (see table 10). Crimes against property, such as auto theft, burglary, and "other theft," represented more than half of all offenses, while status offenses such as truancy, runaway, and "ungovernability" counted for roughly one-

Table 10. Harris County delinquency referrals by age, race, sex, and offense, 1962

Offense	Boys				Girls				
	White	Black	Latino	Total	White	Black	Latino	Total	Overall
Auto theft	233	99	69	401	17	1	0	18	419
Robbery	39	28	13	80	4	4	3	11	91
Burglary	549	297	172	1,018	30	33	17	80	1,098
Other theft	530	353	197	1,080	62	66	24	152	1,232
Truancy	81	102	45	228	51	25	16	92	320
Runaway	202	113	75	390	262	156	112	530	920
Ungovernable	61	31	10	102	42	34	17	93	195
Sex offense	70	59	22	151	60	38	9	107	258
Drugs	6	0	3	9	9	9	0	18	27
Assault	78	64	27	169	9	21	6	36	205
Malicious mischief	154	66	52	272	20	17	1	38	310
Traffic violation	20	11	3	34	0	0	1	1	35
Arson	3	1	2	6	0	0	0	0	6
Other	318	170	141	629	132	79	54	265	894
All	2,185	1,290	765	4,240	640	463	256	1,359	5,599

Figures do not include 411 "pending referrals," which brings total to 6,010.
Source: Harris County Juvenile Probation Department, *Annual Report for 1962* (Houston, 1963).
Courtesy of the Houston Metropolitan Research Center, Houston Public Library.

fifth the total. Boys comprised four-fifths of all offenders and outnumbered girls in nearly every offense category with the exception of runaway and drug offenses (the latter a negligible number). Murder arrests went unrecorded, presumably because such cases were transferred to adult court, while the number of assaults registered on the lower end of the spectrum. The major differences across racial and ethnic lines came not with juvenile arrests but with disposition decisions after arrest (see tables 11 and 12). A higher percentage of whites (22.8) than Latinos (21.0) or blacks (18.1) were referred to juvenile court; however, the percentage of blacks committed to the TYC was nearly three times as high (33.0) as that of whites (12.0) and much higher than Latinos (20.0). Whites seems to have been far more likely (248) than blacks (84) or Latinos (64) to be placed on probation in the custody of their families. Even more starkly, once boys and girls are counted together, African Americans outnumbered the *combined* total of whites and Latinos (108 to 104) committed to a TYC training school.[18]

The rise in juvenile crime elicited two responses in the late 1950s and early 1960s. A broad debate erupted over the inadequacy of child welfare and delin-

Table 11. Harris County male delinquency referrals processed through juvenile court, 1962

	White	Black	Latino	Total
Total cases referred	499	233	161	893
Committed to Texas Youth Council	61	77	33	171
Committed to county	35	0	20	55
Probation to family	248	84	64	396
Cases pending	129	54	35	218
Foster placement	2	0	0	2
Petition denied	24	18	9	51

Figures do not include 229 boys already in Gatesville at beginning of year.
Source: Harris County Juvenile Probation Department, *Annual Report for 1962* (Houston, 1963).
Courtesy of the Houston Metropolitan Research Center, Houston Public Library.

Table 12. Harris County male delinquency referrals, dispositions to Texas Youth Council by race and ethnicity, 1962

	White	Black	Latino	Total
Total referrals	2,185	1,290	765	4,240
Total court cases	499	233	161	893
Percent referred to court	22.8	18.1	21.0	
Committed to Texas Youth Council	61	77	33	171
Percent committed to Texas Youth Council	12.0	33.0	20.0	

Source: Harris County Juvenile Probation Department, *Annual Report for 1962* (Houston, 1963).
Courtesy of the Houston Metropolitan Research Center, Houston Public Library.

quency prevention services. State and local chapters of the National Mental Health Association mounted a media campaign on behalf of expanded clinical services for children. A 1958 film, *Help Wanted*, portrayed children rotting in the county's dilapidated juvenile detention ward and called for the construction of a new facility.[19] The political climate was far from receptive to such proposals. While far-right "Minute Women" had seized control of the Houston school board, a regionally potent "anti–mental health movement" had fueled suspicion of child welfare services and guidance counseling programs, peaking in 1959 when school officials publicly burned psychological survey data gathered from Houston high school students. An even greater divide stood between child-serving professionals and the city's business class, whose members not only wielded political influence but also filled the boards of directors of virtually all of Houston's service agencies. In 1959, the Houston Community Council published the results of an opinion survey taken of both groups. It revealed that board members were twice as likely as their professional staffs to favor "punishment" over "treatment" for "childhood deviations" and to interpret delinquent behaviors as "causes" rather than "effects" of a child's social environment. Board members also preferred that social services be supported by private charity, while their staff voted for a greater use of tax-based funds. The two groups also disagreed over whether existing services were adequate, with business philanthropists asserting that they were, and child-serving professionals and paraprofessionals warning that they were not.[20]

Around this same time, a hue and cry went out for law enforcement and the courts to crack down on juvenile delinquency. In response to the Evans murder of December 1958 (discussed in chapter 4), a newly elected county judge proposed lowering the age at which juveniles could be tried as adults from seventeen to fifteen; two years later, in 1961, Houston district attorney Frank Briscoe "declared war" on juvenile offenders. The atmosphere increasingly appeared to be one of crisis. Newspaper articles regularly featured youth gangs such as the "Black Widows," whose members wore spider tattoos on their legs, or ran bold-faced headlines screaming of "teen-age terrorists" running wild in the city streets.[21] This public discourse contained a racial and ethnic subtext. Comprising a disproportionate percentage of delinquency referrals to TYC institutions, black and Latino youth came to symbolize the scourge of delinquency in the local media. At the same time, however, they also evoked the most explosive racial issue of the day: desegregation of the public schools and other public accommodations. In 1956, a group of black parents filed a lawsuit, *Delores Ross et al. v. Houston Independent School District* (HISD), seeking to end Houston's "dual system" of education, which violated the landmark ruling in *Brown v. Board of Education*. The case prompted a bitter struggle, exacerbated two years later when Hattie Mae White became the first African American to win election to the HISD School Board.[22] White voters responded by electing an openly segregationist mayor, Lewis Cutrer. Rather than quell the budding civil rights movement, however, Cutrer found himself forced to accommodate it. In March 1960, students from the all-black Texas Southern University (TSU) waged a successful campaign to integrate downtown Houston. Chartered by the Texas legislature in 1947, TSU had represented an effort to forestall court-ordered integration of the state's universities in advance of the *Sweatt v. Painter* case. Instead, ironically enough, the school became a launching pad for a series of direct action protests, including sit-ins and boycotts, which began the successful desegregation of drugstore lunch counters, department stores, restaurants, and theaters. Led in part by TSU student Curtis Graves, who would later win election to the Texas legislature, black students formed the Progressive Youth Association as an effective protest group in the mold of the Student Non-Violent Coordinating Committee (SNCC) in the early 1960s.[23] The struggle for racial equality, combined with the increased visibility of young black activists, formed a crucial, if never mentioned, backdrop for the shift to "get-tough" solutions to juvenile delinquency. The escalating rhetoric of law and order drowned out voices of caution, such as juvenile court judge Mills, who called for increased social services rather than stiffer punishments. Mills argued against "get tough shortcuts" and in favor of rehabilitation, warning that the court had the "unusual responsibility" of preserving the constitutional rights of youth who lacked legal counsel or a jury trial. Mills raised questions that undoubtedly made many Houstonians squirm:

> The real question is to know what can or should be done to provide legally and adequately for them. How can they be protected, properly guided and saved from further delinquency and possible adult crime, and at the same time safeguard the public welfare? These questions cannot be answered by merely handing out legal doses of justice. Not more than twenty per cent of all children before our Juvenile Court are repeaters. This percentage could be further reduced if our cases were better diagnosed and the court had adequate local facilities and/or better state resources to properly treat and rehabilitate many of the children long recognized as problems in schools and known for years to social and welfare agencies. The big gap continues to be between what we *know* about juvenile delinquency and dependency and what facilities are available to meet even the minimum needs of many court wards.[24]

He also decried that homes for dependent and neglected children "completely ignored" black and Latino youth, as well as "boys and girls who are too easily thought of as being retarded."[25] As a result, these children were more likely to be labeled delinquents rather than dependents and thus more likely to be placed in a TYC facility.

Even as city officials debated the funding of services and the proper response to juvenile delinquency, social agencies that worked directly with inner-city youth attempted to demonstrate what could be done with more funding. Leading the charge was the NCA's Rusk Settlement House, which had deep roots in one of the city's oldest Mexican American barrios and had helped promulgate the notion that delinquency represented a problem of shared social responsibility (see chapter 2). However, by the late 1950s, that outlook had begun to give way to one that isolated high-crime neighborhoods from the city as a whole and emphasized the role of local residents as both the causes and solutions to problems of poverty, unemployment, crime, and delinquency. Reformers who advocated delinquency prevention now viewed the problem as bounded within particular communities rather than as a shared responsibility across communities, which in turn promulgated different diagnoses and solutions. Emblematic of this new focus was Rusk's "Neighborhood

Development" initiative, launched in 1957. The program focused on the Clayton Homes public housing project, a series of low-rise apartment buildings built six years earlier. NCA director Harbach had advocated tirelessly for the construction of Clayton Homes as a replacement for the dilapidated shotgun shacks that had once dotted the area's landscape.[26]

In 1957, Rusk's Neighborhood Development program began providing child and youth services at Clayton Homes. The program began modestly with a recreation room and a child-care center, but the area's mostly "young families" refused to avail themselves of these seemingly much-needed services. An NCA study described local residents as "indifferent"; teenage boys told staff that their older relatives had warned them that the agency was affiliated with the police. Such reports exasperated longtime Rusk staffers because youth gangs were on the rise in the neighborhood; in contrast to past eras, even "good" boys who had been regular participants in Rusk's programs were drifting toward gang membership. Even some local residents agonized over the situation; as one youth counselor wondered, "Just where do we lose our hold on our boys as they grow into manhood?"[27] Its Clayton Homes program had underscored Rusk's declining success in preventing and controlling juvenile delinquency. Baffled and frustrated, Rusk staffers wondered what had changed. A 1959 NCA report identified a structural cause: the replacement of an upwardly mobile, urban working class with what would later have been called a permanent underclass.[28] Men who in earlier generations would have filled unskilled factory jobs found them foreclosed by automation; families who once might have looked forward to the good life now remained mired in "extremely complicated [and] long histories of sub-standard existence."[29] Rusk's social workers found families lacking "mental and physical health, employment, education, legal and protective services, housing, and vocational training." The report punctuated its findings with vivid anecdotes of working families headed by two parents or single mothers struggling with low incomes, long hours, and exhausting labor. Most of these families suffered from untreated mental and physical disorders whose causes ranged, in the report's view, from obvious health problems to ambiguously defined "cultural" or moral personal failings. At the same time, the report demonstrated Rusk's shifting focus on changing individual behaviors within its area population, rather than addressing the structural inequalities that produced bad schools, poor job opportunities, and inadequate social services. Emblematic of this new approach was the report's labeling of the Clayton Homes residents as "hard-to reach" or "multi-problem" families.[30]

To turn the project around, the NCA concluded it had to share power more equitably with the people it sought to help. In 1960, the NCA created the Clayton Homes Neighborhood Development Program Committee, whose members were elected by neighborhood residents. Energized by community participation, the Clayton Homes project began to make concrete accomplishments. A mass cleanup of the housing project's grounds led to successful petitions that the city's sanitation department provide pest-control services and halt the excessive dumping of garbage in the area. The NCA assisted with the opening of a locally owned grocery store; staged an enrollment drive for children in preschool, kindergarten, and elementary school; and sponsored adult students in night classes at the local high school.[31] Community leaders also hit upon a solution to "the problem of teenagers" during a polio vaccination drive that placed local youths in leadership positions. In March 1963, nearly two hundred teenagers voted to create a youth leadership committee, whose members attended a two-day "training retreat" sponsored by the NCA. Since parties, dances, and field trips were "hardly ever" offered at their local school, the youth committee organized their own under NCA auspices. A vocational program trained youth in typing, filing, auto repair, and other skills and placed several young residents in jobs. All this work led to what the county juvenile probation department praised as "a noticeable reduction" in referrals from the neighborhood.[32]

The Clayton Homes program also attracted the attention of national experts at the Ford Foundation and the National Institutes of Health, each of which were experimenting with community-based delinquency prevention projects.[33] Animating many of these endeavors was an abiding belief that delinquency arose from a "culture of poverty," a phrase popularized by the cultural anthropologist Oscar Lewis and the social activist Michael Harrington.[34] As the policy historian Alice O'Connor has noted, Lewis defined the culture of poverty largely in behavioral terms, arguing that exaggerated qualities such as "resignation, dependency, present-time orientation, lack of impulse control, weak ego structure, sexual confusion, and instant gratification" mired the poor in a "vicious cycle" spanning generations.[35] Indeed, Lewis served as the keynote speaker at an event attended by the Clayton Homes' residents, the Conference on Citizenship in a Democracy held at Texas A&M University in 1963.[36] The culture of poverty comported with the shift that had taken place in Houston, away from the "city as a whole" philosophy of shared community responsibility for delinquency and toward its isolation in specific neighborhoods. Even the well-intentioned Clayton Homes project found itself grappling with the notion that delinquency was one of many social ills arising from a deviant culture that existed separately from the middle-class mainstream of postwar America. While discrimination, inequality, and material poverty did not disappear completely from public discussions of delinquency in cities such as Houston, as they did in the public discourse surrounding the TYC, they did increasingly take a back seat to psychological and cultural explanations. These tensions were on full display when, in 1962, Houston became one of the first cities to win federal funding under President John F. Kennedy's Committee on Juvenile Delinquency and Youth Crime.

Houston Action for Youth: "Fighting Down" Delinquency

Established in February 1962, Houston Action for Youth represented the state's most significant response to urban juvenile delinquency since the TSYDC's early years. The city was one of ten to receive federal funds appropriated under the Juvenile Delinquency and Youth Offenses Control Act of 1961, under which thirty million dollars was administered by a committee whose members were appointed by President Kennedy. Led by former officials from the Ford Foundation's "gray areas" project, the president's committee awarded eighteen-month planning grants to applicants who had the political support of local elected officials and who promised to mount a "comprehensive" attack on juvenile delinquency. Statewide and local youth agencies had failed to stem delinquency, it was believed, because they too often had operated in isolation from one another. Therefore, the task of HAY and its counterparts in other American cities was to coordinate and thus more effectively deliver an array of youth services to the populations that needed them most. This endeavor was to focus on a specific neighborhood, labeled the "demonstration area," preferably one in which delinquency rates ran highest, which ideally would inspire emulation across the city and region. Under the committee's guidelines, HAY was expected to emphasize "community action" by enlisting community residents in diagnosing local needs, mapping out a response, and governing the program once it was under way.[37]

The president's committee also emphasized "opportunity theory," a term coined by the sociologists Richard Cloward and Lloyd Ohlin in their 1960 book *Delinquency and Opportunity*. The authors' experiences working with Mobilization for Youth had led them to dissent from the prevailing assumptions of 1950s' sociology, which held that urban delinquency represented either a form of pathology or a conscious opposition to middle-class values.[38] Instead, Cloward and Ohlin argued that delinquency stemmed from a lack of opportunity for licit social mobility. In their view, the postwar influx of African American and Puerto Rican youth, the flight of white ethnics and industrial jobs, and an increasingly unresponsive education system in New York City had combined to close off traditional pathways to breadwinning adult manhood. They called for a more responsive and comprehensive delivery of social services, especially vocational and job training for adolescent males, and increased partnerships with local businesses. Opportunity, they reasoned, would promulgate a sea change in the "ghetto culture" that encouraged gang membership, self-defeating behaviors, and "negative identities."[39]

This evolving theoretical perspective guided the thinking of the president's committee's Demonstration Review Panel, which selected Houston as the only southern city to receive a planning grant. Championing Houston's application was panel member Robert Sutherland, the director of the Hogg Foundation for Mental Health at the University of Texas. During World War II, Sutherland had advocated for expanded programs in children's mental health and delinquency prevention, using the language of shared social responsibility. However, in an article published in the March 1957 issue of *Federal Probation*, Sutherland had distinguished inner-city delinquency from more predictable adolescent misbehavior. Belonging to a "subculture . . . at odds with the larger community," urban "cultural" delinquents differed from their better-off "emotional" counterparts, who suffered from psychological disorders that were often treatable.[40] Thus, although delinquency existed in "some of the better neighborhoods," it included less serious, "reckless behavior opposed by family, church, and school." Sutherland's typologies subsequently appeared in two major studies of Texas youth sponsored by the Hogg Foundation: *Tomorrow's Parents* (1965), a survey of suburban high school youth in central Texas, and *Delinquency in Three Cultures* (1969), which compared delinquency among working-class white and Mexican American youth in San Antonio, and Mexican youth in Monterrey. These studies drew further distinctions between delinquents from different racial, ethnic, economic, and geographic backgrounds that also surfaced in HAY, which equated "cultural deprivation" with a lack of economic opportunity in Houston's poorest neighborhoods.[41]

HAY's proposal thus included all the standard points of emphasis for the president's committee: opportunity theory, the demonstration model, comprehensiveness, and community action. However, it also reflected unique challenges identified by the project's administrators, the University of Houston and the Community Council of Houston and Harris County. Chief among their concerns was a long-standing hostility among city leaders toward publicly funded social services, as noted earlier in this chapter. However, some forms of public persuasion had been successful; the 1958 film *Help Wanted* was credited in part with the construction of a new juvenile detention center in 1962, a lesson that was not lost on HAY, particularly its principal investigator, Richard Evans.[42] A professor of psychology at the University of Houston, Evans hosted a weekly program on the local public television station, one of the first of its kind in the nation. From the late 1950s into the 1970s, Evans interviewed several leading lights of child psychology on his program, including Erik Erikson and Kenneth Clark. As early as 1955, Evans had moderated televised panels that specifically discussed juvenile delinquency.[43] Based on his experiences with television, Evans devoted a substantial portion of HAY's initial $260,582 planning grant to a media campaign. Educating the public, Evans believed, was crucial to winning support for the kinds of comprehensive services that HAY planned to showcase in its demonstration area. In fact, so important was this public relations campaign that it antedated the selection of a demonstration area. Thus HAY's vision of an "all-out, comprehensive action program to fight down juvenile delinquency" included a significant attempt to shape public opinion on delinquency's causes and solutions, without offering specific plans of its own.[44]

To run the public relations campaign, Evans hired Jane Brandenberger, a spokesperson for the local United Fund, and Mary Ellen Goodman, a professor of cultural anthropology at the University of Houston. Goodman was a nationally known expert on race, education, and childhood. While completing her doctorate at Columbia University in the early 1950s, Goodman had researched the impact of school segregation on the self-esteem of white and black children. Her work had complemented the more famous "doll studies" conducted by Kenneth and Mamie Clark, part of a body of social psychological research in the postwar era that had attacked racial inequality for its emotional toll on children. Indeed, one of Goodman's former mentors, Otto Klineberg, praised her first study, *Race Awareness in Young Children* (1952), as "a classic investigation" that had "played a part in the Supreme Court's desegregation decision" in *Brown v. Board of Education*.[45] Goodman, it was expected, would bring a "child's-eye view" to the media campaign, while Brandenberger would assemble a multipronged package of television programs, radio spots, print advertisements, and a monthly newsletter mailed to agencies and professionals that served youth. Brandenberger enlisted the cooperation of practically every key social agency in the city, including the Houston Police Department, juvenile court judge J. W. Mills, and the Harris County school board.[46]

In December 1962, HAY launched a twelve-part television series titled *Target: Delinquency* to air in prime time on all three of Houston's commercial networks, as well as the public station housed at the University of Houston.[47] The university's drama program provided actors for the first three installments, which were docudramas based on the case files of the Harris County Juvenile Probation Department. In the first film, *The Lonely Ones*, viewers meet three teenagers from very distinct social backgrounds: "Jimmy Johnson," the lower-class white son of a single mother; "Susie Jamison," the wealthy daughter of an oil executive; and "Johnny Garcia," a "Latin-American" son of immigrants. The film begins with two brief addresses to the audience.[48] First, HAY principal investigator Evans warns that while the film is based on "true stories," delinquency is "far more complex than any single film could portray." He is followed by Houston congressman Albert Thomas, who advises that

Figure 14. Promotional still shot from *The Lonely Ones*. Caption: "Old friends . . . a stolen car . . . a bottle of booze . . . and trouble was back in Jim's life." (Sutherland [Robert L.] Papers. Courtesy of the Dolph Briscoe Center for American History, University of Texas at Austin.)

"only three percent" of local teenagers break the law, but "these eight thousand children cost you and me thousands of dollars every year." Taken together, these statements sought to assure viewers that their own teenagers were not part of the problem, much the way that the opening disclaimer to the controversial juvenile delinquency film *The Blackboard Jungle* had distanced its fictionalized inner-city vocational school from most American high schools. The genre of "juvenile delinquency films" that became popular in the late 1950s often featured similar disclaimers meant both to stave off criticisms of sensationalism and to reassure audiences that their own children were not delinquents.[49] In order to elicit compassion, *The Lonely Ones* first had to remind its viewers that delinquent youth were the exception rather than the rule—the "others" who may have looked and acted somewhat like middle-class teenagers but who were definitively not like them.

In the first act, a Houston probation officer narrates the story of "Jimmy," who is shown leading a group of teenagers on a drunken joyride in a stolen car (figure 14). Their erratic driving attracts the attention of the police; a car chase results in a crash that kills all of the passengers except Jimmy. A flashback explains how Jimmy

Figure 15. Film still from *The Lonely Ones*. Caption: "At the Texas Youth Council correctional institution in Gatesville, Texas, Jimmy went to school." (Sutherland [Robert L.] Papers. Courtesy of the Dolph Briscoe Center for American History, University of Texas at Austin.)

arrived at this moment. As a child, he had lived in the San Felipe Courts, a public housing project located in one of the poorest neighborhoods in the city (and in HAY's eventual demonstration area). But the film avoids lingering on Jimmy's poverty; instead, it focuses on his family situation. The head of Jimmy's household is a single mother with five children fathered by four different men. She has routinely paraded men in front of Jimmy; in one scene, she ushers a strange man into the bedroom while a troubled Jimmy looks on. Abruptly, the story jumps forward to a scene of Jimmy in juvenile court, the result, viewers are told by the narrator, of years of petty crime and underage drinking. Portraying himself, Harris County juvenile court judge J. W. Mills sentences Jimmy to the Gatesville School for Boys. Shot on location, the film portrays the notoriously overcrowded facility as a clean and orderly setting, where Jimmy finds in his shop teacher a fatherly mentor along the lines of *Rebel*'s Officer Roy (figure 15). After lavishing on Jimmy an unlikely level of individual attention, Gatesville paroles him to a "loving" foster family on a country ranch. Surely this type of setting, which child-saving reformers had held up as the ideal site of rehabilitation for delinquent youth for over a century, would nurture Jimmy's better angels. And indeed, Jimmy finds happiness in the form of "loving parents," a state of affairs that proves all too fleeting. Upon his return to school, Jimmy "immediately" falls in with "the wrong kind of friends." After an argument with his foster parents, Jimmy flees back to Houston, where the lure of petty crime is irresistible. Successive scenes depict Jimmy snatching a car, joyriding with his friends, stealing gasoline, and vandalizing property. As the story returns to the car crash, the camera lingers on the bloodied bodies of Jimmy's friends while the narrator laments his passengers' lost potential. He explains that Jimmy is the product of a "lifetime of deprivation," defined by his rebellion against "the lonely position." Jimmy's neglectful mother, not his material poverty, have doomed his prospects from the start, rendering it impossible for the school system, juvenile justice, or foster care to help him.

The "lonely condition" also plagues the next character, Susie, who is the illegitimate daughter of an alcoholic heiress and a deceased businessman. Neglected by her mother, Susie is sexually abused by her mother's second husband, a nightclub singer intent on hustling the family out of its inheritance. By the age of fifteen, Susie has "slowly turned into a wanton little creature" who is sexually precocious and emotionally unstable. In successive scenes, the film shows Susie picking a fight with another girl at school and later "dancing suggestively" with boys, while the narrator describes her as "a wild, sensual youngster on the surface" who has been "scarred" by her home life. Put off by Susie's "sudden twists in attitude," local service agencies like the YWCA throw up their hands; in any case, their assistance smacks too much of poverty for a child of wealth. "I'm no poor slob from the slums," Susie sneers at a YWCA staffer, "looking for a hand-out from you social workers." Without such help, however, Susie soon descends into addiction and prostitution and lands in a slum apartment with a junkie for a boyfriend. Susie's final destination is the county juvenile detention ward, where she is shown suffering through detoxification in a cell. The point is clear: Juvenile delinquency knows no boundaries of social class. Like Jimmy, Susie is a victim of parental abuse and neglect, exacerbated by the assumption that wealthy children do not need social services.

The film's final story features fifteen-year-old Johnny Garcia, who is introduced by the probation officer-narrator as his "first Latin-American case." Johnny's father, a widower, appears as a hard-working provider but poorly educated and overwhelmed by responsibility. Unlike Susie, Mr. Garcia eagerly accepts assistance in scenes showing a social worker from the Rusk Settlement House teaching him how to budget his meager income. Despite his poverty and lack of parental attention, Johnny's greatest challenge in the film is coping with "the plight of the Latin, who finds the cultural background and patterns of the Anglo-American quite varied and different from his own." Illustrating this struggle to "adjust" is a scene in which

Johnny picks a fight during a Little League baseball game. Against a backdrop of swinging fists and dust clouds, the narrator explains to viewers that Johnny is irrational, "hot-blooded," and physically small—a lethal combination. Although he is "good-hearted," Johnny suffers from a severe inferiority complex exacerbated by his inability to acculturate—a classic American immigration narrative tinged with worn stereotypes about Latinos. The long-standing association of Latino youth with gang activity in Houston frames Johnny's first serious crime, committed at the age of twelve. Johnny stabs a boy in a knife fight and is placed on probation for two years. At school, "patient teachers" seek not only to educate Johnny but to build up his "self-esteem," with little success. Where Jimmy falls in with a bad crowd, Johnny attracts it, even becoming "the brains" of a youth gang. "As angry with society as he had ever been," viewers are told, his new friends "rekindle[d] . . . his old fear and rage of being born underprivileged . . . [and] denied the love of his mother." In rapid-fire fashion, images of the boys committing all manner of petty crimes flash across the screen, concluding with the boys ransacking the rock-and-roll section of a record store.

Loud rock and roll music provides the soundtrack for Johnny's final act, which begins with Johnny and his friends getting drunk. When the conversation turns to jokes about Johnny's small size, he explodes in a "distorted fury" and launches a "swift and savage" knife attack. Consumed with rage, Johnny unwittingly kills not his main tormentor in the gang but his best friend, whose life expires as the music fades to the abrasive sound of a "scratching needle." As the scene fades to black, the narrator explains that Johnny has been "caught . . . not by the police . . . but by his own conscience." While the victim's body is carted off in the background, Johnny's probation officer learns by phone that he has committed suicide—a conclusion that further highlights the film's portrayal of Johnny as an "emotional delinquent" who suffers less from poverty or discrimination than from "maladjustment." The onus for Johnny's problems falls more on Johnny himself than on the adults and institutions that surround him.

The Lonely Ones borrows liberally from the emerging genre of teenage films, featuring three youthful protagonists who rebel against adult society. Like the teenagers in *Rebel without a Cause*, the film's delinquents suffer largely from poor or nonexistent parenting, and find understanding only from juvenile justice authorities. However, where popular films tended to grant agency to youth, *The Lonely Ones* portrays them in naturalistic fashion as hapless victims of their environment. Their respective rebellions appear predictable and self-destructive. With scarcely any dialogue allotted to the teenagers themselves, the film focuses less on the "delinquent's own story" than on parental failures. In *Rebel*, suburban middle-class youth "from good families" stand in for the typical juvenile delinquent; in *The Lonely Ones*, youth from various social classes share similar problems that lead to delinquent behavior. In their own distinctive ways, each film constructs an environment where class, gender, race, and ethnicity take a back seat to psychology. The lack of childhood self-esteem, which once had convinced the Supreme Court that segregated schools fostered feelings of inferiority in black children, here is used to explain the delinquent career of a Mexican American teenager from the barrio who, in real life, likely would have attended a segregated school and encountered individual discrimination on a regular basis. Even more striking is the complete absence of African American youth, the most overrepresented group in Harris County's juvenile court and probation statistics, as we have seen. Clearly, HAY's media campaign "whitened" delinquency, for reasons that were unclear. In Houston, a southern city with a long history of racial discrimination, segregation, and hostility to taxpayer-funded social services, such a strategy might have animated HAY's choices for *The Lonely Ones*.

In any case, the film provoked disagreement among HAY's top-level staff. Shortly before the film aired, Jane Brandenberger and Mary Ellen Goodman resigned, protesting its portrayal of delinquency as "too soft."[50] According to Goodman, she "had urged the project to deal with juvenile problems at various economic levels as well as in depressed and underprivileged areas—and to have the program presented to inspire a big community response as opposed to one [that] might merely be imposed on the community."[51] Although she never publicly clarified this objection, Goodman's last published work (she died in 1969), a study of Mexican American children and families in Houston, was suggestive. In it she employed the participant-observation method to describe a "child's-eye view" of life in the ghettos and barrios of Houston, suggesting that she took community perspectives more seriously than she felt the filmmakers had. Goodman rejected theories of "peer culture" and "the culture of poverty" as "self-fulfilling prophecies" generated by experts who took middle-class American models of family and childhood as universal norms.[52] Such a critique was only partially applicable to *The Lonely Ones*, which for all its flaws did highlight youth agency even as it downplayed the inner-city environment inhabited by most of Houston's at-risk and delinquent youth. Too often, as other critics have noted, antidelinquency and antipoverty projects emphasized behavior largely as the cause rather than the effect of the urban environment.[53] This phenomenon fed into existing narratives of juvenile delinquency, which had reduced causation to individual and family psychology in the previous decade, a tendency perpetuated in *The Lonely Ones*.

In the following weeks, HAY films presented a day in the life of a Harris County juvenile probation officer (*The Wasted Youth*), which focused on "school dropouts" and "their lack of job opportunities"; a biopic of a teenager's struggles with his caring but misunderstanding parents (*The World of Billy Joe*); and nine "white paper" programs that featured HAY's Richard Evans interviewing local experts, public officials, and community leaders. HAY later defended the investment in these films by claiming that they had moved public opinion significantly. In its first annual report, HAY published two opinion surveys that suggested the film series had moved public opinion favorably.[54] In the first survey, conducted before the film series had aired, "community leaders" overwhelmingly agreed that juvenile delinquency was a serious problem requiring far more prevention programs than the city had sponsored previously. Echoing those sentiments were five hundred respondents from the general public, over half of whom had watched at least one installment of the series. Nearly all (94 percent) viewed delinquency as "serious"; three-quarters (75 percent) believed it was being handled poorly; and a large majority (84 percent) favored a raise in taxes to pay for intervention programs. However, most respondents (90 percent) blamed "the family" rather than "poverty" as the main cause for delinquency and agreed on the need to restore "traditional family values, including discipline and even corporal punishment." While the same percentage supported job training and educational programs, the results suggested an ambiguous response at best, one that may have been encouraged by HAY's choice to highlight family dysfunction at the expense of socioeconomic inequalities in its vignettes of individual youth. Despite these potential warning signs, HAY touted *Target: Delinquency* as an overall success.

Underscoring the flaws of *Target: Delinquency* was HAY's later admission that the series bore "no specific relationship to the action program." Indeed, *The Lonely Ones* aired the very same month that HAY identified its demonstration area, a broad region just north of downtown Houston encompassing the Fourth, Fifth, and Sixth Wards. According to the 1960 U.S. Census, African Americans comprised just over half (51 percent) of the seventy-five thousand people who inhabited this "old city area," with whites and Latinos each making up about a quarter of the population.[55] The area's median income, educational attainment level, and quality of housing were in the lowest quarter of the city. Over a third of the area's teenagers had dropped out of school and were unemployed, helping to explain juvenile crime rates that were consistently the city's highest. In the face of such grim figures, HAY's first major report, published in January 1964, reflected more directly than the film series the influence of "culture of poverty" thinking. In explaining the problem of school dropouts, for instance, HAY primarily blamed parents for failing to encourage "studying and the value of education" and cited widespread "anti-school feelings" among families generally, spurred by distrust of "representatives of the school system."[56] Nowhere does it mention the legacy of racial segregation in Houston or the ongoing and quite bitter struggle to provide a modicum of equal resources to inner-city schools.[57] Similarly, HAY described the area as "disorganized" and "isolated from activities involving conventional norms."[58] According to HAY, "the area exhibit[ed] the classic social and psychological characteristics found in current descriptions of the culture of poverty such as social and economic deprivation; alienation from the dominant community, with accompanying attitudes of hostility, antagonism, defeatism, fear and distrust; and limited access to the opportunity system."[59]

The "hostility" identified by HAY developed into organized expressions of community discontent over the next two years, particularly in the majority-black neighborhoods of Houston's Fifth Ward. HAY narrowed its focus to this area as a consequence of its absorption into the federally funded Harris County Community Action Association (HCCAA) between 1965 and 1967. While administering Head Start, Job Corps, and Neighborhood Youth Corps programs, HAY increasingly found itself embroiled in conflicts between black residents and city authorities. By 1967, Texas Southern University had become the center of local protest and the local Black Power movement, a shift that mirrored changes in national civil rights organizations. Where TSU's students once had engaged in nonviolent protest to integrate public accommodations, they now embraced a more militant stance for black empowerment and radical social change. This was particularly in evidence in April 1967, when the Student Non-Violent Coordinating Committee came to Houston. At TSU, students fought with administrators for recognition of a chapter of the national "Friends of SNCC" as an official campus organization. Meanwhile, outspoken SNCC leader Stokely Carmichael addressed a large crowd at the nearby University of Houston.[60] The heightened presence of SNCC helped fuel a series of protests. TSU students blockaded Wheeler Avenue, the main thoroughfare that bisected the campus, to pressure the school to close the road to through traffic. In May, the drowning of a small child in a landfill located in the nearby Sunnyside neighborhood had galvanized local anger over the placement of city dump sites in black areas. Around that time, the expulsion of a group of black students for fighting with whites at a local middle school touched off a round of protests over unequal treatment.

However, residents of the Fifth Ward reserved their greatest anger for the nearly all-white Houston Police Department. In addition to failing to patrol black neighborhoods or recruit black officers adequately, the department had a checkered history of police brutality. Tensions had run so high that the regional Office of Economic Opportunity (OEO) office had organized its entire antipoverty campaign in Houston around the goal of preventing urban violence. Nonetheless, the situation erupted into tragedy on the night of May 16, 1967, when Houston police engaged in a shootout with students on the TSU campus. Police fired several thousand rounds of ammunition into two men's dormitories, but the only person they hit was one of their own, rookie officer Louis Kuba, who was killed by a ricocheting bullet. In the aftermath, five hundred students were arrested, five of whom were charged with Kuba's murder.[61] The incident aroused intense public anger as well as national attention. Bill Elliott, the former juvenile court judge who had called for tougher sentencing laws, charged "outside agitators" with planning the "riot" at TSU. Similar calls for the restoration of "law and order" in Houston came from Mayor Louis Welch, local congressman George Bush, and Texas governor John Connally.[62] However, they competed with others who viewed the TSU incident through the lenses of generational conflict and youthful immaturity. In a lengthy feature piece, *Newsweek* magazine likened the firefight to the race riots that were sweeping through American cities at the time. Dubbing it "a Happening of the Stokely Generation," the article quoted several students who "wished they had" fired on the police.[63]

More emphatic on this score were the conclusions of Blair Justice, a sociologist and special advisor to Mayor Welch on race relations. Based on surveys of black high school and college students taken before and after the TSU incident, Justice, echoing Eriksonian adolescent psychiatry, argued that local African American youth had embraced "negative identities" as emotional compensation for their frustration with persistent inequality. In Justice's view, these identities could be reduced to two general archetypes: "the black revolutionary," a leadership figure who sublimated his insecurity over competing with better-educated whites into Black Power slogans, and "the rebel without a cause," a follower who engaged in mob action as an outlet for generalized frustration and cheap thrills.[64] Based in part on Justice's conclusions, the HCCAA in summer 1967 launched "Project Go," a campaign to enlist local militants in antipoverty efforts. However, when it was discovered that two of those militants, Trazewell Franklin and Floyd Nichols, were among the five TSU students indicted in the Kuba shooting, the HCCAA became the object of intense criticism. That November, as part of its inquiry into urban violence, the Senate Permanent Subcommittee on Investigations held hearings on the TSU affair that put the HCCAA on the defensive. Soon after, OEO officials forced the HCCAA to close down Project Go; by the early 1970s, the HCCAA had retreated into less controversial youth vocational and educational programs.[65] By that time, what had begun as a campaign to curb delinquency nearly a decade earlier had expanded into a broad-based antipoverty and civil rights endeavor that bore little relationship to concerns about the root causes of inner-city delinquency or the disproportionate commitment of nonwhite youth to the TYC.

A Widening Gulf

Houston's postwar struggles with juvenile delinquency were significant in that it was Texas's largest city, with its largest youth population. With a juvenile crime rate that rose faster than the national average, Houston found itself committing more youth to TSYDC custody than any other Texas city. This phenomenon was driven largely by disproportionate rates of commitment for African American and Latino youth, who experienced poverty at much higher frequencies than white youth. Hampered by its legacy of racial segregation, discrimination, and hostility to tax-supported social services, Houston nevertheless managed to nurture some experimentation with community-based delinquency prevention. However, the character of prevention was changing in the 1950s, as social reformers and experts increasingly approached impoverished urban areas from psychological and anthropological perspectives, which caused them initially to objectify rather than empathize with the people they purported to help. In the Clayton Homes case, reformers sought to empower youth and families from a working-class and poor Latino community to improve their own neighborhood and, in the process, curb delinquency and gang membership. By contrast, Houston Action for Youth attempted to mobilize broad public support for a vaguely defined antidelinquency campaign that tended to misrepresent the typical juvenile delinquent in Houston. Once HAY confronted a more representative sample of at-risk youth in its demonstration area, it resorted to "culture of poverty" interpretations that stigmatized inner-city populations as members of a deviant subculture who were largely to blame for their own troubles.

The end of HAY's story reflected a national pattern in the 1960s that has received substantial attention from historians. In the usual telling, the federal War on Poverty broadened the scope of the community-based delinquency prevention programs launched at the beginning of the decade. The result was social and political polarization, often pitting white-dominated city governments against African American and Latino communities. This strife has been widely credited with provoking a backlash that included expansion of prisons, police crackdowns on inner-city neighborhoods, and a reduction in federal and state social welfare programs. However, HAY and similar programs also promoted community-based prevention and rehabilitation models that visibly though indirectly contradicted the TYC's institutional model. Moreover, as we shall see in chapter 6, because of their focus on inner-city youth, community programs not only overlapped with civil rights activism but also drew attention to the growing racial and ethnic disparities in the administration of juvenile justice. The gulf was widening between the TYC's own imperatives for expanded incarceration and local communities increasingly concerned about not only the welfare but also the rights of children and youth. While national experts and urban reformers promoted alternatives to incarceration for juvenile offenders and warned of grave violations of their civil rights, the TYC mounted a major campaign to expand its institutional capacity.

SIX

Circling the Wagons
The Struggle over the Texas Youth Council, 1965–1971

On March 22, 1961, Bert Kruger Smith, a consultant with the Hogg Foundation for Mental Health at the University of Texas, took a guided tour of the Gatesville State Schools for Boys training school complex.[1] To her own surprise, Smith was generally impressed with what she saw. Although overcrowding remained a problem, seven distinct units housed and schooled boy inmates according to age, behavior, and intelligence. Modern-looking buildings with sparkling clean interiors outnumbered the (still in use) crumbling wood and brick structures built in the previous century. Teachers, guards, and administrators appeared more patient and competent than Gatesville's prior reputation would have suggested. Daily life for the boy inmates observed by Smith seemed to be "the opposite" of the "extreme regimentation and social deprivation" that had characterized Gatesville since its inception. Most of the individual inmates encountered by Smith exhibited a disciplined but self-assured demeanor. Indeed, the scene's tidiness was so complete that it aroused Smith's suspicion; she was well aware that in the past, officials had orchestrated similar tours for prominent "outsiders" as a means of forestalling public criticism. Therefore, Smith speculated about what she might have been missing. After watching a classroom of seventh graders perform at only about a "third grade" level of competence, Smith wondered about the quality of schooling. Smith also noted that her tour had not included the dormitories "where the 'others' live, the bad boys and the Negroes," those who comprised a plurality of Gatesville's inmates. Smith departed Gatesville still uncertain about the extent to which the TYC had improved the substance, and not merely the appearance, of its rehabilitation program.

Smith's lingering doubts echoed those of Weldon Brewer, a TYC board member and her tour guide that day. Behind the scenes, Brewer had been a lone dissenter from the TYC's expansion of secure institutions. Instead, Brewer advocated a "dynamic" program that emphasized community-based prevention and rehabilitation—a return to the agency's founding rhetoric, never truly put into practice.[2] In a measure of how completely the TYC had abandoned its original mission, Brewer explicitly invoked not the agency's recent history but the national discovery of inner-city poverty. Incarceration in a training school, he warned, failed to address the "economic deprivation" of the urban areas from which most TYC commitments came and to which they most likely would return.[3]

As it had in prior periods, the renewed skepticism about juvenile justice stemmed from the desire to protect youth from prisonlike conditions. Critics in the 1960s, however, expanded substantially on their predecessors' criticisms. They argued that the juvenile court, the detention center, and the training school undermined adolescent "adjustment" to a normal environment because they constituted abnormal environments themselves. Would-be delinquents adjusted to life in the "total institution," which did not equip them for life in the outside world. Moreover, reformers of the 1960s were more willing to view the youth who fell within the purview of juvenile justice by the same social and cultural standards applied to "normal" teenagers. In this approach, they differed from their predecessors in important ways. First, these reformers wished to extend the protections of adolescent status to actual juvenile inmates rather than fictional images devised for public consumption. Rather than frame delinquent and at-risk youth as prematurely adult criminals or simply omit them from public discussion altogether, youth advocates of the 1960s insisted on portraying them, too, as misguided, immature, and impressionable. If adolescence was truly a universal life stage, then all children were entitled to experience it equally, along with the same generous margin of error that often was extended to more-privileged youth. Second, influenced by the youth culture, campus uprisings, and social movements of the decade, their conception of adolescent identity formation envisioned more autonomy and agency for youth than had the early postwar generation of reformers. To some critics, youth were not merely helpless victims to be defended against state abuse; they were also citizens with individual rights to be upheld. The language of rights, so prevalent in the period, charged a new effort to reform juvenile justice. Nationally, campaigns against child abuse, due process violations in juvenile courts, and imprisonment for status offenses dovetailed with compelling revelations of abused inmates in Texas's training schools. The TYC responded at it always had, by tarring their critics as naive, ideological, or self-interested. Unbeknown to the agency, the ensuing struggle would come to represent the last gasp of a dying regime.

"All I Learned Was How to Hate"

On August 27, 1964, TYC director James A. Turman sounded a dire warning before the budget committee of the Texas House of Representatives: a rising tide of delinquency threatened to engulf the state's still badly overcrowded training schools.

In large part, Turman attributed the problem to relaxed moral strictures toward youthful misbehavior. "With nudity becoming fashionable, alcohol being accepted, and obscenity and lewd entertainment being permitted by adults," impressionable teenagers were being coddled, led astray, and ultimately getting arrested in greater numbers.[4] The TYC lacked the resources to handle the resulting increase in delinquency referrals. Turman requested and received a biennial budget of over eighteen million dollars, nearly double that of the previous biennium and a sixfold increase over operating expenses in 1957, the year that the TYC was reconstituted as an independent agency. The increased funds would allow the TYC to expand its institutional capacity and its fledgling juvenile parole program, inaugurated in 1961, which Turman contended had already helped lower recidivism rates, despite employing only fourteen officers who had supervised 1,139 parolees during the previous year.[5] The record on the TYC's juvenile parole program is spotty. It seems that the legislature approved it due to lobbying from local jurisdictions as well as the Texas chapter of the National Council on Crime and Delinquency, but it remained an underdeveloped part of the TYC's overall program throughout the decade.[6] To peruse the minutes of the TYC board in the early 1960s is to be reminded of the Texas Board of Control reports from the 1920s and 1930s: short, dry, and preoccupied with the minutiae of quarterly budgets and construction costs for new facilities. There was very little recorded discussion of juveniles, treatment issues, or the overall health of the program.

However, the fiscal year beginning in summer 1963 had not been a good one for the TYC. It began with the forced resignation of Gatesville superintendent O. F. Perry in July 1963, following the discovery that Perry had been permitting widespread use of corporal punishment. A "slow-moving, affable ex-school teacher, administrator, and coach," Perry had been popular with local citizens, who denounced the TYC for his ouster, accusing the agency of running Gatesville by "remote control."[7] A more serious protest erupted a few months later, when former employees charged the TYC with running Gatesville "like a concentration camp."[8] In May 1964, a group of parents and former staff members mailed written complaints to President Lyndon B. Johnson, Attorney General Robert F. Kennedy, and Governor John Connally, alleging that inmates suffered regularly from physical abuse, including the use of dogs, and routine denial of medical care. TYC board members and a detail of Texas Rangers visited Gatesville but "failed to find any evidence" to support the charges.[9] For the first time, the federal government intervened, sending FBI agents to investigate Gatesville, also, however, to no avail. Thus, the TYC was under assault from various directions at the time of its "whopping" budget request. In a lengthy article, the *Dallas Morning News* revealed the contents of a confidential employee questionnaire commissioned by the Texas State Auditor's Office. Staff complained that the TYC was ignorant of "the actual problems facing employees," and that Gatesville "simply stored boys out there with no thought of educating, rehabilitating or developing a work habit for them."[10] Some legislators, led by Representatives David Crews of Conroe and Ben Barnes of DeLeon, proposed transferring authority over the training schools to the Texas Department of Corrections, which recently had opened a much-touted unit for "young first offenders." However, Turman, with the support of Gatesville's legislative delegation, beat back all of the TYC's critics. The agency maintained its authority over the training schools and received funding to expand them further.

Although these attacks brought no immediate consequences, they reinforced the agency's existing insularity against outside criticism. In some respects, this tendency was a holdover from the pre-TYC era. But it reached new heights thanks in large part to Turman himself, who approved policies clearly intended to discourage public access to the training schools. In addition to the aforementioned limits on researchers and reporters, Turman had coauthored an intake policy that was openly contemptuous of inmates' families—in direct contravention to virtually all the advice given the TYC by national experts in its formative years, but very much in keeping with official hostility to "meddling" families and attorneys in the pre-TYC era. Caseworkers were instructed to meet with parents and give "a frank but objective explanation of any faulty family patterns or relationships which [had] led to the present difficulties."[11] Sharp restrictions on parental visits and communications stemmed from a belief that they hampered an inmate's rehabilitation:

> Another common error made by parents is to write a child in this vein: "Don't you worry. We will get you out of there in a few weeks. We have hired a lawyer and he is writing the Governor." Such an attitude on the part of parents can only cause trouble. The child will likely assume an attitude of cocksureness, see no reason to try to learn or be cooperative, make no attempt to settle down and adjust to the institutional routine. He boasts to the other children that he will be out of there in a couple of weeks. . . . For a parent to circulate a petition requesting that a child be released will cause the same sort of trouble. Such a petition will serve no useful purpose whatsoever and is a complete waste of time. . . . Many parents never seem able to accept the fact that their child has been committed to the State, but continue to fight the people who are trying to help their child, are critical and difficult, and never permit the child to settle down and accept the situation. . . . Parents can be disturbed and frustrated and hostile the same as their children.[12]

Increasingly, the TYC pitted itself against "outsiders," including parents, supposedly driven by self-interested motives that were unrelated to actual problems in the institutions. By the mid-1960s, the accumulation of criticism from both proponents of punishment and advocates for child welfare hardened an existing penchant for secrecy and defensiveness into a reflexive worldview. "We've had just about all this nonsense we're going to tolerate," declared Turman in a speech to a Gatesville civic club shortly before the House budget hearings.[13] Supporting Turman throughout this period were TYC chairman Robert Kneebone and board member Louis Henna, businessmen and philanthropists with extensive experience on the boards of child welfare agencies. Kneebone, a consulting vice president at the Texas Commerce Bank of Houston, had served as dean of the Graduate School of Banking at Southern Methodist University, president of the Houston United Fund, and president of the Texas Tourist Council. Henna, who had joined the TSYDC in 1952, owned auto dealerships in the Austin area, had served as mayor of nearby Round Rock, and had helped found the Texas Baptist Children's Home for orphaned and dependent children.[14] Both men regularly made unscheduled inspections of the TYC's training schools and gave them glowing reviews. The only major recorded criticism came from Henna, who objected to the absence of reading materials, especially the Bible, from the isolation wards at Gatesville, Mountain View, and Crockett.[15] Otherwise, Kneebone and Henna lent Turman their unqualified support, joining him in circling the wagons against outside criticism of any sort.

That attitude faced its stiffest test due to the circumstances surrounding a fifteen-year-old Gatesville inmate from Houston named Eddie Kellar Jr.[16] In fall 1968, Kellar's mother and his stepfather, Dartman Evans, were summoned to the Gatesville infirmary. They arrived to find their son in "a coma," with an armed guard stationed outside his room. According to Evans, the boy's body was covered in bruises, his mouth was "busted," and his chest was marked with "a boot print." Gatesville officials told Evans that Kellar's attackers had been "two Negro boys with sexual motivation"; however, when Evans pressed for more information, this story changed several times, until finally it was admitted privately that a guard had been responsible for Kellar's injuries. Absent an official investigation, no criminal charges were filed. While his parents pursued a seventy-five-thousand-dollar civil lawsuit against the TYC, Kellar spent the next two months convalescing in a nearby hospital with his mother at his side. Because the TYC refused to release any official information about his injuries, Kellar's family was forced to rely on their son's own testimony, which he was too "terrified" to give to authorities. TYC director Turman would later claim, defiantly, that Gatesville's doctors had "not found a scratch" on Kellar—"not one." In any case, Kellar's parents were unable to prevent his return to Gatesville to finish out his sentence. During their first family visit after the incident, Kellar's stepfather was greeted by the very guard responsible for the beating, "settin' there with his cowboy boots on."[17]

The local media became interested in Kellar's story. Robin Lloyd and Tad Dunbar, two television journalists from Corpus Christi, interviewed Kellar's family for an investigative report on the TYC. Lloyd and Dunbar had even managed to secure permission from the usually secretive TYC to film at Gatesville and Mountain View, apparently by avoiding mention of their interest in uncovering abuses. The result was what one newspaper later called a "horror series" that aired over a three-week period in December 1968.[18] Images of Mountain View's prisonlike exterior—its high double barbed-wire fence ringed with security lights and armed guards on horseback—alternated with confused TYC officials lamely answering questions and angry former employees giving eyewitness accounts of beatings.[19] One of the fiercest critics to appear in the series was the Reverend Frank Briganti, who had served as a Catholic chaplain at Mountain View for the seven months from July 1964 through January 1965. After witnessing two beatings and counseling fearful boys covered in bruises, Briganti began cataloging incidents of abuse. He noticed that inmates were placed in solitary confinement for minor offenses, such as speaking Spanish. One day, while Briganti watched, a gym instructor stopped exercises because a boy was lagging behind the rest of the class. In an "utterly routine fashion," the boy put his hands behind his back and allowed the instructor to punch him in the chest several times. When Briganti complained to the superintendent, he was fired; soon afterward, he confronted Turman in his Austin office. Turman refused to launch an investigation because, as he admitted to Briganti, he was "too close to some of the men at Mountain View and might not be objective." Briganti then joined the group of parents and former employees who had contacted the Texas Department of Public Safety and the FBI, which had launched a probe that yielded no actionable results.

However, the political landscape had changed dramatically between the time of Briganti's initial complaint in 1965 and his televised interview in late 1968. His story hit the airwaves amid a heightened sensitivity to the plight of children in institutions. Spurred in part by widely reported instances of "battered child syndrome," a diagnostic category endorsed in 1962 by the American Pediatric Association and the U.S. Children's Bureau, the federal government had begun requiring that child welfare agencies report cases of child abuse more stringently.[20] This concern echoed the position of the United Nations, which in its 1959 Declaration of the Rights of the Child had urged its member nations to take preventive measures against "neglect, cruelty, or exploitation." "Wherever possible," it had insisted, even dependent or delinquent youth should remain with their families or be placed in settings conducive to their "healthy and normal" development.[21] In the eyes of a growing chorus of critics, the large training schools in use in several states offered the exact opposite of a normal environment. Led by Erving Goffman and Howard Becker, academic social scientists identified such places as "total institutions" that fostered adjustment not to society but to institutional norms themselves.[22] The state legislatures of California and New York established new procedural guidelines intended to reserve training schools for only the most violent and serious juvenile offenders. In all other cases, juvenile courts were encouraged to seek "the least restrictive dispositional alternative" to institutionalization. New York took this approach further in its 1962 Family Court Act, which formally classified less serious and younger offenders as Persons in Need of Supervision (PINS).[23] That same year, in Texas, a study conducted by the National Council on Crime and Delinquency and the Junior Leagues of Texas concluded that the TYC had failed to mount effective noninstitutional programs. Calling for "smaller regional training schools," the Junior League distributed two short documentary films based on its research, *Christina's Doll* (1962) and *A Theft of Tomorrows* (1965).[24] "How unfair it is to the already unhappy boys and girls," a press release lamented, "if there are not properly trained officials to help them and adequate facilities to house them if they are taken from their homes."[25] The federal government concurred; in 1967, the President's Commission on Law Enforcement and the Administration of Justice issued a report endorsing the notion of the juvenile court as essentially a court of last resort in which older, more serious offenders received due process protections.

Unlike prior waves of juvenile justice reform, this one concerned itself substantially with civil liberties. The New York and California statutes had mandated the right to counsel and parental notification. These and other due process reforms received federal sanction in a series of key rulings by the United States Supreme Court: *Kent v. U.S.* (1966), *In re Gault* (1967), and *In re Winship* (1970). Perhaps the most celebrated of these was the *Gault* case, in which a fifteen-year-old boy had received an indeterminate sentence of up to six years for the crime of making obscene phone calls—a crime that, for an adult, would have resulted in a fine of fifty dollars and a maximum of sixty days in jail. Warning that "the condition of being a boy does not justify a kangaroo court," the *Gault* ruling extended to juvenile offenders the right to counsel, to confront witnesses, and to be notified of charges.[26] In Texas, the decision set off a round of litigation to courts of civil appeals. In May 1968, the Court of Civil Appeals for Houston reversed the commitment of a twelve-year-old girl who was a habitual runaway. The court ruled that a local juvenile parole officer had interviewed the girl without counsel present, then used her words against her in commitment proceedings. Although it admitted uncertainty about interpreting *Gault* in light of Texas's "overly vague" juvenile code, the court stated that judges were taking juvenile cases more seriously when decisions resulted in institutionalization.[27] Even more confusion surfaced one month later, when another civil appeals court ordered a new trial for a fourteen-year-old Lubbock boy accused of rape. Here the court agreed with an argument that *Gault* mandated the adult court's standard of proof beyond a reasonable doubt rather than the juvenile code's less stringent "preponderance of the evidence." Although other juvenile appeals courts cited this ruling, the Texas Supreme Court overturned it a year later, suggesting an unprecedented confusion about the juvenile court even among the state's highest legal authorities.[28]

In response, the Texas House of Representatives established the Interim Committee on Juvenile Crime and Delinquency, tasked with bringing the state's juvenile code into compliance with *Gault*. Instead, however, the committee embarked on an investigation of the TYC based on the public allegations of abuse circulating in late 1968. The committee chairman, Vernon Stewart of Wichita Falls, met with Corpus Christi reporters Lloyd and Dunbar. Stewart himself had also received firsthand reports from former Mountain View inmates in his district. So too had committee member Curtis Graves, who became perhaps the fiercest critic of the TYC in the legislature. A veteran civil rights activist and graduate of Texas Southern University, Graves had been elected to the Texas House in 1966 as one of only two African American state legislators since Reconstruction. During his election campaign, Graves's opponent had tarred him as a criminal by circulating a police mug shot taken after Graves's arrest during the TSU student sit-in protests.[29] Attuned by experience to the discriminatory use of police power against African Americans, Graves represented the city that long had sent by far the most juvenile commitments to state custody. Moreover, Graves's main constituency, the African American residents of Houston's Fifth Ward, were more likely than any other social group to see their children sent off to Gatesville or Mountain View. By the late 1960s, black youth comprised nearly one-third of the inmate population, but only about one-tenth of the high school–age population of Texas.[30] Having received "hundreds" of complaints from his constituents, Graves, along with Chairman Stewart, became the driving forces behind the subsequent investigation.

The TYC did not receive word of the committee's intentions until the day before hearings were set to begin, January 3, 1969. Morning testimony featured the TYC's critics: the Kellar family, the Corpus Christi reporters, and Reverend Briganti. It was revealed that the TYC had fired eighty-seven guards from Gatesville and Mountain View in the previous five years for violating the agency's use-of-force policy, which prohibited physical force except in cases of "imminent danger" to the safety of staff, inmates, or state property.[31] To critics, an average of more than one such firing a month bolstered their claims that abuse was the rule rather than, as the TYC maintained, the exception. And yet anecdotal evidence suggested the ineffectiveness of even these precautions. Reporter Dunbar recounted the story of one guard, fired for beating an inmate, who "came back every night for a week and beat up the boy again and again until the guard who was letting the fired guard in was himself fired."[32] Briganti testified that the staff's response to one inmate who suffered from epileptic seizures was to confine him in an isolation cell with a "tear-gas bomb." (No mention is made in any of the TYC's records indicating exactly when the agency began authorizing the use of Mace, a chemical agent marketed to law enforcement and prison agencies in the early 1960s.) Another critic, Shirley Tyler, who taught math at a Houston junior high school and worked as a volunteer tutor for Gatesville parolees, claimed to have fielded "more than 200" abuse complaints from former inmates over a six-year period. Boys who had never met one another told her similar tales of arbitrary beatings, for "smiling and not smiling" and for "not standing up straight enough and standing up too straight." Tyler also described a punishment area called "the pit," an open sewage ditch in which boys were forced to wade and sometimes, she claimed, wrestle one another for the guards' amusement.

After a morning filled with such graphic testimonials, the committee spent the entire afternoon questioning TYC director Turman. In his rebuttal, Turman characterized the "parroted" complaints as part of a "campaign to discredit the agency" tainted by self-interest and ignorance.[33] In Turman's portrayal, Briganti was a disgruntled former employee whose allegations had been disproved by an FBI investigation, while Tyler was an overly emotional mother of seven frustrated because the TYC had rejected her attempts to adopt parolees as foster children. Even less trustworthy, according to Turman, were the claims of inmates' parents, such as the Kellars, who were obviously biased in favor of their children. Repeating what had been the official view since at least the second decade of the century, Turman reminded the committee that juvenile inmates would happily tell their parents whatever they wanted to hear in order to secure release. By contrast, the TYC subjected inmate complaints to greater scrutiny, investigating each one carefully. In such cases, Turman boasted, inmates typically had recanted their claims in the end, though he admitted firing guards who had "lost their temper and hit the boys." The not-so-subtle implication was that the TYC filled a void created by a lack of parental discipline. Behind most family complaints lay their own failures, which, Turman suggested darkly, included abuse at home. "There's no need for us to kick them around," he maintained. "They've been kicked around by experts before they ever come to us."[34] These well-worn attempts at blanket denial and blame shifting backfired; rather than assuaging the committee's skeptics, as they might have in past years, they reinforced the perception of a cover-up. Indeed, at the conclusion of Turman's testimony, Chairman Stewart suggested that TYC officials either knowingly approved of abuses or remained blissfully unaware of day-to-day events at their own facilities.

Committee members quickly decided that the only way to ascertain the truth was to see the facilities for themselves in as unvarnished a fashion as possible. The very next day, a Saturday, the legislators conducted a surprise inspection of Gatesville and Mountain View. Accompanied by reporters, who had been sworn to silence, the committee quietly departed from Austin in an airplane owned by the Department of Public Safety. At the training school compound, they split up into four "teams" to interview "as many inmates as possible" and to examine institutional records. One group met with four inmates, including Kellar, who were confined in isolation cells. Immediately the legislators were confronted with visual evidence of abuse—black eyes, swollen faces, bruised bodies, and blood-stained walls—that rendered the inmates' statements nearly beside the point. Late that night, visibly "shaken" committee members held an angry press conference on the tarmac before boarding their return flight. Stewart expressed his belief in the veracity of abuse allegations, promising an "extremely critical report" and a "full-blown investigation" in the upcoming legislative session.[35]

However, the TYC and its allies, having caught wind of the committee's visit to Gatesville, were determined to halt a wider investigation, and they were politically well connected enough to act accordingly. When Stewart's group landed back in Austin, it was greeted by Ben Barnes, the lieutenant-governor-elect and outgoing speaker of the House. A former proponent of transferring the training schools to the jurisdiction of the Texas Department of Corrections, Barnes had shown little inclination to fret over prisonlike conditions in the training schools. At the urging of Senator J. P. Word and Representative Bob Salter, both legislators from Coryell County, Barnes declared that the committee had exceeded its original mandate and moreover lacked the legal authority to conduct what had become essentially a criminal investigation. In the "wee hours" of the next morning, Barnes led his own "midnight inspection" of Gatesville and Mountain View with a hastily assembled entourage that included Stewart, the TYC board, TYC director Turman, and a contingent of Texas Rangers. The same group of guards and inmates questioned previously by the Stewart committee underwent a "grilling" led by TYC board member Louis Henna. Meanwhile, Rangers administered polygraph tests to several juvenile inmates at their regional office in nearby Waco, under the supervision of the Coryell County district attorney.[36] Such circumstances did not encourage truth telling; although the test results were never made public, one can surmise an environment of intimidation that produced an outcome more favorable to the TYC. Indeed, as Turman had bragged to the committee, several boys recanted or modified their earlier testimonies. For instance, one seventeen-year-old inmate revised his prior assertion that a group of guards had held him down and hit him in the face several times to the less serious statement that one guard had "kicked [him] lightly on the leg." In his triumphal return to Austin, Barnes held a well-attended

Figure 16. "Contraband weapons," undated, ca. 1960s. (Box 2007/23-17, Records, Texas Youth Commission. Courtesy of the Texas State Library and Archives Commission.)

press conference that amounted to a propaganda offensive on behalf of the TYC in which he focused particularly on the Mountain View facility for "violent and serious" offenders. While Barnes admitted that one boy's bruises "looked serious," he explained that they had occurred in the context of a mass escape plot that had included the planned murder of a guard—all uncovered with the use of polygraph testing.[37] To illustrate this point, Barnes posed for a photograph with an assortment of "jiggers," "shivs," and other weapons made by inmates, an image that appeared on the front pages of several newspapers. Such images had surfaced intermittently throughout the TYC era (figure 16). Citing the inmates' long rap sheets, which included charges of armed robbery and assault, Barnes scolded the TYC's critics for confusing them with "Little League ball players who [had] run away from a Little League ball game."[38] Barnes went on to praise Mountain View's "spotless" facilities and to call for across-the-board pay raises for TYC staff.

Although the Stewart committee dropped its investigation of specific abuse charges, its members remained undeterred by Barnes's maneuvers from their intent to publish a report critical of the TYC. Over the next few days, a series of heated behind-the-scenes negotiations took place in Barnes's office between the committee, Barnes, and Gatesville-area legislators. At one point, Dr. George Beto, head of the Texas prison system, met with the participants to advise them on the possibility of placing the training schools under his supervision—a proposal undoubtedly advanced by Barnes himself (Beto opposed the idea).[39] Meanwhile, on the pages of the state's newspapers, a public debate raged over conditions in the training schools. Gatesville superintendent M. D. Kindrick, who had been with the institution since World War II, complained that the investigation and negative publicity had disrupted institutional order and inspired a rash of escape attempts.[40] The *Fort Worth Star-Telegram* conducted its own polygraph examination of two former inmates, both twenty years old, which substantiated their claims that beatings were "a way of life down there": "We were beaten until we fell down, then we were kicked. And then to explain the cuts and bruises and puffed lips and faces, we had to sign an incident report saying we fell down accidentally or that we got into a fight with another inmate."[41]

Finally, the tense week ended with a closed-door meeting of the Stewart committee and TYC board members Henna and Kneebone. The committee presented three official recommendations: the stationing of Texas Rangers at the training schools; an outside evaluation of the TYC by a private organization such as the National Council on Crime and Delinquency; and unspecified "revisions" in the organization of the TYC (probably a reference to replacing Turman and the TYC board).[42] Gatesville-area legislators continued to play the same role that their forebears had done during the last major reform push in the 1940s. They derided the entire investigation as sensational and dishonest; however, revealingly, their chief complaint was that the decision to leave them uninformed of the investigation suggested "that they thought [Gatesville-area legislators] knew that there was in fact brutal treatment at the schools and . . . condoned it."[43] For their part, TYC officials openly mocked the idea of an outside investigation unless it was made by "competent experts" from Texas. TYC board member Jerry Kolander, a former Amarillo juvenile court judge, exhorted his colleagues across the state to have "no qualms whatsoever about ordering a juvenile confined either in Gatesville or Mountain View."[44] At the end of a week of charges and countercharges, the TYC emerged victorious in a press conference to announce what was officially billed as a compromise solution. With Stewart and TYC officials at his side, Barnes announced plans for a future study to be completed at an unspecified date, omitting two of the committee's three original recommendations and leaving any future action very much in doubt. Any study was unlikely to proceed under the auspices of the Texas House, set to begin a new legislative session dominated by the TYC's political allies. One of the TYC's staunchest supporters was the powerful chairman of the House Appropriations Committee, William S. Heatly of Paducah (known informally as the "Duke of Paducah"). His brother, M. D. Heatly, worked for the TYC as a part-time psychiatrist, although he received a full-time annual salary of twenty-thousand dollars, a blatant violation of the state's nepotism laws. Only weeks after the TYC investigation ended, Chairman Heatly engineered passage of a bill funding the construction of a new training school located in Giddings, a town about an hour's drive northeast of Austin, which happened to lie in the district of Gus Mutscher, the incoming speaker of the House.[45]

The TYC's critics reacted with palpable frustration. Representative Graves appeared on several Houston television stations to denounce the "whitewashing" of the investigation in a quid pro quo arrangement with the TYC. Fort Worth juvenile court judge Scott Moore, who had served as a lay member of the Stewart committee, leveled similar accusations.[46] Robert McKenzie, a former Gatesville guard who had passed information to the committee, warned that TYC officials were "covering up" a system of "concentrated terror."[47]

As the political fight drew to a close in mid-January 1969, it seemed that the TYC had succeeded in thwarting its critics. However, the media kept the story alive through a series of investigative reports that appeared in big-city newspapers in late January 1969.[48] Although sympathetic to the TYC, the reports qualified their support with several criticisms. The *Post* obtained records of recent staff firings, which listed causes such as slapping, kicking, and paddling boys; in one extreme case, a guard was found to have "whipped all the boys in his dorm with an electric cord." In interviews, Mountain View superintendent M. D. Kindrick and his assistant superintendent Mack O. Morris categorically denied ever beating inmates. Morris insisted that Mace was used sparingly, only six times in the previous decade, and that only the "gate security guards" at Mountain View carried it. "The reform school boys often make up horrendous stories, or exaggerate accounts of actual incidents and shade them to their advantage in talking to their parents and others," explained Clinton Kersey, the TYC's director of paroles. "Very often lie detector tests or thorough investigations find the truth to be otherwise." In an unwittingly incriminating endorsement, prison director George Beto agreed that brutality had declined in the training schools, observing that discussion of it had declined among "Gatesvillers graduated to his prison system." Interviewees told the *Post* that the investigation had served only to heighten tensions at the facilities and to embitter the staff, who felt misunderstood. Contrasting the unarmed guards with "tough, rebellious, and dangerous" boys, Turman complained, "A lot of people making irresponsible charges don't seem to understand that these kids have to be controlled." Turman also touted improvements in staffing; the TYC had redefined "guards" as "Youth Activities Supervisors" and increased the educational requirements for the position. The typical hire held at least a high school or general equivalency diploma (GED) and underwent a two-week "indoctrination" program designed by Sam Houston State University. Cut from "a better class" than in the past, TYC employees were younger on average, advanced through a six-step classification system, and wore uniforms. However, as even Turman, Kindrick, and Kersey admitted, these advances were tempered by the entrenched problem of high staff turnover. "Not enough people are being trained," lamented Turman, "and if they are they won't work for what we pay." Low salaries combined with isolated locations (about 30 percent of Gatesville's staff commuted from another county) to produce a 50 percent turnover rate; most employees held second jobs "farming, ranching, working in grocery stores or filling stations." The staff shortage was especially pronounced for caseworkers, who faced average monthly caseloads of seventy-five, about a quarter more than the nationally recommended number.

Even more damning was a series of interviews with former TYC inmates published in the *Texas Observer*, a liberal weekly magazine based in Austin.[49] Here, for the first time, episodes of racial and ethnic discrimination appeared alongside tales of abuse. Although the TYC nominally had integrated its facilities, inmates were kept separated whenever possible. For instance, guards enforced segregated seating at the cafeteria, while routinely addressing racial epithets to black and Latino youth. Indeed, Mexican American informants provided the *Observer* with some of its most bitter testimonials. Ronaldo Suarez recalled being beaten by a guard, notoriously for his hatred of "wetbacks," the day before his parole. After being struck "twenty times on each leg from knee to thigh," Suarez was left unable to walk without a limp. Under threat of parole revocation, Suarez had signed a false incident report stating that he "got hurt playing football." For many of the *Observer*'s informants, complicity in abuse was the coin of the realm: the key to gaining release. Frank Vargas, a nonviolent repeat offender from Houston, had been part of the group of inmates interviewed by the Stewart committee. According to Ben Barnes, Vargas had played a central role in the alleged escape plot uncovered by polygraph testing. Fearing for their son's safety after the public blow-up, Vargas's parents had traveled to Austin to confront TYC director Turman, who dismissed their concerns while issuing bland assurances that beatings were rare. This promise gave cold comfort to the *Observer*'s interviewees; one parolee who had served a two-year sentence in Gatesville could not recall a single visit from Turman. However, he did receive a letter from Barnes, conceding that most TYC inmates were "not criminals" but confused teenagers "in need of guidance, protection, and understanding rather than harsh punishment." For Vargas, echoing several other interviewees, the lesson was bitter indeed: "I learned to hate. . . . I wasn't that way [before]."

Who was the typical TYC inmate by the late 1960s? According to a 1969 survey by the Texas Senate, that inmate was a fifteen-year-old boy (up slightly from the average over previous years, as shown in table 13), on his first commitment for a crime against property, from a metropolitan area (72 percent of all TYC inmates in the previous year). He was likely to have been referred by a law enforcement

Table 13. Median age of commitment to the Texas Youth Council for boys, 1935–1970

1935	1940	1945	1950	1955	1960	1965	1970
14.1	14.3	14.4	14.5	15.1	15.4	15.5	15.1

Source: Dana Buckley MacInerney, "A Statistical Survey of Commitments to the Gatesville State Training School for Boys and the Gainesville State Training School for Girls, 1936–1945" (MA thesis, University of Texas, 1951); *Annual Report of the Texas Youth Council* (Austin, 1949–71).

officer, to have come from a "broken home," and to be roughly two years behind grade level in school.[50] In other words, the typical TYC inmate closely resembled the delinquent youth represented in the Houston Juvenile Probation Department statistics over the previous decade (see chapter 5). Despite official and media warnings to the contrary, youth were not demonstrably more violent or dangerous than they had been ten or twenty years earlier. Neither, if the firsthand accounts being published in the Texas media were to be believed, had the TYC's facilities changed much—except to multiply and to be more prisonlike than previously.

Less than a month after these accounts appeared, TYC director Turman appeared before the Senate Finance Committee. In a preemptive move, Turman sent reporters and legislators copies of an extremely favorable outside evaluation of the TYC conducted the previous November. Lavishing praise on the TYC's "significant progress," the report touted it as "the outstanding state agency for juveniles" nationally, ranking second only to the California Youth Authority. Stunningly, the author of the study was none other than Austin MacCormick, executive director of the Osborne Foundation and a long-standing national authority on juvenile corrections. A former crusader against abusive conditions in adult and juvenile prisons, MacCormick had helped design the "youth authority model" for the American Law Institute in the 1930s and had advised the reformers who created both the California Youth Authority and the Texas State Youth Development Council in the 1940s. However, by the 1960s, he had become more a defender than a critic of the correctional agencies that he had, after all, helped to create. During that decade, he produced four separate but similarly worded evaluations of the TYC (1962, 1964, 1967, 1969), each of which suggested areas for improvement while lauding the agency's well-intended efforts.[51] Summing up the reception of this latest report, one Fort Worth juvenile judge likened it to "Mary Poppins—perfect in every way."[52] Equally unimpressed, Senator Don Kennard of the Finance Committee accused Turman of "institutionalizing people rather than treating them."[53] Kennard, a Democrat from Fort Worth, noted that the TYC's budget request devoted more funds to the construction of the new Giddings training school than to the combined costs of the agency's entire payroll and its probation and prevention programs. Echoing sentiments expressed at the TSYDC's conception two decades earlier, Kennard argued that smaller, urban facilities could prove cheaper and more effective than training schools located in remote backwaters.[54]

The legislature's final stab at reforming the TYC came in May 1969, when the Senate Youth Affairs Committee released a lengthy report titled *Services to Youth in Texas*. The report struck an all-too-familiar chord; calling for "decentralization of boys' training school facilities," it recommended the construction of two smaller centers located in or near major cities.[55] Noting that the main intake center for boys remained at Gatesville, the committee "could find no persuasive arguments for the physical location of the reception and classification centers at relatively isolated institutions" instead of in metropolitan areas where professionals and resources were more available. For instance, one boy sent to Gatesville from Dallas was seen by a part-time TYC psychiatrist who commuted once a week from Dallas.[56] Regional intake, the committee suggested, could foster more continuity in sentencing and diagnoses, possibly even allowing more of the less serious offenders to remain in their home communities in a supervised "diagnostic parole." Indeed, such a regional facility could double as a "pre-release center" for inmates reentering the community.

More individualized programming was also essential, the committee asserted, because the TYC's inmate population mixed repeat offenders on their first or second commitment with mentally ill or retarded youth "dumped" into a correctional facility by rural counties lacking in services to diagnose or treat them appropriately. The Senate committee report presented detailed recommendations for improving academic, vocational, and rehabilitation programs. It also called for higher staff pay; the typical employee worked forty-eight hours per week while holding a second job. The staff-student ratio (1:40) led to "a depressingly constant use of control techniques." The committee investigated six specific abuse complaints and found four of them credible. Investigators found "a strong climate of suppression, repression, and fear" pervading the training schools, along with "a well-developed and highly sophisticated subculture, or contraculture" among the boy inmates, "with its own rules and its own vocabulary," that extended "far beyond the confines of the training schools into the urban communities and even, reportedly, into the Texas Department of Corrections."[57] Finally, the committee scolded the TYC for touting "the mere existence of unprosecuted investigations" as evidence of a positive program: "Neither the Texas Rangers nor the [FBI] is . . . in the business of evaluating the rehabilitation programs at Texas training schools for juveniles who have been adjudged delinquent. Neither should these agencies be expected to enforce the policies of the state training schools relating to the use of physical force."[58]

Despite this fairly comprehensive and critical report and the rising chorus of objections, the TYC won its immediate battle. The agency's allies rammed its budget through the legislature, and construction began on yet another juvenile facility in a politically advantageous location. However, the TYC's victory proved to be short-lived. The inaction of the executive and legislative branches left only one channel open to reformers: the judiciary.

Interfering with a "Little Family Decision"

The next attack on the TYC began not from the state legislature or a large city like Houston, but rather with a lawsuit against the El Paso Juvenile Court, located hundreds of miles to the west of the training schools. Within months, this seemingly isolated affair would mushroom into a federal class-action lawsuit, *Morales v. Turman*, which culminated with the release of several hundred juvenile inmates, the downfall of the existing TYC administration, and by the end of the decade, the closure of Gatesville and Mountain View. The case would have national implications for the treatment of juvenile offenders placed in state custody that continue to command attention.[59]

The lead attorney in the case, Steven Bercu, headed the juvenile division of the El Paso Legal Aid Society, an agency funded by the federal Office for Economic Opportunity. A native of Dallas, Bercu had graduated from the University of Texas law school in 1965 and obtained a master's degree in international relations in Denmark. His mother had served as the first female city attorney in Dallas; upon her retirement in the early 1960s, she joined that city's legal aid office.[60] In summer 1970, shortly after Bercu began working in El Paso, he received a steady stream of complaints from parents who had committed their children to the TYC and now wanted them returned home. Bercu soon discovered the existence of an arrangement by which parents used the county probation office for assistance in disciplining their children. Misbehaving youth could be placed in the county juvenile detention center several times; if this failed to "scare them straight," the juvenile court stepped in and recommended commitment to a state training school. As it turned out, the probation department grossly misled parents about both the nature of TYC facilities and parents' ability to retrieve their wayward children. As one mother explained to Bercu, "I took him to [the detention center] because he was bad, and when he came back home, he still didn't mind me, so I took him back and Mr. Raley sent him to Gatesville. . . . They said when he got straightened out we could get him to come back home. And I need him back home now to do some work, and they're telling me he can't come home."[61]

Eager to rid themselves of their problem children, many parents were all too willing to be misled about living conditions at the training schools. Probation officers described Gatesville "as a prep school," complete with "a swimming pool . . .

nice clothes and good food and a good education."[62] It would seem that parents had little reason to believe such promises. The state training schools' notoriety bordered on legend; closer to home, the county detention center struck fear into teenagers for its run-down, vermin-ridden buildings, as well as its abusive staff. The "D-Home," as teenagers called it, had opened in 1950 with input from the TSYDC's traveling consultants. Seeking an alternative to jail, the home's founders hoped to provide education and nurture to "wayward and underprivileged youths."[63] According to one brochure, the home operated on a medical model of delinquency as "a behavior disorder . . . symptomatic of emotional maladjustment."[64] This description would seem to call for a therapeutic program run by psychologists and psychiatrists; however, the county juvenile probation department never seems to have hired such personnel. On its watch, the home's physical plant fell into disrepair; classrooms went unused and finally served as makeshift storage spaces; and "disgusting" isolation cells harbored long-vanquished diseases such as tuberculosis.[65] Apparently ignorant of these conditions, parents used the D-Home as a kind of babysitter; teenagers, for their part, learned to despise it. "I'd rather be dead than go back to the D-Home," exclaimed one girl upon her release. "The way they treat you there, all it does is make you hate the person who put you in."[66]

The checkered history surrounding the D-Home extended to its administrators, particularly Morris Raley, the chief of juvenile probation. In the early 1960s, Raley, whose resume included stints as a farmhand and a security guard, had headed the Juvenile Patrol, a police task force plagued by scandal. In 1966, forcible rape charges against two of Raley's subordinates caused the patrol to be disbanded. Upon becoming chief of juvenile probation, Raley hired an unemployed truck driver for the position of superintendent of the detention home. He advised, "95 percent of the kids that come through here don't need psychologists or psychiatrists. Most of them are just kids who can't talk things out."[67] His aversion to hiring employees with an iota of training or experience in working with troubled teenagers, however, made it unlikely that kids "talked things out" during their stays in the detention home. Indeed, as Bercu's case gained steam, the county's child protective services division was in the midst of investigating charges that two of Raley's employees had abused *their own* children.[68]

The practice that landed Raley in court, however, was the "agreed judgment," which Bercu had learned about from the parade of parents who passed through his office. This informal mechanism allowed parents to commit their children to state custody without a hearing in juvenile court and represented an obvious violation of the Supreme Court's ruling in the *Gault* case three years earlier. Signed by the parent, Raley, and the county judge, the document appeared to uninitiated readers as the product of an actual courtroom proceeding. The agreed judgment was a boon to the judge, allowing him to open his courtroom to juvenile cases a mere "one afternoon every two weeks."[69] So routine was this practice that it accounted for over one-third (twenty-four of seventy) of juvenile delinquency commitments from El Paso County in the year preceding Bercu's involvement. With only about 3 percent of the high school–age population in Texas, the county supplied almost 15 percent of new commitments to the Gainesville School for Girls alone.[70]

In October 1970, Bercu filed cases on behalf of several teenagers who had been sent to the state training schools. He also raised a "furor" that slowly gathered a great deal of attention. The *El Paso Times* ran an investigative series that expanded on Bercu's discoveries, won a Pulitzer Prize, and elicited a public repudiation of agreed judgments from the district attorney. Parents' reactions ranged from "indifferent to moderately hostile," according to Bercu: "I was interfering with their little family decision that they wanted little Mary or little Billy . . . gone for the problems they had caused."[71] The father of Alicia Morales, the fifteen-year-old girl who became the lead plaintiff in the case, was an alcoholic angered because his daughter refused to turn over her wages. Other parents, however, expressed guilt to reporters. "I don't know why I sent her there," mused one mother, while another hoped her son could forgive her for sending him to "a prison."[72]

At least one parent decided to get involved on her child's behalf. Martha Brown had committed her fifteen-year-old son Johnny for reasons that were at once unique and all too typical. Johnny had run away from home several times to visit his sweetheart, a fourteen-year-old girl who had been deported to Juarez, just across the border from El Paso. At her wits' end, Martha had sent her son to the D-Home more than once. But then Johnny threatened to marry his girlfriend, sending his mother into a panic. She committed him to Gatesville based on information given to her by probation officer Raley. However, she soon realized that she had made a mistake and hired Bercu to secure his release. Shortly after that, she received a letter from Johnny in which he described being beaten by his caseworker. In January 1971, Martha Brown visited her son and found him shaking and covered in bruises. Fearing more bad publicity, the TYC immediately fired Johnny Brown's caseworker, a move that angered the staff at Gatesville. A week later, Martha witnessed her son and over one hundred other boys flee the Gatesville complex while guards stood idly by: a staged escape. In the past, as we have seen, the TYC had reserved this tactic for frightening the public away from investigations or reforms of the training schools. This time, however, guards had acted alone in support of the fired caseworker. They sent a clear message that the cost of such firings to the TYC's public image could be much steeper than the benefits. Unlike officials in Austin, rank-and-file guards rarely felt the need to apologize for what they did. "I slapped that boy for his own good," explained the fired caseworker to a reporter. "That's the way you have to handle the boys."[73] The incident likely would never have occurred had it not been for Martha Brown's decision to publicize her son's ill treatment and to visit Gatesville at that fortuitous moment.[74]

From the outset, the case in El Paso attracted the attention of the national television media. In early October 1970, NBC News contacted TYC director Turman. The network planned a feature on American juvenile justice and wished to profile the Texas Youth Council. A representative assured Turman that NBC viewed the Texas program as "among the best in the country."[75] On November 1, Turman met NBC production coordinator Peter Freedberger at the Austin airport and drove him to Gatesville for a guided tour. During the return trip to Austin, Freedberger abruptly asked if he could film inside Gatesville. He specifically wished to interview juvenile inmates from El Paso, even naming individual boys for whom Steve Bercu had filed petitions for release. An angry Turman refused the request, suspecting a coordinated effort between NBC and Bercu to draw the TYC into the El Paso lawsuit.[76] Turman had become aware of the El Paso case because Roland Green, the assistant attorney general for the State of Texas, had flown to El Paso to assist with the county's defense. Spying the seeds of a larger case, Green warned Turman to "be on the lookout for Mr. Bercu."[77]

Although Bercu later denied any collaboration with NBC, he was well aware of the training schools' reputation. Moreover, he kept pace with debates in expert circles over the definition of criminal responsibility, the efficacy of "total institutions," and the civil rights of children and adolescents. Just prior to filing suit in El Paso, Bercu had traveled to Chicago to attend a conference on "juvenile prison systems" cosponsored by the OEO and the Youth Law Center. Formed in the wake of the *Gault* ruling, the Youth Law Center served as a "back-up center" for the OEO's legal aid offices around the country.[78] It joined other newly formed organizations such as the Children's Defense Fund in providing academic research, political lobbying, public advocacy, and legal aid on behalf of young people from poor and historically disadvantaged groups. When Bercu realized that he had a major civil rights case on his hands, he called the center for assistance.[79]

Not without reason, Turman came to view himself as under siege from all directions. He continued to field requests from NBC News to film in Gatesville. El Paso's state senator forwarded a letter from NBC that trumpeted the film credits of producer Martin Carr, which included the award-winning *Hunger in America* and *Migrant: An* NBC White Paper.[80] These films had dramatized the plight of vulnerable groups and galvanized public action on their behalf. *Hunger in America*, for example, came during a political fight for an expanded national food-stamp program.[81] The program had stirred controversy in Texas because it juxtaposed malnourished children in San Antonio with the county commissioner, A. J. Ploch, who casually dismissed the problem by saying, "You'll always have hunger. . . . You've got to have Indians and chiefs." Ploch later complained that he had been "mistreated" by unscrupulous ideologues who were not "really looking for the truth."[82] Given this history, Carr's resume doubtlessly confirmed Turman's worst fears. Although he refused to respond to NBC's written requests submitted between November 1970 and January 1971, Turman scribbled his answers by hand in the margin spaces. These notes track Turman's intransigence, as well as his growing irritation with incursions into his control over information. Over the course of the correspondence, the quality of his handwriting declined noticeably; by the final letter, one can barely decipher Turman's vehement objections and invocations of state laws. Next to a paragraph requesting permission to shoot exterior footage of Gatesville and Gainesville: "[We] agreed to this at the time of [NBC's] visit to Gatesville, they did not choose to do it!!!" Later: "NBC's sole interest has been to interview students, which state law *does not permit according to the attorney general!*"[83] Turman ignored NBC's first written request; the network sent it again by certified mail.[84] When Turman finally responded to NBC, he maintained his dismissive stance, acidly stating that "only a court of competent jurisdiction" could order the TYC to allow interviews.[85]

The biggest surprise was yet to come, however. While Turman sparred with NBC, attorney Bercu had decided to seek personal interviews with his juvenile clients, many of whom had no inkling of his efforts on their behalf. In an El Paso courtroom, the state's lawyer countered that Bercu's clients preferred to remain in training school. Bercu obtained a court order allowing him to depose his clients; the TYC, in his recollection, "had no idea what was coming next."[86] On January 27, 1971, Bercu and William P. Hoffman Jr. of the Youth Law Center arrived at the Gainesville School for Girls. They showed their court order to Superintendent Thomas Riddle. Appointed in 1966 to replace the reformer Maxine Burlingham, Riddle, the first male superintendent in Gainesville's history, was an "old football player" with little experience in juvenile corrections.[87] Soon Bercu and Hoffman found themselves in a conference call with TYC director Turman and assistant attorney general Green. At Green's suggestion, the attorneys were permitted to interview their clients under Riddle's supervision; two days later, the same restrictions applied at Gatesville. Green unwittingly had given Bercu and Hoffman what they had wanted all along—an opportunity to widen the scope of the case. "We were pretty sure [that] we were going after the school as soon as we went in," recalled Bercu; "continuing the lawsuit" until they could find a way to expand it became their primary goal.[88] Within weeks, they sought an injunction in the district court whose jurisdiction included Gainesville, where the presiding judge, William Wayne Justice, seemed most likely to be sympathetic to the juvenile plaintiffs. At that time, Bercu and

Hoffman also filed a class-action lawsuit to prevent juvenile judges across Texas from committing minors to the TYC's custody without due process.[89]

As its setbacks mounted in the courtroom, the TYC lost even more ground in the area of public relations. In May 1971, NBC aired *This Child Is Rated X* on its Saturday night *White Paper* news magazine. The broadcast took viewers to a Chicago juvenile detention center, an Indiana state juvenile training school, and finally to El Paso. While the film offered critical yet mixed portrayals of Chicago and Indiana, it reserved its harshest indictments for Texas. Two former juvenile inmates from El Paso described their experiences in Gatesville. While his father looked on, Philip Workman, a delicate-looking Anglo boy of fifteen, recounted how guards "whipped" the arches of his feet with a steel rod. Ricky Reed exited a bus after eight months in Gatesville and was greeted by NBC cameras along with his family. According to Reed, guards weighing "close to three hundred pounds" beat boys at random. He described a climate of terror in which boys never knew when a guard might "jump on" him. Reed also spent time in the isolation ward of the El Paso D-Home, which he described as "smelly . . . with roaches everywhere, no one to talk to," commenting, "You start to lose your mind."

The story then shifted abruptly to El Paso probation chief Morris Raley, whose appearance in the film surely ranked as a case study in unintentional self-defamation. Of the D-Home he remarked: "It isn't intended as a resort vacation." He gestured toward a large ball of string displayed on his desk, the result of a boy who had unraveled his T-shirt while languishing in solitary confinement. The interviewer suggested that the boy might have been bored; Raley disagreed. "I don't think so," drawled Raley, who found "getting back at any adult, especially his parents" a more likely explanation. For him, the "coddling permissiveness" of parents represented a larger problem than the rough treatment of youth in juvenile facilities. However, parents who appeared in the film expressed bewilderment about their decision to commit their children to TYC custody, like the mother who sheepishly mumbled to the camera, "I don't know why I signed that paper." Bercu also gave an interview, explaining how an "agreed judgment" worked and musing about why parents would "want their children put in a prison." Overall, the film presented a devastating portrait of El Paso's juvenile court and juvenile probation department and suggested that much worse could be found at the TYC, at the moment when a lawsuit threatened to do just that.

Breaking Point

In retrospect, the TYC's exercise of raw political muscle to stave off outside scrutiny and legislative reform seems short sighted. Had the agency's leadership simply

acquiesced to some of the proposals contained in, for instance, the 1969 Senate report, it might have evaded the court-ordered reforms described in the next chapter.
Nothing in the TYC's institutional records suggests that leadership was following
closely the national developments of the 1960s: the growing concern about child
abuse, the emphasis on children's rights, the due process revolution in juvenile justice. The TYC looked mainly to Austin for its cues; indeed, even when the board ac-
knowledged in 1965 that the federal Civil Rights Act would require the desegregation of the girls' training schools at Crockett and Gainesville, TYC director Turman
stipulated that the agency could not act without a directive from the legislature.[90]
Professionally, the agency's degreed experts located themselves mainly within the
field of corrections first and the social and behavioral sciences second—if at all.
This orientation allowed them to fall behind expert opinion in the very fields that
were grappling with new theories of identity formation, social labeling, and the
effects of institutionalization. Increasingly, outside critics and TYC officials seemed
to be speaking past one another because they were drawing on completely different
universes of understanding, as would become painfully apparent over the next
three and a half years of litigation.

SEVEN

Creating a Right to Treatment

Morales v. Turman, 1971–1988

In July 1971, each of the TYC's roughly 2,500 training school inmates received a sealed envelope. In it were a questionnaire and a cover letter from Judge William Wayne Justice, of the Eastern District of Texas, presiding in the case of *Morales v. Turman*. The letter explained that the TYC was standing trial and requested that inmates complete the enclosed survey. Inmates were assured that their responses would be kept confidential, in keeping with the court's interest in protecting their "legal rights."[1] The questions focused on whether inmates had received a court hearing or counsel before being committed to TYC custody. Of the 2,294 respondents, 863 had hearings without legal counsel, while 280 had never set foot in a courtroom. Nearly half of the TYC's inmate population, in other words, had been committed in violation of the due process requirements laid down in the *Gault* ruling.[2] It is possible to view this result as a consequence of the TYC's change in mission during the 1950s. Had the TYC maintained its early role as an arbiter of standard procedures in local juvenile courts, it might have taken the lead in ensuring compliance with *Gault*. However, by withdrawing from the field and narrowing its focus essentially to incarceration, the agency seemed to be barely aware of the problem, let alone concerned about it. Moreover, as if these revelations were not damning enough, about fifty respondents scribbled on the back of their questionnaires handwritten descriptions of abuses suffered at the hands of staff. This information, along with some of the testimonials obtained by Bercu from his initial group of clients, opened the door to expanding the case's focus from due process to conditions of confinement.

Throughout spring and summer 1971, TYC officials struggled to respond to the horror stories that had been circulating publicly in recent years. Their descriptions of juvenile inmates vacillated from ominous warnings about their dangerousness to sympathetic invocations of "hurt, frightened children."[3] From TYC director Turman's perspective, the focus on the agency's most controversial training schools was frustrating. The TYC was also responsible for two orphan homes for dependent children, which had experienced no serious scandals over the years. Equally quiet was the Crockett School for Girls and the recently opened Brownwood facility just west of Austin, which served as the diagnostic intake center for all female commitments and offered an experimental, coeducational rehabilitation program that would later receive praise from the *Morales* litigators and experts. Although only partially implemented over the previous decade, the TYC's juvenile parole program was now staffed with twenty officers working in most of the state's major urban areas. In short, the TYC was doing some things right that were being lost in the whirlwind of abuse scandals and legal actions.

At the same time, as we saw in the 1969 legislative investigations, many Texans were becoming impatient with what they viewed as the TYC's overreliance on large institutions. This anti-institutional critique dovetailed with a national trend. One of the more influential expert witnesses in the *Morales* case was Jerome Miller, who had taken the then-unprecedented step of closing down all of Massachusetts's juvenile training schools during his tenure as director of the state's Department of Youth Services.[4] The move attracted national media attention; in numerous interviews and later a memoir, Miller explained how he had come to Massachusetts to "clean up" its scandal-ridden juvenile facilities. However, he quickly found his efforts frustrated by a staff accustomed to running a prisonlike program of control and custody; community groups fearful of delinquents allowed to run wild due to "permissive" treatment policies; and elected officials with vested economic interests in maintaining the status quo. Miller developed an anti-institutional critique that was also being adopted by analysts of the "prison-industrial complex" spreading across the Sun Belt region and by critics of mental hospitals who believed that the mentally ill and mentally retarded could be integrated into everyday society.[5] He also seemed to identify many of the key obstacles to reform in the troubled history of Texas's juvenile justice system.

However, the overarching reality was that the TYC had failed to keep up with the changing face of juvenile justice. Apathetic to new concerns about child welfare and children's rights, the agency also paid little attention to an issue that increasingly preoccupied national reformers: disproportionate minority confinement. The president's commission had studied the problem in 1967, and it would become a major policy issue for the federal Office of Juvenile Justice and Delinquency Prevention after it was created by the U.S. Congress in 1974. Advocacy groups such as the Youth Law Center and the Children's Defense Fund made it a priority when they began work in the 1970s. From within the juvenile justice system, practitioners lamented how their courts, detention centers, and state facilities had become dumping grounds for poor and nonwhite youth. For instance, Judge Lois G. Forer described poor conditions in a Philadelphia juvenile court in a widely read 1970

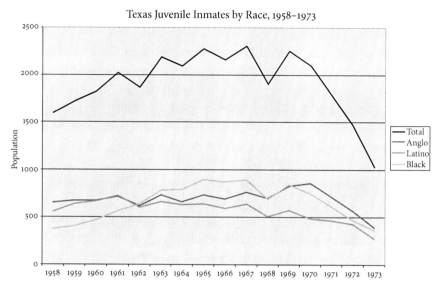

Figure 17. Texas juvenile inmates by race and ethnicity, 1958–1973. Data compiled from *Annual Report of the Texas Youth Council*, 1957–74.

book, which also revealed that 90 percent of the youth were black and were subjected to discrimination in sanctions.[6] The aforementioned NBC television special *This Child Is Rated X* included a segment on the disproportionate incarceration of black youth in the Cook County (Chicago) system. This issue would become important during the *Morales* proceedings, which highlighted the general overrepresentation of nonwhite youth in TYC facilities (see figure 17), as well as the treatment disparities they experienced within those facilities. These revelations would lead the court to conclude that the protections and privileges of American adolescence—represented by the right to treatment—should be extended to all youth regardless of their racial, ethnic, or economic background.

The July 1971 questionnaire would prove to be only the first of many incursions against the authority of TYC staff. An extended discovery phase disrupted the institutional routines at Mountain View, Gatesville, and Gainesville over the next several months, leading to a kind of low-intensity warfare over the question of who truly represented the wishes of the juvenile inmates.

"The Students Now Know It Can Be Done"

On Labor Day morning in 1971, the day before the beginning of court proceedings, what was later described as a "riot" erupted at the Gatesville Schools for Boys. The source of the disturbance was the Sycamore unit, an academic high school program reserved for 240 boys aged fifteen and older classified as "capable" of working at grade level. Large numbers of boys began huddling together during breakfast, which alarmed guards so much that they halted the day's routine and returned everyone to their separate dormitories. This action, however, came too late. Within hours, a group of about ninety boys gathered on the athletic field and marched off the grounds, while a guard supervisor tried in vain to dissuade them. As the marchers approached a nearby highway, they met with a small contingent of guards ready for a fight. In a response that was clearly rehearsed, the boys laughed and casually walked around the blockade. Television cameras arrived on the scene in time to witness highway patrolmen halt the march by firing shotguns in the air. Mere hours after it had started, the protest came to an end.[7]

Nevertheless, the boys had "accomplished their goal" of drawing attention to their plight. The timing was crucial; the upcoming court hearing would decide whether to expand the scope of *Morales* beyond procedural violations in the state's juvenile courts to include conditions of confinement. The protest march therefore irritated and worried Gatesville supervisors as well as top TYC officials. Where past generations of aggrieved inmates had sought escape or release on an individual basis, the Sycamore insurgents had acted collectively; although no information survives about individual participants, their sheer numbers suggest that boys shelved long-standing rivalries and disputes on behalf of their shared interests in gaining their freedom. Officials were also unnerved because the boys had carried off a protest devoid of violence or property damage, which supported the idea that they were at least partially innocent victims rather than hardened criminals. The "peace march," as officials privately referred to it, was more likely to evoke a civil rights protest than a jailbreak. Hard-pressed to label the incident an escape attempt, Gatesville officials instead called it a "riot." They feared that the inmates were taking over the proverbial asylum, not by force but with the assistance of activist attorneys and a sympathetic judge. The notion that juvenile inmates might achieve a collective status as an oppressed social group deeply worried TYC officials. Thus, even though nobody escaped, "the riot was successful," admitted the Gatesville superintendent, M. D. Kindrick, observing moreover, "The students now know it can be done." The protest galvanized even those inmates who did not participate, who were heard cheering loudly while they watched coverage on the local evening news.[8]

In November 1971, over state objections, Bercu obtained permission to conduct one-on-one interviews with all 2,500 inmates in the training schools. The gender divide is worth noting; while boys' cases tended to highlight abusive conditions of confinement, girls' cases were far more likely to call attention to due process violations during commitment to state custody. At that time, roughly 80 percent

Table 14. Percentages of Texas Youth Council admissions by race, ethnicity, and gender, 1971

	African American	Mexican American	White
Male	35	26	39
Female	23	8	58

Source: *Annual Report for the Texas Youth Council for the Fiscal Year Ending August 31, 1971* (Austin, 1971), 23–24.

of the inmate population was male, and 61 percent came from "broken families." Most male referrals—81 percent—had come from a police department, while 78 percent of female referrals had come from a probation officer, a truant officer, or a social worker. As in previous years, 63 percent of male offenses were property crimes such as stealing or auto theft, while 60 percent of female inmates had been committed for vague offenses such as "disobedience." As we have seen, in informal commitment procedures such as the "agreed judgment," parents tended to use probation officers to control and discipline their children. This was especially the case for teenage girls who asserted autonomy, such as the lead plaintiff, Alicia Morales, discussed previously. The racial and ethnic breakdown remained fairly consistent with previous trends toward the overrepresentation of nonwhite offenders (see table 14).

Thus, during the following January and February, over one hundred attorneys and law students from the University of Texas and Southern Methodist University conducted hundreds of interviews in school gymnasiums. The interviews became occasions for minor but revealing clashes between training school staff and aspiring young attorneys. For example, guards who routinely permitted, even encouraged, the act of smoking cigarettes protested when interviewers offered them to inmates. One irate Gatesville guard confiscated a pack of cigarettes from an attorney after she had offered several of them to inmates. TYC officials viewed the incident as an example of the pernicious, peerlike influence of Bercu's youthful assistants.[9] But the school guards made unconvincing opponents of teen smoking. So pervasive was smoking in the training schools that a visiting psychiatrist later singled out "seeing young teenage girls through a thick cloud of cigarette smoke" as her "most vivid memory."[10] Cigarettes long had been integral to the system of rewards and punishments; some dormitory supervisors even recognized smoking as a "recreational" activity. Why, then, the objections to smoking during interviews with attorneys? Already a threat to the guards' authority, lawyers who passed out cigarettes unwittingly seized control over a key element of the reward structure. Cigarettes were as much a form of currency in juvenile institutions as they were in adult prisons, and guards feared that boys would associate the reward of smoking with the deposition process.

TYC lawyers collected other evidence suggesting that the interviews cultivated disrespect for staff. One Gatesville caseworker recalled being informed by a boy that the "staff was not qualified as correctional workers nor did the program rehabilitate boys."[11] Staff expressed fear that inmates who believed their release imminent would defy rules and backslide from their path toward rehabilitation. Others, particularly at Gatesville, claimed to have unearthed intimidation tactics during interviews. An inmate who refused to describe the cleanliness of his meals as anything other than "all right" supposedly goaded his interviewer into a confrontation. When he was accused of lying, the boy allegedly shoved the meeting table into his questioner's chest, then stalked out of the gym. In another interview, an "annoyed" law student demanded that a boy "quit lying" about his treatment from guards. The response, in this telling: "I don't have to answer any questions from you, you long-haired S.O.B."[12]

The use of women interviewers seems to have exacerbated the sense of injury among staff. At Gatesville, this merely underscored one similarity between the training school and the prison. Boys who had never learned how to behave around girls were unlikely to acquire this skill in an all-male environment where survival often depended upon exaggerated displays of masculinity. And yet no reports surfaced of sexual impropriety. The presence of female professionals seems to have disturbed the adult guards far more than the supposedly hypersexual boys. Well-educated and assertive, women interviewers who offered cigarettes to boys, then argued about it with guards, probably posed a threat to authority beyond the mere disruption of established smoking schedules. The effect was quite different with girl informants, who sometimes viewed female attorneys as role models worthy of the kind of respect never given to school staff. One Gainesville girl, given cigarettes contrary to a written order from her father, emerged from her deposition proclaiming her disdain for staff and her desire to "wear pants" like the woman who interviewed her.[13]

As much as the staff resented the incursion of female attorneys, they clearly despised their male colleagues even more. At Gainesville, Bercu's unannounced appearance in a cosmetology class "terribly excited" trainees, who quickly abandoned the haircuts they were in the middle of giving. The flustered instructor then found herself fielding questions from Bercu about her qualifications to teach hairstyling.[14] Bercu's own long hair and "hippie" appearance deeply offended state attorneys, TYC officials, and training school staff. To many of the inmates, however, Bercu's look was a breath of fresh air in a landscape of crew cuts and uniforms. "We looked like rock stars to [the kids]," says Bercu, who "made a point" of irritating the staff by wearing long hair, beard, blue jeans, and unbuttoned shirts on his visits to the training schools.[15] Boys "thought it was pretty cool," while girls "loved it"; employees, meanwhile, struggled to reestablish order after a Bercu visit. At Gainesville, girls became "extremely defiant" and "unusually abusive" toward their captors. Angry claims to "rights," tirades against "God damned M.F. state people," and threats to have the school closed down resulted in a tripling of the number of girls placed in solitary confinement.[16] Equally exciting to inmates was the fact that Bercu wielded real power: "The main thing . . . [was] that we could push these guys around. These were their tormentors. When we came in, everyone got deferential immediately. As far as the kids were concerned, it was . . . unbelievable. We would come in there, a bunch of hippies basically, and everybody would back off."[17]

Although Bercu's appearance angered officials and excited inmates, it apparently meant little to Judge William Wayne Justice. Only one year before the beginning of *Morales v. Turman*, Justice famously had overturned a ban on long hair at Tyler Junior College, a ruling that town fathers had warned would "destroy the college."[18] A native of Tyler, Texas, and an appointee of President Lyndon Johnson, Justice had ordered Robert E. Lee High School in Tyler to replace the school song, "Dixie," and the school flag, the Confederate Battle Flag that many southern schools and government buildings had erected in response to court-ordered desegregation. In another case, Justice agreed with plaintiffs that Tyler High School cheerleader selection practices were discriminatory. He issued several unpopular but key decisions that garnered him a reputation as a judicial activist and, according to his biographer, a defender of individual freedom and dignity against incursions from the state.[19]

In recognition of Justice's concerns, the TYC claimed that legal aid attorneys were exploiting their juvenile clients for personal and strategic gains. For evidence, they produced letters from inmates. "All they do is lie and try to get all the money they can before they say they cannot help you," stated one handwritten note from a Mountain View inmate.[20] In fact, officials had manipulated the situation to produce such letters. Tom Dixon, an associate of Bercu's from Dallas, had filed a series of release petitions in fall 1971. In response, Dallas district attorney Henry Wade informed Dixon in February 1972 of his intention to fight each writ in court and refile charges against juveniles who had already won release. Dixon was forced to solicit funds from inmates' families for court costs, a difficult task given that some parents were less than eager to see their children released from training school. "Your mom says they simply don't have it," explained Dixon in one letter, "and I don't think she wants anything to do with me anyway. You'll need to talk this over with your father in person."[21] Inmates who hailed from the Dallas area received a letter informing them that Dixon would be unable to secure their release, as he had promised.[22] Casting further suspicion on inmate complaints, training school staff had censored outgoing mail to legal aid attorneys, in defiance of a court order, but encouraged letters to TYC lawyers.[23] It was not unusual for refraining from writing to attorneys to be included on the list of inmates' "treatment goals." "As long as I write you," one Gainesville inmate later told Bercu, "is as long as I am going to stay."[24]

Staff believed that inmates were better off in the training schools. "So many of the girls' parents are too permissive," advised one trainee from Texas Woman's University.[25] Her viewpoint echoed that of other TYC officials, including director Turman. He once had lectured Dixon that he "should be less interested in releasing these kids and more interested in their dispositions." But Dixon did indeed worry about the fate of his clients should they be released; many of them, he conceded, had "no place to go." In November 1971, he requested permission for representatives of Dallas-area "halfway houses and religious agencies" to discuss placement options for his juvenile clients. Turman never replied to this inquiry.[26] Turman's staff fed him information designed to squelch any interest in cooperating with Dixon. From Gatesville came retainer invoices and written affidavits from boys. According to these documents, Dixon charged exorbitant fees and encouraged his clients to "mess up" or run away. "I don't give a shit what happens," Dixon supposedly boasted. "I can get you out."[27]

Also, big-city district attorneys awaited any released inmates with new arrest warrants for old offenses. Several unhappy inmates were returned to the training schools, where they were recruited to swear out complaints against Steve Bercu. "I misrepresented the truth because I was desperate to be released," claimed one Gainesville girl who "want[ed] to tell the truth this time."[28] The momentous offense for which she had landed in Gainesville in the first place: writing bad checks. Letters from parents sympathetic to the TYC portrayed legal aid attorneys as meddlers in the disciplining of disobedient youth. "I sincerely cannot understand why they are doing these things," wrote one parent. "I believe that they will only hurt the kids more than help them."[29]

More influential in the courtroom were those parties who believed the opposite was true, that juvenile delinquents suffered far more harm in a training school than they would at home. In December 1972, Judge Justice granted a plaintiff motion to allow expert witnesses to conduct participant-observation studies at the training schools.[30] He also invited the Justice Department to join the case, resulting in the deployment of FBI agents to inspect and photograph the facilities and the grounds. The Mental Health Law Project, a nonprofit legal aid firm, joined the plaintiffs on behalf of the American Psychiatric Association and the American Psychological Association. The influx of such prestigious coplaintiffs allowed Bercu to solicit key testimony from a range of well-known experts on youth and corrections. Gerda Hansen Smith, a psychiatry instructor at the University of Texas Medical Branch in

Figure 18. Michigan dormitory guard station or "cage" interior, Gatesville State Schools for Boys, ca. 1960s. (Box 2007/23-17, Records, Texas Youth Commission. Courtesy of the Texas State Library and Archives Commission.)

Galveston, led a team of researchers who spent two weeks living at the Gainesville School for Girls. Smith was "appalled" by both the physical conditions and the use of language to paper over them. According to the TYC's published literature, inmates lived in "home-like cottages" with "private rooms."[31] The word "cottage," observed Smith, implied "something . . . warm and cozy," while "private room" suggested "a teenager's room . . . my daughter's and my son's room." At Gainesville, however, the interior of the cottage resembled nothing more than a cell block: "dark, narrow corridors with teenage girls looking out a slightly opened door that was chained." Each "private room" contained "a cot projecting from a concrete block wall with a heavy wood door, with a little peephole up at the top, [and] with a window that looked out that had a heavy screen on it."[32] Even less changed from an earlier era were the boys' dormitories, which remained congregate in format, with a guard station in the center (see figure 18).

Similar contradictions bedeviled long-standing descriptions of "house parents" who "functioned much like parents in a home."[33] In any other setting, the brand of parenting that actually existed in the training schools would have drawn charges of child abuse, even in the 1970s. The primary sources of information were the juvenile inmates themselves, who testified in open court and gave depositions in closed-door meetings. The TYC long had insisted on the untrustworthiness of such statements, claiming that they were tainted by the obvious prospect of release, an innate proclivity for lying, and adolescent immaturity. These arguments now fell flat, in large part due to the efforts of Jerome Miller, who helped convince Judge Justice of the value of inmate testimony. The TYC and its training schools looked all too familiar to Miller, who had several years of experience interviewing juvenile inmates in Massachusetts. By this time, Miller had left Massachusetts and become director of the Illinois Department of Child and Family Services.[34] His decision to get involved in the Texas case only added to Miller's controversial stature within his profession. That June, a meeting of the National Conference of Superintendents of Training Schools and Reformatories voted overwhelmingly to censure Miller. A few weeks later, as Miller addressed a New Orleans meeting of the National Council on Crime and Delinquency, an emissary of the Texas attorney general surreptitiously recorded his comments in the hopes of using them against him in court.[35]

Undeterred, Miller visited the Mountain View School for Boys twice in summer 1973. On his first visit, he received a guided tour from school officials. Certain that he had not seen everything, he approached a boy who was hoeing in a grove of peach trees on the side of a hill. The boy told Miller to look on the other side of the hill, in an area not visible from the front entrance. There Miller found boys "all in a line in these uniforms, hoeing at the open ground in a useless sort of fashion, in unison, [like] the old chain gang."[36] In the isolation ward, he found battered, bruised, and terrified boys, only a few of whom would even whisper their complaints aloud for fear of retribution. Days before the start of the trial phase of *Morales v. Turman*, Miller returned with Judge Justice in tow, taking him straight to the isolation ward, or Security Treatment Center (STC), at Mountain View. Any doubts the judge might have harbored about the veracity of inmate testimony paled in the face of what he saw. Miller's former informants, shaking with fear and covered in fresh bruises, begged him to leave. It was all too obvious what had taken place since Miller's last visit. According to Justice's biographer, "it was a very unsettling experience" for him; most of the boys looked "so young" to be in such a secure facility.[37] Although the TYC provided no data on the age of STC inmates, it did provide some incomplete offense records. In 1972, Mountain View inmates were placed in the STC most often for fighting, attacking staff, and sexual misconduct. Of the latter, there were seventeen such offenses in 1972, mainly "sodomy" and "masturbation."[38] The STC was undoubtedly a grim place, and for an inmate, to testify about it was to risk life and limb. "All of the pressures are on him not to say anything," argued Miller. In Massachusetts, it was typical for a boy to confide privately to Miller about abusive treatment. "When we got to taking a formal statement, with his knowledge that generally he's going to be in that system awhile, face to face with the people he's accusing," however, the average inmate did the "prudent" thing: "clam up."[39]

Even as the court dispersed experts to study the training schools, the TYC attempted to counter with yet another report by Austin MacCormick, issued at the end of March 1972. The report expressed deep contempt for the views of the TYC's critics, sneeringly referring to "so-called community-based programs and services," and defended staff-on-inmate abuse as "inevitable." MacCormick cited the combination of boys who "know a hundred ways to try the patience of an adult" and guards with "very short tempers" who "have been accustomed to impose physical punishments on their own children." MacCormick's defense peaked with the following tirade:

> Nowadays the correctional field is being subjected to harsh criticism in the press and on the air as it has never been before. It is usually directed at prisons . . . but juvenile institutions have had their share. Sometimes the criticism is warranted, although the critics seldom recognize the enormous improvements that have been made in the last 40 years, as I know from having had a hand in it. More often than not the criticism comes from people who do not know what they are talking about, believe anything that is told them as long as it is bad enough, and especially accept any statement made by the avowed radicals and revolutionaries in our prisons and their super-radical supporters in the outside world. . . . Sometimes they are made by people in the correctional field who should know better than to accept accusations by inmates. . . . The sad truth is that some of them do not care whether they are true or not, as long as they are exciting and interesting to readers and listeners.[40]

"A Very Unsettling Experience": Inmate Testimony

Inmates were sometimes deposed privately, but most of them gave testimony in open court during a sweltering six-week period in July and August 1973. During the trial, juvenile inmates feared for their safety, despite reassurances from representatives of the Texas attorney general. The crowds that filled the courtroom, which included reporters and TYC officials, added to their trepidation. Occasionally, when witnesses seemed too paralyzed with fear to speak, Judge Justice cleared the courtroom. Then they told their stories, horror tales far more graphic than the many that had been presented in various forums over the decades of the training schools' existence. Observers from the national media were both "astonished" at the terrible things the inmates described and awestruck at testimonials that indicted school guards and officials who often were sitting only a few feet away.[41]

One of the worst stories was that of C.W., who had entered Gatesville at the age of fourteen. New inmates such as C.W. were considered "fresh fish," meaning they had to fight to win acceptance in the dormitory.[42] One might expect to find an adult staff that struggled to contain this practice and tolerated it only grudgingly. Instead, guards turned out to be willing overseers of all manner of ritualized fighting between inmates. After "about ten" fights, C.W. fled Gatesville but was recaptured two months later. He stayed at the Gatesville Reception Center, a temporary detention facility for boys awaiting placement in one of the seven "schools" that comprised the Gatesville campus. One day, without warning, C.W. and five other boys were put in handcuffs and leg irons and herded onto a truck. Their destination was Mountain View, the facility built for "violent and serious offenders" but informally used as a form of punishment for boys who attempted to run away from or otherwise cause trouble at Gatesville. Transfer to Mountain View was used routinely as a form of punishment even for Gatesville inmates who were status or nonviolent offenders.

Upon arrival, C.W. and his companions lined up against a concrete wall in a supervisor's office, while a group of guards loudly informed them of the rules. Next to C.W., a Latino boy raised his hand; he spoke almost no English and had not understood the rules. Not surprisingly, he also did not respond to an order to lower his hand. What happened next shocked and frightened C.W. The supervisor walked up to the boy and punched him several times while the others watched. C.W. was escorted to his dormitory, where once again he was a "fresh fish." Again a guard looked on as C.W. fought with a fellow inmate. But his initiation into Mountain View was only beginning. After halting the fight, the guard walked C.W. into a side room, ordered him to stand against a wall with his hands in his pockets, and punched him several times in the stomach. The "racking," as this practice was known, was so pervasive that it came up in the testimony of every single Mountain View inmate. C.W.'s guard proved especially sadistic; the day after the "racking," he presided over a beating administered by eight boys that lasted over an hour and ended long after C.W. was unconscious. One boy who witnessed the incident recalled that the guard had intervened because he did not want "a dead fish on his hands."[43]

As one might expect, stomach-turning stories such as this one almost always drew attention to the staff. What right-thinking adult, wondered observers on all sides (including some members of the TYC's own defense team) could visit such horrors on adolescent boys, regardless of their offenses? How could trained professionals, including some with doctoral degrees in psychiatry and psychology, countenance such practices, which so obviously went against practically everything they should have learned about children's mental health? The answers begin, as they had in Massachusetts, in the area of political economy. The TYC had recruited a nearly all-white staff from Gatesville and other small towns in the region. For many guards, a job at Gatesville or Mountain View paid so little that it served only to supplement income earned elsewhere, either from a second job or a military pension. Several supervisors were "retired army people" from nearby Fort Hood.[44] Academic or professional training was the exception rather than the rule. For example, Mack O. Morris, the assistant superintendent of Mountain View, held only a high school equivalency diploma. Like several of his employees, Morris had taken a few courses in corrections at Sam Houston State University, a growing center for the education of employees in the Texas prison system.[45] This curriculum choice betrayed the fact that much of the TYC's staff, as well as their superiors, viewed their work through the lens of adult prison rather than juvenile rehabilitation. In any case, professional qualifications mattered little for career mobility. Dwain Place, a former accountant at Pan-American Petroleum Corporation, began pursuing a master's degree in corrections long after he became the superintendent of Gatesville.[46] In 1957, his right-hand man Morris had landed his first Gatesville job as a cook. Within five years, he rose through the ranks of guard dormitory supervisor to become assistant superintendent.[47]

Morris's tenure was unusual; few workers stayed long enough to earn a promotion. Guards clearly found few satisfactions in their jobs. They received low pay, worked long hours, endured stressful situations that were rarely resolved in the space of a single shift, and probably enjoyed little in the way of social status outside the training school. These factors could have contributed to the guards' unforgivable actions. Their power over the boys may have afforded at least some guards a kind of horrible compensation; "poor white trash" on the outside, they became feared enforcers inside the training school. Few boys could hope to stand up physically to the average guard, despite TYC director Turman's insistence that "any seventeen-year-old kid in Mountainview [sic] . . . with his bare hands can take any man there apart."[48] In one description that echoed countless others, a guard who stood over six feet tall and weighed about three hundred pounds attacked a boy less than half his size.[49] Guards also wielded symbolic power deriving in part from their black uniforms, cowboy hats, and cowboy boots, an ensemble that caught the attention of experts who visited Mountain View. "I found myself saying yes, sir, and no, sir, and being very polite," recalled one visitor. "All I could see was the uniform."[50] Marking staff as prison guards rather than counselors or mentors, uniforms put the lie to job titles like "youth activities supervisor" and "house parent." One child psychiatrist noted that the Mountain View uniform could hardly promote rehabilitation in the institutional context when it so clearly signified "control and punishment" everywhere else.[51]

Physical abuse at Gatesville and Mountain View was part of a spectrum of punishments that enforced conformity to an unforgiving regimen that only loosely resembled the military drill format introduced in the second decade of the century. Boys wore crew cuts and uniforms, marched in formation, and observed strict rules of conduct. Military practices sometimes appeared in exaggerated and grotesque forms. Rule breakers were assigned to work details conducted in enforced silence for several hours at a time. Unlike military work or even prison labor, juvenile work details consisted of "make-work" tasks so designed for maximum punishment that they failed even to contribute to the upkeep of the institution or its grounds. Lacking any constructive purpose, the duties were thus not scheduled to follow any set pattern; boys were just as likely to "pull grass" one day as to shovel dirt pointlessly between two piles the next. The most notorious exercise was "picking." Boys in orange uniforms "lined up foot to foot, heads down . . . were required to strike the ground with heavy picks, swung overhead as the line moved forward."[52] Boys worked for hour-and-a-half stretches; during fifteen-minute breaks, they sat "in a line with their heads between their legs, looking down; they were not allowed to look in either direction or to talk."[53] When FBI agents arrived to photograph the work detail, one boy remembered being ordered to "keep [his] head up, not down."[54] Uneducated they may have been, but the guards clearly made distinctions between practices that seemed to require concealment and those that did not.

They also proved quite adept at devising and enforcing an intricate set of regulations governing work details, many of which increased the likelihood of violations. On a regular basis, boys collapsed after several hours of swinging a pick, shoveling dirt, or pulling grass. C.W. testified that "at least ten times" he saw such boys taken to a supervisor's office, only to return with visible bruises and welts.[55] Sixteen-year-old T.A. recalled one time that he had bent his knees after several hours of pulling grass. For this "resting" violation, he was "racked" by a guard supervisor who outweighed him by nearly two hundred pounds. His attacker then wrote out a bogus incident report and forced T.A. to sign it, another indication that guards knew what they were doing was illegal if not immoral.[56]

Although it represented a form of punishment, the work detail also served ideological purposes, and here we return to the question of how a well-educated officialdom that theoretically should have known better could permit the Mountain View regime. TYC officials viewed hard labor as essential to rehabilitation and defended punishments for boys who could not or would not work. Deeply ingrained in daily life, hard labor had acquired meanings fluid enough to accommodate a variety of explanations. To guards, work detail made the time pass by quicker; "busy work [was] better . . . than doing nothing."[57] Officials restated this sentiment more bluntly. "Work is required," asserted TYC director Turman matter-of-factly;

allowing some inmates to work less than others, he warned, would be "untenable in any correctional institution."[58] In this view, relieving boys who collapsed on the job would inspire others to feign exhaustion or illness; soon no one would be working. The worst crime a boy could commit, refusal to work, brought out the harshest reprisals. Turman referred to this act as a "mutiny" that had to be crushed immediately to prevent a mass revolt.[59] Inmates who engaged in solitary strikes against the work detail were likely to be teargassed. One supervisor admitted spraying Mace in a boy's face while two guards held him down.[60] In another case, a boy who attempted a peaceful sit-down protest in his cell was locked in with an activated can of Mace. Journalist Kenneth Wooden tracked down a former inmate nicknamed "Tweetybird" at an insane asylum; his body was covered in chemical burns caused by repeated gassings at close range. Privately, FBI agents told Wooden they were "astounded" that the TYC would approve the use of Mace on juveniles in a closet-sized isolation cell.[61] Only Turman defended the practice, citing training seminars for guards conducted by the Texas Department of Public Safety. On the witness stand, however, Turman stubbornly refused to confront the substance of such incidents:

Q: Have you ever been tear gassed, Dr. Turman?

A: Yes, sir.

Q: Have you ever tried to work after you've been tear gassed?

A: Yes, sir.

Q: Were you able to work?

A: Yes, sir.

Q: Were you able to work five hours with a pick axe in the manner that I've described earlier, do you think?

A: I didn't have to do a pick axe . . . but I had to work.

Q: Was it pleasant?

A: No.[62]

All tear-gas incidents at Mountain View transpired in the separate housing for inmates on work detail, an isolation ward paradoxically named the Security Treatment Center. The typical cell was eight-by-ten feet and contained only an open toilet and a steel bed. The walls were painted black and lit only by a lamp that resembled a car headlight except that it remained lit at all hours. Air-conditioning was provided for guard stations but not cells, which reached sweltering temperatures during the long, hot Texas summers.[63] Schoolbooks and visitors were prohibited.[64] The barren, uncomfortable cell that greeted a boy after five or six hours of grueling labor invited him to collapse in exhaustion. But he had to stay awake or suffer further punishment; rules prescribed that STC inmates remain awake, in

Figure 19. James A. Turman, executive director of the Texas Youth Council, 1957–73. (Box 1999/087-11, Records, Texas Youth Commission. Courtesy of the Texas State Library and Archives Commission.)

total silence, until ten o'clock at night. This presented problems for the numerous inmates dosed with sleep-inducing drugs like Thorazine or barbiturates, many of whom fell asleep early and earned themselves more time in the STC-work detail.[65] Asked for his view of the STC, Turman (figure 19) observed tartly that it was "not a place for people to loaf."[66]

It was, however, an easy place to gain entry. Among the transgressions that landed boys in the STC were "gambling for candy," "writing love letters to a lady academic teacher," "throwing a bar of soap at a boy," "laughing in church," and "calling Mr. Morris a rat."[67] Asked to explain such a wide range of infractions, many of which seemed minor, Turman offered only anecdotes of extreme behavior that did not match up with any of the violations documented in the Mountain View files.[68] Although he claimed to have spoken with STC inmates "every few days," it was clear that Turman had little inkling of what had transpired on his watch. Not once did he refer to a printed manual or handbook, because most of those that did exist had been developed in the 1950s and early 1960s and never updated. Over the years, the TYC board had added rules and regulations piecemeal, compiling them in a massive volume of handwritten notes that Turman called "the minutes" but which were really a mishmash of policy directives and meeting minutes. Judge Justice pored over these notes but found nothing of value, concluding that the TYC suffered from "the very evident absence of any central leadership, direction, or planning."[69]

The process by which inmates got out of the STC stripped away the veneer of orderly procedure to reveal something much more disturbing. Some inmates languished for weeks and months in cells ostensibly intended for, at most, a few days' stay. Twice a week, a discipline committee composed of school officials considered individual cases in meetings that were brief and perfunctory. Neither caseworkers nor the boys themselves participated in these deliberations. Inmates appeared just long enough to learn the committee's final decision and received no explanation of how it was reached. They were not permitted to address the committee, an almost needless rule given the perverse ritual that preceded inmates' appearance at a hearing. Inmates ran barefoot from their cell to the meeting room, chased by a guard who "racked" those who ran too slowly.[70] Small wonder that inmate witnesses in court could not identify rules of conduct or paths to being declared "rehabilitated" by their captors. Upon entering Gatesville, fifteen-year-old M. learned from fellow inmates to "just go along, keep your mouth shut, and listen." These precepts helped M. survive daily life, though he "hadn't figured out" how to make parole.[71] At this time, the TYC reported that the average length of stay for a Mountain View inmate was about eighteen months, while the average age of new admissions was 15.9 years old (see table 15). Only 4.9 percent of all male juvenile offenders had committed a violent crime against a person (sixty-six crimes, including eleven homicides).[72]

It was clear that the line between rehabilitation and punishment, if it ever truly existed, had blurred beyond recognition in both theory and practice. Revealingly, one thing that TYC director Turman shared with juvenile inmates was a seeming inability to offer a clear criterion for what constituted rehabilitation. Expert witnesses were certain, however, that it could not be found at Mountain View. Jerome

Table 15. Length of stay in months for Texas Youth Council inmates, 1973

	Median	Longest
Crockett	12.3	38
Gainesville	12.4	29
Brownwood	12.0	21
Gatesville	10.0	26
Mountain View	18.8	30

Source: *Morales v. Turman*, 383 F. Supp. 53, 1974 U.S. Dist. (August 30, 1974), at 5.

Miller declared it "the most brutal disciplinary unit" he had ever seen.[73] Even more damning were the conclusions of corrections consultant Howard Ohmart of the California-based American Justice Institute, who produced a report for the case in 1972. Ohmart, who had evaluated over twenty prisons, including the notorious Angola State Prison in Louisiana, described Mountain View as "punitive, regimented, and oppressive."[74] Guards wore "police-type uniforms" that, in Ohmart's estimation, discouraged the ability of staff to function as "substitute parents," as the TYC claimed they did. Epitomizing Mountain View's worst qualities was its "Security Treatment Center," reserved for rule breakers. Here boys lived in isolation cells and worked on a "punitive work squad." Ohmart recalled:

> As we approached the work squad the nine coverall-clad figures (with the "security" emblem emblazoned on the back) were seated on the ground taking the carefully timed "break." Elbows on knees, head between hands, they sat staring at the ground, forbidden to either talk or look at each other. Shortly after our arrival, one of the two supervising officers gave the work signal and without a word the group arose, still in line and started swinging their heavy hoes. The hoe comes high overhead and chops into the earth, in a pointless and completely unproductive exercise. Three or four swings and the line moves forward in unison, wordless, and with faces in a fixed, blank expressionless mask.[75]

Ohmart then observed the boys eating lunch, in total silence, heads bowed down, on the floor of their isolation cells (see figure 20). Ultimately, he concluded, "We have never seen anything quite as depressing, or anything that seemed so deliberately designed to humiliate, to degrade and debase. It is surely oppression in its simplest and most direct form."[76] One of the most revealing documents to survive this case was TYC director Turman's copy of Ohmart's report. Turman scribbled angry margin notes that argue with nearly every statement in this sixty-page report. Next to the paragraph quoted above, Turman wrote: "This is called discipline." Next to Ohmart's criticism of the staff uniforms, Turman wrote: "The stu-

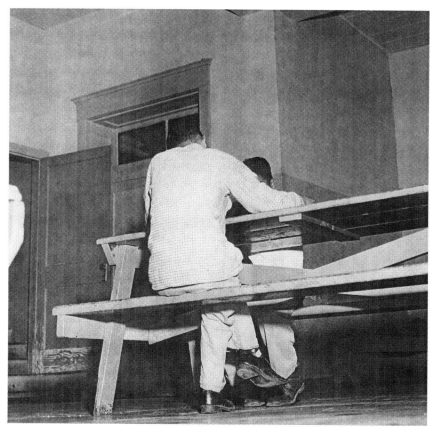

Figure 20. Sitting in silence, Gatesville State Schools for Boys, ca. 1960s. (Box 2007/23-17, Records, Texas Youth Commission. Courtesy of the Texas State Library and Archives Commission.)

dents in our schools have learned that clothes do not make a man." In many places he simply retorted "stupid" or "false."[77]

The "Control" System and the Construction of Deviance

Ohmart's report pointed to the TYC's adaptation of the "control model," a central feature of the Texas prison system and one that has remained controversial among prison historians and corrections experts. George Beto, the head of the Texas Department of Corrections, had earned a reputation as a sort of corrections guru for his refinement of the control model, which relied on strict regimentation of daily life enforced in part by some of the inmates themselves. Functioning as deputies to the guards, these "building tenders" enjoyed special privileges in exchange for their services. In the late 1960s and early 1970s, when prison riots in New York and California made headlines, the Texas prisons seemed like models of efficiency and order. Years later, this image would be shattered by a prisoners' rights case, *Ruiz v. Estelle*, that exposed abuses similar to those uncovered in the juvenile training schools. Nevertheless, scholars have continued to debate the merits of the control model. Its most vocal defender, criminologist John J. DiIulio, viewed the era of the control model as a veritable "golden age" when prisoners suffered little physical abuse, benefited from strict regimentation, and learned skills that lowered recidivism. Other observers disagreed, arguing that the use of building tenders helped conceal a host of abuses even as it more efficiently delivered physical punishment to disobedient inmates.[78]

The counterpart to the building tender in the juvenile training school was the "office boy," who functioned in almost precisely the same way. The resemblance was no accident; according to one study of Texas prisons, "some of these same 'office boys' would go on to become building tenders."[79] They supervised work details, administered punishments, doled out privileges, and occasionally even performed more official duties such as writing incident reports. Inmates feared office boys almost as much as the guards. Any inmate who chose to speak with attorneys or visiting experts risked vengeance from the office boys, who were on the lookout for "snitches." Even Steve Bercu once found himself cornered in a Mountain View bathroom by three large boys who were clearly acting on orders from adult staff.[80]

Attempts to enforce a code of silence during the court case revealed a secondary role for the office boys as the rulers of an inmate caste system based partly on race. Shortly after a visit from child psychiatrist Leonard Lawrence in March 1973, over one hundred boys were involved in what inmates later described as a "gang fight" between blacks and whites. Although interracial fighting was common, this incident seemed different.[81] According to J.H., the fighting began when a "tall white boy" sucker-punched a black inmate for no apparent reason. Afterward, office boys wrote incident reports that penalized black inmates.[82] The fight was just the tip of the proverbial iceberg. Office boys often supervised work details without adults present, an opportunity that they used to inflict pain on black inmates; they "kick[ed] them and beat them just like the men."[83] Adult guards sanctioned and protected this behavior. One day Jimmy Lee Jones, a gym instructor at Mountain View, complained to his superiors that he had witnessed office boys beating black inmates outside his office window. He was told to "find another job" if he disapproved of what he had seen. Jones was a rarity among the Mountain View staff. He was younger than most teachers, and he was African American. Moreover, Jones actually brought proper credentials to the job for which he was hired. He held a bachelor's degree in physical education, had worked with boys at a YMCA youth center in Houston, and had served a tour of duty in Vietnam.[84]

The office boys operated within an institutional subculture that made the train-ing school into a conduit between the state's urban neighborhoods and its prisons, as noted in the 1969 Texas Senate Youth Affairs Committee report. An oft-cited ex-ample of the delinquent subculture was the "counting system," in which those who "counted" belonged to and enjoyed the protection of inmate gangs. Membership brought benefits, but it also placed inmates in "abrasive and irreconcilable situa-tions." For instance, "a boy who [was] about ready to be recommended for parole and who [was] a 'counter' [was] subjected to almost unbearable pressures in efforts to induce him to 'mess up' . . . his opportunity for favorable parole consideration."[85] In this view, the inmate subculture prevented rehabilitation and glorified crime; if inmates would only cooperate with the program, order and salvation would fol-low. Adult staff expressed hopelessness about the situation: "One caseworker said he had once discouraged boys from trying to 'count' but no longer did so because he felt it met a need for some of them."[86] This statement psychologized tangible benefits as emotional "needs" and rationalized away the role of adult guards in perpetuating the gang system. Office boys were granted sweeping powers, allowing favored inmates to function with, if anything, more impunity than a street gang. Whether they had been a response or a spur to existing inmate gangs, the office boys clearly controlled "turf" and made organization for self-protection a necessity for their fellow inmates.

An unofficial sexual classification system organized inmates in more insidious and damaging ways. Guards were charged with the responsibility of separating "punks" from the general inmate population. Starting in the early twentieth cen-tury, the word "punk" has carried several meanings, according to prisoner-turned-historian Stephen Donaldson. In prison usage, it has referred to "a young, usually smaller and heterosexual, male who is exploited as a female surrogate by older, tougher, more powerful . . . males, or 'jockers.'" Outside the prison, a "punk" was also "a juvenile delinquent, a young outlaw, a young hoodlum"—precisely the kind of person who "ended up in jails and as the youngest were particular targets for 'turning out.'"[87] To be a "punk," then, was to occupy the lowest rung of a social structure defined by physical size, strength, and experience in "personal combat." Most "punks" were first-time offenders convicted for "nonviolent or victimless" crimes who lacked the necessary attributes to survive without suffering rape. Ac-cording to Donaldson, "juvenile institutions" have contained a "high proportion" of "punks," who have been misunderstood completely by adult officials. They were al-most always unwilling victims in a drama of masculine power that often expressed ethnic or racial dominance as well. When "punks" succumbed to sexual assault and became the property of a "daddy" or "jocker," officials viewed this "survival driven" behavior as willing consent and interpreted the rapist as an "aggressive homosexual" rather than a heterosexual confined to a place without women.[88]

Virtually all the practices described by Donaldson surfaced during courtroom scrutiny of the boys' training schools. Two "punk dorms" housed not only all the allegedly "homosexual" inmates at Mountain View but also boys sent over by Gatesville staff. This practice was hardly a secret; the *Fort Worth Star-Telegram* had reported it shortly before the start of *Morales v. Turman*.[89] Moreover, as Donaldson has observed, "jailhouse sexuality" usually operated openly, with full knowledge of guards, despite being forbidden by disciplinary codes.[90] In fact, at Mountain View, guards exercised hands-on control over it, although they did so informally and without recourse to any written policy. They placed "aggressive" and "passive" homosexuals in separate dormitories. A closer look showed that all the "aggressive homosexuals" were "larger, stronger" black inmates, while their "passive" partners were "smaller" Anglo and Latino inmates. TYC director Turman defended this pattern by citing "cultural" differences in the expression of what he called "homosexual tendencies." They had to be separated from one another as well as the general inmate population, he asserted, to protect against their "strange form of jealousy."[91] Asked to identify the defining features of sexual "deviance," Turman mumbled vaguely about "aberrant behavior" with "symptoms."[92] The guards restated Turman's views more bluntly. "You can tell if they look like a queer," one guard told an incredulous Miller during his visit.[93] Austin MacCormick, one of the few experts to defend the TYC, expressed his wish to "straighten out a few of them, except that nowadays nobody wants to be straightened out. They want to be accepted as homosexuals."[94]

MacCormick's comment raised a secondary question: Was homosexuality a legitimate identity choice during adolescence? The issue had recently divided the membership of the American Psychiatric Association (APA), which was considering the removal of homosexuality from the list of mental disorders published in its *Diagnostic and Statistical Manual of Psychiatric Disorders* (DSM).[95] The previous year, in nearby Dallas, the APA annual meeting took the controversial step of inviting gay rights activists to speak on the subject.[96] Around the same time, the APA joined the *Morales* case on the side of the juvenile inmates. This stance put the APA at odds with a longtime member of its state and national chapters, TYC director Turman. It also suggested a rejection of the argument, advanced by many older APA members, that the DSM deletion would "encourage" homosexuality in teenagers. Some clinicians complained that they could not steer "sexually confused" adolescents toward a normative heterosexuality unless homosexuality remained a disorder.[97] In addition to its deconstruction of the meanings of sexuality in a total institution, *Morales v. Turman* also participated in the era's debate over gay rights and identity.

A nebulous term in psychiatric clinics, "sexual confusion" described an even broader range of behaviors in a setting such as Mountain View. It included activities that have come to typify the everyday lives of teenage boys: masturbating, talking about sex, or comparing penis sizes. The backwardness of diagnosing these behaviors as "homosexual" would be funny had it not brought such severe consequences. "Deviant" boys usually were medicated and separated from the rest of the inmate population. Some ended up in a "punk dorm"; others found themselves placed in the isolation ward, which meant days spent on the grueling work detail.

This dynamic of superficial diagnosis and physical separation also took place, accompanied by emotional rather than physical abuse, at the girls' training schools. Gainesville staff harassed girls who held hands, combed each other's hair, or simply spent too much time together. One girl, G.G., had acquired the nickname "Love Business" among staff. Her caseworker had explained that "being a homosexual means you are no longer concerned about boys. You're always concerned about girls."[98] Another girl, M., remembered a "house mother" who warned her about "lesbian initiations" when she first arrived at Gainesville. No such thing ever took place.[99] Scenes like "two girls walking down the hall with their arms around each other" were enough to send staff into a panic.[100] At both the Gainesville and the Crockett girls' schools, the staff used a system of rules and rewards to discourage any "queer" behavior. For example, the enactment of a dress code that allowed girls to wear their own clothing rather than uniforms permitted only fashions and hairstyles that "looked feminine."[101]

Inmates recalled the awkward and painful feelings that came with being labeled "homosexual." G.G., for one, found it "hard to make friends or have emotions" without needling from staff about "being an L.B."[102] For boys, a "homosexual" diagnosis might come before or after a sexual assault; regardless, it signified physical weakness and emasculation as much as a supposed preference for other boys. To be designated a "punk," remembered C.W., was to be told that "you were small and everyone could run over you."[103] C.W. lived in the "punk dorm" reserved for "passive homosexuals," all of whom were "smaller boys" but not self-identified homosexuals. The African American inmates who lived in the other "punk dorm" objected even more strenuously to their official diagnosis. One of them, J.H., insisted that he was a "dude" rather than a "punk." To draw the distinction clearly, he mentioned "Slut," a smaller boy to whom he attached the pronouns "her" and "she."[104]

Adolescents so well versed in the sexual language of the prison presented expert witnesses with textbook examples of the emotional damage wrought by the training school. Too often, they argued, the "homosexual" tag became a self-fulfilling prophecy. Boys placed in Mountain View's "punk dorms" inexorably "succumb[ed] to the defined situation" and in so doing internalized an identity as a "sexual deviant."[105] At Gainesville, "staff fear of homosexuality [made] it an attractive form of rebellion," giving rise to "an 'underground culture' with a special jargon and ritual."[106] TYC staff misunderstood and distorted expressions of the sexual curiosity that typified adolescence, according to child psychiatrist Leonard Lawrence, who ran a residential clinic for children and adolescents in San Antonio. Bans on even the most innocuous behaviors taught that "thinking about sex" made one "a bad person," a lesson that took on added meaning in an environment where "legitimate decisions [about] sexual preference" were impossible. According to Lawrence, some inmates were doubly traumatized—first by sexual assault and again by the guilt feelings that arose from being stigmatized as a "deviant." In the guise of preventing sexual deviance, adult staff nurtured "negative identity formation," with inmates believing that they were irredeemably strange.[107] Lawrence added that many "normal" boys had experimented sexually with male and female partners, a claim known to psychiatrists and indeed most Americans (however much they may have disagreed) since the time of Alfred Kinsey's famous reports on male and female sexual behavior. Opposed to this possibility, TYC director Turman insisted that youthful sexual experimentation occurred only in "preadolescent puberty"—a bizarre invention, given that the onset of puberty usually marked the beginning of the developmental stage of adolescence.[108]

Sex and sexuality were key areas for adolescent identity formation, and the acceptable borders for exploration had been expanding throughout the previous decade. One of the ways in which schools had sought to harness and control this phenomenon was through sex education programs. However, it was discovered that the sex education program offered to girl inmates at Gainesville failed to offer anything approaching useful information. Psychiatrist Gerda Hansen Smith, who had visited Gainesville as part of the court-ordered participant-observation team, pronounced the class "a sham" that substituted old-time moral absolutism for sound reproductive information. Classes consisted of an instructor who nervously "just kind of read a few newspapers" aloud. When a new girl described how she had engaged in unprotected sex and worried that she might be pregnant, the teacher turned knowingly to Smith and muttered about "the new permissiveness."[109] Another girl told Smith that she was unable to discuss sexual problems with her caseworker without being exhorted to "put [her] faith in God." Shortly after that confession, Smith began to notice that Christianity played an inordinate role in the school's program. She met several caseworkers who "only wanted to talk about religion . . ., the love of the Christian life, and Christian attitudes."[110] Girls were required to attend Sunday church services, which for many of them constituted the only outdoor activity of the weekend.[111]

Gainesville's poor handling of sex education translated into dangerous treatment of girls who were unfortunate enough to enter the training school pregnant. Inmates approaching their due date were furloughed in time for childbirth but returned within the month. This policy separated young mothers from their infant children for periods that could last as long as two years. Girls whose families could not or would not help them found themselves in an untenable position; some considered putting their newborns up for adoption. TYC officials expressed little remorse over this situation; Austin MacCormick blamed the girls' "stupid and ignorant" families.[112] Lending a eugenicist cast to such statements were stories of abortions induced through either the incompetence or connivance of Gainesville staff. The evidence, though inconclusive, strongly suggested that induced abortions were an informal but regular practice at Gainesville. Three girls testified that they miscarried after the school nurse coerced them into ingesting unidentified white pills.[113] Other girls corroborated these claims; Gainesville's use of the procedure was "common knowledge" even in the home communities of parolees.[114] G.A., who was four months' pregnant, took "ten white pills" under the threat of solitary confinement. She began to bleed four days later, in a cruel irony while languishing in "pregnancy class," and finally miscarried that evening. Although allowed to recuperate in the Gainesville clinic for two weeks, G.A. saw no doctor until a month after the miscarriage. Staff faithfully foiled G.A.'s attempts to notify the fetus's biological father. Her housemother confiscated G.A.'s mail and placed it in her official file, informing her that she was "entitled to [her] opinion." Only because a caseworker took the initiative to summon G.A.'s mother did Judge Justice hear a believable eyewitness account of the episode; he seems to have discarded similar stories for lack of evidence, though transcripts show that he found them persuasive.[115] His final opinion gave no mention of the pills, noting only that G.A., like other pregnant inmates, had received "inadequate" medical attention.[116]

With the introduction of the coeducational Brownwood facility in 1970, Gainesville had become the site for older, "more sophisticated" female offenders.[117] While black inmates reported being subjected to racial epithets by white staff, Mexican American inmates were penalized regularly for speaking Spanish, particularly to one another. White girls received special privileges that brought them into more frequent contact with staff, who felt comfortable enough to vent their racial hostilities in what they assumed was friendly company. One such girl, M., recalled hearing daily complaints about black inmates who "got on their nerves."[118] White inmates who befriended blacks might be directed to "act like a white girl."[119] At the same time, staff closely monitored black inmates who acted "too black," a phrase that referred to cultural or political expressions that might lead to individual or collective rebellions. Black girls who entered Gainesville wearing an Afro or plaited hair (cornrows) were "encouraged" to cut or straighten their hair.[120] A directive from the Gainesville superintendent prohibited the circulation of Black Panther literature; staff were ordered to take "preventive measures" against any "advocation [sic] of black power or Chicano power."[121] One such measure prevented black girls from sitting together during meals in groups larger than two, even though the cafeteria tables only seated four.[122]

G.G. complained frequently enough about these practices to be labeled a "troublemaker." In return, her "house mother" prevented visits from her actual mother, whom she called "an unfit bitch." When TYC consultant Austin MacCormick visited Gainesville, G.G. informed him of her troubles; his only response was to call her "a damn liar."[123] G.G. reserved her deepest bitterness, however, for the older African Americans who worked at Gainesville in the positions of caseworker, recreational supervisor, and house parent. In court, G.G. explained why they were no better than their white counterparts:

> Q: Would you feel better if there were more black staff at Gainesville?
> A: Yeah, if they act black.
> Q: Would you feel better if there were more black house parents?
> A: Same goes for them. If they act black.
> THE COURT (interjecting): Maybe you can explain to me what you mean by that.
> WITNESS: Well, they think they're better than us black girls. They think they are so high up.[124]

The divide was both generational and regional; the fact of shared skin color could not overcome barriers of experience. Older, rural blacks were almost as likely as their white coworkers to overreact to black teenagers from large and midsized cities who were assertive and listened to "loud music."[125] The superintendent of the Crockett School for Girls, Pete Harrell, was a case in point. Until 1965, Crockett had served at the Jim Crow school for black girls, and Harrell had been the lone black official of any stature in the TYC hierarchy. During his court testimony, he warned of a "more sophisticated, more destructive, and more vicious" generation of juvenile delinquents.[126] But a glance at the statistics on offenses in the early 1970s showed that violent crime was the exception rather than the rule for juveniles. While only 5 percent of boy inmates were violent offenders, over 60 percent of girls were committed for "disobedience" to parents or school officials.[127] Surprisingly for a time when many American parents were fuming at the rise in drug use among teenagers, the TYC kept no figures on drug-related arrests. However, one can speculate that many adolescent girls who found themselves in a training school in the early 1970s were charged with "cultural" offenses—precocious sexuality, drug experimentation, nonconformity in dress or music taste, or simply a more pronounced rebellious attitude toward adults.[128] Arriving at a place like Gainesville, such girls likely confronted a staff that, if anything, seemed even more out of touch with their problems than their own parents and teachers had been on the outside.

Gainesville employees who could not speak the language of youth cultures proved even less adept at communicating with Spanish-speaking inmates, who comprised between one-quarter to one-third of the inmate population. In fact, they did not have to try. A long-standing English-only policy covered every conceivable interaction between inmates and workers. In court, the Gainesville superintendent defended this policy as an educational tool to promote English-language facility; in practice, it was all too clear that ban functioned to prevent Mexican American inmates from secretly mocking staff, conspiring to commit mischief, or holding any kind of truly private conversation.[129] Girls caught speaking Spanish were subject to disciplinary action. Gainesville's discipline records for 1969–73, which were turned over to the court, suggest that the ban provided endless opportunities for punishment. At the same time, individual offenses were so routine sounding that one suspects the ban proved unenforceable at times. Entries for one girl included offenses such as "called me a *puta* & then denied it," "talking in Spanish, dirty talk," and "sassy & impudent." This particular girl was placed in isolation several times, without any specific reason, suggesting that it was a last resort for exasperated workers.[130] Another girl, cited five times in two weeks for speaking Spanish, received after-school detention and had her smoking privileges revoked. Only when she was caught "lying about" speaking Spanish was she placed in isolation.[131]

Again, it is important to underscore that the staff's shortcomings merely reflected those of their lettered superiors. William M. Lovejoy, a psychiatrist employed part-time at Gainesville, admitted that he long had struggled in one-on-one sessions with Mexican American girls because he could not speak Spanish. His only exposure to the language came from Spanish instructional cassettes played during weekly drives between his Dallas psychiatric clinic and Gainesville.[132] For the professionals, the language barrier was only the most visible aspect of a larger cultural gulf separating them from the adolescents they purported to help. Lovejoy, an elderly psychiatrist trained in the 1930s, seemed well intentioned but incapable of relating to girl inmates of color. His assurances that he understood "black dialect" and "poor ghetto families," as well as "Mexican American culture," rang hollow.[133] Similarly, Austin MacCormick had a "hard time relating to Chicanos . . . [and] Blacks"; he further conceded that he could only "guess" at their treatment, a statement that seemed to severely undercut his ringing praise for the Texas training schools throughout the preceding decade.[134]

TYC officials all but admitted that they were unable or unwilling to take seriously the variety of identities that juvenile delinquents brought into the training schools. They presided over institutions that cast some boys as "punks," most girls as lesbians, and teenagers of color as inherently inferior. Even "normal" white inmates received a severely restricted brand of education. Girls learned to cook, clean, and care for the babies of working-class men, even as they were denied information about their own reproductive systems. For boys, the Texas prison system cast a huge shadow over every aspect of their experiences. Most of the worst features of adult prison appeared in some form in Gatesville and Mountain View: military regimentation, hard labor, inmate rape, racially motivated gang violence, and extended solitary confinement. At Gainesville, girls learned what they likely already knew, that their life choices were extremely limited and possibly tethered to a male provider. The boys received a harsher education seemingly intent on making them into inmates rather than citizens, a process made all the more offensive by the lack of remorse shown by those who administered and benefited from it. Founded ostensibly on the principles of children's mental health and steered by experts trained in psychiatry, psychology, and social work, the Texas Youth Council somehow had gone terribly awry. In fact, the TYC's failures to live up to its own therapeutic precepts had brought about its downfall.

At the end of the trial phase, on August 31, 1973, Judge Justice issued an emergency injunction restricting the use of corporal punishment, banning the use of Mace, prohibiting racial segregation, and setting forth strict guidelines for the use of solitary confinement. The injunction declared the TYC's existing practices in each of these areas to be "unacceptable to contemporary society" and in violation of various provisions of the Constitution.[135] Judge Justice ordered that the new guidelines be posted in TYC facilities and appointed Gatesville social worker Charles Derrick as the court's ombudsman to ensure that the order was followed. In response, TYC director Turman complained publicly about the order, stating that it could not be enforced. Gatesville staff permitted an inmate riot to erupt, claiming that their hands were tied by Justice's directives. There was some implication that staff were acting with the sanction, if not the outright encouragement, of top TYC officials. The riot was widely viewed as a clumsy attempt by the TYC to embarrass the court; however, it had the opposite effect.[136] The consensus view had shifted considerably against the TYC's use of large and virtually unaccountable institutions. State newspapers wondered about the national impact of the case's outcome, even reviving the 1969 Texas Senate report that had called for "decentralization."

A harsh rebuke from Judge Justice was followed by the abrupt resignation of director Turman and board chairman Kneebone, elevating Brownwood facility superintendent Ron Jackson to the position of interim (and eventually permanent) director of the agency. Brownwood had opened in 1970 and was the only TYC institution to escape any significant criticism during the case. Housing both the statewide reception center and a cottage-style facility for less serious female offenders, Brownwood had quickly established a reputation for a "dynamic and individualized program" and earned praise from advocates for the *Morales* plaintiffs.

Jackson's successful work at Brownwood made him an obvious choice to lead the TYC through the coming period of court-ordered reform.[137]

Nearly a year later, on August 30, 1974, Judge Justice issued his complete ruling. The opinion decried not only the "physical" but also the "psychological" damage inflicted on juvenile inmates in the state's care. More broadly, the ruling held that juveniles taken into the TYC's custody had a "right to treatment," based on the TYC's own mission statement, the Eighth Amendment's prohibition against cruel and unusual punishment, and the Fourteenth Amendment's due process clause. Justice went on to define treatment on the basis of normative expectations for adolescence, focusing on the importance of self-esteem and mental health. "The acquisition of a positive identity," he declared, was "one of the primary tasks of adolescence."[138] In the detailed sixty-page opinion, Justice listed all the services that TYC would be required to provide. It was almost a verbatim repetition of items listed in the 1969 Senate report and the 1949 TYC enabling legislation. For instance, staff hirings were to be based on professional training, psychological testing, and racial and ethnic diversity. Institutions that had long functioned according to separate and inconsistent rules were to share well delineated guidelines for diagnosis, treatment, and parole. The court abolished corporal punishment, the use of tear gas, and stoop labor. It also limited solitary confinement to days rather than weeks in isolation, and specified the few situations where it was appropriate. Juveniles were entitled to individual treatment plans, bilingual education, assessments for learning disabilities, career guidance services, and appropriately trained personnel.[139]

Court-Supervised Reform, 1974–1988

The most immediate result of the ruling was the closing of Mountain View in 1975 and Gatesville in 1979, "because effective rehabilitation treatment at the facilities had become impossible."[140] Judge Justice ordered a shift to community-based facilities, citing the "least restrictive alternative" model put forward in the 1967 president's commission and the 1974 federal Juvenile Justice and Delinquency Prevention Act.[141] In 1975, the Texas legislature appropriated nine million dollars for the development of community-based treatment programs. That same year, the state appealed *Morales* to the Fifth Circuit, which ordered a new trial on the basis that the case should have been heard by a three-judge panel. The TYC promptly fired ombudsman Derrick and withdrew from ongoing negotiations with the plaintiffs' attorneys for a settlement. Ultimately, the U.S. Supreme Court reversed the ruling and sent it back to the Fifth Circuit for a consideration of the merits. In a separate but related case concerning conditions in institutions for the mentally ill, *Donaldson v. O'Connor*, the Supreme Court ruled against a right to treatment yet suggested that rehabilitating juveniles was "desirable." Thus, the Court limited the scope of Judge Justice's ruling to the prohibition on cruel and unusual punishment in the Eighth Amendment.[142]

However, even as the case was mired in appeal, the TYC was changing under Jackson's leadership. By 1976, the agency was operating halfway houses in Austin, Corpus Christi, Dallas, and Houston. The following year, the Texas Department of Public Welfare certified the TYC's Residential Contract Program as a "child-placing agency," allowing it to contract with counties for foster homes, group homes, and residential treatment centers.[143] The TYC also established a four-pronged Community Services Division, budgeted at roughly twelve million dollars, which in many respects harkened back to the agency's original program in 1949. The division included the Community Assistance Program to keep "pre-delinquent youth" in their communities; supervised parole; and managed TYC-operated and privately operated residential sites. The stated goal, "to develop meaningful corrections programs for pre-delinquent and delinquent youth without taking [them] a long distance from their homes," signaled a major shift in emphasis.[144] Between 1974 and 1981, the number of TYC youth placed in community-based programs had risen from 81 to 2,168, with nearly two-thirds of all TYC commitments in noninstitutional settings (either on parole or in a residential program).[145]

As for *Morales*, wishing to avoid the expense of further litigation, both sides moved toward a settlement agreement, which was approved by Judge Justice in April 1984. The settlement created a Morales Consultant Committee to monitor TYC's progress over a multiyear period until mandated improvements had been made. The committee issued its final report in 1988, proclaiming TYC's makeover to be a success. Not only was the TYC found to be in compliance with the provisions of the *Morales* settlement agreement, but it had become a national model for juvenile correctional programs elsewhere.[146] By that time, the legislature had enacted a new Texas Family Code, which set forth guidelines separating status offenders from more-serious offenders in court; it had also created the Texas Juvenile Probation Commission in 1981 to carry out the important service of state support and standardization of local juvenile justice systems, which the TYC had historically proven unable to provide. Reflecting on the *Morales* case in 2003, attorney Bercu suggested that its most important legacy was that "for decades, thousands and thousands of kids ... didn't get shipped to these places that [they] would have under the prior regime."[147] By then, however, the pendulum had swung yet again in the direction of punishment, challenging the TYC's ability to adhere to the treatment principles laid down in the *Morales* settlement.

Epilogue
The New American Dilemma

The summer of 2002 found the state of Texas far removed from the reforms envisioned in *Morales v. Turman*. Instead, the state had attracted bitter condemnations from national and international critics for its administration of the death penalty to juvenile offenders. That summer, the state executed three African American men—Napoleon Beazley, T. J. Jones, and Toronto Patterson—for crimes they had committed at the age of seventeen. Of the three, Beazley's case provoked the deepest soul-searching, largely because his case defied practically every stereotype about "super-predators" who kill without conscience. Beazley hailed from a two-parent, middle-class household in Grapeland, an East Texas town where the races historically had lived separately and mingled infrequently. However, Beazley had managed to break down old social barriers. According to a lengthy profile in *Texas Monthly*, Beazley was "the first black kid ever to be accepted by whites" and "a bright teenager with a loose-limbed confidence and a dazzling smile." An honors student, star athlete, and president of his senior class at Grapeland High School, Beazley had dreamed of attending Stanford Law School.[1]

His many successes, however, exacted a price: Beazley was resented and ostracized by his peers in "the Quarters," the historically black neighborhood where he had grown up. He later complained of experiencing worse racial taunts from "other black kids" than from whites. Soon he fell in with an older cousin, a mid-level drug dealer who offered Beazley the street credibility he had desired. Beazley began to lead a double life, selling and using drugs by night while winning school accolades by day. Finally, one night in April 1994, Beazley participated in a carjacking in the nearby city of Tyler (the site of the *Morales* trial two decades earlier). Riding with his cousin and another man, Beazley followed an older white couple in a Mercedes to their garage, where the runner-up for "Mr. Grapeland High" shot and killed an unarmed man. Weeks later, as he was preparing for his graduation, Beazley was arrested by police, to the shock of virtually the entire community.[2]

News of the crime stirred unusual passions, not least because the victim, John Luttig, was a retired oilman and the father of Judge J. Michael Luttig, a conservative Republican who sat on the D.C. Circuit Court of Appeals. The case seemed to validate the worst fears about a generation of "thrill-killers" whose actions called for maximum punishment, and Beazley was quickly sentenced to death. However, as his case made its way through the appeals process, Beazley had several defenders, including his former schoolteachers, the attorney from his home county who had originally prosecuted him, and the judge who had presided over his trial. Each asked for a commutation of his sentence to life in prison. In early 2002, as Beazley's execution date approached, Texas governor Rick Perry fielded clemency petitions from Amnesty International and South African archbishop Desmond Tutu. CNN produced an hour-long special, *Scheduled to Die*, that showcased the controversy over Beazley's case. Beazley openly admitted his guilt and expressed unswerving remorse for his crime. "I was old enough to know what I was doing," he insisted. "Any explanation I tried to give would sound like an excuse, and there's no excuse for what I've done."[3] Beazley maintained this position until his final statement, given the day before his death by lethal injection on June 7, 2002, in which he lamented his "senseless" and "heinous" crime but warned that his execution would repeat his own errors of judgment.[4]

Citing neurological research on the "teenage brain," several local commentators decried the application of the ultimate adult punishment to juvenile offenders. "Teenagers are redeemable and able to be rehabilitated," protested Alberta Phillips of the *Austin American-Statesman*, because of "social and physiological differences between adolescents and adults."[5] An article in the *Texas Law Review* phrased the problem more directly: Had "kids who kill" forfeited the age-based protections built up over a century of legal and cultural practice? Had they in fact forfeited their childhood?[6]

The debate over the juvenile death penalty, punctuated by cases such as Beazley's, reflect a growing disaffection with the trajectory of juvenile justice among legal experts, professionals, and academics. On the one hand, as Jeffrey Fagan has noted, the increasing number of juveniles transferred to adult court since the 1970s has presupposed that adolescents ought to be held to the same standard of criminal responsibility as adult offenders.[7] At the same time, the juvenile court too often has become, in Barry Feld's words, "a scaled-down, second-class criminal court that provides young offenders with neither therapy nor justice."[8] As noted earlier, abuse scandals in facilities for juvenile offenders, both privately and publicly run, have become less unusual occurrences in recent years. The impact of those conditions has fallen disproportionately on African American and Latino youth. According to the federal Office of Juvenile Justice and Delinquency Prevention, in 2001 African

Americans comprised just 17 percent of the juvenile population but 43 percent of all juvenile arrests.[9] In a May 2000 study by researchers from the National Council on Crime and Delinquency, black juvenile offenders were significantly more likely than whites to be referred to court, detained while awaiting trial, incarcerated in juvenile facilities, and sentenced as adults. This pattern held even when blacks and whites committed identical crimes. For instance, in drug-related arrests, white youth comprised nearly two-thirds of cases but stood only a one in three chance of being waived to adult court. The reverse was true for black youth in the study, a disparity made all the more striking by the continued miscounting of Latino offenders as "white" in some jurisdictions (a practice discontinued by the U.S. Census Bureau over two decades ago).[10]

Greater awareness of this "cumulative disadvantage" may set the stage for a new cycle of juvenile justice reform. I would suggest that it confronts us with an American dilemma for the twenty-first century. In 1944, Gunnar Myrdal's massive study of American race relations, *An American Dilemma*, set forth a challenge to a nation at war. Myrdal argued that the "American creed" of equal citizenship was belied by the realities of racism, segregation, lynchings, and institutional discrimination. Rectifying those historical injustices, he suggested, would fulfill the promises embodied in the Declaration of Independence and the Constitution and enable the nation to live up to the Four Freedoms that represented the official war aims as spelled out by President Franklin Delano Roosevelt in World War II. Famously depicted in a series of Norman Rockwell illustrations, the Four Freedoms envisioned a society whose members shared equally in free expression, religious tolerance, a middle-class standard of living, and a sense of shared security. Indeed, the modern civil rights movement grew out of a wartime campaign to extend these benefits to African Americans and in the process win "double victory" over Nazism overseas and Jim Crow at home.[11]

Even as the struggle for racial equality made enormous strides in the wake of the historic *Brown v. Board of Education* ruling, the pattern in juvenile justice has trended in the opposite direction. This century's dilemma is to extend the privileges and protections of childhood and adolescence to all youth, regardless of social background; to make the reality of juvenile justice hew more closely to its founding rhetoric; and to break the deeply ingrained habit of viewing even the worst youthful offenders as if they were fully responsible adults. This ambition was put forward clearly in Judge Justice's 1974 ruling in *Morales v. Turman*, but many of the principles he expressed have been reversed in the years following the 1988 settlement, for reasons to which we now turn.

While the TYC was implementing the settlement guidelines for community-based programs, the nation as a whole began moving in the opposite direction.

Law-and-order critics of juvenile justice argued that the introduction of due process protections historically afforded to adult defendants had weakened an already porous juvenile system. Therefore, violent and serious juvenile offenders who enjoyed adult protections should face adult penalties or, in an oft-repeated 1980s slogan, "adult time for adult crime." In 1980, the State of Washington adopted new sentencing guidelines based on a "point system" that gave judges discretionary authority to transfer youth to adult court or to issue determinate sentences that could extend a youth's commitment beyond the age of eighteen.[12] Prompted in part by the crack cocaine epidemic of the late 1980s, other states emulated Washington's policy shift. In 1987, Texas adopted a determinate sentencing statute making it easier to transfer juvenile offenders from the TYC to adult prison for up to thirty years for violent crimes (such as murder, rape, aggravated assault) and allowed judges to transfer juveniles as young as ten years of age to adult court. In its 1991 *Uniform Crime Reports*, the FBI issued a twenty-five-year study of violent juvenile crime that showed a 27 percent increase between 1980 and 1991, which it described as "an unrivaled period of juvenile violent crime."[13] That same year, the Texas Attorney General's office released a report stating that about one-third of TYC referrals were members of "named gangs" and another third "belong[ed] to a circle of friends who think of themselves as a gang."[14] In 1995, the legislature reported that between 1985 and 1993, juvenile arrests in Texas had increased by 43 percent, and juvenile homicides had tripled. Juvenile arrests for violent offenses, often gang related, rose by a quarter nationally, and by as much as 40 or 50 percent in some states.

Between 1990 and 1996, forty states passed new legislation expanding the categories of juvenile cases that could be transferred to adult court.[15] State legislatures began investing millions of dollars in the expansion of large, maximum-security "youth prisons." Democratic President Bill Clinton backed a federal crime bill that allocated millions of dollars for juvenile boot camps, a fashionable solution for the "out-of-control teens" featured regularly on daytime talk shows. Meanwhile, in Texas, Republican George W. Bush won the 1994 gubernatorial race on a platform that called for getting tough on juvenile crime. "So long as we've got an epidemic of crime," he declared memorably in January, 1994, "I think we ought to forget about rehabilitation and worry about incarceration."[16] The legislature turned Bush's campaign promise into a reality the following year, in HB 327, an omnibus juvenile justice reform act. It increased the list of offenses eligible for determinate sentencing, expanded transfer into the adult criminal system for incarcerated juveniles, and lowered the age at which a juvenile could be tried in adult court from fifteen to fourteen. In an attempt to standardize juvenile sentencing around the state, the bill also included a progressive sanctions model that was to guide juvenile judges and probation departments in their decision making. The 1996–97 state budget increased juvenile justice spending by nearly $200 million, including approximately $55 million in bond proceeds to almost triple the TYC's institutional capacity from 1,686 in 1995 to 4,358 in 2005.[17] At the time, experts were predicting a 73 percent increase in the number of incarcerated juveniles by 2002. This would prove to be inaccurate, however; TYC commitments reached their peak in 1998 with 3,188 new commitments, but by 2006 that number had dropped to 2,638.[18]

Even as the TYC expanded its secure institutions, rates of abuse began climbing. In 2005, prompted by allegations of abuse in the nearby Evins Regional Juvenile Justice Center in Edinburg, the *McAllen Monitor* published a series of articles by journalist Elizabeth Pierson exploring the reasons behind the high rates of violence in TYC facilities. Pierson's research showed that from 1999 to 2005, youth in TYC institutions experienced steadily increasing levels of abuse; by 2005, three out of every one hundred youth had been abused by TYC employees.[19]

In the wake of the 2007 sex abuse scandal, the legislature was moved to take sweeping action. On May 28, the legislature unanimously passed SB 103, omnibus juvenile justice legislation aimed at improving conditions in the TYC and preventing further abuse of incarcerated youth. The legislation established public reporting of cases of abuse, a parents' bill of rights, the Office of the Inspector General to investigate criminal allegations within TYC institutions, and the Office of the Independent Ombudsman to serve as an advocate for incarcerated youth. It also increased preservice training requirements for staff, required a youth-to-staff ratio of 12 to 1, mandated that the TYC provide specialized treatment to youth who needed it, and prohibited the commitment to the TYC of youth who had engaged in misdemeanor-level delinquent conduct. The bill also directed the state's Sunset Advisory Commission to explore the possibility of developing a regionalized system with smaller facilities closer to children's communities. Last, the 2008–9 biennial budget also provided $47 million in increased funding to the Texas Juvenile Probation Commission to support community-based alternatives to incarceration in TYC facilities. However, as in past reform periods, implementation would not come easily. Governor Rick Perry appointed as TYC conservator Ed Owens, a career prison official, who in turn began importing personnel and practices from the Texas prison system. Most controversially, Owens, along with the TYC's acting executive director Dimitria Pope, instituted a policy directing staff to use pepper spray as a first resort for controlling disobedient inmates. The pepper spray directive provoked a new round of lawsuits and protests, largely from youth advocates and juvenile justice experts, who argued that curbing abuses called for the reduction, rather than the increase, of prisonlike features. Pope also discarded a study commissioned by the TYC to propose ways to reform the agency. In September 2007, this Blue Ribbon Task Force released its report, which singled out the pepper-spray policy for special criticism. Urging "a shift in culture away from punishment and towards a treatment approach," the report put forth a plan for smaller, regionally located treatment centers that emphasized family and community involvement in the rehabilitation of juvenile offenders.[20]

While one must be careful not to oversimplify the troubled history of juvenile justice in Texas, the cyclical pattern of abuse and scandal—from humanitarian reform, to juvenile crime panic, to "get-tough" crackdown—emerges with painful clarity. The litany of errors is long, beginning with the all-too-common willingness to view juvenile offenders as fully responsible adults, even in the face of scientific evidence suggesting otherwise. Public fears of "teenage terrorists" in the 1950s and 1960s and of "super-predators" in the 1980s and early 1990s have propelled the growth of expensive lockdown facilities that have failed to deter juvenile crime but have succeeded with startling consistency in offending the conscience. Since the 1940s, experts have largely concurred on the superior effectiveness of smaller, community-based, therapeutic programs as compared to remote, secure institutions for the rehabilitation of troubled youth. However, Texas has consistently failed to sustain its investment in such programs, preferring instead to attempt reform of a broken system within the framework of an institutional status quo. Such reform efforts have proven inadequate in challenging those deeply ingrained institutional practices that focus on security, control, and punishment to the exclusion of effective rehabilitative programming, often out of structural necessity as much as ideology. Surely these are errors upon which we can improve.

NOTES

Introduction

1. In this book, the acronym TYC refers to both the Texas Youth Council (1957–83) and its successor agency, the Texas Youth Commission (1983–present).

2. Nate Blakeslee, "Hidden in Plain Sight," *Texas Observer*, February 23, 2007 (first published online February 16, 2007). See also Blakeslee, "Sins of Commission," *Texas Monthly*, May 2007, 150.

3. "Sex Abuse Reported at Youth Jail," *Dallas Morning News*, February 18, 2007.

4. "Sexual Abuse Scandal Rocks Texas Juvenile Prison System," Associated Press, March 6, 2007; "Texas, Addressing Sexual Abuse Scandal, May Free Thousands of Its Jailed Youths," *New York Times*, March 24, 2007; "In Texas, Scandals Rock Juvenile Justice System," *Washington Post*, April 7, 2007; "Two Indicted for Abuse at Texas Detention Center," NPR *Morning Edition*, April 11, 2007.

5. Texas Youth Commission, *Texas Youth Commission: Report from the Conservator*, prepared by Jay Kimbrough (Austin, 2007); "Youth Abuse Hotline Quickly Gets 1,100 Complaints," *El Paso Times*, March 26, 2007; "Juvenile Justice on Trial in Texas," *Chicago Tribune*, March 27, 2007; "Injuries of Teen Inmates Probed," *USA Today*, May 14, 2007; "Feds Knew about TYC Abuse Cases," *Dallas Morning News*, August 5, 2007.

6. Joint Select Committee on the Operation and Management of the Texas Youth Commission, *Preliminary Report of Findings and Initial Recommendations: A Report to the Lieutenant Governor and the Speaker of the House*, 80th Tex. Leg. (Austin, 2007).

7. "$5M Lawsuit Filed in TYC Scandal," *Dallas Morning News*, March 19, 2007.

8. "My Case Freed 500 Teens from Prison!" *Seventeen*, September 2007; see also Howard Witt, "To Some in Paris, Sinister Past Is Back," *Chicago Tribune*, March 12, 2007; "Cotton Tells Story to Teen Magazine," *Paris News*, August 19, 2007.

9. "Sex Abuse Reported at Youth Jail," *Dallas Morning News*, February 18, 2007.

10. Histories of the juvenile court tend to highlight its many contradictions. Among the early works, see Steven Schlossman, *Transforming Juvenile Justice: Reform Ideals and Institutional Realities, 1825–1920* (1977; repr., DeKalb: Northern Illinois University Press, 2005); David J. Rothman, *Conscience and Convenience: The Asylum and Its Alternatives in Progressive America* (1980; repr., New York: Aldine de Gruyter, 2002), 236–92; Robert M. Mennel, *Thorns and Thistles: Juvenile Delinquents in the United States, 1825–1940* (Hanover, N.H.: University Press of New England, 1973); and Anthony M. Platt, *The Child Savers: The Invention of Delinquency*, 3rd ed. (Camden, N.J.: Rutgers University Press, 2008). More-recent studies include Mary E. Odem, *Delinquent Daughters: Protecting and Policing Adolescent Female Sexuality in the United States, 1880–1925* (Chapel Hill: University of North Carolina Press, 1995); Barry C. Feld, *Bad Kids: Race and the Transformation*

of the Juvenile Court (New York: Oxford University Press, 1999); David S. Tanenhaus, *Juvenile Justice in the Making* (Cambridge: Oxford University Press, 2005); Anne Meis Knupfer, *Reform and Resistance: Gender, Delinquency, and America's First Juvenile Court* (New York: Routledge, 2001); and Tamara Myers, *Caught: Montreal's Modern Girls and the Law, 1869–1945* (Toronto: University of Toronto Press, 2007).

11. John J. DiIulio Jr., "The Coming of the Super-Predators," *Weekly Standard*, November 27, 1995.

12. See, for instance, Henry A. Giroux, *Fugitive Cultures: Race, Violence, and Youth* (New York: Routledge, 1996).

13. A good synthesis of the growing literature on the history of childhood is Steven J. Mintz, *Huck's Raft: A History of American Childhood* (New York: Oxford University Press, 2005).

14. Ben B. Lindsey and Rube Borough, *The Dangerous Life* (1931; repr., New York: Arno Press, 1974), 90.

15. "Sex Abuse, Violence Alleged at Teen Jails across U.S.," CNN *Presents* (broadcast April 4, 2008), http://www.cnn.com/2008/CRIME/04/04/juvenile.jails/index.html.

16. See most notably Elizabeth S. Scott and Laurence Steinberg, *Rethinking Juvenile Justice* (Cambridge, Mass.: Harvard University Press, 2008).

One. The Other Lost Generation

1. The names of juveniles in this chapter are pseudonyms only if they did not appear in published or publicly available sources.

2. The following story of Jimmy's offense is taken from "Mr. Jones" to R. B. Walthall, March 12, 1927; Jones to Governor Dan Moody, March 15, 1927; and court documents attached to Charles E. King to H. H. Harrington, May 14, 1927, in Chairman R. B. Walthall files, 1924–29 (letters) and Chairman H. H. Harrington files, 1917–28 (court documents), Texas State Board of Control Board member's files, Archives and Information Services Division, Texas State Library and Archives Commission, Austin (archive hereafter cited as TSLAC).

3. This paragraph draws on two letters from Jimmy Jones to his father, both dated February 25, 1927, and Mr. Jones to R. B. Walthall, March 10, 1927, both in Chairman R. B. Walthall files, TSLAC.

4. Mr. Jones recounted this meeting months after it happened. Jones to H. H. Harrington, June 23, 1927, Chairman H. H. Harrington files, TSLAC.

5. Daniel J. Moody Jr. to TBC, March 22, 1927; TBC to Charles E. King, March 25, 1927, both in Chairman H. H. Harrington files, TSLAC.

6. The following description draws on the report of J. E. McCoy to TBC, March 31, 1927, Chairman H. H. Harrington files, TSLAC.

7. TBC to C. E. King, April 5, 1927, Chairman H. H. Harrington files, TSLAC.

8. A. D. Chestnut to H. H. Harrington, April 3, 1927, Chairman H. H. Harrington files, TSLAC.

9. J. A. Farqhuar to H. H. Harrington, April 19, 1927, Chairman H. H. Harrington files, TSLAC.

10. Judge W. H. Thompson to TBC, May 11, 1927, Chairman H. H. Harrington files, TSLAC.

11. C. E. King to H. H. Harrington, May 14, 1927, Chairman H. H. Harrington files, TSLAC.

12. Lorene Moon to Judge Thompson, May 30, 1927, Chairman H. H. Harrington files, TSLAC.

13. Mr. Jones to H. H. Harrington, June 2, 1927; Jones to Harrington, June 4, 1927; Harrington to Jones, June 6, 1927; Jones to Harrington, June 8, 1927, all in Chairman H. H. Harrington files, TSLAC.

14. Harrington to Jones, June 6, 1927.

15. Governor Moody to C. E. King, June 16, 1927; TBC to King, June 16, 1927; Mr. Jones to H. H. Harrington, June 23, 1927, all in Chairman H. H. Harrington files, TSLAC.

16. H. H. Harrington to C. E. King, August 13, 1927, Chairman H. H. Harrington files, TSLAC.

17. *Report of the Commissioners and Trustees of the House of Correction and Reformatory, located at Gatesville, Coryell County* (Austin: State Printing House, 1888), 1–2; Texas Youth Commission Facilities and Programs History and Information Notebooks, Archives and Information Services Division, TSLAC.

18. It is unclear whether Gatesville was the first statewide juvenile institution of its kind in the South, although that claim is advanced in Donald R. Walker, *Penology for Profit: A History of the Texas Prison System, 1867–1912* (College Station: Texas A&M University Press, 1988), 72. At the very least it was among the earliest; see Vernetta D. Young, "Race and Gender in the Establishment of Juvenile Institutions: The Case of the South," *Prison Journal* 73, no. 2 (June 1994): 244–65; and John Garrick Hardy, "A Comparative Study of Institutions for Negro Juvenile Delinquents in the Southern States" (PhD diss., University of Wisconsin, 1946).

19. *Report of the Trustees to the Governor, December 18, 1888* (Austin: State Printing Office, 1888).

20. Zelma Scott, *A History of Coryell County, Texas* (Austin: Texas State Historical Association, 1965), 58.

21. Ibid., 135. See also Randolph B. Campbell, *Gone to Texas: A History of the Lone Star State* (New York: Oxford University Press, 2004), 292–351.

22. T. A. Saunders testimony, "Testimony of Officers and Employees of the State Juvenile Training School to the Legislative Investigating Committee on November 19th and 20th, 1917," reprinted in *Biennial Report of the State Juvenile Training School, 1916–1917* (Austin, 1917), 8–31, here 13.

23. *Biennial Report of the State Juvenile Training School, 1913–1914* (Austin, 1914), 37.

24. Ibid., 38–40.

25. *Biennial Report of the State Juvenile Training School, 1917–1918* (Austin, 1918).

26. Paula S. Fass, *The Damned and the Beautiful: American Youth in the 1920s* (New York: Oxford University Press, 1977); Kathy Peiss, *Cheap Amusements: Working Women and Leisure in New York City, 1880–1920* (Philadelphia: Temple University Press, 1986); Beth L. Bailey, *From Front Porch to Back Seat: Courtship in Twentieth-Century America* (Baltimore: Johns Hopkins University Press, 1988); John Modell, *Into One's Own: From Youth to Adulthood in the United States, 1920–1975* (Berkeley: University of California Press, 1989), 67–120; Joseph M. Hawes, *Children between the Wars: American Childhood, 1920–1940* (New York: Twayne, 1997), esp. 1–28.

27. Robert S. and Helen Merrell Lynd, *Middletown: A Study in Modern American Culture* (New York: Harcourt, Brace, and World, 1929), 131–52.

28. Michael Phillips, *White Metropolis: Race, Ethnicity, and Religion in Dallas, 1841–2001* (Austin: University of Texas Press, 2006), 57–76; Bernadette Pruitt, "'For the Advance-

ment of the Race': The Great Migrations to Houston, Texas, 1914–1941," *Journal of Urban History* 31, no. 4 (May 2005): 435–78; Arnoldo De León, *Ethnicity in the Sunbelt: A History of Mexican Americans in Houston* (Houston: University of Houston, 1989); and James M. SoRelle, "Race Relations in 'Heavenly Houston,' 1919–45," in *Black Dixie: Afro-Texan History and Culture in Houston*, ed. Howard Beeth and Cary D. Wintz (College Station: Texas A&M University Press, 1992), 175–91.

29. Judith N. McArthur, *Creating the New Woman: The Rise of Southern Women's Progressive Culture in Texas, 1893–1918* (Urbana: University of Illinois Press, 1998), 54–75; *Handbook of Texas Online*, s.v. "Women and Politics" http://www.tsha.utexas.edu/handbook/online/articles/ww/pwwzj.html.

30. *The Juvenile Offender and Texas Law: A Handbook*, rev. ed., (Austin: Hogg Foundation for Mental Health, 1966), 1–5. For a discussion of the Chicago court's evolving model of child protection, see David S. Tanenhaus, *Juvenile Justice in the Making* (New York: Oxford University Press, 2004), 23–54.

31. Quoted in *Biennial Report, 1913–1914*, 22.

32. *Juvenile Offender and Texas Law*; see also "Juvenile Training School Proposed," *Dallas Morning News*, February 13, 1909.

33. "Gatesville Training School Resignations," *Dallas Morning News*, November 28, 1912.

34. "Training School Hybrid Institute," *Dallas Morning News*, December 1, 1912.

35. *Biennial Report of the State Institution for the Training of Juveniles, 1908–1910* (Austin, 1910), 17.

36. Mrs. E. W. Bounds, "The Transformation of the State Juvenile Training School," address to the Texas Conference of Charities and Corrections, November 30, 1913, reprinted in *Biennial Report, 1913–1914*, 45.

37. HB 27, *General and Special Laws of the State of Texas*, 33d Leg., 1st Sess., 1913, 7–12 (hereafter *Juvenile Act of 1913*).

38. Ibid.

39. *Ex Parte Raymond Brooks*, 85 Tex. Crim. 252, 211 S.W. 592, 1919 Tex. Crim. App., April 30, 1919.

40. *Ex Parte Maurice Gordon*, 89 Tex. Crim. 125, 232 S.W. 520, 1920 Tex. Crim. App., October 23, 1920.

41. White House Conference on Child Health and Protection, *The Delinquent Child: Report of the Committee on Socially Handicapped Delinquency* (section 4, 1930), reprinted by the U.S. Children's Bureau as *The Delinquent Child* (New York: Century, 1932), 325–26.

42. *Biennial Report of the State Institution for the Training of Juveniles, 1910–1911* (Austin, 1911), 22.

43. Ibid., 23.

44. "Marlin Man to Head State Training School," *Dallas Morning News*, January 15, 1913; "Eddins Thorough School Man," *Dallas Morning News*, January 17, 1913.

45. *Delinquent Child*, 305. On the prestige of juvenile judges, see David J. Rothman, *Conscience and Convenience: The Asylum and Its Alternatives in Progressive America* (1980; repr., New York: Aldine de Gruyter, 2002), 236–60.

46. Address by A. W. Eddins to the Texas State Conference of Charities and Corrections, November 30, 1913, at Fort Worth, reprinted in *Biennial Report, 1913–1914*, 37–43. An example of press coverage was the article "Assails Schools for Neglect of Delinquent Boys," *San Antonio Express*, November 29, 1914, "Juvenile Delinquency" Vertical File, Center for American History, University of Texas at Austin.

47. The following information is taken from *Biennial Report, 1913–1914* and *Biennial Report of the State Juvenile Training School, 1915–1916* (Austin, 1916).

48. For examples, see Paula S. Fass, *Outside In: Minorities and the Transformation of American Education* (New York: Oxford University Press, 1989); and John Bloom, *To Show What an Indian Can Do: Sports at Native American Boarding Schools* (Minneapolis: University of Minnesota Press, 2000).

49. *Biennial Report, 1915–1916*, 26.

50. *Biennial Report, 1917–1918*, 16–20.

51. Robert S. Miller, "Better Boys," *Austin Statesman*, March 12, 1916; the editorial is reprinted in *Biennial Report, 1915–1916*, 22–26; the military drills are also described in Ted Winfield Brumbalow, "An Analysis of the Educational Program of the State Juvenile Training School" (MA thesis, University of Texas, 1937), 34–36.

52. *Biennial Report, 1916–1917*, 29–30.

53. *Biennial Report, 1914–1915*, 19–20.

54. *Juvenile Act of 1913*, 11–12.

55. "The Transformation of the State Juvenile Training School," in *Biennial Report, 1913–1914*, 44–48.

56. In addition to Young, "Race and Gender," and Hardy, "Comparative Study of Institutions," see more recently Geoffrey K. Ward, "Color Lines of Social Control: Juvenile Justice Administration in a Racialized Social System, 1825–2000" (PhD diss., University of Michigan, 2001).

57. The data are reproduced in *Delinquent Child*, 322–24.

58. See Ward, "Color Lines of Social Control," esp. 40–117; Jennifer Trost, *Gateway to Justice: The Juvenile Court and Progressive Child Welfare in a Southern City* (Athens: University of Georgia Press, 2004); and David M. Oshinsky, *Worse Than Slavery: Parchman Farm and the Ordeal of Jim Crow Justice* (New York: Free Press, 1997), esp. 46–48.

59. Trost, *Gateway to Justice*, 152–55.

60. Brumbalow, "Analysis of the Educational Program," 58.

61. *Biennial Report of the State Board of Control, 1932–1934* (Austin, 1934), 66. This exact phrase appeared in practically every biennial report of the 1920s and 1930s.

62. *Delinquent Child*, 350.

63. *Biennial Report, 1917–1918*, 15–16.

64. *Report of the State Board of Control to the Governor and the Legislature, 1920–1924* (Austin, 1924), 87–92.

65. *George W. Brown v. the State of Texas*, 99 Tex. Crim. 70, 268 S.W. 460, 1925 Tex. Crim. App., January 28, 1925.

66. *First Annual Report of the State Board of Control to the Governor and the Legislature* (Austin, 1920), 117–18.

67. Ibid.

68. The literature on female delinquency is vast, much of it focused on the early decades of the juvenile court. See Steven Schlossman and Stephanie Wallach, "The Crime of Precocious Sexuality: Female Juvenile Delinquency in the Progressive Era," *Harvard Educational Review* 48, no. 1 (February 1978): 65–94; Ruth M. Alexander, *The Girl Problem: Female Sexual Delinquency in New York, 1900–1930* (Ithaca, N.Y.: Cornell University Press, 1995); Mary E. Odem, *Delinquent Daughters: Protecting and Policing Adolescent Female Sexuality in the United States, 1885–1920* (Chapel Hill: University of North Carolina Press, 1995); Anne Meis Knupfer, *Reform and Resistance: Gender, Delinquency, and America's*

First Juvenile Court (New York: Routledge, 2001); and Tamara Myers, *Caught: Montreal's Modern Girls and the Law, 1869–1945* (Toronto: University of Toronto Press, 2007).

69. Carrie Weaver Smith obituary, *Publisher's Weekly* 141 (1942): 2213.

70. Miriam Van Waters, "Where Girls Go Right," *Survey* 48, no. 9 (May 27, 1922): 361–76.

71. Ibid., 366–67.

72. Ibid., 371.

73. Carrie Weaver Smith, "The Unadjusted Girl," *Social Hygiene* 6, no. 3 (July 1920): 401–6.

74. *First Annual Report of the State Board of Control*, 120.

75. "Hookworm at County Home for Girls: Report Made to County Officials by Dr. Carrie Weaver Smith," *Dallas Daily Times Herald*, February 23, 1916, p. 5.

76. *First Annual Report of the State Board of Control*, 124.

77. Ibid., 126.

78. Ibid., 127.

79. Ibid., 118–19.

80. "Finishing Schools," *Time* 30, no. 19 (November 8, 1937), describes Smith as "kindly" and "hard-working" and much beloved by the girl inmates, who rioted for several days in protest of her dismissal.

81. Smith obituary.

82. See Lewis L. Gould, *Progressives and Prohibitionists: Texas Democrats in the Wilson Era* (Austin: University of Texas Press, 1973); and Norman D. Brown, *Hood, Bonnet, and Little Brown Jug: Texas Politics, 1921–1928* (College Station: Texas A&M University Press, 1984). For James Ferguson's views on correctional reform, see Robert Reps Perkinson, "The Birth of the Texas Prison Empire, 1865–1915" (PhD diss., Yale University, 2001), 361–67.

83. "A. W. Eddins Resigns Place at Gatesville," *Dallas Morning News*, April 6, 1915.

84. A *Dallas Morning News* article describes King as having been "endorsed by Governor J. E. Ferguson" (ibid.); see also *Biennial Report, 1915–1916*, 3–5.

85. See *Biennial Report, 1917–1918*, 16–17.

86. "Says 29 Lose Jobs at State Training School," *Dallas Morning News*, September 2, 1925.

87. C. A. Mayberry to H. H. Harrington, Texas State Board of Control, December 26, 1926; Harrington to Mayberry, January 4, 1927; Frank Wilson to Harrington, April 3, 1927; Harrington to Wilson, April 5, 1927; A. D. Chestnut to Harrington, April 3, 1927; J. A. Farqhuar to Harrington, April 19, 1927; Harrington to Farqhuar, April 22, 1927, all in Chairman H. H. Harrington files, TSLAC.

88. J. P. Kendrick to the Texas State Board of Control, July 30, 1927; C. E. Gandy to TBC, July 31, 1927; H. C. Dollins to TBC, August 1, 1927; E. J. Brooks to TBC, August 11, 1927; J. A. Farqhuar to TBC, August 11, 1927, all in Chairman H. H. Harrington files, TSLAC.

89. The use of this adjective, roughly synonymous with "charitable," suggests that the state at least nominally separated juvenile offenders from adult criminals. Eleemosynary institutions included all dependent populations except for the prisons, which operated under the Penitentiary Commission.

90. A 1946 study of six state training schools in Alabama, Arkansas, Georgia, North Carolina, Tennessee, and Virginia found each of them under the supervision of a state board of control. See Hardy, "Comparative Study of Institutions."

91. This description draws on the following sources: *H. G. Twyman v. the State of Texas*, 1924 Tex. Crim. App.; "Training School Case Is Closed by Vote of Board Sustaining King," *Dallas Morning News*, November 6, 1921; and "Testimony of Boys regarding Punishments

at Gatesville," Texas State Board of Control hearing notes, undated, circa October–November 1921, Chairman R. B. Walthall files, TSLAC.

92. "Releases Are Asked for Boys in Gatesville School," *Dallas Morning News*, October 2, 1921; "Square Deal for Boys Advocated," *Dallas Morning News*, November 7, 1921; "Federation Asks for Change at School," *Dallas Morning News*, November 16, 1921; "Public Is Blamed for Death of Boy," *Dallas Morning News*, November 18, 1921.

93. "Superintendent of Gatesville School Resigns Position," *Dallas Morning News*, November 19, 1921.

94. "List of Boys Buried in the Gatesville Cemetery," compiled in 1967, Morales case files, Texas Youth Commission, Archives and Information Services Division, TSLAC.

95. *Biennial Report, 1917–1918*, 22–23.

96. *First Annual Report of the State Board of Control*, 116.

97. Brumbalow, "Analysis of the Educational Program," 67.

98. "Dying Boy Is Given Parole," *Dallas Morning News*, October 28, 1927; and Mrs. Linn to Governor Dan Moody, April 9, 1927; Moody to Linn, April 12, 1927; H. H. Harrington to Linn, April 16, 1927, both in Chairman H. H. Harrington files, TSLAC.

99. Lorene Moon to H. H. Harrington, April 19, 1927; Harrington to Dan Moody and Mrs. Linn, April 22, 1927, both in Chairman H. H. Harrington files, TSLAC.

100. Memo, Mrs. Hunt, Gatesville Registered Nurse, to Mrs. Wilson, September 7, 1927, Chairman H. H. Harrington files, TSLAC.

101. Mrs. Wilson to Dan Moody, October 11, 1927, Chairman H. H. Harrington files, TSLAC.

102. Dan Moody to Mrs. Wilson, October 17, 1927; H. H. Harrington to Wilson, October 22, 1927, both in Chairman H. H. Harrington files, TSLAC.

103. Notarized Statement of Dr. Ralph Bailey, MD, to Charles E. King, October 25, 1927; H. H. Harrington to C. E. King, October 24, 1927; King to Harrington, October 25, 1927; Harrington to Mrs. Wilson, October 27, 1927, all in Chairman H. H. Harrington files, TSLAC.

104. The quotation is from Mrs. Wilson to Dan Moody, July 25, 1928; the events preceding Leland's death are recounted in Mrs. Wilson to H. H. Harrington, January 19, 1928; Harrington to Wilson, January 19, 1928, all in Chairman H. H. Harrington files, TSLAC.

105. *Report of the State Board of Control, 1920–1924*, 87–92; see also *Biennial Report, 1917–1918*.

106. W. P. Bockem to Dan Moody, November 16, 1927, Chairman H. H. Harrington files, TSLAC.

107. Dan Moody to W. P. Bockem and Texas State Board of Control, November 19, 1927; H. H. Harrington to Bockem, November 21, 1927; Bockem to Harrington, November 28, 1927; Harrington to Bockem, December 3, 1927, all in Chairman H. H. Harrington files, TSLAC.

108. All the figures in this paragraph are from Brumbalow, "Analysis of the Educational Program," 43–48.

109. *Delinquent Child*, 311.

110. S. M. N. Marrs to R. B. Walthall, May 6, 1929; Decision, *Donald B. Gregg v. Board of Trustees of the State Juvenile Training School*, May 6, 1929, both in Chairman R. B. Walthall files, TSLAC.

111. Studies of vocational education include Herbert M. Kliebard, *Schooled to Work: Vocationalism and the American Curriculum, 1876–1946* (New York: Teacher's College

Press, 1999); Harvey A. Kantor, *Learning to Earn: School, Work, and Vocational Reform in California, 1880–1930* (Madison: University of Wisconsin Press, 1988); and Harvey A. Kantor and David B. Tyack, eds., *Work, Youth, and Schooling: Historical Perspectives on Vocationalism in American Education* (Stanford, Calif.: Stanford University Press, 1982).

112. *Delinquent Child*, 311–13.

113. *Report of the State Board of Control to the Governor and the Legislature, 1924–1926* (Austin, 1926), 122–24.

114. "Work Better Than Courts," *State Boys*, March 31, 1928.

115. "The Attitude of the Institution toward the Juvenile Offender," *Report of the State Board of Control, 1924–1926*, 113.

116. C. E. King to R. B. Walthall, August 16, 1927, Chairman R. B. Walthall files, TSLAC.

117. Brumbalow, "Analysis of the Educational Program," 63–65.

118. King to Walthall, August 16, 1927.

119. R. B. Walthall to Lorene Moon, April 30, 1928, Chairman R. B. Walthall files, TSLAC.

120. Lorene Moon to R. B. Walthall, May 3, 1928, Chairman R. B. Walthall files, TSLAC.

121. R. B. Walthall to Lorene Moon, May 4, 1928; Moon to Walthall, May 8, 1928, both in Chairman R. B. Walthall files, TSLAC.

122. R. B. Walthall to Lyman J. Bailey, May 10, 1928, Chairman R. B. Walthall files, TSLAC.

123. *Biennial Report, 1917–1918*, 16.

124. Ibid., 13.

125. H. H. Harrington to Charles E. King, August 16, 1927; T. A. Saunders to Harrington, September 12, 1927; Harrington to Saunders, September 15, 1927; "Resolutions Are Passed Regarding Training School," *Gatesville Messenger*, September 16, 1927, all in Chairman H. H. Harrington files, TSLAC.

126. "Juvenile Peons of Texas," *Galveston Tribune*, September 12, 1927.

127. Ibid.

128. "Tribune Stand Declared Right," *Galveston Tribune*, September 14, 1927. On Cohen, see *Handbook of Texas Online*, s.v. "Cohen, Henry," http://www.tsha.utexas.edu/handbook/online/articles/CC/fco13.html; and Perkinson, "Birth of the Texas Prison Empire," 383–86. On convict leasing in Texas and the South generally, see Walker, *Penology for Profit*; and Alex Lichtenstein, *Twice the Work of Free Labor: The Political Economy of Convict Labor in the New South* (New York: Verso, 1996).

129. H. H. Harrington to *Galveston Tribune*, September 16, 1927 (published September 17), Chairman H. H. Harrington files, TSLAC.

130. Henry Cohen to H. H. Harrington, September 19, 1927, Chairman H. H. Harrington files, TSLAC.

131. The following anecdote is taken from Judge Charles G. Dibrell to Henry Cohen, November 1, 1927; Affidavit of Joey O'Connor, November 1, 1927; Cohen to H. H. Harrington, November 3, 1927; Harrington to C. E. King, November 5, 1927; King to Harrington, November 8, 1927; Harrington to Dibrell, November 15, 1927, all in Chairman H. H. Harrington files, TSLAC.

132. "El Paso Club of Reform School Boys Formed," *El Paso Herald*, March 15, 1929.

133. Ibid.

134. "Charge School 'Masquerades,'" *El Paso Herald*, March 29, 1929; "Moody Recognizes Mestrezat's Charges," *El Paso Herald*, March 30, 1929.

135. J. P. Mestrezat to Claude Teer, May 2, 1929, Chairman Claude Teer files, 1929–1939, Texas State Board of Control Board member's files, Archives and Information Services Division, TSLAC.

136. Dr. Grover C. Wood memo, June 30, 1927; G. O. Bateman to Governor Dan Moody, August 23, 1927; John W. Mackey to H. H. Harrington, September 28, 1927, all in Chairman H. H. Harrington files, TSLAC.

137. Bateman to Moody, August 23, 1927.

138. H. H. Harrington to C. E. King, September 30, 1927; King to Harrington, October 13, 1927; Harrington to J. W. Mackey, October 15, 1927, all in Chairman H. H. Harrington files, TSLAC.

139. Dr. G. A. Trott to Governor Dan Moody, July 16, 1928; Moody to Trott, July 24, 1928, both in Chairman R. B. Walthall files, TSLAC.

140. Mrs. M. H. Witt to Governor Dan Moody, January 22, 1928; R. B. Walthall to C. E. King, February 3, 1928, both in Chairman R. B. Walthall files, TSLAC.

141. Mrs. Richards to Governor Dan Moody, July 19, 1928; Moody to Richards, July 20, 1928; J. B. Hearn to R. B. Walthall, July 24, 1928; Richards to Moody, July 28, 1928; Moody to Richards, July 31, 1928, all in Chairman R. B. Walthall files, TSLAC.

142. Mr. Baker to H. H. Harrington, April 6, 1927; Harrington to Baker, April 9, 1927; Harrington to C. E. King, April 9, 1927; Lorene Moon to Harrington, April 11, 1927, all in Chairman H. H. Harrington files, TSLAC.

143. For a summary, see Robert S. Birchard, *Cecil B. DeMille's Hollywood* (Lexington: University Press of Kentucky, 2004), 227–32.

144. "Notes on the Passing Show," *Dallas Morning News*, April 12, 1929.

145. C. E. King to Cecil B. DeMille, November 26, 1927; George Ellis to H. H. Harrington, November 29, 1927; Harrington to Ellis, December 3, 1927, all in Chairman H. H. Harrington files, TSLAC.

146. Birchard, *Cecil B. DeMille's Hollywood*.

147. "Giving Juvenile Delinquents a Chance," *Dallas Morning News*, April 14, 1929.

148. This description is taken from the following sources: Statement of Roy Catlett, December 11, 1929; E. H. Nesbitt to R. B. Walthall, December 26, 1929, all in Chairman R. B. Walthall files, TSLAC.

149. Statement of Dr. I. F. Johnson, December 11, 1929; Dr. T. M. Hall to E. H. Nesbitt, December 11, 1929; Hall to Nesbitt, December 24, 1929, all in Chairman R. B. Walthall files, TSLAC.

150. Statement of Dr. H. F. Connally, December 21, 1929; E. H. Nesbitt to R. B. Walthall, December 26, 1929; Walthall to Nesbitt, December 29, 1929, all in Chairman R. B. Walthall files, TSLAC.

151. Statement of Connally, December 21, 1929.

Two. Socializing Delinquency

1. Texas Board of Control, *Survey and Report of an Examination of the Gatesville State School for Boys, Gatesville, Texas, for the Period from September 1, 1939, to August 31, 1941* (Austin, 1941), 12, Chairman Weaver H. Baker files, 1941–47, Texas State Board of Control Board member's files, Archives and Information Services Division, Texas State Library and Archives Commission, Austin (hereafter cited as Chairman Weaver H. Baker files).

2. Ibid., 11–17.

3. Texas Board of Control, *Survey and Report, September 1, 1939, to August 31, 1941*, 8–10, Chairman Weaver H. Baker files.

4. Michael Willrich, *City of Courts: Socializing Justice in Progressive Era Chicago* (Cambridge: Cambridge University Press, 2003). On shared social responsibility, see Linda

Gordon, *Pitied but Not Entitled: Single Mothers and the History of Welfare, 1890–1935* (New York: Free Press, 1994), 287–306.

5. Report quoted in David S. Tanenhaus, *Juvenile Justice in the Making* (New York: Oxford University Press, 2005), 131. Other recent discussions of the role of child welfare services in juvenile justice include Tamara Myers, *Caught: Montreal's Modern Girls and the Law, 1869–1945* (Toronto: University of Toronto Press, 2006), 89–134; Jennifer Trost, *Gateway to Justice: The Juvenile Court and Progressive Child Welfare in a Southern City* (Athens: University of Georgia Press, 2005); Tanenhaus, *Juvenile Justice in the Making*, 111–38; and Anne Meis Knupfer, *Reform and Resistance: Gender, Delinquency, and America's First Juvenile Court* (New York: Routledge, 2001), 13–64.

6. In addition to Trost, *Gateway to Justice*, see also Lee S. Polansky, "I Certainly Hope That You Will Be Able to Train Her: Reformers and the Georgia Training School for Girls"; and Joan Marie Johnson, "The Colors of Social Welfare in the New South: Black and White Clubwomen in South Carolina, 1900–1930," both in *Before the New Deal: Social Welfare in the South, 1830–1930*, ed. Elna C. Green (Athens: University of Georgia Press, 1999), 138–80.

7. U.S. Census figures reproduced in Char Miller and David R. Johnson, "The Rise of Urban Texas," in *Urban Texas: Politics and Development*, ed. Char Miller and Heywood T. Sanders (College Station: Texas A&M University Press, 1990), 3–32, here 6–8.

8. Ibid; see also Randolph B. Campbell, *Gone to Texas: A History of the Lone Star State* (New York: Oxford University Press, 2004), 360–64; and Bruce J. Schulman, *From Cotton Belt to Sun Belt: Federal Policy, Economic Development, and the Transformation of the South, 1938–1980* (New York: Oxford University Press, 1991), 135–73.

9. George Fuermann, *Houston: Land of the Big Rich* (Garden City, N.Y.: Doubleday, 1951), 83–84; see also his *Reluctant Empire* (Garden City, N.Y.: Doubleday, 1957). For overviews of Houston's history, see David G. McComb, *Houston: A History* (Austin: University of Texas Press, 1981); Joe R. Feagin, *Free Enterprise City: Houston in Political-Economic Perspective* (New Brunswick, N.J.: Rutgers University Press, 1988); Beth Anne Shelton et al., *Houston: Growth and Decline in a Sunbelt Boomtown* (Philadelphia: Temple University Press, 1989); and Marguerite Johnston, *Houston: The Unknown City, 1836–1946* (College Station: Texas A&M University Press, 1991).

10. Robert B. Fairbanks, "Public Housing for the City as a Whole: The Texas Experience, 1934–1955," *Southwestern Historical Quarterly* 103, no. 4 (April 2000): 402–24; for more-nuanced portrayals of Houston's philanthropists, see Johnston, *Houston*; Don E. Carleton, *A Breed So Rare: The Life of J. R. Parten, Liberal Texas Oilman, 1896–1992* (Austin: Texas State Historical Association, 1998); and Kate Sayen Kirkland, "Envisioning a Progressive City: Hogg Family Philanthropy and the Urban Ideal in Houston, Texas, 1910–1975" (PhD diss., Rice University, 2004).

11. Kirkland, "Envisioning a Progressive City," 173–88.

12. For an overview of American settlement houses, see Judith Ann Trolander, *Professionalism and Social Change: From the Settlement House Movement to Neighborhood Centers, 1886 to the Present* (New York: Columbia University Press, 1987).

13. Corrine S. Tsanoff, *Neighborhood Doorways* (Houston: Neighborhood Centers of Houston and Harris County, 1958), 1–8; Judith N. McArthur, *Creating the New Woman: The Rise of Southern Women's Progressive Culture in Texas, 1893–1918* (Urbana: University of Illinois Press, 1998), 79–81.

14. Jane Addams, *The Spirit of Youth and the City Streets* (New York: Macmillan, 1909), 20.

15. McArthur, *Creating the New Woman*, 82–83. See also Kay Walters Ofman, "The Practice of Social Welfare: A Case Study in Dallas, 1890–1929" (PhD diss., University of Michigan, 1999).

16. Margarita B. Melville, "Mexicans," in *The Ethnic Groups of Houston*, ed. Fred R. von der Mehden (Houston: Rice University Press, 1984), 42–61, here 47; Arnoldo De León, *Ethnicity in the Sunbelt: A History of Mexican Americans in Houston* (Houston: University of Houston, 1989), 44–46.

17. Tsanoff, *Neighborhood Doorways*, 18–36.

18. De León, *Ethnicity in the Sunbelt*, 70–94. See also Benjamin Márquez, LULAC: The Evolution of a Mexican American Political Organization (Austin: University of Texas Press, 1993). For a related study of Los Angeles, see George J. Sánchez, *Becoming Mexican American: Ethnicity, Culture and Identity in Chicano Los Angeles, 1900–1945* (New York: Oxford University Press, 1993). For more on the association of delinquency with youth of Mexican origin, see Eduardo Obregón Pagán, *Murder at the Sleepy Lagoon: Zoot Suits, Race, and Riot in Wartime L.A.* (Chapel Hill: University of North Carolina Press, 2003), esp. 19–44.

19. Edgar W. Ray, *The Grand Huckster: Houston's Judge Roy Hofheinz, Genius of the Astrodome* (Memphis: Memphis State University Press, 1980), 60–75; on crime prevention, see David B. Wolcott, *Cops and Kids: Policing Juvenile Delinquency in Urban America* (Columbus: Ohio State University Press, 2005), 126–45. The phrase "cult of judicial personality" borrows from David J. Rothman, *Conscience and Convenience: The Asylum and Its Alternatives in Progressive America*, rev. ed. (New York: Aldine de Gruyter, 2002), 236–60.

20. The description relies on the following articles from the *Houston Post*: "County Grand Jury Recommends Stricter Control of Honky-Tonks," December 1, 1942; "Slaying in Café Here Is Laid to Gang Activity," January 11, 1943; "Roundup of Youths Suspected of Being Petty Gangsters Begins," January 17, 1943; "Teen-Age Gangsters," June 10, 1943; "42 Boys, Many Carrying Knives, Arrested Here," June 13, 1943; "Zoot Suiters at Negro Dance," August 5, 1943; "Mexican-American Gangs," August 21, 1944. The gang problem is also discussed in De León, *Ethnicity in the Sunbelt*, 105–10.

21. Edward J. Escobar, *Race, Police, and the Making of a Political Identity: Mexican Americans and the Los Angeles Police Department, 1900–1945* (Berkeley: University of California Press, 1999). On Houston, see Dwight Watson, *Race and the Houston Police Department, 1930–1990: A Change Did Come* (College Station: Texas A&M University Press, 2005), 1–36; and James M. SoRelle, "Race Relations in 'Heavenly Houston,'" in *Black Dixie: Afro-Texan History and Culture in Houston*, ed. Howard Beeth and Cary D. Wintz (College Station: Texas A&M University Press, 1992), 175–91. On "curbside counselors," see Eric C. Schneider, *Vampires, Dragons, and Egyptian Kings: Youth Gangs in Postwar New York* (Princeton, N.J.: Princeton University Press, 1999).

22. Houston Council of Social Agencies, "Juvenile Delinquency in Houston: A Preliminary View," *Social Statistics* 1, no. 2 (December 1944), Houston Metropolitan Research Center, Houston Public Library (hereafter cited as HMRC); De León estimates that the city's population of Mexican origin in the 1940s ranged between 6 and 10 percent (*Ethnicity in the Sunbelt*, 110).

23. Flyer, undated, "Junior LULAC Be-Bop Dance," box 40, Papers of LULAC Council 60 (microfilm), HMRC; De León, *Ethnicity in the Sunbelt*, 75.

24. Letter to the editor, *Houston Post*, September 13, 1944.

25. For a succinct discussion of the rise of the "teenager," see Steven Mintz, *Huck's Raft: A History of American Childhood* (Cambridge, Mass.: Harvard University Press, 2004),

265–68. The problems posed by home-front children are explored in William M. Tuttle Jr., *Daddy's Gone to War: The Second World War in the Lives of America's Children* (New York: Oxford University Press, 1993), esp. 30–90. On teen canteens, see Grace Palladino, *Teenagers: An American History* (New York: Basic Books, 1996), 80–95. See also Kelly Schrum, *Some Wore Bobby Sox: The Emergence of Teenage Girls' Culture, 1920–1945* (New York: Palgrave Macmillan, 2004).

26. "Teen-Age Canteen Dances Will Start Friday Night," *Houston Post*, March 16, 1944; "Teen-Age Canteen Success," *Houston Post*, March 18, 1944.

27. *Our Community* 1, no. 2 (June 1944), materials of the Community Chest and Council, Council of Social Agencies, and United Way (3 boxes), HMRC.

28. William I. Thomas and Florian Znaniecki, *The Polish Peasant in Europe and America* (1918; repr., New York: Alfred A. Knopf, 1927); Frederic Thrasher, *The Gang: A Study of 1,313 Gangs in Chicago* (Chicago: University of Chicago Press, 1927); Clifford Shaw et al., *Delinquency Areas* (Chicago: University of Chicago Press, 1929); Harvey Zorbaugh, *The Gold Coast and the Slum* (Chicago: University of Chicago, 1929). For a history, see Martin Bulmer, *The Chicago School of Sociology: Institutionalization, Diversity, and the Rise of Sociological Research* (Chicago: University of Chicago Press, 1984).

29. *Our Community* 1, no. 2 (June 1944); 1, no. 6 (October 1944); and 2, no. 2 (June 1945), materials of the Community Chest and Council, HMRC.

30. The quotations in the paragraph are from "A Little Journey to the Rusk Settlement," radio transcript, Saturday, April 15, 1944, Papers of Franklin Israel Harbach, HMRC (hereafter cited as Harbach Papers).

31. "Priorities for Youth," Houston Council of Social Agencies, November 1942, Materials of the Community Chest and Council, HMRC.

32. F. I. Harbach to Irene Franklin, March 25, 1964, Harbach Papers.

33. Harbach is mentioned briefly in a published history of Henry Street; see Helen Hall, *Unfinished Business: In Neighborhood and Nation* (New York: Macmillan, 1971), 222. See also "Memorials," chap. 11, in *Annual Proceedings of the Philosophical Society of Texas* (Dallas: Philosophical Society of Texas, 1998). The discussion of Harbach's activities in Houston draws on W. E. Moreland, HISD Superintendent, to F. I. Harbach, March 17, 1944; Maude Cashin to F. I. Harbach, March 24, 1945; Petition of Magnolia Park Improvement Association to Mayor and City Council of Houston, August 19, 1947; F. I. Harbach to Felix Tijerina, March 23, 1948, all in Harbach Papers.

34. "Preventing Wartime Delinquency" (pamphlet) (Austin: Hogg Foundation for Mental Hygiene, August 1943), Papers of the UT (University of Texas) Hogg Foundation for Mental Health, 1940–present, Center for American History, University of Texas at Austin (hereafter cited as UT Hogg Foundation Papers).

35. *The Hogg Foundation Reports: A Summary of Three Years' Work—A Forecast of Next Steps* (Austin: Hogg Foundation for Mental Hygiene, 1944). Although the "circuit-rider" allusion here is taken from the author's interview with Wayne Holtzmann, October 23, 2003, it was first made in a February 1941 article in the DeLeon Free Press, as recounted in *The Hogg Foundation for Mental Health: The First Three Decades* (Austin: University of Texas Press, 1970), 15. For an analysis of the "psychiatric perspective," see Elizabeth Lunbeck, *The Psychiatric Persuasion: Knowledge, Gender, and Power in Modern America* (Princeton, N.J.: Princeton University Press, 1994).

36. Clifford Whittingham Beers, *A Mind That Found Itself: An Autobiography* (New York: Longmans, Green, 1908); Gerald N. Grob, *Mental Illness and American Society, 1875–1940* (Princeton, N.J.: Princeton University Press, 1983), 144–72; Nathan G. Hale Jr.,

The Rise and Crisis of Psychoanalysis in the United States: Freud and the Americans, 1917–1985 (New York: Oxford University Press, 1995), 170–72. The Texas mental hygiene survey can be found in Gerald N. Grob, ed., *Public Policy and Mental Illness: Four Investigations, 1915–1939* (New York: Arno Press, 1980).

37. In addition to Grob, *Mental Illness and American Society*, the following discussion draws on Kathleen W. Jones, *Taming the Troublesome Child: American Families, Child Guidance, and the Limits of Psychiatric Authority* (Cambridge, Mass.: Harvard University Press, 1999); Margo Horn, *Before It's Too Late: The Child Guidance Movement in the United States, 1922–1945* (Philadelphia: Temple University Press, 1989); and Theresa Richardson, *The Century of the Child: The Mental Hygiene Movement and Social Policy in the United States and Canada* (New York: State University of New York Press, 1989).

38. Jones, *Taming the Troublesome Child*, 103.

39. Ibid., 91; Hale, *Rise and Crisis*, 87.

40. Jones, *Taming the Troublesome Child*, 106–8; see also Kriste Lindenmeyer, *A Right to Childhood: The U.S. Children's Bureau and Child Welfare, 1912–1946* (Urbana: University of Illinois Press, 1997), 139–62.

41. Horn, *Before It's Too Late*, 61–69.

42. "Dallas Child Guidance Clinic for the Study and Treatment of 'Problem' Children," undated, circa 1930, UT Hogg Foundation Papers.

43. *Annual Report of the Child Guidance Center of Houston* (Houston: Child Guidance Center of Houston, 1931), UT Hogg Foundation Papers. Much of the center's early documentation has been destroyed; for an overview of its history, see Kirkland, "Envisioning a Progressive City," 198–219.

44. Unless specifically noted, the following section relies on these sources: Kirkland, "Envisioning a Progressive City"; Greta Anderson, *More Than Petticoats: Remarkable Texas Women* (Guilford, Conn.: Globe Pequot Press, 2002), 63–72; Gwendolyn Cone Neeley, *Miss Ima and the Hogg Family* (Dallas: Hendrick-Long, 1992); Louise Iscoe, *Ima Hogg: First Lady of Texas* (Austin: Hogg Foundation for Mental Health, 1976); *Handbook of Texas Online*, s.v. "HOGG, IMA," http://www.tsha.utexas.edu/handbook/online/articles/HH/fho16.html. For more on James Hogg, see Robert Cotner, *James Stephen Hogg, A Biography* (Austin: University of Texas Press, 1959). On Will C. Hogg, see John Avery Lomax, *Will Hogg, Texan* (1940; repr., Austin: Hogg Foundation for Mental Health, 1956).

45. Neeley, *Miss Ima*, 24. The Hogg family library included several books on mental health and illness, including the following: Henry Maudsley, *Responsibility in Mental Disease* (New York: Appleton, 1878); William B. Carpenter, *Principles of Mental Physiology* (New York: Appleton, 1881); and Hugo Munsterberg, *Psychology and Life* (Boston: Houghton Mifflin, 1898). The entire list can be found in *Dedication Program, Will C. Hogg Building* (Austin: Hogg Foundation for Mental Health, 1968).

46. "Interview with Miss Ima Hogg, August 24, 1970," UT Hogg Foundation Papers.

47. "Conversation between Dr. Robert L. Sutherland and Miss Ima Hogg," May 10 and 13, 1967, p. 13, UT Hogg Foundation Papers.

48. Ibid.; see also "Transcription of Meeting at Miss Hogg's Home," March 8, 1962, pp. 2–3, UT Hogg Foundation Papers.

49. Robert Lee Sutherland, "An Analysis of Negro Churches in Chicago" (PhD diss., University of Chicago, 1930).

50. Robert Lee Sutherland, "Negro Youth: A Review of the Problems, Summary of Research, and a Recommended Program," October 1937; Sutherland, "A Proposed Study

of Negro Youth Recommended to the American Youth Commission," undated, ca. winter 1937–38; Minutes, First Meeting of the Advisory Committee on the Negro Project, Washington, D.C., January 8, 1938, Sutherland (Robert Lee) Papers, 1937–73, Center for American History, University of Texas at Austin. The AYC monograph series includes Allison Davis and John Dollard, *Children of Bondage: The Personality Development of Negro Youth in the Urban South* (Washington, D.C.: American Council on Education, 1940); E. Franklin Frazier, *Negro Youth at the Crossways: Their Personality Development in the Middle States* (Washington, D.C.: American Council on Education, 1940); Charles S. Johnson, *Growing Up in the Black Belt: Negro Youth in the Rural South* (Washington, D.C.: American Council on Education, 1941); and Robert L. Sutherland, *Color, Class, and Personality* (Washington, D.C.: American Council on Education, 1942).

51. On the American youth problem and the federal response in the 1930s, see Mintz, *Huck's Raft*, 233–53; and Richard A. Reiman, *The New Deal and American Youth: Ideas and Ideals in a Depression Decade* (Athens: University of Georgia Press, 1992). See also Eleanor Roosevelt, "Facing the Problems of Youth," *Journal of Social Hygiene* (October–December 1935): 393–94; Eleanor Roosevelt, foreword to *American Youth: An Enforced Reconnaissance*, ed. W. Thatcher Winslow and Frank P. Davidson (Cambridge, Mass.: Harvard University Press, 1940); Winslow, *Youth, A World Problem* (Washington, D.C.: U.S. Government Printing Office, 1937), xi; and Homer P. Rainey, *How Fare American Youth?* (New York: D. Appleton-Century, 1938), 159.

52. Robert L. Sutherland, "Society's Responsibility for Protecting the Mental Health of Children," *Texas State Journal of Medicine* 37 (February 1942): 658–61.

53. Charlotte Helen Towle, *Common Human Needs: An Interpretation for Staff in Public Assistance Agencies* (Washington, D.C.: U.S. Government Printing Office, 1945).

54. Elizabeth Borgwart, *A New Deal for the World: America's Vision for Human Rights* (Cambridge, Mass.: Harvard University Press, 2005), 76–85.

55. *Essentials of a Community Mental Health Program: Tentative Guideposts for Community Planning* (Austin: Hogg Foundation for Mental Hygiene, 1945).

56. "Outline of Conference of District and County Judges Held at the Gatesville State School for Boys on August 29, 1942," Chairman Weaver H. Baker files.

57. Survey schedule attached to memo, H. L. Lackey, Gatesville Sociologist, to R. N. Winship Jr., January 26, 1942, Chairman Weaver H. Baker files. The data sets also appear in Dana Buckley MacInerney, "A Statistical Survey of Commitments to the Gatesville State Training School for Boys and the Gainesville State Training School for Girls, 1936–1945" (MA thesis, University of Texas, 1951).

58. "State Training School Is Testing Ground for New Plan for Delinquent Boys," *Fort Worth Star-Telegram*, March 11, 1942.

59. R. N. Winship Jr., "The Coordination of Institutional Care for Children at the Gatesville State School for Boys with Services in the Community," presentation, Austin, Tex., October 1941, Chairman Weaver H. Baker files.

60. Ibid.

61. "State Training School," *Fort Worth Star-Telegram*, March 11, 1942.

62. "Legislative Report on Gatesville State School for Boys," in *Report of the Committee to Investigate State Eleemosynary and Reformatory Destitution*, 48th Texas Legislature (February 1, 1943), 199–209.

63. W. H. Baker to R. N. Winship Jr., January 14, 1942; Winship to Baker, January 17, 1942; Harry Flentge to Baker, January 24, 1942, all in Chairman Weaver H. Baker files.

64. Senator Karl L. Lovelady to W. H. Baker, January 8, 1942; Baker to Lovelady, January 9, 1942; Representative Earl Huddleston to Baker, April 20, 1942, all in Chairman Weaver H. Baker files.

65. C. E. Gandy to Governor Coke Stevenson, February 1, 1942; Stevenson to Gandy, February 4, 1942; W. J. Caruth to TBC, February 14, 1942, all in Chairman Weaver H. Baker files.

66. Unless otherwise noted, the following discussion relies on Meeting Minutes, Texas Board of Control, February 3, 1942, Chairman Weaver H. Baker files.

67. W. H. Baker to Harry Flentge, February 5, 1942, Chairman Weaver H. Baker files.

68. F. A. Morris Jr. to Earl Huddleston, May 4, 1943; Huddleston to Baker, May 6, 1943; Huddleston to TBC, June 2, 1943; W. H. Baker to R. N. Winship Jr., June 4, 1943; Baker to Huddleston, June 4, 1943; Baker to Senator Karl Lovelady, June 4, 1943; Lovelady to Huddleston, June 5, 1943, all in Chairman Weaver H. Baker files.

69. Earl Huddleston to Governor Coke Stevenson, June 5, 1943; Stevenson to Huddleston, June 9, 1943, both in Chairman Weaver H. Baker files.

70. W. H. Baker to Earl Huddleston, July 12, 1943, Chairman Weaver H. Baker files.

71. "State School Head Dies at Gatesville," *Dallas Morning News*, September 4, 1943.

72. Unfortunately, none of the available documents provide ironclad evidence of Johnston's guilt or innocence. R. B. Johnston to W. H. Baker, March 24, 1944; Judge Clarence O. Kraft to Howard Lackey, March 29, 1944; Lackey to Kraft, April 4, 1944; Lackey to TBC, April 4, 1944; W. H. Baker to Kraft, April 10, 1944; Baker to Coryell County Sheriff Joe White, April 20, 1944; Kraft to Baker, May 6, 1944; Johnston to Lackey, June 15, 1944; Inmate Affidavit, June 15, 1944; Lackey to Baker, June 18, 1944; Baker to R. E. Blair, June 19, 1944; Clyde Vinson to Baker, July 24, 1944; Baker to Vinson, July 26, 1944, all in Chairman Weaver H. Baker files. As Johnston's defense attorney, Vinson received permission from the TBC to interview boy inmates individually and in the presence of a Gatesville employee, a policy that would later be held to violate a juvenile's right to counsel.

73. Texas Division of Child Welfare, *Report on the Gainesville State School for Girls* (Austin, 1942).

74. "State Girls' School Head Charged with Forgery," *Dallas Morning News*, October 20, 1942; Ray Winder, Cooke County Attorney, to TBC, May 5, 1943; W. H. Baker to Winder, May 6, 1943, all in Chairman Weaver H. Baker files. The details appear in *Mary A. Stone v. State of Texas*, 147 Tex. Crim. 489, 182 S.W. 2d 400, 1944 Tex. Crim. App., June 14, 1944.

75. W. H. Baker to Margie Mizell, December 10, 1942; Mizell to Mrs. W. C. Lear, Austin Police Department, December 12, 1942, both in Chairman Weaver H. Baker files.

76. Bell Turner Johnson to W. H. Baker, April 6, 1943; Baker to Johnson, April 8, 1943, both in Chairman Weaver H. Baker files.

77. "Punishment at Girls' Training School Revealed," *Gainesville Daily Register*, May 12, 1943; Margie Mizell to W. H. Baker, May 13, 1943; Baker to Mizell, May 17, 1943, letters in Chairman Weaver H. Baker files.

78. Charles F. Arrowood to TBC, August 26, 1943; J. W. Calhoun to TBC, August 30, 1943, both in Chairman Weaver H. Baker files.

79. Unless otherwise noted, all juvenile names are pseudonyms. Anne's anecdote relies on the following sources: Pearl Chadwell to Judge Will McLean, April 10, 1944; McLean to Chadwell, April 12, 1944; J. B. Sallas to Chadwell, May 29, 1944; Chadwell to Sallas, June 1, 1944; Judge McLean to Chadwell, June 10, 1944; Chadwell to Mr. Ricks, June 12, 1944; Sallas to Chadwell, June 15, 1944; Chadwell to Sallas, June 20, 1944; Sallas to W. H. Baker,

July 8, 1944; Baker to Sallas, July 10, 1944; Baker to Chadwell, July 10, 1944; Chadwell to Baker, July 12, 1944; Baker to Chadwell, July 14, 1944, all in Chairman Weaver H. Baker files.

80. Affidavit of Laverne McCrary, Gainesville Assistant Superintendent, October 10, 1946; Selma Jones to TBC, October 11, 1946; Lucy T. Furlow to TBC, October 11, 1946, all in Chairman Weaver H. Baker files.

81. The quotations in the paragraph are from "Inspection of Gainesville State School for Girls, December 8–10, 1945," Chairman Weaver H. Baker files.

82. "Martineau's Blast Draws Sharp Replies," *Corpus Christi Caller*, July 30, 1946; and R. E. Blair to W. H. Baker, July 27, 1946, Chairman Weaver H. Baker files.

83. E. J. Wallace, Waco Humane Society, to TBC, August 9, 1946; W. H. Baker to Wallace, August 12, 1946; R. E. Blair to Wallace, August 21, 1946, all in Chairman Weaver H. Baker files.

84. "Fatherly Attitude Found in Use at Gatesville School for Boys," *Dallas Morning News*, October 13, 1946; for another example, see "Impressed by Training School for Girls, Gainesville," *Waxahachie Daily Light*, December 1, 1945.

85. Mrs. W. W. Goodson, First Methodist Church of Strawn, Texas, to TBC, November 25, 1946; W. H. Baker to Goodson, December 11, 1946; C. A. Mangham, Pastor, Pleasant Valley Baptist Church, to TBC, January 15, 1947; Ida Thompson to Governor Beauford Jester, October 12, 1947; Jester to Thompson, October 16, 1947; Loma Lowe to Jester, October 12, 1947; Jester to Lowe, October 16, 1947, in Chairmen Lanning, Logan, Ashley, and Baker files, 1939–53, Texas State Board of Control Board members files, Archives and Information Services Division, Texas State Library and Archives Commission, Austin (hereafter cited as Chairmen Lanning, Logan, Ashley, and Baker files).

86. "Report of the Legislative Investigating Committee on Eleemosynary and Reformatory Institutions," March 7, 1947 (photocopy), Chairmen Lanning, Logan, Ashley, and Baker files.

87. Ibid., emphasis in original.

88. "Report of Visit to Gatesville State School for Boys, Saturday, March 8, 1947," Chairmen Lanning, Logan, Ashley, and Baker files.

89. R. E. Blair to TBC, March 10, 1947, Chairmen Lanning, Logan, Ashley, and Baker files.

90. R. E. Blair to Carlos C. Ashley, March 10, 1947, Chairmen Lanning, Logan, Ashley, and Baker files.

91. Harry W. Flentge to Hall H. Logan, May 2, 1947; Logan to R. E. Blair, May 2, 1947; Logan to Judge Floyd Ziegler, May 2, 1947; Logan to "Superintendents, All Institutions," May 3, 1947; Floy E. Lyon, MD, to TBC, May 5, 1947; memo, "Visit to Gatesville," Logan to TBC, July 17, 1947; Logan to Ziegler, August 12, 1947; memo, "Visit to Gainesville," Logan to TBC, November 20, 1947, all in Chairmen Lanning, Logan, Ashley, and Baker files. Newspaper articles include "Evils Found at State's Institutions," *Dallas Morning News*, April 29, 1947; "State School Brutality Bared," *Houston Chronicle*, April 29, 1947; "Gatesville Draws O.K. from Ashley," *Tyler Morning Telegraph*, April 30, 1947; "Reform School Survey Ordered," *Dallas Morning News*, May 2, 1947; "Bad Boys Must be Strapped, House Told," *Dallas Morning News*, May 6, 1947; "Ban on Whip Gets Setback," *Dallas Morning News*, May 29, 1947.

92. Notes from H. H. Logan phone conversation with Hugo Carroll, May 7, 1947; notes from phone conversation with "Illinois Training School for Boys," May 9, 1947; Logan

to Whittier State Industrial School, September 2, 1947, all in Chairmen Lanning, Logan, Ashley, and Baker files.

93. Judge Floyd Ziegler to Logan, October 9, 1947, Chairmen Lanning, Logan, Ashley, and Baker files.

94. Mimeographed press release, November 4, 1947, Chairmen Lanning, Logan, Ashley, and Baker files; "Seven Named to Revamp Reformatory Laws," *Dallas Morning News*, November 5, 1947.

Three. Juvenile Rehabilitation and the Color Line

1. *First Annual Report of the State Board of Control to the Governor and the Legislature* (Austin, Tex., 1920), 117–18.

2. The following brief overview draws on Jacquelyn Dowd Hall, *Revolt against Chivalry: Jessie Daniel Ames and the Women's Campaign Against Lynching*, rev. ed. (New York: Columbia University Press, 1993), 107–28; *Handbook of Texas Online*, s.v. "Texas Association of Women's Clubs," http://www.tsha.utexas.edu/handbook/online/articles/TT/vet1 .html; and "Compiled History of Brady State School," August 10, 1990, Youth Commission Facilities and Programs History and Information Notebooks, Texas Youth Commission files, Archives and Information Services Division, Texas State Library and Archives Commission, Austin (hereafter cited as TYC files).

3. Hall, *Revolt against Chivalry*, 134–35.

4. "Verily, Times Are Really Changing!" *Houston Defender*, May 14, 1938. The incident is also described in "Membership Report," NAACP Houston Youth Council, June 17, 1938, NAACP Youth File, Youth Council, Texas, 1936, 1938–39, Papers of the NAACP, part 19, Youth File, series A (microfilm), 1919–139 (Bethesda, Md.: University Publications of America, 1994) (hereafter cited as NAACP Youth File).

5. Dwight Watson, *Race and the Houston Police Department, 1930–1990: A Change Did Come* (College Station: Texas A&M University Press, 2005), 1–36; and Robert D. Bullard, *Invisible Houston: The Black Experience in Boom and Bust* (College Station: Texas A&M University Press, 1987), chap. 9.

6. "Houston Chapter of Youth Council Has Fine Program," *Houston Defender*, May 28, 1938.

7. Membership Applications and Reports, NAACP Youth File.

8. "Incarceration of Negro Girl Presents Perplexing Problem," *San Antonio Express*, May 25, 1939; *Biennial Report of the State Board of Control to the Governor and the Legislature* (Austin, 1938), 85–86.

9. Earl W. Alexander, San Antonio Youth Council, to Frederic Morrow, NAACP Branch Coordinator, May 26, 1939; Morrow to Alexander, June 2, 1939, both in NAACP Youth File.

10. Weaver H. Baker to Judge Charles G. Dibrell, April 18, 1944, Chairman Weaver H. Baker files, Archives and Information Services Division, Texas State Library and Archives Commission, Austin (hereafter cited as Chairman Weaver H. Baker files).

11. Maude H. Gerhardt, Nueces County Probation Department, to TBC, June 6, 1943; W. H. Baker to Gerhardt, June 8, 1943, both in Chairman Weaver H. Baker files.

12. Quoted in "Negro Girl Won't Be Punished for Murder of Boy Friend—Texas Has No Prison for Her," *Corpus Christi Times*, June 5, 1943.

13. Judge C. G. Dibrell to W. H. Baker, April 26, 1943, and April 17, 1944; other complaints include Joe C. Gladney, District Attorney, Rusk County, to TBC, June 10, 1943; and

Judge H. Buescher, Colorado County, to TBC, January 19, 1944, all in Chairman Weaver H. Baker files.

14. Gretchen Abbott to W. H. Baker, July 24, 1944; Baker to Abbott, July 25, 1944; Margaret Yates, Dallas Council of Social Agencies, to Baker, July 25, 1944; Robert Raibel, First Unitarian Church of Dallas, to Baker, August 1, 1944; Rita M. Fleming, San Antonio chapter of the American Association of Social Workers, to Baker, August 2, 1944; Gerald J. Schepp, President, San Antonio Social Workers Association, to Baker, August 2, 1944; R. C. Tompkins, Nagodoches County Welfare Board, to Baker, August 11, 1944; Mrs. Earl F. Walborg, Houston YWCA, to Baker, August 12, 1944; San Antonio Community Welfare Council to Baker, August 14, 1944; Baker to Council, August 15, 1944; and Harold Braun, Austin Community Chest, to Baker, August 17, 1944, all in Chairman Weaver H. Baker files.

15. William M. Ryan to W. H. Baker, July 28, 1944; Baker to Ryan, July 29, 1944. Similar sentiments were expressed in other correspondence; see E. E. Hall, Houston Council of Social Agencies, to Baker, July 31, 1944; Baker to Hall, August 2, 1944; Douglas MacGregor to Baker, August 8, 1944; Baker to MacGregor, August 9, 1944; A. D. Simpson, Houston Chamber of Commerce, to Baker, August 19, 1944; Baker to Simpson, August 21, 1944, all in Chairman Weaver H. Baker files.

16. On the image and reality of the "V-girl" scare, see, for instance, Grace Palladino, *Teenagers: An American History* (New York: Basic Books, 1996), 74–76, which argues that fewer than 2 percent of adolescent girls were sexually active in the early 1940s. The starting point for the extensive literature on female sexual delinquency, referenced in chapter 1, is Steven Schlossman and Stephanie Wallach, "The Crime of Precocious Sexuality: Female Juvenile Delinquency in the Progressive Era," *Harvard Educational Review* 48, no. 1 (February 1978): 65–94.

17. "Home for Negro Girls," *Houston Post*, October 3, 1943; "Army Asks Strong Drive," *Houston Post*, November 21, 1943; "Detention Home Funds," *Houston Post*, December 3, 1943.

18. W. M. Ryan to W. H. Baker, July 28, 1944, Chairman Weaver H. Baker files.

19. "As We See the Problem in Houston," statement attached to Marjorie Wilson to W. H. Baker, August 4, 1944, Chairman Weaver H. Baker files.

20. Nellie M. Hall to W. H. Baker, August 14, 1944, Chairman Weaver H. Baker files.

21. For a penetrating analysis of alternate constructions of black and white female sexuality, see Rickie Sollinger, *Wake Up Little Susie: Single Pregnancy and Race before Roe v. Wade*, 2nd ed. (New York: Routledge, 2000).

22. Marjorie Wilson to W. H. Baker, January 29, 1945, Chairman Weaver H. Baker files.

23. Adolph I. Salsburg to TBC, October 17, 1946, Chairman Weaver H. Baker files.

24. Marjorie Wilson to W. H. Baker, February 7, 1945; Baker to Senator R. C. Lanning, March 12, 1945; Baker to Representative John Hoyo, April 18, 1945, all in Chairman Weaver H. Baker files.

25. "Compiled History of Brady State School.".

26. Gunnar Myrdal, *An American Dilemma: The Negro Problem and Modern Democracy* (New York: Harper and Bros., 1944); for a historical examination of the study, see Walter A. Jackson, *Gunnar Myrdal and America's Conscience: Social Engineering and Racial Liberalism, 1938–1987* (Chapel Hill: University of North Carolina Press, 1990).

27. Myrdal, *American Dilemma*, 634.

28. B. D. Geslin to Governor Coke Stevenson, June 20, 1946, Chairman Weaver H. Baker files.

29. W. H. Baker to Representative O. C. Fisher, September 18, 1945; Brady Chamber of Commerce to TBC, September 22, 1945; Baker to Brady Chamber of Commerce, September 24, 1945, all in Chairman Weaver H. Baker files.

30. Judge Wiley Caffey to W. H. Baker, October 26, 1945. Other examples include Judge Harlee Morrison, Kaufman County, to TBC, April 19, 1946; R. E. Neely, Harris County (Houston) Probation Department, to W. H. Baker, July 16, 1946; George M. Cusick, Galveston County Probation Office, to Baker, July 17, 1946; Irma Thompson, Tyler-Smith County Child Welfare Unit, to Baker, July 24, 1946; W. E. Robertson, Harris County Probation Department, to Baker, August 9, 1946, all in Chairman Weaver H. Baker files.

31. Family Welfare Bureau of Galveston to TBC, August 28, 1946, and September 7, 1946, both in Chairman Weaver H. Baker files.

32. V. L. Pitman to TBC, October 9, 1946, Chairman Weaver H. Baker files.

33. Marzelle C. Hill to W. H. Baker, December 11, 1945, Chairman Weaver H. Baker files.

34. Janie Jones to W. H. Baker, October 3, 1946, Chairman Weaver H. Baker files.

35. For a discussion of Smith's activities, see Michael Phillips, *White Metropolis: Race, Ethnicity, and Religion in Dallas, 1841–2001* (Austin: University of Texas Press, 2006), 112–18.

36. A. Maceo Smith to W. H. Baker, June 12, 1946, Chairman Weaver H. Baker files.

37. Lillie Portley, Fifth Ward Civic Club, to W. H. Baker, September 5, 1946, Chairman Weaver H. Baker files.

38. Mrs. V. C. Tedford, TFCWC, to TBC, July 3, 1946; W. H. Baker to Tedford, July 8, 1946, both in Chairman Weaver H. Baker files.

39. Memos, TBC to Governor Coke Stevenson, February 4 and December 3, 1946, both in Chairman Weaver H. Baker files.

40. "Compiled History of Brady State School."

41. The motto appears in several documents, most prominently in the *Student-Staff Handbook for the Brady State School* (1948), Chairman Weaver H. Baker files. On self-help, see Kevin K. Gaines, *Uplifting the Race: Black Leadership, Politics, and Culture in the Twentieth Century* (Chapel Hill: University of North Carolina Press, 1996).

42. Minutes, Brady State School staff meeting, February 8, 1947, Chairmen Lanning, Logan, Ashley, and Baker files, 1939–53, Texas State Board of Control Board members files, Archives and Information Services Division, Texas State Library and Archives Commission, Austin (hereafter cited as Chairmen Lanning, Logan, Ashley, and Baker files).

43. *National Negro Health Week, 33rd Observance, March 30–April 6, 1947*, United States Public Health Service pamphlet (copy), Chairmen Lanning, Logan, Ashley, and Baker files.

44. "Community-Wide Cooperation for Better Health and Sanitation," radio broadcast transcript, Sunday, March 30, 1947, Chairmen Lanning, Logan, Ashley, and Baker files.

45. "National Negro Health Week Schedule, Brady State School," undated, March 1947; W. H. Baker to I. W. Rowan, April 3, 1947, both in Chairmen Lanning, Logan, Ashley, and Baker files.

46. Carl M. Tibbitts to Hall H. Logan, February 4, 1947, Chairmen Lanning, Logan, Ashley, and Baker files.

47. "Training School for Negro Girls Readied near Brady," *San Angelo Standard-Times*, February 12, 1947.

48. H. H. Logan to C. M. Tibbitts, March 7, 1947, Chairmen Lanning, Logan, Ashley, and Baker files.

49. All quotations are from "Training School for Negro Girls Readied."

50. "General Rules and Regulations for the Administration and Operation of the Brady State School," March 1947, Chairmen Lanning, Logan, Ashley, and Baker files.

51. C. M. Tibbitts to H. H. Logan, March 19, 1947, Chairmen Lanning, Logan, Ashley, and Baker files.

52. I. W. Rowan to H. H. Logan, April 10, 1947, Chairmen Lanning, Logan, Ashley, and Baker files.

53. U. V. Christian, Chair, Advisory Board, to H. H. Logan, April 29, 1947, Chairmen Lanning, Logan, Ashley, and Baker files.

54. H. H. Logan to I. W. Rowan, May 3, 1947, Chairmen Lanning, Logan, Ashley, and Baker files.

55. Meeting Minutes, Advisory Board of the Brady State School, June 11, 1947, Chairmen Lanning, Logan, Ashley, and Baker files.

56. "Brady State School, 1947–1950: Final Report," February 10, 1950, TYC files.

57. I. W. Rowan to H. H. Logan, August 13, 1947; November 24, 1947; December 1, 1947; January 2, 1948; February 2, 1948; February 29, 1948; March 31, 1948; May 6, 1948, all in Chairmen Lanning, Logan, Ashley, and Baker files.

58. I. W. Rowan to H. H. Logan, April 30, 1947, Chairmen Lanning, Logan, Ashley, and Baker files.

59. H. H. Logan to I. W. Rowan, May 3, 1947; Logan to Rowan, May 14, 1947; Logan to Rowan, May 26, 1947, all in Chairmen Lanning, Logan, Ashley, and Baker files.

60. Unless otherwise indicated, the following story draws on these sources: "Hearing Held in the Office of the State Board of Control," August 29, 1947; and "Investigation at Brady State School," September 4–12, 1947, both in Chairmen Lanning, Logan, Ashley, and Baker files.

61. "Rose Thompson" is a pseudonym, as are all juveniles' names unless otherwise noted.

62. Dr. D. W. Jordan to I. W. Rowan, May 15, 1947, Chairmen Lanning, Logan, Ashley, and Baker files.

63. All four girls testified to the events during and after their escape from Brady; the following description is a composite of their testimonies. "Investigation at Brady," Chairmen Lanning, Logan, Ashley, and Baker files.

64. "Brady State School, 1947–1950: Final Report," TYC files.

65. I. W. Rowan testimony, "Hearing Held in the Office of the State Board of Control," August 29, 1947, Chairmen Lanning, Logan, Ashley, and Baker files.

66. Dr. D. W. Jordan to I. W. Rowan, September 1, 1947, Chairmen Lanning, Logan, Ashley, and Baker files.

67. "Rose Thompson" testimony, "Investigation at Brady State School," September 4–12, 1947, Chairmen Lanning, Logan, Ashley, and Baker files.

68. Meeting Minutes, Advisory Board of the Brady State School, November 28, 1947; and Memo, "Visit to Brady State School," H. H. Logan to TBC, December 16, 1947, both in Chairmen Lanning, Logan, Ashley, and Baker files.

69. *To Secure These Rights: The Report of the President's Committee on Civil Rights* (Washington, D.C.: U.S. Government Printing Office, 1947), 140–41.

70. "A Practical Health Program for Myself and My Family," radio broadcast transcript, April 4, 1948, Chairmen Lanning, Logan, Ashley, and Baker files.

71. Memo, "Visit to Brady State School," H. H. Logan to TBC, May 4, 1948, Chairmen Lanning, Logan, Ashley, and Baker files.

72. I. W. Rowan to H. H. Logan, May 6, 1948, Chairmen Lanning, Logan, Ashley, and Baker files.

73. Marzelle C. Hill to H. H. Logan, May 26, 1948, Chairmen Lanning, Logan, Ashley, and Baker files.

74. Emma Harrell to H. H. Logan, June 8, 1948, Chairmen Lanning, Logan, Ashley, and Baker files.

75. Carter Wesley, "Austin and Brady," *Dallas Express*, June 5, 1948.

76. Ibid.

77. Memo, H. H. Logan to TBC, January 5, 1949, Chairmen Lanning, Logan, Ashley, and Baker files.

78. "Compiled History of Brady State School," TYC files.

79. "Brady State School, 1947–1950: Final Report," TYC files.

80. Ibid.

81. Hall H. Logan invitation card, October 27, 1949, Chairmen Lanning, Logan, Ashley, and Baker files. The school held a second graduation the next year. Commencement program, May 23, 1950, TYC files.

82. *Annual Report of the Brady State School, August 31, 1948* (1948), 9–10, Chairmen Lanning, Logan, Ashley, and Baker files.

83. "Brady State School, 1947–1950: Final Report.".

84. "Success" and "The Real You," *Brady State News*," vol. 1, November 19, 1948, Chairmen Lanning, Logan, Ashley, and Baker files.

85. "Brady State School, 1947–1950: Final Report."

86. "Juvenile Delinquency," in *Brady News*, vol. 2, March 2, 1949, Chairmen Lanning, Logan, Ashley, and Baker files.

87. "Behavior Problems," in *Brady News*," vol. 3, June 6, 1949, Chairmen Lanning, Logan, Ashley, and Baker files.

88. "Check Upon Yourself," in *Brady News*," vol. 1, November 18, 1949, Chairmen Lanning, Logan, Ashley, and Baker files.

89. "Brady State School, 1947–1950: Final Report."

90. "Report on Students with Unusual Behavior," E. Harrell to I. W. Rowan, May 7, 1948, Chairmen Lanning, Logan, Ashley, and Baker files.

91. For a discussion of this diagnosis in the context of juvenile training schools, see Anne Meis Knupfer, *Reform and Resistance: Gender, Delinquency, and America's First Juvenile Court* (New York: Routledge, 2001), 140–42.

92. "Report on Students with Unusual Behavior."

93. E. Harrell to W. E. Robertson, Chief Probation Officer for Harris County (Houston), June 2, 1948; Harrell to H. H. Logan, June 3, 1948, both in Chairmen Lanning, Logan, Ashley, and Baker files.

94. "Report on Students with Unusual Behavior."

95. "Report on Girls 18 Years Old or near 18 Years Old," August 1948, Chairmen Lanning, Logan, Ashley, and Baker files.

96. E. Harrell to H. H. Logan, August 9, 1948, Chairmen Lanning, Logan, Ashley, and Baker files.

97. Erwin K. Stork to H. H. Logan, August 13, 1948; Logan to E. Harrell, August 18, 1948, Chairmen Lanning, Logan, Ashley, and Baker files.

98. E. Harrell to H. H. Logan, August 9, 1948, Chairmen Lanning, Logan, Ashley, and Baker files.

99. The following paragraph draws on whipping reports submitted by E. Harrell to TBC, July 1948–September 1949, Chairmen Lanning, Logan, Ashley, and Baker files.

100. Population figures are from "Population Report, Brady State School," August 1949, Chairmen Lanning, Logan, Ashley, and Baker files.

101. "Crockett Asks Negro Girls' School," *Austin American*, March 24, 1950; "Crockett Site for Delinquent Negroes Studied," *Houston Chronicle*, March 29, 1950; "Crockett Picked for Delinquent Girls' Center," *Austin American*, July 2, 1950.

102. D. W. Kennedy Jr. to H. H. Logan, June 20, 1950, Chairmen Lanning, Logan, Ashley, and Baker files.

103. Earle P. Adams to H. H. Logan, June 19, 1950, Chairmen Lanning, Logan, Ashley, and Baker files.

104. "Job of Negro Girls' School Well Done," *Houston Post*, November 27, 1952.

105. "Crockett State School Opens With 29 Girls," *Crockett Democrat*, January 4, 1951; "Crockett State School Superintendent Gives Resumé of Ten Years' Operation," *Crockett Democrat*, January 31, 1957.

106. E. Harrell to H. H. Logan, December 11, 1948, Chairmen Lanning, Logan, Ashley, and Baker files.

107. "Compiled History of Crockett State School," August 10, 1990, TYC files.

Four. James Dean and Jim Crow

1. "Jester Will Recommend Adoption of Extensive Youth Program," *Houston Chronicle*, February 6, 1949; "16-Member State Youth Council Urged," *Houston Post*, February 6, 1949; "Jester Will Offer Delinquency Plan," *Big Spring Herald*, February 6, 1949; "Integration of State and Local Child Agencies Urged by Group," *Fort Worth Star-Telegram*, February 8, 1949; "New Plan for Youths," *Abilene Reporter-News*, February 15, 1949; "Youth Development Measure Filed with Aim of Correcting Delinquency," *Austin American-Statesman*, February 18, 1949.

2. "Youth Council's Importance Cited in Shivers Talk," *Austin American-Statesman*, May 23, 1950; "Committee Begins Choosing Delegates to the White House," *Austin Statesman*, June 24, 1950.

3. The film was based on a best-selling memoir by a former mental patient: Mary Jane Ward, *The Snake Pit* (New York: Random House, 1946).

4. Albert Deutsch, *Our Rejected Children* (Boston: Little, Brown, 1950). Deutsch was the best known of several postwar critics of juvenile justice; see also Paul Tappan, *Delinquent Girls in Court* (New York: Columbia University Press, 1947); and Benjamin Fine, *1,000,000 Delinquents* (Cleveland: World, 1955). On the postwar movement for community mental health clinics, see Gerald N. Grob, *From Asylum to Community: Mental Health Policy in Modern America* (Princeton, N.J.: Princeton University Press, 1991); and Ellen Herman, *The Romance of American Psychology: Political Culture in the Age of Experts* (Berkeley: University of California Press, 1995).

5. Federal Bureau of Investigation, *Uniform Crime Reports, Annual Bulletin for 1954* 15, no. 2 (1955): 111.

6. James Gilbert, *A Cycle of Outrage: America's Reaction to the Juvenile Delinquent in the 1950s* (New York: Oxford University Press, 1986).

7. Richard Clenenden and Herbert W. Beaser, "The Shame of America," *Saturday Evening Post*, January 8–February 5, 1955.

8. For example, see "How American Teen-Agers Live," *Look*, July 23, 1957; or "Our Good Teen-Agers," *Newsweek*, November 23, 1959. For a broad overview, see Grace Palladino, *Teenagers: An American History* (New York: Basic Books, 1996), 96–135, 154–73.

9. *Rebel without a Cause*, directed by Nicholas Ray (1955); for one film reviewer, the "shock impact" came from the film's location in "a pleasant middle-class community" (*Variety*, October 26, 1955, p. 6). See also Thomas Doherty, *Teenagers and Teenpics: The Juvenilization of American Movies in the 1950s*, rev. ed. (Philadelphia: Temple University Press, 2002); and Leerom Medovoi, *Rebels: Youth and the Cold War Origins of Identity* (Durham, N.C.: Duke University Press, 2005), 177–91.

10. Transcript, "Meeting of the Texas Training School Code Commission Held in the State Capitol, Austin, Texas, June 19, 1948," Chairmen Lanning, Logan, Ashley, and Baker files, 1939–53, Texas State Board of Control Board members files, Archives and Information Services Division, Archives and Information Services Division, Texas State Library and Archives Commission, Austin (hereafter cited as Chairmen Lanning, Logan, Ashley, and Baker files).

11. Clenenden's assessment echoed existing critiques of Gatesville's threadbare vocational program. "Vocational Weakness Found at State Boys' School," *Austin American*, February 13, 1948; and "Texas' Crime School," *Houston Post*, July 18, 1948.

12. Transcript, "Meeting of the Texas Training School Code Commission."

13. Mimeographed press release, November 4, 1947, Chairmen Lanning, Logan, Ashley, and Baker files; "Seven Named to Revamp Reformatory Laws," *Dallas Morning News*, November 5, 1947; "Reform School Kids Given Break," *Dallas Morning News*, November 12, 1947; "A Crusader for Freedom," *Dallas Herald*, October 21, 1962; "Walter K. Kerr" Vertical File, Center for American History, University of Texas at Austin; Walter Kinsolving Kerr, "Juvenile Detention in Austin and Travis County" (MA thesis, University of Texas at Austin, 1949).

14. "Kerr Attends Parley on Delinquents," *Austin American*, February 11, 1948.

15. National Conference on Prevention and Control of Juvenile Delinquency, *Report on Institutional Treatment of Delinquent Juveniles* (Washington, D.C.: U.S. Government Printing Office, 1946), 2–3.

16. Austin H. MacCormick, *The Education of Adult Prisoners, a Survey and a Program* (New York: National Society of Penal Information, 1931). For more on MacCormick, see Steven Schlossman and Joseph Spillane, *Bright Hopes, Dim Realities: Vocational Innovation in American Correctional Education* (Berkeley: National Center for Research in Vocational Education, University of California at Berkeley, 1992), 19–27; Steven Schlossman and Amy R. DeCamp, "Correctional Education," in *Encyclopedia of Educational Research*, ed. Marvin C. Alkin, 6th ed. (New York: MacMillan, 1992), 244–47; and David J. Rothman, *Conscience and Convenience: The Asylum and Its Alternatives in Progressive America*, rev. ed. (New York: Aldine de Gruyter, 2002), 280–81.

17. This discussion draws substantially on Laura Mihailoff, "Protecting Our Children: A History of the California Youth Authority and Juvenile Justice, 1938–1968" (PhD diss., University of California, Berkeley, 2005), esp. 64–126. See also Bertram M. Beck, *Five States: A Study of the Youth Authority Program as Promulgated by the American Law Institute* (Philadelphia: American Law Institute, 1951); and Robert H. Bremner, ed., *Children and Youth in America: A Documentary History*, vol. 3 (Cambridge, Mass.: Harvard University Press, 1974), 1060–68.

18. *Child by Child We Build a Nation: A Youth Development Plan for the State of Texas* (Austin: Texas Training School Code Commission, 1949), 24, Archives and Information Services Division, Texas State Library and Archives Commission, Austin.

19. *Texas Juvenile Court Research Reports*, vol. 3, *Juvenile Court Statistics and Related Services for Texas Children*, Texas Juvenile Court Research Project, State of Texas Board of Public Welfare (Austin, December 1948).

20. *Child by Child We Build a Nation*, 9–25; Pat Wiseman to Hall H. Logan, June 10, 1948; Logan to Pearl G. Chadwell, June 11, 1948; Chadwell to Logan, June 13, 1948, all in Chairmen Lanning, Logan, Ashley, and Baker files.

21. *Child by Child We Build a Nation*, 34.

22. Ibid., 32–33.

23. H. H. Logan to R. E. Blair, July 1, 1948, Chairmen Lanning, Logan, Ashley, and Baker files. The *Amarillo Times* series included the following articles: "Launch Investigation at Gatesville Boys' School," October 27, 1948; "Gatesville Trade Training School under Probe," October 29, 1948; "Juvenile Punishment 'Harsh but Justified,'" October 30, 1948; "Boys Learn Walls at State School Enclose Own World," November 1, 1948; and "State School for Boys Most in Need of Better Teachers, Fun Facilities," November 2, 1948.

24. F. L. King, TBC Educational Director, to TBC, November 24, 1948, Chairmen Lanning, Logan, Ashley, and Baker files.

25. Leslie Jackson to Hall H. Logan, September 10, 1948; Memo, John Freeman to J. B. Head, Gatesville School Principal, February 24, 1949; Bryan District Judge W. S. Barron to Freeman, January 31, 1949; S. L. Bellamy, Travis County Juvenile Court, to Freeman, February 7, 1949; Herman E. Krimmel, Nueces County Juvenile Probation Department, to Freeman, February 7, 1949; W. E. Robertson, Houston Juvenile Probation Department, to Freeman, February 14, 1949; S. M. Davis, Dallas Juvenile Court, to Logan, February 19, 1949; James J. Davis, Bexar County Juvenile Court, to Freeman, March 3, 1949; TBC press release, May 8, 1949, all in Chairmen Lanning, Logan, Ashley, and Baker files.

26. J. Freeman testimony, "Investigation of Gatesville State School for Boys," May 25, 1949; Freeman to H. H. Logan, June 15, 1949, both in Chairmen Lanning, Logan, Ashley, and Baker files.

27. Memo, H. H. Logan to TBC, May 18, 1949, Chairmen Lanning, Logan, Ashley, and Baker files.

28. Ibid.

29. H. H. Logan to R. E. Blair, May 17, 1949; Blair to Logan, May 31, 1949, both in Chairmen Lanning, Logan, Ashley, and Baker files.

30. A. S. "Mack" Hull, "A Report to the Governor of the State of Texas on Conditions in the Gatesville State School for Boys at Gatesville, Texas," May 19, 1949; "Five Gatesville Boys on Lam," *Waco Tribune-Herald*, May 1, 1949; "13 Youths Make Escape at Gatesville," *Fort Worth Star-Telegram*, May 1, 1949.

31. Harry Flentge to James Teague, May 28, 1949; Teague to H. H. Logan, June 8, 1949, both in Chairmen Lanning, Logan, Ashley, and Baker files.

32. Teague testimony, "Investigation of Gatesville," May 25 and June 6, 1949, Chairmen Lanning, Logan, Ashley, and Baker files.

33. Quoted from Edna Mae Lace testimony, in "Investigation of Gatesville." Other employees testified anonymously or through correspondence. W. E. Smith to TBC, undated, circa June 1949, Chairmen Lanning, Logan, Ashley, and Baker files.

34. "Escapes at Gatesville Blamed on Board's New Rules," *Waco Tribune-Herald*, June 12, 1949; "Grand Jury Blames State School Escapes on 'Governing Board,'" *Gatesville Messenger*, June 17, 1949.

35. Memo, H. H. Logan to TBC, June 14, 1949; "Testimony of Mr. R. E. Blair, Superintendent of the Gatesville School for Boys, Given in the Office of Chairman Logan of the Board of Control," June 21, 1949; Memo, Logan to T. B. Warden, June 27, 1949; Warden to Logan, June 29, 1949; Memo, Logan to Tom DeBerry, June 30, 1949; Memo, DeBerry to TBC, July 1, 1949; Logan to John Winters, Executive Secretary, TSYDC, September 13, 1949, all in Chairmen Lanning, Logan, Ashley, and Baker files.

36. Minutes, TSYDC Meeting, November 21, 1949, Minutes, State Youth Development Council and Texas Youth Council, 1949–65, Archives and Information Services Commission, Texas State Library and Archives Commission, Austin (hereafter cited as TSYDC Minutes).

37. Unless otherwise noted, this paragraph draws on Texas State Youth Development Council, *First Annual Report of the State Youth Development Council to the Governor, Fiscal Year Ended August 31, 1950* (Austin, 1950).

38. HB 705, *General and Special Laws of the State of Texas*, 51st Leg., 1st Sess., 1949.

39. Texas State Youth Development Council, *A Community Organization for Children and Youth* (Austin, 1950), Chairmen Lanning, Logan, Ashley, and Baker files.

40. *First Annual Report of the State Youth Development Council*, 7.

41. William Foote Whyte, *Street Corner Society: The Social Structure of an Italian Slum* (Chicago: University of Chicago Press, 1943).

42. "Integration of State and Local Child Agencies Urged By Group," *Fort Worth Star-Telegram*, February 8, 1949, State Youth Development Council Early History Scrapbooks, Texas Youth Commission, Archives and Information Services Division, Texas State Library and Archives Commission, Austin (hereafter TSYDC Scrapbooks).

43. Minutes, TSYDC Meeting, November 21, 1949, TSYDC Minutes. News articles included "Ex-Travis Probation Officer Offered a Top State Youth Job," *Austin American-Statesman*, September 27, 1949; "Bellamy Quits for New Position," *Houston Press*, September 29, 1949; "Bellamy Upheld by Youth Panel Despite Charges," *Austin American-Statesman*, November 22, 1949; "Bellamy Employment by Youth Council Protested," *Houston Post*, November 22, 1949, all in TSYDC Scrapbooks.

44. Minutes, TSYDC Meeting, March 15, 1951, TSYDC Minutes.

45. *Key*, 1, no. 1 (November 1950), TSYDC Scrapbooks.

46. "Youth Leader Praises Movie Trend," *Austin American-Statesman*, May 1, 1950; "Youth Council's Importance Cited in Shivers Talk," *Austin American-Statesman*, May 23, 1950; "Better Law Needed for Child Support," *Dallas Morning News*, October 21, 1950; "Reverend Kerr Reviews Conference Goals for AAUW," *Austin American-Statesman*, November 8, 1950; "Youth Center Made No. 1 Project of Youth Development Council," *Bonham Daily Favorite*, January 23, 1951; "Plans Are Drawn Here for Youth Survey Project," *Port Arthur News*, February 1, 1951; "Survey Planned in Port Arthur on Youth Recreation," *Beaumont Enterprise*, February 6, 1951; "Youth Reform Changes Asked," *Wichita Falls Record News*, February 7, 1951; "The Proper Approach," *Lubbock Avalanche-Journal*, February 8, 1951; "Lufkin Students Request Program of Recreation," *Lufkin Daily News*, March 12, 1951; "Director Says Youth Aid Is Local Problem," *McAllen Valley Evening Monitor*, April 27, 1951; "Smith County to Get Added Juvenile Aid," *Tyler Morning Telegraph*,

May 3, 1951; "Major Needs of Youth Outlined," *Amarillo Globe-News*, May 22, 1951, all in TSYDC Scrapbooks.

47. "Texas Explores Salvage of Youth," *Austin Statesman*, July 6, 1950, TSYDC Scrapbooks.

48. *Our Community* 1, no. 2 (June 1944), Materials of the Community Chest and Council, Council of Social Agencies, and United Way (3 boxes), Houston Metropolitan Research Center, Houston Public Library.

49. Erik H. Erikson, *Childhood and Society* (New York: Norton, 1950), 261–63. Erikson elaborated these ideas in later editions of this book, as well as *Young Man Luther: A Study in Psychoanalysis and History* (New York: Norton, 1958); and *Identity, Youth, and Crisis* (New York: Norton, 1968). For a definitive biography that probes the intellectual roots of Erikson's theories, see Lawrence J. Friedman, *Identity's Architect: A Biography of Erik H. Erikson* (New York: Scribner, 1999).

50. Clifford R. Shaw, *The Jack-Roller: A Delinquent Boy's Own Story* (Chicago: University of Chicago Press, 1930).

51. My usage of "continuum theory" borrows from Gerald N. Grob, *From Asylum to Community: Mental Health Policy in Modern America* (Princeton, N.J.: Princeton University Press, 1991).

52. "Diagnostic Centers," Memo, Harold J. Matthews to TSYDC, November 29, 1950; Matthews to Hall H. Logan, December 5, 1949, both in Chairmen Lanning, Logan, Ashley, and Baker files. Minutes, TSYDC Meeting, December 19, 1949, TSYDC Minutes.

53. "Diagnostic Centers"; Memo, H. J. Matthews to TSYDC, July 6, 1950, Chairmen Lanning, Logan, Ashley, and Baker files.

54. "Two Juvenile Girls to Take 'Spot' Psychological Exams," *Tyler Courier-Times*, March 6, 1951; "Juvenile Diagnostic Clinic to Bring Mobile Unit to Edinburg," *McAllen Valley Evening Monitor*, April 5, 1951; "Youth Council Clinic to Be Here Next Week," *Nagodoches Daily Sentinel*, July 21, 1951, all in TSYDC Scrapbooks.

55. The following anecdotes are from "Mobile Diagnostic Clinic, Summary and Recommendations," in State Youth Development Council, *Third Annual Report of the State Youth Development Council to the Governor, Fiscal Year Ended August 31, 1952* (Austin, 1952), 51–61.

56. "New Look in Juvenile Correction Paying Off," *Fort Worth Star-Telegram*, May 7, 1950; other favorable articles included "Gainesville State School for Girls Declared Progressive Institution," *Houston Chronicle*, June 13, 1949; "Gainesville School Is Being Transformed," *Austin American-Statesman*, October 8, 1949; and "Gainesville State School Girls Learn Practical Subjects in Study Courses," *Austin American-Statesman*, October 11, 1949, all in TSYDC Scrapbooks.

57. Minutes, TSYDC Meeting, February 21, 1952, TSYDC Minutes.

58. Mimeographed Program, Gainesville State School for Girls Open House, May 26–27, 1950; "State School Girls, like Any Other, Enjoy Holding 2-Day Open House," *Austin American-Statesman*, May 27, 1950; "Girls' School Open House," *Fort Worth Star-Telegram*, May 27, 1950, all in TSYDC Scrapbooks.

59. "Gainesville State School," *Houston Chronicle*, June 13, 1949, TSYDC Scrapbooks.

60. All of the habeas corpus petitions were rejected by the county courts, but one reached the state court of appeals, where it was dismissed without any further discussion: *Ex Parte Barbara June Beal and Soyla Cardona*, 157 Tex. Crim. 466, 250 S.W. 2d 221, 1952 Tx. Crim. App.

61. "Houston Mother Rips Gainesville Treatment," *Houston Chronicle*, January 24, 1952, TSYDC Scrapbooks.

62. "Girl Tells of Terror in Reform Schools: Matron Gave Her Goof Balls, Court Is Told," *Houston Chronicle*, February 1, 1952, TSYDC Scrapbooks. For a representative headline on "goof balls," see "Youth Describes 'Goof Ball' Orgy," *Houston Chronicle*, February 16, 1951, "Juvenile Delinquency" Vertical File, Houston Metropolitan Research Center, Houston Public Library.

63. "Official Demands Girl's School Cleanup," *Houston Chronicle*, February 2, 1952, TSYDC Scrapbooks.

64. "'I'll Kill Myself Before I'm Returned,' Girl Vows," *Austin Statesman*, February 7, 1952, TSYDC Scrapbooks.

65. "One-Man Probe of Girl's School Pledged," *Houston Chronicle*, February 3, 1952; "Shivers Opposes Lash as Teener Correction," *Houston Chronicle*, March 14, 1952, both in TSYDC Scrapbooks.

66. "Whipping Ban Blamed for Girls School Riot," *Fort Worth Star-Telegram*, March 20, 1952; "State Schools' Straps Banned," *Houston Post*, April 25, 1952; "Banning the Lash," *Fort Worth Star-Telegram*, April 27, 1952, all in TSYDC Scrapbooks. See also Minutes, TSYDC Meeting, February 21, 1952, TSYDC Minutes.

67. James Atlee interviewed at the TSYDC's December 1949 meeting, Minutes, TSYDC Meeting, December 19, 1949, TSYDC Minutes.

68. "Coryell Due Consideration," *Gatesville Messenger*, December 28, 1949, TSYDC Scrapbooks.

69. *First Annual Report of the State Youth Development Council*, 27–28.

70. Ibid., 43–44; "Fence Worth a Trial," *Gatesville Messenger*, April 28, 1950; "Coryell Jury Blasts Escapes at the Gatesville Boys School," *Waco News-Tribune*, June 9, 1950; "Grand Jury Blames Thefts on State School Escapees," *Dallas Morning News*, June 10, 1950, all in TSYDC Scrapbooks.

71. Minutes, TSYDC Meeting, June 22, 1950, TSYDC Minutes.

72. The following narrative draws on "Austin Youth Held in Affray," *Austin Statesman*, August 16, 1950; "Coryell Wants Gatesville Oust," *Austin Statesman*, August 17, 1950; "Mass Meeting Favors Removal of School from Gatesville," *Fort Worth Star-Telegram*, August 17, 1950; "Walter Mack Better after Gunshot Wound by Walter Johnson," *Coryell County News*, August 18, 1950; "Gatesville Wants Problem Solved," *Dallas Morning News*, August 24, 1950; "Runaway Boys Should Be Whipped," *McKinney Examiner*, August 25, 1950, all in TSYDC Scrapbooks.

73. "Citizens Demand Return to Whip," *Dallas Morning News*, August 17, 1950.

74. Ibid.

75. "Brighter Day Looms for Texas Juveniles," *Austin American*, September 24, 1950, TSYDC Scrapbooks.

76. Minutes, TSYDC Meeting, September 21, 1950, and November 16, 1950, TSYDC Minutes. Also "Small Unit Breakup for Gatesville Set," *Houston Post*, September 22, 1950; "Youth Council Says Split School for Boys to Divide Sheep, Goats," *Austin American*, September 22, 1950; "Real 'Reform': That is Texas' Need," *Lubbock Morning Avalanche*, September 27, 1950; "Youth Council Eyes New Institutions," *Waco Times-Herald*, November 16, 1950; "Reformatory 'Face-Lifting' Planned," *Austin American*, November 16, 1950; "Four Schools Called Gatesville Need," *Dallas Morning News*, November 17, 1950, all in TSYDC Scrapbooks.

77. Minutes, TSYDC Meeting, September 21, 1950, TSYDC Minutes.

78. On the Binet tests, see Elizabeth Lunbeck, *The Psychiatric Persuasion: Knowledge, Gender, and Power in Modern America* (Princeton, N.J.: Princeton University Press, 1994),

54–61. On their use with racial and ethnic minorities, see Anne Meis Knupfer, *Reform and Resistance: Gender, Delinquency, and America's First Juvenile Court* (New York: Routledge, 2001), 35–46.

79. *First Annual Report of the State Youth Development Council*, 51–58.

80. *Second Annual Report of the State Youth Development Council to the Governor, Fiscal Year Ended August 31, 1951* (Austin, 1951), 42–52.

81. *First Annual Report of the State Youth Development Council*, 53.

82. Nowhere in the record is there any mention of a substantial transfer of black inmates from TSYDC facilities to a mental institution. The incidents cited here draw on Minutes, TSYDC Meeting, September 21, 1950, and September 20, 1951, TSYDC Minutes.

83. *Handbook of Texas Online*, s.v. "Abilene State School," http://www.tshaonline.org/handbook/online/articles/AA/sba2.html.

84. TSYDC Policy Directive 19 (August 22, 1952), TSYDC Minutes.

85. "Plan to Break Up Gatesville Boys' Institution into Four Units Proposed," *Brownwood Bulletin*, February 8, 1951; "Two Favor Relocation of Boys' School," *Austin Statesman*, February 16, 1951, both in TSYDC Scrapbooks.

86. "Texas Seeks Remedy for 62-Year Disgrace," *Dallas Morning News*, March 17, 1951, TSYDC Scrapbooks.

87. "$669,000 Will Improve School," *Waco Times-Herald*, May 20, 1951; "Bellamy New Head of Gatesville," *Austin Statesman*, July 20, 1951, both in TSYDC Scrapbooks.

88. Minutes, TSYDC Meeting, May 21, 1953, TSYDC Minutes.

89. *Sixth Annual Report of the State Youth Development Council to the Governor of Texas* (Austin, 1955), 1–2.

90. *Texas' Teenagers in Trouble: 1955 Statewide Delinquency Survey* (Austin, 1956), 3–4.

91. These figures are composites from the TSYDC *Annual Reports*, 1950–60.

92. These figures are from U.S. Bureau of the Census, *Texas: General Social and Economic Characteristics, 1950* (Washington, D.C.: Government Printing Office, 1951), 64–66; and *First Annual Report of the State Youth Development Council*, 36–37.

93. The TSYDC published figures for the two-year period of 1953–55 showing an increase in delinquency rates per 10,000 population among black juveniles, from 16.8 to 21.9, but a small decrease for whites, from 8.8 to 8.6. *Sixth Annual Report of the State Youth Development Council*, 24.

94. *Texas Juvenile Court Statistics for 1958* (Austin, 1959). These surveys were conducted infrequently, using varying survey schedules, in the 1950s and 1960s. After 1958, race vanished from the list of survey schedules, returning only in the 1970s, when data collection became more regularized under the supervision of the Population Research Center at the University of Texas.

95. Minutes, TSYDC Meeting, March 19, 1953, TSYDC Minutes.

96. Minutes, TSYDC Meeting, August 1955, TSYDC Minutes.

97. "Gatesville Boys School Not a Prison," *Dallas Morning News*, February 5, 1957.

98. The *Austin Statesman* series included the following articles: "Delinquency Fight Uses 'Old Broom,'" March 2, 1955; "What Is a Juvenile Delinquent, and How Does He Become That Way?" March 3, 1955; "Goals Lofty, Cash Lagging," March 4, 1955; "And Now What?" March 6, 1955, all in "Juvenile Delinquency" Vertical File, Center for American History, University of Texas at Austin.

99. Minutes, TSYDC Meeting, December 2, 1954, TSYDC Minutes.

100. "Drive Seeks Chapels at Training Schools," *Dallas Morning News*, April 27, 1956. The TSYDC received updates on the chapels at its regular meetings throughout 1956 and 1957, TSYDC Minutes.

101. James Aubrey Turman, "A Comparison of Negro and White Teacher Attitudes toward Non-Segregation" (MA thesis, University of Texas at Austin, 1951).

102. *Sixth Annual Report of the State Youth Development Council*, 26.

103. Minutes, TSYDC Meeting, March 31, 1955, TSYDC Minutes.

104. Minutes, TSYDC Meeting, May 26, 1955, TSYDC Minutes.

105. Minutes, TSYDC Meeting, December 6, 1955, TSYDC Minutes; James Aubrey Turman, "A Comparative Study of Some Selected Solutions to the Problem of Logical-Psychological Continuity in the Educative Process" (PhD diss., University of Texas, 1956).

106. Minutes, TSYDC Meeting, December 6, 1956, TSYDC Minutes.

107. Minutes, TSYDC Meeting, August 2, 1956, TSYDC Minutes.

108. "Youths Accused in Killing," *Houston Chronicle*, December 28, 1957; "Try 15-Year-Olds, Judge Hunt Says," *Houston Chronicle*, January 4, 1958; "Citizens Panel Draws Blueprint Aimed at Curbing Teen Crime," *Houston Chronicle*, January 15, 1958; Bo Byers, "Bigger Reformatories, Tougher Laws Favored," *Houston Chronicle*, January 26, 1958 ; "Are Youngsters Coddled by Law?" *Houston Chronicle*, January 27, 1958; "Capitol A," *Austin American*, February 19, 1958; "Mischief Gives Way to Murder," *Dallas Morning News*, February 23, 1958, all in "Juvenile Delinquency" Vertical File, Houston Metropolitan Research Center, Houston Public Library.

109. "Juvenile Laws Hit by Turman," *Austin Statesman*, March 10, 1958, "Texas Youth Council" Vertical File, Center for American History, University of Texas at Austin.

110. Ibid.

111. "Budget Boost Approved by Youth Council," *Dallas Morning News*, June 1, 1960; "Gatesville Resentment Flares after School Guard's Slaying," *Dallas Morning News*, August 3, 1961; "Gatesville: Country Club for Toughs?" *Dallas Morning News*, August 13, 1961; Minutes, TYC Meeting, May 29, 1962, TYC Minutes.

Five. "Hard to Reach"

1. Minutes, TSYDC Meetings, August 2, and December 6, 1956, TSYDC Minutes, Archives and Information Services Division, Texas State Library and Archives Commission, Austin (hereafter cited as TSYDC Minutes).

2. "Workers Pour by Thousands into City," *Houston Post*, September 4, 1942, p. 1.

3. David G. McComb, *Houston: A History* (Austin: University of Texas Press, 1981), 131–44; Joe R. Feagin, *Free Enterprise City: Houston in Political-Economic Perspective* (New Brunswick, N.J.: Rutgers University Press, 1988), 43–72; Beth Anne Shelton et al., *Houston: Growth and Decline in a Sunbelt Boomtown* (Philadelphia: Temple University Press, 1989), 14–51; Robert D. Bullard, *Invisible Houston: The Black Experience in Boom and Bust* (College Station: Texas A&M University Press, 1987), 41–42, 103–4. For a comparative overview of Houston, Dallas, and San Antonio, see Char Miller and David R. Johnson, "The Rise of Urban Texas," in *Urban Texas: Politics and Development*, ed. Char Miller and Heywood T. Sanders (College Station: Texas A&M University Press, 1990), 3–29.

4. George Fuermann, *Houston: Land of the Big Rich* (Garden City, N.Y.: Doubleday, 1951), 11–24, celebrates the city's "forward-looking culture" based on "individualism, inde-

pendence, and indulgence" drawn from both the Old South and the frontier West; he repeats these themes in *Reluctant Empire* (Garden City, N.Y.: Doubleday, 1957). On postwar inequality, see Bullard, *Invisible Houston*; Howard Beeth and Cary D. Wintz, eds., *Black Dixie: Afro-Texan History and Culture in Houston* (College Station: Texas A&M University Press, 1992), esp. the essays in part 4; and Arnoldo De León, *Ethnicity in the Sunbelt: A History of Mexican Americans in Houston* (Houston: University of Houston, 1989), 98–103.

5. Robert B. Fairbanks, "Public Housing for the City as a Whole: The Texas Experience, 1934–1955," *Southwestern Historical Quarterly* (April 2000): 402–24, here 422.

6. On the juvenile delinquency hearings, see James A. Gilbert, *A Cycle of Outrage: America's Reaction to the Juvenile Delinquent in the 1950s* (New York: Oxford University Press, 1986), 143–61.

7. Joseph L. Zarefsky, "Statistics Relating to Juvenile Delinquency: What Are the Facts for Houston and Harris County?" (Houston: Community Council of Houston and Harris County, 1954), 5–6.

8. Ibid., 18.

9. Roy Hofheinz to Franklin Harbach, November 4, 1953; Harbach to Hofheinz, November 11, 1953; Harbach to W. A. Kirkland, March 25, 1955, all in Papers of Franklin Israel Harbach, Houston Metropolitan Research Center (hereafter cited as Harbach Papers).

10. F. I. Harbach to Lyndon B. Johnson, July 24, 1956, Harbach Papers.

11. David Riesman with Nathan Glazer and Reuel Denney, *The Lonely Crowd: A Study of the Changing American Character* (New Haven, Conn.: Yale University Press, 1950), 66–67, states that "the other-directed child grows up in a small family, in close urban quarters, or in a suburb," but never proceeds from alienation to delinquency. A similar conclusion that correlates the instability of suburban families with "life-adjustment" school curricula is offered in William H. Whyte Jr., *The Organization Man* (Garden City, N.Y.: Doubleday, 1956), 423–34. See also Herbert J. Gans, *The Levittôwners: Ways of Life and Politics in a New Suburban Community* (New York: Pantheon Books, 1967). It is also worth noting that in *Rebel without a Cause*, Jim Stark (James Dean) complains regularly about the family's frequent moves, which are chalked up to his father's corporate job and to a desire to give Jim a fresh start after multiple run-ins with the police.

12. Corrine S. Tsanoff, *Neighborhood Doorways* (Houston: Neighborhood Centers of Houston and Harris County, 1958), 92–99; Judith Ann Trolander, *Professionalism and Social Change: From the Settlement House Movement to Neighborhood Centers, 1886 to the Present* (New York: Columbia University Press, 1987); Helen Hall, *Unfinished Business: In Neighborhood and Nation* (New York: Macmillan, 1971), 173–78.

13. Jean Maxwell to F. I. Harbach, June 24, 1947; Harbach to Maxwell, July 3, 1947; National Federation of Settlements, "Report on Latin-American Cooperative Program" (July 26, 1948); "List of Pan-American Fellows" (July 15, 1955), all in Harbach Papers.

14. F. I. Harbach to G. A. Walls, July 2, 1947, Harbach Papers.

15. F. I. Harbach to Martha Gano Houstoun, January 3, 1948; Lillie M. Peck to Katherine Lenroot, January 3, 1948; Peck to Lenroot, July 7, 1950; Lenroot to Harbach, July 20, 1950, all in Harbach Papers.

16. FBI, *Uniform Crime Reports for the United States, 1960* (Washington, D.C.: Department of Justice, Federal Bureau of Investigation, 1961), 18–19, 54–66, 92–95.

17. These figures are from Zarefsky, "Statistics Relating to Juvenile Delinquency"; and Harris County Juvenile Probation Department, annual reports for 1956–62. See also

"County Juvenile Cases Up 300% in 10 Years," *Houston Chronicle*, May 13, 1962, in "Juvenile Delinquency" Vertical Files, Houston Metropolitan Research Center (hereafter cited as HMRC).

18. Harris County Juvenile Probation Department, *Annual Report for 1962* (Houston, 1963), HMRC.

19. "1958 Mental Health Campaign Publicity Report," Mental Health Association of Houston and Harris County, UT Hogg Foundation Papers, Center for American History, University of Texas at Austin.

20. Houston Community Chest, "Child Welfare Study #4," January 26, 1959, Papers of the Houston Community Chest, HMRC.

21. "Elliott to Seek Criminal Trials at Younger Age," *Houston Chronicle*, December 9, 1958; "Tattooed Punks: Young Toughs Defy Law on North Side," *Houston Chronicle*, December 28, 1960; "Hoodlum Hero Lives for 'Kicks,'" *Houston Chronicle*, February 12, 1961; "D.A. Briscoe Declares War on Former 'Untouchables,'" *Houston Chronicle*, October 9, 1961; "County Juvenile Cases Up 300% in 10 Years," *Houston Chronicle*, May 13, 1962, all in "Juvenile Delinquency" Vertical Files, HMRC.

22. See William Henry Kellar, *Make Haste Slowly: Moderates, Conservatives, and School Desegregation in Houston* (College Station: Texas A&M University Press, 1999), esp. 70–135; and Don E. Carleton, *Red Scare! Right-Wing Hysteria, Fifties Fanaticism, and Their Legacy in Texas* (Austin: Texas Monthly Press, 1985).

23. On the history of Texas Southern University, see John S. Lash, Hortense W. Dixon, and Thomas F. Freeman, *Texas Southern University: From Separation to Special Designation* (Houston: Texas Southern University, 1975). On the sit-in movement, see Brian David Behnken, "Fighting Their Own Battles: Blacks, Mexican Americans, and the Struggle for Civil Rights in Texas" (PhD diss., University of California, Davis, 2007), 124–45; F. Kenneth Jensen, "The Houston Sit-In Movement of 1960–61," *Black Dixie*, 211–22; and Thomas R. Cole, *No Color Is My Kind: The Life of Eldrewey Stearns and the Integration of Houston* (Austin: University of Texas Press, 1997).

24. J. W. Mills, "The Philosophy of the Court of Domestic Relations, the Juvenile Court for Harris County," reprinted in Harris County Juvenile Probation Department, *Annual Report for 1956* (Houston, 1957), emphasis in original.

25. Ibid.

26. Harbach described the area's poor housing in "Report on Magnolia Park," October 1, 1943. His dealings with the mayor's committee are discussed in F. I. Harbach to Lillian Peck, August 3, 1945; Harbach to Martha Gano Houstoun, August 24, 1945; E. W. Blum to Harbach, November 19, 1945. The public housing referendum is discussed in Harbach to Marie McGuire, June 30, 1949; Harbach to E. W. Blum, July 1, 1949; Blum to Harbach, July 11, 1949. McGuire, a former employee of Harbach's, went on to direct the Houston Housing Authority. All documents in Harbach Papers.

27. Tsanoff, *Neighborhood Doorways*, 115.

28. The major formulation of this idea would come in William Julius Wilson, *The Truly Disadvantaged: The Inner City, the Underclass, and Public Policy* (Chicago: University of Chicago Press, 1987). For a historical appraisal, see Michael B. Katz, ed., *The "Underclass" Debate: Views from History* (Princeton, N.J.: Princeton University Press, 1993).

29. "1960 Budget Report for the Neighborhood Centers Association of Houston and Harris County, submitted to the United Fund, May 1, 1959," Harbach Papers, HMRC.

30. Ibid.

31. Corrine S. Tsanoff, "Working Together for Neighborhood Improvement," *Children* 11, no. 5 (September–October 1964): 179–82. The project is also described in "Study of the Clayton Homes Neighborhood Development Program: A Total Neighborhood Approach," grant proposal to the National Institutes of Health, December 4, 1961, Sutherland (Robert Lee) Papers, Sutherland (Robert Lee) Papers, 1937–73, Center for American History, University of Texas at Austin (hereafter cited as Sutherland Papers).

32. Tsanoff, "Working Together for Neighborhood Improvement"; "Study of the Clayton Homes Neighborhood Development Program."

33. Correspondence shows the Ford Foundation's interest in Clayton Homes, although it ultimately received funding from the NIH. Richard W. Boone to F. I. Harbach, September 15, 1961; Robert L. Sutherland to Harbach, December 4, 1961; Sutherland to David Hunter, December 6, 1961; Sutherland to Richard Boone, January 8, 1962, all in Sutherland Papers.

34. "The culture of poverty cuts across regional, rural-urban, and even national boundaries," asserted Oscar Lewis in *Five Families: Mexican Case Studies in the Culture of Poverty* (New York: Basic Books, 1959), 16. Policymakers took him at his word, applying his theory to a host of groups in the 1960s. Michael Harrington outlined a "personality of poverty" more prone to mental illness (*The Other America: Poverty in the United States* [New York: Collier Books, 1962], 121–38).

35. Alice O'Connor, *Poverty Knowledge: Social Science, Social Policy, and the Poor in Twentieth-Century U.S. History* (Princeton, N.J.: Princeton University Press, 2001), 117–18.

36. "COCIAD: Conference on Citizenship in a Democracy," flyer, 1963; Franklin Harbach, "Creating a Neighborhood Climate for Better Mental Health," lecture, the Boston Settlement Council, July 1963; "Settlement Programs with Mental Health Implications for Urban Areas," lecture, National Institute of Mental Health, August 1963, all in Harbach Papers.

37. There is voluminous literature on the antidelinquency and antipoverty community action projects of the 1960s, much of which debates whether they were successful. In addition to O'Connor, *Poverty Knowledge*, 124–38, see Noel A. Cazenave, *Impossible Democracy: The Unlikely Success of the War on Poverty Community Action Projects* (Albany, N.Y.: SUNY Press, 2007), esp. 49–64; Irwin Unger, *The Best of Intentions: The Triumphs and Failures of the Great Society under Kennedy, Johnson, and Nixon* (New York: Doubleday, 1996), 54–69; Thomas F. Jackson, "The State, the Movement, and the Urban Poor: The War on Poverty and Political Mobilization in the 1960s," in *The "Underclass" Debate: Views from History*, ed. Michael B. Katz (Princeton, N.J.: Princeton University Press, 1993), 403–39; Allen J. Matusow, *The Unraveling of America: A History of Liberalism in the 1960s* (New York: Harper and Row, 1984), 108–19; and Joseph H. Helfgot, *Professional Reforming: Mobilization for Youth and the Failure of Social Science* (Lexington, Mass.: Lexington Books, 1981). For an overview of these programs in Texas, see William Stephen Clayson, "Texas Poverty and Liberal Politics: The Office of Economic Opportunity and the War on Poverty in the Lone Star State" (PhD diss., Texas Tech University, 2001).

38. Albert K. Cohen, *Delinquent Boys: The Culture of the Gang* (New York: Glencoe, 1955).

39. Richard Cloward and Lloyd Ohlin, *Delinquency and Opportunity: A Theory of Delinquent Gangs* (Chicago: University of Chicago, 1960). For a historical analysis, see Eric C. Schneider, *Vampires, Dragons, and Egyptian Kings: Youth Gangs in Postwar New York* (Princeton, N.J.: Princeton University Press, 1999). At the time, sociologist Daniel Bell argued that previous generations of European immigrants had used criminal activity to finance their escape from poverty to respectability. Bell, "Crime as an American Way of

Life," in *The End of Ideology: On the Exhaustion of Political Ideas in the Fifties* (New York: Collier Books, 1961), 127–50.

40. Robert L. Sutherland, "Delinquency and Mental Health," *Federal Probation* (March 1957), Sutherland Papers.

41. Bernice Milburn Moore and Wayne H. Holtzman, *Tomorrow's Parents: A Study of Youth and Their Families* (Austin: University of Texas Press, 1965); and Carl M. Rosenquist and Edwin I. Megargee, *Delinquency in Three Cultures* (Austin: University of Texas Press, 1969).

42. "Once-Forlorn Juvenile Ward Now among Best," *Houston Chronicle*, November 17, 1963. The film is described in "1958 Mental Health Campaign Publicity Report," Mental Health Association of Houston and Harris County, in ut Hogg Foundation Papers, Center for American History, University of Texas at Austin.

43. "Delinquency Discussion on Channel 8," *Houston Chronicle*, July 15, 1955. For a compilation of some of Evans's televised interviews, see Richard I. Evans, ed., *The Making of Social Psychology: Discussions with Creative Contributors* (New York: Gardner Press, 1980).

44. "Project: Action for Youth," newsletter 1 of Greater Houston Action for Youth, University of Houston, August 1962, Sutherland Papers. "Houston Sole Applicant in Delinquency Fight," *Houston Chronicle*, February 1, 1962; "Community Council to Support uh Grant Bid," *Houston Post*, February 13, 1962; "School Board Gives ok to Study of Delinquency," *Houston Chronicle*, February 13, 1962; "Delinquency Study by U.H. to Get Review," *Houston Chronicle*, February 28, 1962. Joseph Zarefsky, Houston Community Council, to R. L. Sutherland, February 15, 1962; Sutherland notes to self, May 8, 1962; Sutherland, "Notes from Conference with Richard Evans," July 27, 1962, all in Sutherland Papers.

45. Klineberg foreword to Mary Ellen Goodman, *The Culture of Childhood: Child's-Eye Views of Society and Culture* (New York: Columbia University Teacher's College Press, 1970), xi. See also Goodman, *Race Awareness in Small Children* (Cambridge, Mass: Addison-Wesley Press, 1952); the revised 1964 edition includes an introduction by Kenneth Clark. On Clark's role in the *Brown* case, see Richard Kluger, *Simple Justice: The History of* Brown v. Board of Education *and Black America's Struggle for Equality* (New York: Random House, 1976), 315–39.

46. The details are in Jane Brandenberger, "Communications Outline," Greater Houston Action for Youth Project Folder, October 11, 1962, Sutherland Papers.

47. Ibid.

48. Unless otherwise noted, the following descriptions come from a script for "The Lonely Ones," Greater Houston Action for Youth Project Folder, October 11, 1962, Sutherland Papers. The only known copy of the film itself is in the possession of Richard Evans.

49. Thomas Doherty, *Teenagers and Teenpics: The Juvenilization of American Movies in the 1950s*, rev. ed. (Philadelphia: Temple University Press, 2002).

50. "Resignations Fail to Halt Youth Film," *Houston Chronicle*, December 18, 1962.

51. "2 Quit Youth Program in Policy Differences," *Houston Post*, December 19, 1962.

52. Goodman, *Culture of Childhood*.

53. See, for example, Robin D. G. Kelley, *Yo' Mama's Disfunktional! Fighting the Culture Wars in Urban America* (Boston: Beacon Hill Press, 1997), esp. chap. 1.

54. The following data come from the Greater Houston Action for Youth Project, *Demonstration Action Program: A Community Project to Plan for the Prevention and Control of*

Delinquency Sponsored by University of Houston and Community Council of Houston and Harris County (1964), appendix 3.

55. Greater Houston Action for Youth Project, *Demonstration Action Program*, 443.

56. Ibid., 318.

57. See Kellar, *Make Haste Slowly*; and Behnken, "Fighting Their Own Battles."

58. Greater Houston Action for Youth Project, *Demonstration Action Program*, 316.

59. Ibid., 401.

60. William Clayson, "The War on Poverty and the Fear of Urban Violence in Houston, 1965–1968," *Gulf South Historical Review* 18, no. 2 (Spring 2003): 38–60.

61. Ibid.

62. "5 Charged in TSU Riot Fatal to Young Officer," *Houston Post*, May 18, 1967; "Elliott Claims TSU Riot 'Premeditated,'" *Houston Post*, May 20, 1967. For media accounts more sympathetic to the TSU students, see Bill Helmer, "Nightmare in Houston," *Texas Observer*, June 9 and June 23, 1967; and Leslie Linthicum, "Nightmare at TSU in '67 Still Spawns Controversy," *Houston Post*, May 11, 1987.

63. "The Stokely Generation," *Newsweek*, May 29, 1967, 24–25.

64. Blair Justice, *Violence in the City* (Fort Worth: Texas Christian University Press, 1969).

65. Clayson, "War on Poverty"; *Riots, Civil and Criminal Disorders: Hearings before the Permanent Subcommittee on Investigations of the Committee on Government Operations*, U.S. Congress, 90th Congress, 1st Session, November 1, 2, 3, and 6, 1967, part 1 (Washington, D.C.: U.S. Government Printing Office, 1967), 61–144. A brief summary of the TSU incident appeared in U.S. National Advisory Commission on Civil Disorders, *Report of the National Advisory Commission on Civil Disorders* (New York: Bantam Books, 1968), 40–41.

Six. Circling the Wagons

1. Memo, "Trip to Gatesville," Bert Kruger Smith to Robert L. Sutherland, March 22, 1961, Sutherland (Robert Lee) Papers, 1937–73, Center for American History, University of Texas at Austin.

2. Ibid.

3. Ibid.

4. Quoted in "Texas Youth Council Chief Sounds Warning on Future," *Dallas Morning News*, August 28, 1964.

5. Ibid.; see also *Annual Report of the Texas Youth Council for 1965* (Austin, 1966).

6. Minutes, TYC Meeting, October 3, 1961, Minutes, State Youth Development Council and Texas Youth Council, 1949–65, Archives and Information Services Commission, Texas State Library and Archives Commission, Austin (hereafter cited as TYC Minutes).

7. "Opinions Vary as Perry 'Quits' Boys School Post," *Dallas Morning News*, July 21, 1963.

8. "Youth Council Director Hits Critic of Institution," *Dallas Morning News*, June 3, 1964.

9. Minutes, TYC Meeting, May 6, 1964, TYC Minutes.

10. "Youth Council Due Hearing on Budget Plea for 18 Million," *Dallas Morning News*, July 20, 1964.

11. *Manual on Preparation of Children for Admission to the State Training Schools* (Austin: Texas Youth Council, 1956), 2.

12. Ibid., 4.

13. "Youth Council Director Hits Critic."

14. *Annual Report of the Texas Youth Council to the Governor for the Fiscal Year Ending August 31, 1972* (Austin, 1973), 3.

15. Reports of Kneebone's and Henna's visits appear regularly in the TYC's meeting minutes. For example, in a three-month span in 1965, Henna gave two reports of unannounced visits. On one, he led members of the Texas Optimist Club on tours of Gatesville and Mountain View; they were "very impressed with real progress and good programs." Shortly afterward, he complained of "flagrant disregard of Council policy" at Crockett due to lack of reading materials. Minutes, TYC Meetings, June 8 and June 21, 1965, TYC Minutes.

16. The following anecdote draws on "Priest: Ribs, Jaws Broken," *Houston Post*, January 4, 1969; "Youth Beatings Charged," *Fort Worth Star-Telegram*, January 4, 1969; "'Rubbish,' Says Official to Charges of State Reform School Brutalities," *Austin American-Statesman*, January 4, 1969; and Ronnie Dugger, "Brutality Charges at Gatesville," *Texas Observer*, January 10, 1969.

17. Dugger, "Brutality Charges at Gatesville," 15.

18. Ibid.; see also "Corpus TV 'Horror' Series Initiated Probe," *Houston Post*, January 20, 1969.

19. "Mountain View: 'The Bad Ones . . . We Get the Worst,'" *Fort Worth Star-Telegram*, January 26, 1969.

20. Joseph M. Hawes, *The Children's Rights Movement: A History of Advocacy and Protection* (Boston: Twayne, 1991), 99–105; Lynne Curry, *The DeShaney Case: Child Abuse, Family Rights, and the Dilemma of State Intervention* (Lawrence: University Press of Kansas, 2007), 52–55.

21. United Nations, General Assembly Resolution 1386 (14), November 20, 1959, Official Records of the General Assembly, 14th sess. (Supplement 16, 1960), 19; Paula S. Fass and Mary Ann Mason, eds., *Childhood in America* (New York: New York University Press, 2000), 612–15.

22. Erving Goffman, *Asylums: Essays on the Social Situation of Mental Patients and Other Inmates* (Garden City, N.Y.: Anchor Books, 1961); and Howard S. Becker, *Outsiders: Studies in the Sociology of Deviance* (1963; repr., New York: Free Press, 1973).

23. Christopher P. Manfredi, *The Supreme Court and Juvenile Justice* (Lawrence: University Press of Kansas, 1998), 34–48; Barry C. Feld, *Bad Kids: Race and the Transformation of the Juvenile Court* (New York: Oxford University Press, 1999); Hawes, *The Children's Rights Movement*, 105–8; Laura Mihailoff, "Protecting Our Children: A History of the California Youth Authority and Juvenile Justice, 1938–1968" (PhD diss., University of California, Berkeley, 2005), 302–15.

24. *What to Do about Delinquency in Texas: The Implications of a Factual Study* (1962; repr., Austin: National Council on Crime and Delinquency and the Junior League of Texas, 1965), 20.

25. "Junior Leagues Complete New Film on Delinquency," *Austin Statesman*, September 24, 1965.

26. *In re Gault* 387 U.S. 1 (1967), 28; Manfredi, *Supreme Court and Juvenile Justice*, 125–59; for concise case summaries, see Rolando V. del Carmen, Susan E. Ritter, and Betsy A. Witt, eds., *Briefs of Leading Cases in Juvenile Justice* (Cincinnati: Anderson, 1998), 137–38, 175–80.

27. *Debra Fay Leach v. the State of Texas*, Court of Civil Appeals of Texas, 14th District, Houston, 428 S.W. 2d 817 (May 15, 1968). A similar ruling was given in another Houston

case of an illegal search and inadmissible signed confession. See *J. B. Choate Jr. v. the State of Texas*, Court of Civil Appeals of Texas, First District, Houston, 425 S.W. 2d 706 (March 7, 1968).

28. *George Rivers Santana v. the State of Texas*, Supreme Court of Texas, 444 S.W. 2d 614, 1969; 12 Tex Sup. J. 529 (July 23, 1969). This ruling was cited in the following cases: *Roy Y. Martin, Guardian of Johnny Martin Pruett Jr. v. Texas Youth Council*, Court of Civil Appeals of Texas, Third District, Austin, 445 S.W. 2d 553 (June 11, 1969); and, *E.S.G. v. the State of Texas*, Court of Civil Appeals of Texas, Fourth District, San Antonio, 447 S.W. 2d 225 (October 22, 1969).

29. Chandler Davidson, *Biracial Politics: Conflict and Coalition in the Metropolitan South* (Baton Rouge: Louisiana State University Press, 1972), 71–80. See also *Handbook of Texas Online*, s.v. "African Americans and Politics," *http://www.tshaonline.org/handbook/online/articles/AA/wmafr.html*.

30. Inmate population figures are from *Services to Youth in Texas: Preliminary Report of the Senate Youth Affairs Committee* (61st Texas Legislature, 1969), 17–25. The population numbers are from U.S. Bureau of the Census, *Texas: General Social and Economic Characteristics, 1970* (Washington, D.C.: Government Printing Office, 1971), 45.

31. Use-of-force guidelines reprinted in *Services to Youth in Texas*, 88–104.

32. Dugger, "Brutality Charges at Gatesville."

33. "'Rubbish,' Says Official to Charges of State Reform School Brutalities," *Austin American-Statesman*, January 4, 1969.

34. Ibid.; Dugger, "Brutality Charges at Gatesville."

35. "Solons Visit Reform School; 'Critical' Report Due Today," *Austin American-Statesman*, January 5, 1969.

36. "Boys, Guards Take Polygraph Tests at Gatesville," *Dallas Morning News*, January 6, 1969; "Lie Detector Used in School Probe," *Austin American*, January 6, 1969.

37. "Youths Planned to Kill Guard in Escape Try," *Austin American*, January 7, 1969; "Tests Show Boys' Escape Attempt," *Dallas Morning News*, January 7, 1969.

38. "Lie Detector Used in School Probe."

39. "Gatesville Probers Stay Quiet," *Austin American*, January 8, 1969; "Statement Delayed in Gatesville Probe," *Austin American*, January 9, 1969.

40. "Gatesville 'Runs' Tried," *Austin American*, January 8, 1969.

41. "Former Inmates Talk Up," *Fort Worth Star-Telegram*, January 8, 1969.

42. "House Group Advises Changes at Gatesville," *Fort Worth Star-Telegram*, January 9, 1969.

43. "Brutality Probers Scored," *Austin American*, January 10, 1969.

44. "Panel Sees No Need for Gatesville Study," *Fort Worth Star-Telegram*, January 10, 1969.

45. "Observations," *Texas Observer*, January 24, 1969; "Nepotism Law Disregarded Aplenty," *Dallas Morning News*, April 5, 1969.

46. "Youth Council Programs Face Detailed Study," *Austin American-Statesman*, January 11, 1969; "Outside Group to Study Gatesville Operations," *Fort Worth Star-Telegram*, January 11, 1969; "Procedures for Boys' School Probe Agreed by Panel, TYC," *Houston Post*, January 11, 1969; "Over 50 Complaints Given State Unit," *Houston Chronicle*, January 10, 1969.

47. "Ex-Guard Says Whole Truth Not Told," *Dallas Morning News*, January 12, 1969.

48. The following discussion draws on "Brutality Proven by Records," *Houston Post*, January 19, 1969; "Corpus TV 'Horror' Series Initiated Probe"; "Physical Abuse in Decline,

Officials Say," *Houston Post*, January 21, 1969; "'New' Gatesville Improved, TYC Dissatisfied," *Houston Post*, January 22, 1969; "Boys Find Different World at 'Gatesville State,'" *Fort Worth Star-Telegram*, January 26, 1969; "Mountain View: 'The Bad Ones . . . We Get the Worst,'"; "The System Dictates 'in' Gatesville," *Fort Worth Star-Telegram*, January 28, 1969; and "Official Says Brutality No Longer Found at Gatesville Unit," *Fort Worth Star-Telegram*, January 29, 1969.

49. Unless otherwise noted, the following discussion draws on Ronnie Dugger, "More on Gatesville: Alums Recount Brutality," *Texas Observer*, January 24, 1969, pp.7–13.

50. *Services to Youth in Texas*, 25–27.

51. Austin MacCormick to Robert W. Kneebone, TYC Chairman, September 1, 1962; MacCormick, "State Training Schools for Delinquent Children," October 1964; MacCormick to Kneebone, January 13, 1967; MacCormick to Kneebone, January 21, 1969, all in Morales case files, Texas Youth Commission, Archives and Information Services Division, Texas State Library and Archives Commission, Austin (hereafter cited as Morales Case Files).

52. "Reform School Report Criticized by Judge," *Fort Worth Star-Telegram*, January 31, 1969.

53. Kaye Northcott, "The Gatesville Challenge," *Texas Observer*, February 21, 1969.

54. Ronnie Dugger, "Order," *Texas Observer*, March 7, 1969.

55. *Services to Youth in Texas*, 14–15.

56. Ibid.

57. Ibid., 96–101.

58. Ibid.

59. Scholarly treatments of *Morales v. Turman* include the following: Steve J. Martin and Sheldon Ekland-Olson, *Texas Prisons: The Walls Came Tumbling Down* (Austin: Texas Monthly Press, 1987), 86–88; Mary Frances Reddington, "In the Best Interests of the Child: The Effects of *Morales v. Turman* on the Texas Youth Commission" (PhD diss., Sam Houston State University, 1990); and Frank R. Kemerer, *William Wayne Justice: A Judicial Biography* (Austin: University of Texas Press, 1991), 145–81. For a journalistic treatment, see Kenneth Wooden, *Weeping in the Playtime of Others: America's Incarcerated Children*, 2nd ed. (Columbus: Ohio State University Press, 2000), 3–22.

60. Author interview with Steven Bercu, June 23, 2003.

61. Mother's statement as related by Bercu in Reddington, "In the Best Interests of the Child," 50–51.

62. Author interview with Bercu; see also Bill Payne, "The Great Sycamore Jailbreak," *Texas Observer*, March 12, 1971.

63. Bill Payne, "EP Detention Home Fails to Meet Founders' Hopes," *El Paso Times*, October 26, 1970.

64. Ibid.

65. Ibid.

66. Bill Payne, "'Babysitting' by D-Home Seen Danger," *El Paso Times*, October 29, 1970.

67. Bill Payne, "Personnel Qualifications Often Questioned," *El Paso Times*, October 28, 1970.

68. Ibid.

69. Bill Payne, "Questions about Handling Offenders Involve Workings of Juvenile Court," *El Paso Times*, October 27, 1970.

70. Wooden, *Weeping in the Playtime of Others*, 4.

71. Author interview with Bercu.

72. *This Child Is Rated X: An* NBC *White Paper on Juvenile Justice* (National Broadcast Corporation, May 1971).

73. Payne, "Great Sycamore Jailbreak."

74. In our interview, Steven Bercu credited Martha Brown with an "important" role in convincing many other parents that the case against the TYC had merit.

75. Affidavit of James A. Turman, 1973, Morales Case Files.

76. Ibid.

77. Affidavit of Roland Daniel Green III, December 1972, Morales Case Files.

78. Author interview with Bercu.

79. No published history of the Youth Law Center exists, apparently not even within the organization itself. The center continues to operate from San Francisco and Washington, D.C. See http://www.ylc.org/.

80. Peter Freedberger to Senator Joseph Christy, November 20, 1970, Morales Case Files.

81. The film is summarized in Nick Kotz, *Hunger in America: The Federal Response* (New York: Field Foundation, 1979), 10.

82. "Bexar Official Vindicated, CBS Hit on Hunger Show," *Dallas Morning News*, May 26, 1970.

83. Patrick E. Higginbotham to James A. Turman, December 16, 1970, emphasis in the original, Morales Case Files.

84. P. E. Higginbotham to J. A. Turman, January 4, 1971, Morales Case Files.

85. J. A. Turman to P. E. Higginbotham, January 5, 1971, Morales Case Files.

86. Author interview with Bercu.

87. Minutes, TYC Meeting, January 13, 1966, and August 31, 1967, both in TYC Minutes.

88. Author interview with Bercu.

89. Kemerer, *William Wayne Justice*, 147–48.

90. Minutes, TYC Meeting, March 5, 1965, TYC Minutes.

Seven. Creating a Right to Treatment

1. Letter from Justice, reproduced in Mary Frances Reddington, "In the Best Interests of the Child: The Effects of *Morales v. Turman* on the Texas Youth Commission" (PhD diss., Sam Houston State University, 1990), 55.

2. *Morales v. Turman*, 383 F. Supp. 53; 1974 U.S. Dist. (August 30, 1974), at 35.

3. Bill Payne, "'Hurt, Frightened Children,'" *Texas Observer*, March 12, 1971.

4. Unless otherwise noted, the following discussion of Jerome Miller and his "Massachusetts Experiment" comes from his autobiographical *Last One over the Wall: The Massachusetts Experiment in Closing Reform Schools* (Columbus: Ohio State University Press, 1991). For an early analysis of Massachusetts, see Robert B. Coates, Alden D. Miller, and Lloyd E. Ohlin, *Diversity in a Youth Correctional System: Handling Delinquents in Massachusetts* (Cambridge, Mass.: Ballinger, 1978).For a critical review that reflects changing opinion in the 1990s, see John J. DiIulio, "Deinstitutionalized Delinquents," *Public Interest* 107 (Spring 1992): 130.

5. Ruth Wilson Gilmore, "Globalisation and U.S. Prison Growth: From Military Keynesianism to post-Keynesian Militarism," *Race and Class* 40 (1998/99): 171–88; see also Christian Parenti, *Lockdown America: Police and Prisons in an Age of Crisis* (New York: Verso, 1999).

6. Lois G. Forer, *No One Will Lissen: How Our Legal System Brutalizes the Youthful Poor* (New York: John Day, 1970). See also several of the essays in Beatrice and Ronald Gross, eds., *The Children's Rights Movement: Overcoming the Oppression of Young People* (Garden City, N.Y.: Anchor Books, 1977).

7. Statement of M. B. Kindrick, Superintendent, Gatesville School for Boys, "given shortly after the riot on September 6, 1971," submitted to the Texas Attorney General, August 29, 1972, Morales Case Files, Texas Youth Commission, Archives and Information Services Division, Texas State Library and Archives Commission, Austin (hereafter cited as Morales Case Files).

8. Statement of Sycamore Riot Discipline Committee, undated, 1972, Morales Case Files.

9. Statement of Paul F. Bromser, Unit Superintendent, Gatesville School for Boys, August 28, 1972; Statement of T. F. Schloeman, Unit Superintendent, Gatesville, August 23, 1972, both in Morales Case Files.

10. Deposition of Gerda Hansen Smith, Instructor in Neurology and Psychiatry, University of Texas Medical Branch, May 21, 1973, Morales Case Files.

11. Statement of Jesse L. Smith, Casework Supervisor, Gatesville School for Boys, undated, 1972, Morales Case Files.

12. Statement of Leonard C. Winters, Youth Activities Supervisor, Gatesville School for Boys, August 28, 1972, Morales Case Files.

13. Statement of Wanda Wallace, Dorm Supervisor, Gainesville School for Girls, May 21, 1971, Morales Case Files.

14. Statement of Dorothy Moore, Instructor, Gainesville School for Girls, August 4, 1972, Morales Case Files.

15. Author interview with Steven Bercu, June 23, 2003.

16. Statement of James L. Braswell, Director, Security Treatment Center, Gainesville School for Girls, August 4, 1972, Morales Case Files.

17. Author interview with Bercu.

18. Paul Burka, "The Real Governor of Texas," *Texas Monthly*, June 1978, 113–200, here 189; this article is discussed in Steve J. Martin and Sheldon Ekland-Olson, *Texas Prisons: The Walls Came Tumbling Down* (Austin: Texas Monthly Press, 1987), 88.

19. Frank R. Kemerer, *William Wayne Justice: A Judicial Biography* (Austin: University of Texas Press, 1991).

20. Statement of anonymous inmate at Mountain View School for Boys, undated, 1972, Morales Case Files.

21. Thomas A. Dixon to Mountain View inmate, undated, 1972, Morales Case Files.

22. Dixon to "TYC Clients in Gatesville," December 16, 1971, Morales Case Files.

23. Statement of Joe Sasse, Dormitory Supervisor, Mountain View School for Boys, August 23, 1972, Morales Case Files.

24. Deposition of sixteen-year-old inmate at Gainesville School for Girls, July 11, 1973, Morales Case Files.

25. Deposition of Pam Armstrong, Caseworker, Gainesville School for Girls, August 4, 1972, Morales Case Files.

26. Letter, Thomas H. Dixon to James A. Turman, November 29, 1971, Morales Case Files.

27. Memo, Dwain Place, Superintendent, Gatesville School for Boys, to J. A. Turman, December 15, 1971, and December 21, 1971, both in Morales Case Files.

28. Statement, anonymous Gainesville inmate, May 3, 1971, Morales Case Files.

29. Letter from anonymous parent to "Miss McGowan," Gainesville School for Girls, undated, ca. summer 1971, Morales Case Files.

30. *Morales v. Turman*, 59 F.R.D. 157, 1972 U.S. Dist. (December 14, 1972).

31. *Annual Report of the Texas Youth Council to the Governor for 1971* (Austin, 1972), 29.

32. Deposition of Gerda Hansen Smith.

33. *Annual Report . . . for 1971*, 29.

34. Ibid.

35. Ibid., 214–15.

36. Deposition of Jerome Miller, June 19, 1973, Morales Case Files.

37. Kemerer, *William Wayne Justice*, 156–57.

38. Attorney Interrogatory (AI) 3–12 and 4–63, Morales Case Files.

39. Deposition of Jerome Miller.

40. Evaluation report, Austin H. MacCormick to Robert W. Kneebone, March 31, 1972, Morales Case Files.

41. Kenneth Wooden, *Weeping in the Playtime of Others: America's Incarcerated Children*, 2nd ed. (Columbus: Ohio State University Press, 2000), 6.

42. Testimony of "C.W.," sixteen-year-old former inmate at Mountain View and Gatesville Schools for Boys, July 19, 1973, Morales Case Files. C.W.'s testimony also receives brief mention in Judge Justice's final opinion, *Morales*, 383 F. Supp. 53, at 44.

43. Testimony of "H.," fifteen-year-old inmate at Mountain View, July 19, 1973, Morales Case Files. Judge Justice repeated this phrase in *Morales*, 383 F. Supp. 53, at 44.

44. Deposition of Mack O. Morris, November 14, 1972, Morales Case Files.

45. Deposition of George P. Pulliam, Chief Clinical Social Worker, Division of Child and Adolescent Psychiatry, University of Texas Medical Branch in Galveston, May 22, 1973, Morales Case Files. He questioned the applicability of corrections training for staff in a youth-serving facility, scornfully referring to such staff as "the so-called professionals" throughout.

46. Deposition of Dwain Place, Assistant General Superintendent, Gatesville School for Boys, November 16, 1972, Morales Case Files.

47. Ibid.

48. Deposition of Dr. James A. Turman, Executive Director, Texas Youth Council, May 1–2, 1973, Morales Case Files.

49. Testimony of "B.," sixteen-year-old inmate at Mountain View, July 19, 1973, Morales Case Files.

50. Deposition of George P. Pulliam.

51. Deposition of Dr. Leonard Lawrence, Professor of Child and Adolescent Psychiatry, University of Texas-San Antonio, May 22, 1973, Morales Case Files.

52. *Morales*, 383 F. Supp. 53, at 64.

53. Ibid., 65.

54. Testimony of "D.," seventeen-year-old inmate at Mountain View, July 19, 1973, Morales Case Files.

55. Testimony of "C.W."

56. Testimony of "T.A.," sixteen-year-old inmate at Mountain View, July 19, 1973, Morales Case Files.

57. Deposition of George Pulliam.

58. Deposition of James A. Turman.

59. Ibid.

60. The admission appears in *Morales*, 383 F. Supp. 53, at 32.

61. Wooden, *Weeping in the Playtime of Others*, 13–14.

62. Deposition of James A. Turman.

63. Testimony of "B."

64. *Morales*, 383 F. Supp. 53, at 63–64.

65. Ibid.; also discussed in Testimony of "D."

66. Deposition of James A. Turman.

67. Ibid.; a summary list appears in *Morales*, 383 F. Supp. 53, at 62.

68. Deposition of James A. Turman.

69. *Morales*, 383 F. Supp. 53, at 13–16.

70. Ibid., at 65–66.

71. Testimony of "M.," fifteen-year-old inmate, Gatesville School for Boys, July 5, 1973, Morales Case Files.

72. *Annual Report of the Texas Youth Council to the Governor for the Year Ending August 31, 1973* (Austin, 1973), 29–31.

73. Deposition of Jerome Miller.

74. Howard Ohmart, *State Juvenile Incarceration in Texas: An Assessment* (Sacramento, Calif.: American Justice Institute, 1972), Morales Case Files.

75. Ibid.

76. Ibid.

77. J. A. Turman copy of Ohmart report, Morales Case Files.

78. John J. DiIulio Jr., ed., *No Escape: The Future of American Corrections* (New York: Basic Books, 1991). For an alternative view, see Robert Reps Perkinson, "The Birth of the Texas Prison Empire, 1865–1915" (PhD diss., Yale University, 2001), epilogue.

79. Martin and Ekland-Olson, *Texas Prisons*, 91.

80. Author interview with Bercu.

81. Testimony of "C.W."

82. Testimony of "J.H.," seventeen-year-old inmate at Mountain View, July 19–20, 1973, Morales Case Files.

83. Testimony of "T.A."

84. *Morales*, 383 F. Supp. 53, at 80–81. Testimony of Jimmy Lee Jones, July 20, 1973, Morales Case Files.

85. *Services to Youth in Texas: Preliminary Report of the Senate Youth Affairs Committee* (61st Texas Legislature, 1969), 98–99.

86. Ibid.

87. Stephen Donaldson, "Punk," in *Encyclopedia of Homosexuality*, ed. Wayne R. Dynes, 2 vols. (New York: Garland, 1990), 2:1085–86. In 1972, after being jailed for trespassing on White House property during an antiwar protest, Donaldson (known in prison as "Donny the Punk") was raped sixty times in two days. Imprisoned again in the early 1980s, he contracted AIDS from being raped. Now deceased, Donaldson was a former leader for Stop Prisoner Rape, an organization that has advocated on behalf of prisoners since 1980. See "Stop Prisoner Rape: A Brief History," http://www.spr.org/.

88. Stephen "Donny" Donaldson, "A Million Jockers, Queens, and Punks," in *Prison Masculinities*, ed. Don Sabo, Terry A. Kupers, and Willie London (Philadelphia: Temple University Press, 2001), 118–26.

89. "Being a 'Punk' No Fun at Mountain View," *Fort Worth Star-Telegram*, January 28, 1969.

90. Donaldson, "Million Jockers," 124.

91. Deposition of James A. Turman.

92. Ibid.

93. Deposition of Jerome Miller.

94. Deposition of Austin H. MacCormick, Executive Director, Osborne Foundation, May 7, 1973, Morales Case Files.

95. Ronald Bayer, *Homosexuality and American Psychiatry: The Politics of Diagnosis* (New York: Basic Books, 1981), 147–48.

96. Ibid., 107–11.

97. Ibid. Prior to the APA's change of opinion, treatment of adolescent sexuality was guided by studies such as Irving Bieber et al., *Homosexuality: A Psychoanalytic Study of Male Homosexuals* (New York: Basic Books, 1962), which purported to "cure" some of its subjects. Bieber was on the losing side of the APA decision on homosexuality but went on to inspire the National Association for Research and Therapy of Homosexuality (NARTH), an organization of mental health professionals who continue to insist that homosexuality is a curable and damaging disorder. See http://www.narth.com.

98. Testimony of "G.G.," sixteen-year-old inmate, Gainesville School for Girls, July 11, 1973, Morales Case Files.

99. Testimony of "M.," fifteen-year-old inmate, Gatesville School for Boys, July 5, 1973, Morales Case Files.

100. Testimony of Thomas J. Riddle, Superintendent, Gainesville School for Girls, November 20, 1972, Morales Case Files.

101. Deposition of Ernest Leonard Sharp, Chief of Social Services, Crockett School for Girls, November 27, 1972, Morales Case Files.

102. Testimony of "G.G."

103. Testimony of "C.W."

104. Testimony of "J.H."

105. Deposition of Jerome Miller.

106. *Morales*, 383 F. Supp. 53, at 132.

107. Testimony of Dr. Leonard Lawrence, July 23, 1973, Morales Case Files.

108. Deposition of James A. Turman. It is possible that he believed that juvenile delinquents were abnormal in that they experienced sexual feelings prematurely, that is, before "normal" adolescents did.

109. Deposition of Gerda Hansen Smith.

110. Ibid.

111. Ibid.

112. Deposition of Austin H. MacCormick.

113. Testimony of "T.," seventeen-year-old inmate at Gainesville, July 11, 1973; Testimony of "G.," seventeen-year-old inmate at Gainesville, July 11, 1973; Testimony of "G.A.," July 11, 1973, all in Morales Case Files.

114. "M." stated that she was "stunned" upon arrival to learn about the pills. Although they were "common knowledge" among the girls, an unspoken rule forbade speaking with adults about them. Testimony of "M.," seventeen-year-old inmate, Gainesville School for Girls, July 11, 1973, Morales Case Files.

115. Testimony of "G.A."

116. *Morales*, 383 F. Supp. 53, at 138.

117. Deposition of Robert Chilton, Chief of Casework Services, Gainesville School for Girls, November 20, 1972, Morales Case Files.

118. Testimony of "M.," seventeen-year-old inmate, Gainesville School for Girls, July 11, 1973, Morales Case Files.

119. Testimony of "G.G."

120. Ibid.; Deposition of Thomas J. Riddle, Superintendent, Gainesville School for Girls, November 20, 1972, Morales Case Files.

121. Deposition of Thomas J. Riddle.

122. Ibid.

123. Testimony of "G.G.," Morales Case Files.

124. Ibid.

125. Deposition of Robert Chilton.

126. Deposition of Pete Harrell, Superintendent, Crockett School for Girls, November 27, 1972, Morales Case Files.

127. These figures are fairly consistent in the 1971, 1972, and 1973 annual reports of the Texas Youth Council.

128. This disparity prompted Steven Schlossman and Stephanie Wallach, in the 1970s, to research female sexual delinquency. See "Symposium: 'The Crime of Precocious Sexuality: Female Juvenile Delinquency in the Progressive Era,'" *Journal of the History of Childhood and Youth*, 2, no. 1 (Winter 2009): 85–124.

129. Deposition of Thomas J. Riddle.

130. Gainesville discipline reports on girls speaking Spanish, 1969–73, Morales Case Files.

131. Ibid.

132. Testimony of William M. Lovejoy, July 31–August 1, 1973, Morales Case Files.

133. Ibid.

134. Deposition of Austin MacCormick.

135. *Morales v. Turman*, 364 F. Supp. 166, 1973 U.S. Dist. (August 31, 1973), at 2.

136. "Social Worker: Gatesville Riot Was Preventable," *Houston Chronicle*, September 13, 1973; for a full description of the incident, see Kemerer, *William Wayne Justice*, 161–62.

137. "Top TYC Chiefs Quit Position," *Brownwood Bulletin*, September 23, 1973; "Compiled History of Brownwood State School," August 28, 1990, Youth Commission facilities and programs history and information notebooks, Texas Youth Commission, Archives and Information Services Division, Texas State Library and Archives Commission, Austin; *Annual Report of the Texas Youth Council to the Governor for the Fiscal Year Ending August 31, 1970* (Austin, 1970).

138. *Morales*, 383 F. Supp. 53, at 108.

139. Ibid.

140. "Last State School Boy Sent Home," *Gatesville Messenger*, June 28, 1979; "Gatesville School Ends Long Service," *Waco Tribune-Herald*, July 7, 1979.

141. *Juvenile Justice and Delinquency Prevention Act*, 42 U.S.C. 5601 (1974). OJJDP's twin tasks were to promote best practices in the dizzying number of public and private juvenile justice agencies across the nation, implement the deinstitutionalization of status offenders, and after 1988, address the growing problem of Disproportionate Minority Confinement (DMC). For more, see "About OJJDP" on its official site: http://ojjdp.ncjrs.org/about/legislation.html.

142. Kemerer, *William Wayne Justice*, 168–73, summarizes the appeals process.

143. TYC Press Release, June 16, 1977, Morales Case Files.

144. TYC Press Release, April 18, 1978, Morales Case Files.

145. *Annual Report of the Texas Youth Commission for 1981* (Austin, Tex.: Texas Youth Commission, 1982).

146. Texas Youth Commission, *The Response of the Texas Youth Commission to the Fourth Year Report of the Morales Consultant Committee* (Austin, March 8, 1989). Detailed accounts of the settlement negotiations and processes can be found in Kemerer, *William Wayne Justice*, 174–80; and Reddington, "In the Best Interests of the Child," 84–130.

147. Author interview with Bercu.

Epilogue

1. Pamela Colloff, "Does Napoleon Beazley Deserve to Die?" *Texas Monthly*, April 2002.

2. Ibid.

3. Transcript, CNN *Presents*, Saturday, May 25, 2002. A Lexis-Nexis search for "Napoleon Beazley" yielded hundreds of articles from newspapers all over the world, as well as transcripts from national television programs. Similar searches for "Toronto Patterson" and "T.J. Jones" brought only a dozen or so hits from Texas newspapers.

4. Colloff, "Does Napoleon Beazley Deserve to Die?"; Bob Ray Sanders, "Condemned Man's Own Words Best Condemn Capital Punishment," *Fort Worth Star-Telegram*, June 8, 2002.

5. Alberta Phillips, "We Must Draw the Line at Executing Juvenile Offenders," *Austin American-Statesman*, September 1, 2002.

6. Elizabeth S. Scott and Laurence Steinberg, "Blaming Youth," *Texas Law Review* 81, no. 3 (February 2003): 799–841. The "teen brain" research was cited by Justice Kennedy in his majority opinion outlawing the juvenile death penalty. See *Roper v. Simmons*, 125 S. Ct. 1183, 161 L. Ed. 2d 1, 2005 U.S. Lexis 2200.

7. Jeffrey Fagan, "Adolescents, Maturity, and the Law," *American Prospect Online* (August 24, 2005).

8. Barry C. Feld, "The Honest Politician's Guide to Juvenile Justice in the Twenty-First Century," *Annals of the American Academy of Political and Social Science*, vol. 564, "Will the Juvenile Court System Survive?" (July 1999): 10–27. See also Margaret K. Rosenheim et al., eds., *A Century of Juvenile Justice* (Chicago: University of Chicago Press, 2002).

9. Howard N. Snyder, "Juvenile Arrests 2001," *OJJDP Juvenile Justice Bulletin* (December 2003), http://www.ojjdp.ncjrs.org.

10. Eileen Poe-Yamagata and Michael A. Jones, "And Justice for Some" (Building Blocks for Youth, April 2000), http://www.buildingblocksforyouth.org. On Latino juvenile delinquents, see Francisco Villarruel and Nancy Walker, "Donda Esta La Justicia? A Call to Action on Behalf of Latino and Latina Youth in the U.S. Justice System" (Building Blocks for Youth, July 2002). Most recently, see Darnell F. Hawkins and Kimberly Kempf-Leonard, eds., *Our Children, Their Children: Confronting Racial and Ethnic Differences in American Juvenile Justice* (Chicago: University of Chicago Press, 2005); and *America's Cradle to Prison Pipeline: A Report of the Children's Defense Fund* (Washington, D.C.: Children's Defense Fund, 2007). On the counting of Latinos in the census, see Margo J. Anderson, *The American Census: A Social History* (New Haven, Conn.: Yale University Press, 1988), 223–29. For a dissenting view, see Paul E. Tracy, *Decision Making and Juvenile Justice: An Analysis of Bias in Case Processing* (Westport, Conn.: Praeger, 2002).

11. For summaries, see Ronald Takaki, *A Different Mirror: A History of Multicultural America* (Boston: Little, Brown, 1991), 395–99; and David M. Kennedy, *The American People in World War II: Freedom from Fear, Part II* (New York: Oxford, 1999), 335–51. For a close study, see Beth Bailey and David Farber, "The Double-V Campaign in World War II

Hawaii: African Americans, Racial Ideology, and Federal Power," *Journal of Social History* 26, no. 4 (Summer 1993): 817–44.

12. "Washington's New Juvenile Code," *Corrections Magazine*, February 1980; Kay Hopper, "Placement in the State of Washington: The Primary Example of the Movement to 'Get Tough' with Serious Juvenile Offenders" (TYC Dept. of Program Evaluation and Research, June 17, 1980), Morales Case Files, Texas Youth Commission, Archives and Information Services Division, Texas State Library and Archives Commission, Austin.

13. *Uniform Crime Reports for the United States* (Washington, D.C.: Federal Bureau of Investigation, U.S. Dept. of Justice, 1991), 279.

14. *Gangs in Texas Cities* (Austin: Texas Attorney General's Office, 1991).

15. Introduction to *The Changing Borders of Juvenile Justice: Transfer of Adolescents to the Criminal Court*, ed. Jeffrey Fagan and Franklin E. Zimring (Chicago: University of Chicago Press, 2000), 2. See also John J. DiIulio, "The Coming of the Super-Predators," *National Review*, November 1995; Paul J. McNulty, "Natural Born Killers? Preventing the Coming Explosion of Teenage Crime," *The Heritage Foundation Policy Review* 71 (Winter 1995); interview with DiIulio, National Public Radio, July 8, 1996 (LEXIS transcript 2268-10).

16. "Emphasis on Rehabilitation Puts State on Cutting Edge of Corrections Theory," *Austin American-Statesman*, January 16, 1994.

17. Isela Gutiérrez, *The Case for Rebuilding the Texas Youth Commission* (Austin: Texas Coalition Advocating Justice for Juveniles, 2007), 1; General Appropriations Act, HB 1, 74th Legislature, Regular Session. (1995), 8–12, V-35, V-55, and B-37.

18. Texas Youth Commission, *TYC Population Trends*, 2007, http://www.tyc.state.tx.us/research/growth_charts.html.

19. "Little Boys, Big Time: Abuse on the Rise in Texas Juvenile Prisons," *McAllen Monitor*, March 19, 2006; "Elected Officials Express Concern over TYC Abuse," *Brownsville Herald*, March 20, 2006; "Trouble at Evins," *Brownsville Herald*, March 19, 2006; "First Stop in Youth Prison System Is Most Abusive, Records Show," *McAllen Monitor*, March 20, 2006; "Guards on the Defensive," *Brownsville Herald*, March 19, 2006.

20. David W. Springer et al., *Transforming Juvenile Justice in Texas: A Framework for Action*, Blue Ribbon Task Force Report (Austin: University of Texas at Austin, School of Social Work, 2007), 48–49. See also Barry Krisberg, "For Youths' Sake, Change TYC Policy," *Austin American-Statesman*, August 28, 2007; "TYC Rejects Many of Own Task Force's Suggestions," *Dallas Morning News*, September 13, 2007; "Groups File Lawsuit Targeting Texas Youth Commission's Use of Pepper Spray," *Austin American-Statesman*, September 13, 2007; "TYC Is Finding New Leaders—in State's Troubled Prison System," *Dallas Morning News*, September 16, 2007; and David Springer, "Follow the Roadmap for Reform," *Austin American-Statesman*, September 21, 2007.

INDEX

Politics and Culture in the Twentieth-Century South

A Common Thread: Labor, Politics, and Capital Mobility in the Textile Industry
by Beth English

"Everybody Was Black Down There": Race and Industrial Change in the Alabama Coalfields
by Robert H. Woodrum

Race, Reason, and Massive Resistance: The Diary of David J. Mays, 1954–1959
edited by James R. Sweeney

The Unemployed People's Movement: Leftists, Liberals, and Labor in Georgia, 1929–1941
by James J. Lorence

Liberalism, Black Power, and the Making of American Politics, 1965-1980
by Devin Fergus

Guten Tag, Y'all: Globalization and the South Carolina Piedmont, 1950–2000
by Marko Maunula

The Culture of Property: Race, Class, and Housing Landscapes in Atlanta, 1880–1950
by LeeAnn Lands

Marching in Step: Masculinity, Citizenship, and The Citadel in Post-World War II America
by Alexander Macaulay

Rabble-Rousers: The American Far Right in the Civil Rights Era
by Clive Webb

Who Gets a Childhood? Race and Juvenile Justice in Twentieth-Century Texas
by William S. Bush

9 780820 337197